I0445313

THE
STRUGGLE
FOR
UTOPIA

A History of Jewish,
Christian and Islamic Messianism

First published 2022
Copyright © 2022 by Arnold Slyper
All rights reserved
Cover and book design: BenHerskowitz.com

Paperback ISBN: 979-8-9865478-0-0
Hardcover ISBN: 979-8-9865478-1-7

No part of this publication may be translated, reproduced, stored in a retrieval system, or transmitted in any form or by any means, electronic, mechanical, photocopying, recording, or otherwise, without the prior permission in writing from the copyright holder, except in the case of brief quotations embedded in critical articles or reviews.

Published and distributed by
Kochav Press
Mitzpe Nevo 118/6
Ma'ale Adumim, 9841126
Israel
Website: Kochavpress.com

TABLE OF CONTENTS

The Torah is a prophetic book, and the fulfillment of its prophecies constitutes strong evidence for its Divine nature. The Torah uses two main names for God: Elohim is the God of all humanity and Y-H-V-H (yod he vav he or in Hebrew Hashem, the Name) was the God of the Jewish forefathers and will become the tribal God of the Israelites. According to the Torah, the mission of Abraham and the Jewish people is to bring material and spiritual blessing to all mankind. Exile, oppression and redemption will be part of their history. The Jewish people are an eternal people, and the Land of Israel has been bestowed upon them for eternity. The Torah's potential golden age is grounded firmly in this world and not in a heavenly eschatological future.

Abraham was chosen by God because he believed in God's existence and was prepared to disseminate the concept of monotheism to the world. He also believed in God's involvement in the world, in His individual providence, and of His desire to establish a relationship with man. Abraham held that the role of the Jewish people was to build an ideal society based on the way of God and the practice of justice and righteousness. The Sodom and Gomorrah story illustrates that God conducts the world with a combination of justice and righteousness. The way of God will become the basis of Judaism's ethics. The Land of Israel cannot abide injustice, unrighteousness and sexual perversions. The practice of righteousness, justice, love, and loving kindness in their own land will bring material and spiritual blessing to the Jewish people and to all nations prepared to follow in this path.

Moses had engaged in social activism in Egypt although his efforts had been unsuccessful. He married a Midianite woman but did not feel part of Midianite society. The significance of the name of God Y-H-V-H was revealed to him at the Burning Bush and through him to the Jewish people. This name is based on the verb "to be," and signifies that God "will be" with Moses in his mission and subsequently with the Israelites. One of the purposes of the Ten Plagues was to reveal to the Jewish people, and through them to humanity, God's ability to control nature and influence human history. God controls nature by controlling chance, and His laws of quantum physics enable Him to do this at a subatomic level. The story of the Exodus is about how God freed the Israelites from serving a human master, Pharaoh, so that they could serve Him. The Exodus was the first step in the creation of an egalitarian utopian society under the sovereignty of God. The details of how this would be accomplished were revealed at Mount Sinai.

A verse in the Book of Kings states that there were 480 years between the Exodus from Egypt to the beginning of the building of Solomon's Temple. Based on this, the Exodus can be dated to 1446 BCE. Four hundred and eighty years is also internally consistent with the rest of the Bible. The story of the Israelite slavery and Exodus as told in the Torah fits in well with what we know about the history of the pharaohs of the 18th dynasty. It is suggested that Ahmenhotep II was the pharaoh of the Exodus. He became the pharaoh in approximately 1446 BCE. His military expeditions and Temple-building activity were far less extensive than those of his predecessors, indicating that he may have lost his slaves at the Exodus and his chariots at the Sea of Reeds. The commonly accepted date for the Israelite conquest of Canaan at the end of the 13th century BCE and the beginning of the Iron Age fits in poorly with the archeological record. However, a conquest during the Late Bronze Age in about 1400 BCE fits in well with the archeological findings at Jericho and Temple inscriptions found in Egypt.

Isaiah the son of Amoz preached that a Jewish kingdom that failed to practice justice and righteousness was doomed to destruction and exile. However, a remnant of the Jewish people would be redeemed. In beautiful soaring poetry, he described a future utopian existence on earth at the End of Time. His words of consolation have been of considerable comfort to generations of Jews. His belief that the enemies of Israel were appointed by God led him to a non-interventional approach to foreign policy when advising royalty, although his advice was not heeded. The prophet Micah may have been part of Isaiah's prophetic school and he accepted Isaiah's messianic vision, although not his passivism. There have been questions as to what exactly Isaiah meant and how many authors wrote his book. Isaiah's ideas have been extremely influential on Jewish eschatological thought, and through Jesus of Nazareth and early Jewish Christians on that of Christianity.

Jeremiah prophesied during the end of the monarchial period, from the reign of King Josiah until the last of the three Judean exiles during the rule of Zedekiah. His prophecies are in the main about the impending destruction of Judah and the exile of its people. However, his book also contains several chapters of consolation about the return to the land after 70 years of exile. He prophesied that Babylon would be destroyed, that the exiled northern tribes would return, that the seed of David would rule with righteousness and justice, and that an enduring covenant between the Jewish people and God would be established. These prophecies have traditionally been interpreted as being messianic prophecies regarding the End of Time. Alternative ideas have also been proposed and these are discussed.

The return to Judea from Babylon was non-miraculous and very different from that foretold by Isaiah. Given their initial difficulties, the people may well have questioned as to whether this return was truly a God-directed redemption and whether the Temple was destined to be rebuilt. Isaiah had reassured them that Cyrus, the new Persian king, was an agent of God. The Book of Ezra also accepted this. The prophets Haggai and Zechariah reassured the people that they should continue rebuilding the Temple, a project that had been terminated 18 years previously by Cyrus. The arrival of the scholar and leader Ezra 82 years after the first immigration initiated a new phase of rabbinic Judaism. Zachariah's apocalyptic visions, together with those of Daniel, Joel and Ezekiel, marked the beginning of an apocalyptic tradition in Judaism. This is the belief that God will intervene in a cataclysmic struggle between the forces of good and evil to save an elected faithful and this will be the beginning of a new world era.

Chapter 8 Apocalypse According to the Essenes of Qumran, John the Baptist and Jesus of Nazareth 143

Based on the Biblical apocalyptic prophets, the Essenes at Qumran, John the Baptist and Jesus of Nazareth held that an apocalyptic struggle would herald a messianic Kingdom of God on earth. John and Jesus were more inclusive than the Essenes of Qumran and believed that everyone who repented would inherit the Kingdom of God, while the Essenes believed that this was reserved for their followers. The role of John the Baptist is given little emphasis in the New Testament, but it is likely that his second cousin, Jesus of Nazareth, was initially one of his followers. Jesus preached individual virtue, lowliness and humbleness. He taught that wealth had no purpose other than to be given away and family relationships had no relevance while preparing for the Kingdom of God. It is likely that John and Jesus saw their roles as messengers of God proclaiming the imminent arrival of His Kingdom.

Chapter 9 Paul of Tarsus and Christian Messianism 159

Paul of Tarsus gave new meaning to the terms resurrection, salvation and messianism. He held that resurrection would be as spiritual, rather than material, bodies. He believed that Christ's death and subsequent resurrection would bring expiation from sin for those mystically joined with Christ. He suggested that Jew and gentile could together form a new Israel believing in the messianic mission of Jesus. Mosaic Law was therefore irrelevant, even for Jews. The Gospel of Luke introduced the idea that a heavenly Kingdom of God could be entered at death, at which time there would be reward or punishment. All these ideas were far from those of Jesus. Nevertheless, it was the ideas of Paul that took hold within the Roman Empire. Within Paul's supersession ideas and the need for Christianity to define itself in relation to Judaism were unintentionally the seeds of Christian hatred towards Jews. The differing Christian interpretations of the Book of Revelation provide the framework for understanding the varying approaches of Christianity to their eschatology and messianism. This in turn will have implications regarding their relationship with Jews and the State of Israel.

Chapter 10 Rabbi Akiva and the Bar Kochba Revolt 185

Rabbi Akiva was instrumental in collating the Jewish Oral Law and, together with other sages, for charting the direction of Judaism after the destruction of the Second

Temple. He held that everything that God did was for the best. He believed that Jewish sovereignty and rebuilding the Holy Temple would occur through a messianic process, and as the leading rabbinic figure of the time he crowned Bar Kochba the Messiah. Although initially successful, the Bar Kochba Revolt was a disaster and led to the deaths of hundreds of thousands of Jews and the desolation of Judea. Rather than redemption, this revolt was the first step in 2,000 years of Jewish exile. The Bar Kochba revolt was a sobering experience for the Jewish people, and the promotion of messianic activism will not be advocated in primary Jewish books such as the Talmud. Nevertheless, Rabbi Akiva's anticipation of a natural messianic redemption persists in Jewish texts and has been a source of inspiration to Jews throughout the centuries.

Chapter 11   Muhammad and the Jews   203
Muhammad did not accept the authenticity of the Torah and believed that only the Qur'an contained the true revelation from God. He also held that he was the last of the true prophets. The Qur'an contains Biblical stories and midrashim, presented in a manner that reflected the priorities of Muhammad. The basis of Islamic ethics is the Qur'an and the words and actions of Muhammad as reported in the hadiths, whereas the basis of Jewish ethics is a Biblical code reflecting the ways of God. The goal of all Muslims is to achieve a blissful existence in the World to Come. One of the tenets of early Islam was militant *jihad*, warfare with a spiritual significance, aimed at forcibly persuading pagans to adopt Islam.

Chapter 12   The Messianic Era and World to Come According to Maimonides and Nachmanides   219
Based on post-Biblical texts, both Maimonides and Nachmanides believed that the next redemption would be messianic. Maimonides held that the Jewish people would achieve sovereignty during the messianic era in a natural, non-miraculous way, including the realization of global peace and the elimination of poverty. He considered the miraculous nature of the messianic era described by Isaiah to be allegorical. He thought the World to Come would be a heavenly world of souls. Nachmanides disagreed with much of what Maimonides wrote on these topics, arguing that his ideas did not agree with the words of the sages recorded in the Talmud and midrashim. Nachmanides believed that the messianic era and the World to Come would occur miraculously and would be accompanied by a change in the nature of man. He held that the World to Come would be on earth and not in heaven and that resurrected physical bodies on earth would survive without sustenance.

Chapter 13   Kabbala, Messianism and the Vilna Gaon   239
Lurianic kabbala developed in the 1500s as an answer to the frailty of Jewish life, by providing a means of hastening redemption through completing cosmic perfection. Despite the warning of the Talmud, kabbalists were not averse to predicting a date for the onset of messianic times. Hasidism was a revivalist messianic movement that popularized the use of Lurianic kabbala and swept across Eastern Europe. The Vilna Gaon was a scholar and recluse who assumed a leadership role in the dispute between the rabbis of Poland and the Hasidic movement. This dispute hinged on Hasidism's

popularization of kabbala and use of prayer as a means of mystical union with God as an alternative to Torah study. The Vilna Gaon promoted the idea that settling the Land of Israel and becoming involved in its agriculture would hasten the messianic redemption, and 500 of his followers immigrated to Palestine at the beginning of the 1800s. Their relative lack of influence in the country would be a small but incremental step in directing the modern-day return to Zion in a secular, rather than messianic, direction.

Contrary to a commonly-held view, the Dreyfus affair in France was not the precipitating factor in Herzl's efforts to found a Jewish homeland in Palestine. Herzl had been thinking about European antisemitism for many years, and ascribed it to economic factors. His first Zionist book *Der Judenstaat* (*The Jewish State*) was published in 1896 and became a best seller. As a result of its success, he organized the first Zionist Congress in 1897 in Basel, Switzerland. Subsequent congresses elected dues-paying delegates, formed an executive committee and established a financial structure to sell shares and bonds. His novel *Altneuland* contained a utopian, but secular, vision of a Jewish state. *Altneuland* was never the official blueprint for the Jewish state, but it became a foundational text for the Zionist movement, and its liberal, egalitarian and humanistic values were those adopted by the state. It is suggested that Herzl's vision was an appropriate one for that historic time. Nevertheless, the Bible has a dim view of the ability of mankind to create utopian societies based entirely on human-derived values.

Rav Avraham Yitzchak Kook (1865-1935) immigrated to Jaffa in Palestine in 1904 at the beginning of the Second Aliya. He was a mystic, kabbalist and visionary who brought messianic ideas into the modern age. He believed that the Jewish people were at the beginning of a messianic, non-miraculous redemption. He approached the relationship between Orthodoxy and the Jewish rebellions of modernity in a dialectic, rather than antagonistic, fashion. He supported a harmonizing approach to the secular Zionist pioneers and considered them part of God's plan for redemption, even though most of them were not interested in being redeemed. Rav Kook described an innate spiritual force driving the messianic process forward. He suggested that every aspect of life for a Jew was inferior outside the Land of Israel. The yeshiva movement he founded has been influential in training orthodox rabbis equipped to deal with the modern world. On the other hand, he was a mystic who wrote in lofty terms but left no systematic philosophy for his followers that would have enabled them to spearhead a popular messianic renewal. His son, Rav Zvi Yehuda Kook, was the spiritual father of the *Gush Emunim* movement, a messianic movement that promoted Jewish settlement in Judea and Samaria.

Amin al-Husseini was one of the founding members of the Muslim Brotherhood and supported their vision of a pan-Islamic state of which Palestine would be a part. Despite being on the payroll of the British as mufti of Jerusalem and president of the

Supreme Muslim Council, he was partially or completely responsible for a number of anti-Jewish pogroms in Palestine. He was employed by the Nazis as a propagandist for the Axis Powers in Berlin during World War II and made regular broadcasts to the Arab world. He was very familiar with the Holocaust, and together with the Germans planned the extermination of Palestine's Jews in anticipation of Field Marshal Rommel's Afrika Korps' defeat of Great Britain. By mobilizing the Arab world against a Jewish state, al-Husseini was indirectly responsible for Israel's emergence as a military superpower. Islamic antisemitism is currently being maintained by its apocalyptic literature. Iran, Hezbollah and Hamas hold apocalyptic beliefs and regard the murder of Jews and elimination of Israel as a prelude to the Day of Judgment and World to Come. ISIS and al-Qaeda believe in creating an Islamic caliphate at the expense of global stability. Neither Hamas nor the Palestinian Authority is able to make an end of the conflict agreement with Israel because of its messianic beliefs.

Chapter 17   The Messianic Struggle for the Temple Mount   319

The area on which the Temples once stood is considered to have extreme holiness in Judaism, even though there are only Islamic structures there. Israel's Chief Rabbinate forbids Jews from ascending the Temple Mount and Rav Kook's followers have agreed with this in the past. However, the Yesha Council has issued a new ruling encouraging Jews to ascend the Temple Mount and their program has had considerable success. The Yesha Council is not advocating for drastic changes but their aims are nevertheless messianic in scope. God commanded the Israelites to build a Sanctuary so He could dwell and walk amongst them. King Solomon prayed to God that his Temple should not only be the focus for sacrifice but also for Jewish prayer. Muslims will never agree voluntarily to share the Temple Mount. The eschatological aims of Judaism and Islam on the Temple Mount are in total conflict with each other. This, and the increasing number of Jews ascending the Temple Mount, almost guarantee continuing conflict.

PROLOGUE

Why would anyone want to read a book about messianism? After all, the subject is abstruse and irrelevant to most people's concerns.

This book will attempt to show that the very opposite is true. Judaism, Christianity and Islam are messianic religions and their messianic goals have profoundly shaped, and continue to shape the lives of individuals and the direction of the world we live in.

The messianic eschatological beliefs of the three major monotheistic faiths are also at odds with each other, and this has led, and continues to lead, to conflict, hate and violence. Not infrequently, Jews have been the victims of these conflicts. Not all hatred of Jews has its roots in eschatology, but much of it does. Hence, to fully understand antisemitism and why, for example, the State of Israel is so frequently singled out in the United Nations as the world's most racist, apartheid, human-rights violator one has to appreciate the eschatological dimensions behind this hate.

Many of the conflicts initiated by the Islamic world in our present era are messianic struggles. Fundamentalist Islamic movements such as the Islamic State, the Muslim Brotherhood, the Taliban, and al-Qaeda are messianic movements. Israel is currently locked in struggles with Iran, Hezbollah and Hamas which are nothing but messianic. It is not always appreciated that Israel's long-standing conflict with the Palestinians also has eschatological dimensions that are even more consequential than the territorial ones.

Before going further, I should define what I mean by messianism. A standard dictionary definition is belief in a Messiah as a savior of mankind. Another definition used in common speech is religious devotion to an ideal or cause, although this is not one I will be using since it is too broad for this book. A definition I do use, although not quite a standard dictionary definition, is belief that a utopian existence will be created by miraculous or non-miraculous means under the sovereignty of God, with or without the involvement of a messianic-like figure. This definition does not link messianism to the end of the world, although it does not preclude it.

It was Abraham who discovered the religious fundamentals underlying the creation of an ideal society, and the Torah posited that these could be adopted by all humanity. Following the Exodus of the Israelites from Egypt, this notion was given concrete form at Mount Sinai in the form of a covenant between God and the Jews. The laws in this covenant, particularly as related by Moses in the Book of Deuteronomy, contain the blueprint for creating an ideal egalitarian society that imitates the way of God through its practice of righteousness, justice and acts of kindness.

The notion of a messianic future as traditionally understood first made its appearance at the time of the prophets of Israel, particularly Isaiah the son of Amoz and Micah, both of whom lived in the Kingdom of Judah in the 700s BCE. Their prophesies constitute interpretations of the Torah and have been understood in *midrashic*, talmudic and later Jewish texts as foretelling the appearance of a Messiah from the dynasty of King David who will achieve religious and political goals that a regular person would be unable to accomplish, either because the mission is not feasible or because historical circumstances prevent their realization. Since the situation verges on the impossible, the main actor in this drama will be God and the Messiah will be His assistant. Thus, in messianic times God will intervene in human history on front stage, rather than behind curtains as He has done throughout human history.

Specifically, God will bring dispersed Jewish exiles back to the Land of Israel. He will enable the Messiah to increase Jewish religious observance, resolve all contentious issues of Jewish law (*halacha*), successfully fight all Israel's enemies, rebuild the Temple, bring about the recognition of God and a God-based morality to all humanity, and achieve world peace. This will be the first stage in the end of the world as we know it and the beginning of a new world order.

The notion that the world will have a glorious end is an attractive one. Both science and the Torah agree that the universe had a beginning. According to the Torah the world also has direction, and the role of the Jewish people is to create a utopian society that will influence the rest of mankind. It is logical to assume, therefore, that the world also has an end, and this will be something other than humanity annihilating itself in a global shower of radioactivity. A scenario in which God despairs of everything He has created and permits humanity to destroy itself would contradict every vision of the future that the prophets of ancient Israel envisaged and the message of hope they promoted. Rather, Jewish belief from the time of the prophets is that the world is heading towards a messianic existence at the end of history in which God will be acknowledged as sovereign over all His creation.

An aspect of messianism related to the end of the world is apocalypticism. This is the notion that there will be a cataclysmic stage in the messianic future when evil will be defeated, and it represents an even greater intervention of God in the historic process. This struggle will result in the survival of the righteous, the end of the world as we know it and the beginning of the World to Come. The notion of an apocalyptic struggle was introduced by Jewish prophets such as Ezekiel, Zechariah, Joel, Zephaniah, and by Daniel, and was held in Second Temple times by the Essenes and religious leaders such as John the Baptist, Jesus of Nazareth and Paul of Tarsus.

Messianism in Judaism was often linked by the prophets of Israel to redemption, and the belief has arisen over this last 2,000-year exilic period that the next redemption of the Jews from exile will be a messianic one. This idea became even more entrenched as redemption seemed ever more distant, and the Jewish exile exceeded 1,000 and then 2,000 years. Hence, many religious Jews today regard the return of Jews to Israel from throughout the world as indicating the beginning of messianic times, or at least the pre-beginning or "footsteps" of the messianic era.

Nevertheless, the words of the prophets of ancient Israel were far from explicit, and it is by no means certain that this is what they meant. It is quite possible they were discussing a glorious future that would come about in their own times and which had nothing to do with the end of the world. Hence, not all Jewish sages in the past agreed that the messianic era would be miraculous and the beginning of the End of Time. The prominent sage Rabbi Akiva lived at a time when Judea was subjugated by Rome, and he frequently promoted messianic ideas. In his mind this meant that the Jewish people would achieve autonomy from Rome, rebuild the Temple and reinstitute the sacrificial rites. God would direct this process, but not in an overtly miraculous way.

Based on this and his own understanding of messianic times, the influential Jewish philosopher and *halachist* (expert on Jewish law) Maimonides in the 12th century CE suggested that the messianic era would not be a miraculous one, and he interpreted allegorically those statements of the prophets that seemed to indicate otherwise. It has also been suggested that the messianic words of the prophets constitute visions of hope rather than prophecies.

This book traces the evolution of the messianic concept via sketches of the individuals most influential in developing it for the three monotheistic faiths. Since messianism began as a Jewish concept, I begin with Judaism and relate the messianic beliefs of Christian and Muslim visionaries to their Judaic antecedents. This means that these chapters do present a Jewish perspective on these individuals. Each chapter can be read as an independent unit, but I also link them together as an epic saga that began more than 4,000 years ago at the time of Abraham and continues to the present day.

The topics in this book pose many fundamental questions for the three main monotheistic faiths. So let me say at the outset that I am answering none of them. I am a teller of history of religious ideas, of the events that shaped these ideas and how these ideas influenced later history. My aim, as in all my teaching, is to stimulate thinking and debate, but not to force my own ideas into this conversation.

Far from being abstruse and irrelevant, the messianic idea has been, and continues to be, one of the most powerful forces in world history. It is not difficult to see why. In a world of misery and violence, the notion that a utopian future beckons is an extremely powerful one. Pauline Christianity and Islam saw their messianic future mainly in a spiritual or heavenly realm. However, millennia before this, Judaism proposed that one should not despair of this world despite its imperfections and each generation needs to strive towards the creation of a more perfect world under the sovereignty of God. This idea introduced to civilization the hope for a better future and facilitated its moral, scientific and material progress.

Chapter 1

ABRAHAM'S MISSION AND THE UNIVERSAL MESSAGE OF JUDAISM

The epic story to be narrated in this book began in the Middle Bronze Age, somewhere between 1950 to 1800 BCE, when a remarkable individual called Abraham was told by God to make a break with everything he was familiar with and leave his country, his birthplace and his family to initiate a project that would change the course of world history (Genesis 12:1).

Abraham was a counter-cultural iconoclast. This typified his life and his beliefs. He also held that his ideas should be spread by persuasion and not by conquest or coercion and this would become a feature of the religion he initiated we call Judaism.

The mission Abraham was recruited for by God is described in the Torah in the context of seven blessings.[1] These blessings contain promises relevant not only to the Jewish people but to all humanity. They also contain two covenants that encompass the entirety of Jewish history.

Many people consider Divine authorship of the Torah to be no more than a belief. I would argue with this. The Torah contains many prophecies about the Jewish people, and 3,500 years later it can be seen that all of them have been fulfilled.[2] No other body of literature about any other

---

1   The seven blessings are found in the following places in Genesis: Genesis 12:1-3, 12:7, 13:14-17, 15:1-20, 17:1-14, 17:15-22, and 22:15-18. The text from Genesis 17:1-22 does seem like one long blessing, but there is a paragraph space in the middle, effectively making it two blessings.

2   Some of the prophecies in the Torah are overt, such as the blessings given to Abraham currently under discussion. The Torah also contains blessings and curses related to the Jewish people's adherence or lack of adherence to the covenant established at Mount Sinai, and they are frightful in their predictions (Leviticus 26:3-46 and Deuteronomy 28:1-69). All of these have come to pass. The Torah also describes real or metaphysical struggles against adversarial nations seeking to destroy the Jewish people *"from generation to generation"* such as Amalek (Exodus 17:14-16). Many of the stories in Genesis are more indirect in their prophetic messages, in that they can be considered as indicators of the direction of Jewish history. Nachmanides describes this as *"the deeds of the forefathers are a sign to their children"* (ma'ase avot siman lebonim) (Commentary of Nachmanides to ibid., 12:6). Hence,

nation can make this claim. This is strong support for the Divine origin of the Torah.

These blessings tell us that the world we live in was not created for the sake of those adhering to one particular faith, but for all humanity. However, God can only provide blessing to nations that abide by the moral code that governs the world. Abraham's discoveries about God and how he should lead his life are to be the paradigms for how material abundance can be bestowed upon mankind. Moreover, once poverty and strife are eliminated, the nations of the world will be able to devote themselves to spiritual pursuits. As an important Jewish prayer, the Aleinu prayer, says:

> When all humanity will call on Your name, to turn all the earth's wicked toward You. All the world's inhabitants will realize and know that to You every knee must bow and every tongue swear loyalty.

However, before examining four of these seven blessings in detail we need to review two commonly misunderstood aspects of Torah exegesis:

(i). The names of God used by the Bible.

The Torah uses different names for God, corresponding to His various attributes. The three most commonly found names are *Y-H-V-H*, *Elohim* and *El Shaddai*. Readers of the Bible not familiar with Hebrew may be unaware that different names of God are being used since in English they are usually considered synonyms and translated as the same words – God or the Lord.

Elohim is the God of all humanity. The word El is a general term for deity in the Semitic language and was also the name of a Canaanite god. This name has the meaning of a force within nature. The Hebrew name Elohim is in the plural form since God created and controls all the forces within nature. Nevertheless, when Elohim is used in the Torah to describe the One God, the associated verb is usually in the singular. At times the word may mean the Deity or even judges.

In the first creation account Elohim created the universe for all mankind. In the Noah story Elohim promised never again to destroy the world. In the context of the Abrahamic blessings, the name Elohim relates to the universal mission of Judaism.

---

when Jacob wrestled with an angel it was not only Jacob who was wrestling with God and overcoming Him, but the Jewish people who will also wrestle against adverse forces and overcome them (Genesis 32:33). In this way, much of Jewish history is "played out" through the stories of Genesis.

Elohim's relationship with mankind is somewhat distant, and this aspect of God is termed His transcendence. One never finds in the Torah, for example, the expression "love of Elohim" since this is not how humanity relates to Elohim. Rather, man's relationship with Elohim is based on awe or fear.

Another name for God found throughout the Bible is *Y-H-V-H*, these being its four Hebrew letters. In Hebrew, people often use the word *Hashem* – meaning the Name. This name was pronounced in full in the Temple, but its correct pronunciation was lost following the Temple's destruction. One relates to Y-H-V-H with either love or awe. In the second account of creation that takes place in the Garden of Eden we learn that Y-H-V-H is close to individuals and has a relationship with them. This closeness is called His immanence. Y-H-V-H will become the God of Abraham and his family and will subsequently become the national God of the Jewish people.

The attributes of God in relation to these two names are compared in the following table:[3]

The attributes of Elohim	The attributes of Y-H-V-H
A transcendent God	An immanent God
The Creator of the world	A God who relates to individuals
A God concerned with general providence	A God concerned with individual providence
A God who is addressed as "He"	A God who can be addressed as "You"
A God of judgment	A God of mercy
The God of all humanity	The national God of the Jewish people
The God of philosophers in the Biblical wisdom literature	The God of the prophets

The name of God *El Shaddai* appears occasionally in the Bible and is found in the first sentence of the fifth blessing given to Abraham. The meaning of this name is debated. It may well relate to God's aspect of bestowing fertility.[4] Support for this comes from the following passage from the Book of Ruth, in which Ruth's mother-in-law Naomi talked about her inability to bear further sons for her bereaved daughters-in-law because of her age: "*Do*

---

3   This table is based on the chapters in the book *The Documentary Hypothesis and the Composition of the Pentateuch* by Umberto Cassuto. Shalem Press, Jerusalem and New York, 2006.

4   This issue is discussed in the "Commentary to Exodus 6:3" in *A Commentary on the Book of Exodus* by Umberto Moshe David Cassuto, 78. Varda Books, Illinois, 2005.

not call me Naomi (pleasant one), call me Mara (embittered one), for Shaddai has dealt very bitterly with me. I was full when I went away, but Y-H-V-H has brought me back empty. Why should you call me Naomi; Y-H-V-H has testified against me, and Shaddai has brought misfortune upon me" (Ruth 1:20-21).

Why did the Torah use different names for God? Our puzzlement as moderns that One God has several names is a testimony to the success of the Bible in directing us to the appreciation of the unity of God. However, it is suggested that the ancients would have had difficulty in conceptualizing the notion that the same God who created the universe was interested in developing relationships with His created beings. Pagan gods, for example, never communicated with individuals, other than perhaps with a king.[5] Thus, the Torah presented new ideas about one God in a way that was easy for people at that time to conceptualize. The Torah also wished to differentiate between the universal and the tribal aspects of God's messages.

Since the early 1800s, many Biblical scholars have espoused the view of higher Biblical criticism that the Torah is constructed from different sources put together at some period by a redactor. These sources can often be distinguished by the name of God that was used and in particular whether it was Y-H-V-H or Elohim. However, from the perspective I have presented, it can be appreciated that higher Biblical criticism is based on a total misunderstanding of Biblical literary form and the messages it was trying to convey.

(ii). The use of numbers in the Torah:

The people of ancient Mesopotamia loved mathematics. Mathematics is a fundamental aspect of civilization, and civilization began in Mesopotamia. However, to the Mesopotamians numbers had more than just utilitarian value; certain numbers had meaning. The number seven, for example, represented the perfection of the Divine. Because the Torah is a book about the relationship between God and man, it is not surprising that aspects of the number seven are found throughout the Torah. Sometimes the presence of this number may not be at all obvious. For example, a word related to an aspect of God may be repeated seven times within a paragraph to emphasize that it is a keyword.[6]

---

5   In the Noah story God spoke freely to Noah. However, in the very similar Gilgamesh myth, the god Ea could only communicate with Upnapishtim about building an ark by speaking to the brick wall of his reed hut. See "Gilgamesh Tablet XI" in *Myths from Mesopatamia. Creation, the Flood, Gilgamesh and Others* by Stephanie Dalley, 110. Oxford University Press, Revised edition 2000.

6   In the passage about the rainbow being a sign of the covenant (ibid., 9:8-17), the word

The Bible did not invent the significance of the number seven. The ziggurat in Babylon on which the Biblical Tower of Babel story is based had seven stories, and the temple of the god Marduk was at its top on its seventh story. The number seven is also found several times in Tablet XI of the Epic of Gilgamesh that contained the well-known Mesopotamian flood story. The Gilgalmesh flood lasted seven days; there were seven days between the boat coming to rest on a mountain and a dove being released; and a pair of seven jars was offered as a sacrifice. It may be that the first two sevens had no more significance than being the period of a week, but the pair of jars indicates that number seven also had religious significance.

Similarly, to bow to someone seven times was to acknowledge his divine status. The Amarna letters were diplomatic missives sent to the administration of the 18th dynasty of ancient Egypt by vassals in Canaan and other countries. They often began their letter with the sentence "*I bow to my lord seven times,*" acknowledging in this way the divine nature of the pharaoh and their subservience to him.

God bestowed seven blessings on Abraham – seven because this number emphasizes God's imprint on the fulfilment of each of these promises. For the same reason the number seven occurs repeatedly within the blessings themselves.

If number seven is the domain of the holy, then one above seven, number eight, represents an even stronger bond of dedication to God. The meaning of this number is uniquely Jewish. The significance of number eight was first revealed when Abraham was told to circumcise his son on the eighth day from birth as a demonstration of his future commitment to the covenant (Genesis 17:12).

We will now look in detail at four of these seven blessings:

GOD'S FIRST BLESSING TO ABRAHAM –
BRINGING MATERIAL BENEFIT TO THE WORLD

The first communication and directive received by Abraham from God will change not only the direction of the world but also the tone of the Bible. The world blessing occurs in this passage five times and is clearly a key word. The word curse occurs five times in the previous 11 chapters of Genesis.[7] From

---

covenant is repeated seven times and can be considered a keyword.

7   The word curse, either *arur* or *lekalel,* is found in five places in the preceding chapters of Genesis: with respect to the soil (5:24 and 8:21), the serpent (3:14 and 4:11), and the person Canaan (9:25).

this point on, the Bible becomes more upbeat since what was previously an aimless world now has direction through the example of Abraham and his descendants.

The blessing reads as follows:

God [Y-H-V-H] said to Abram, "Go yourself from your land, from your birthplace and from your father's house to the land that I will show you.[8]

#1. I will make of you a great nation,

*#2. I will **bless** you,*

#3. I will make your name great;

*#4. and you shall be a **blessing**.*

*#5. I will **bless** those who **bless** you,*

#6. and him who curses you I will curse;

*#7. and all the families of the earth shall be **blessed** through you"* (Genesis 12:1-3).

This blessing contains seven promises, each of which I have labelled for convenience #1 to #7. These are contained in two sentences, each of which contains two or three promises describing what God will do, and are followed at the end of the sentence by the consequence of these promises. Hence, the consequence of the three blessings in the first sentence is *"and you shall be a blessing."* In the fifth and sixth blessing of this second sentence, God promises Abraham that the success of others will depend on how they relate to him and whether they bless or curse him. Those who appreciate what he stands for and bless him will be rewarded with material success. Those who denigrate Abraham's/God's message will be cursed. The consequences of these two blessings will be *"and all the families of the earth shall be blessed through you."* In other words, the spiritual insights that Abraham has discovered, either on

---

8   Abraham was directed to leave Haran to go to the *"land"* that God will show him. Jewish commentators discuss the significance of the pronoun *"to you"* in the phrase *"Go to you (lech lecho) from your land"* when the sentence could equally well have opened with the single word *"Go!"* (Hebrew *lech*) without the words *to you*. The commentator Rashi translates these words as *go for yourself* and links them to the subsequent blessings. Hence, *go for your pleasure and for your benefit*. However, Cassuto points out that there are other places in the Bible where this use of the pronoun *to* cannot have this meaning. Rather, he suggests it means to go alone or with those close to you and make a clean break from everything with which you are familiar.

his own or with the help of God, will bring in their wake benefit to the entire world.[9]

The importance of this message "*and all the families of the earth shall be blessed through you*" is evident from the fact that it is repeated several times in the Torah. Six chapters later we learn: "*And Abraham will surely become a great and mighty nation and all the nations of the earth will be blessed through him*" (18:18). His son Isaac is told that "*all the nations of the earth shall bless themselves by your offspring*" (26:4), and Isaac's son Jacob is also told that "*all the families of the earth shall be blessed through you*" (28:14). We will also soon learn that blessing will be forthcoming to all humanity not only by virtue of the activities of Abraham but also through his descendants.

But how will this blessing come about? Is it like the touch of Midas in that any contact with Abraham is sufficient to bring about blessing? Possibly – but unlikely. Rather, those who bless Abraham support his moral values and make an effort to imitate them. This in turn will bring them blessing through their acceptance of the foundational moral laws that govern the world. His descendants will also form a "*great nation*" that will enable them to have influence in the world.

The Fourth Blessing: exile and oppression

The fourth blessing made to Abraham contains the first of two covenants made by God. The difference between a covenant and a promise is that a covenant is more formal and is often accompanied by a sign, or in this case a ceremony, so that it will be easily recalled by the Jewish people or by humanity. For example, the sign of the rainbow which appeared to Noah after the flood was also part of a covenant made by God. This covenant made to Abraham, called the "Covenant between the Pieces" is about Jewish exile and redemption to the

---

9   There are other explanations by Jewish commentators as to the meaning in this sentence of "*and you shall be a blessing*," besides the one I have provided based on literary grounds. It could be a directive (Radak) or even a summary of the blessings preceding it. Nachmanides suggests that Abraham will become the standard by which blessings are bestowed upon others. People who wish to bless their son will say: "God should make you like Abram!" because of the *great* name he has acquired. Rashi, following a midrash, suggests that Abraham will have the power of blessing in his hands. Alternatively, blessing will be bestowed on all who come in contact with him. Midrash Raba 39:11 gives two examples: A person who wanted to buy a cow from Abraham would be blessed even before the value of the cow had been assessed; Abraham would pray for a barren woman and the woman would conceive. My explanation for "*all the families of the earth will be blessed through you*" is that of Rabbi Samson Raphael Hirsch who writes: "*But God asserts that finally all the peoples of the world will participate in this blessing inasmuch as they will also found their lives on the same foundation on which you are to found yours*" (Commentary to Genesis 12:3).

land of Canaan. Exile and redemption are an integral part of Jewish history, and since they will take place within the framework of world history, they will also become an integral part of world history. This notion will be discussed further in the next chapter.

The blessings given to Abraham were bestowed at turning points or times of crisis in his life. The circumstances of this fourth blessing are that following God's directive to Abraham to walk through the land, he moved south to Hebron to the Plains of Mamre. There he was informed that Mesopotamian kings have attacked a Canaanite coalition that rebelled against them and captured his nephew Lot from Sodom. Accompanied by a small war party, Abraham struck the kings at night in a surprise raid, rescued Lot, took captives and booty and pursued the fleeing Mesopotamian army as far as Syria. On his return, he restored to the king of Sodom everything that belonged to his city and provided a share of the booty to colleagues who joined him in this attack. He kept nothing for himself.

Abraham then experienced a prophetic vision. At first glance, this passage looks as if it is in two parts, but it should be considered a single unit linked through the word *inheritance*. Its opening is structured around who will do the inheriting, and its second part discusses the circumstances by which his inheritance will be obtained:

> *Part 1. After these events, the word of God (Y-H-V-H) came to Abram in a vision, saying: "Fear not, Abram, I am your shield, your reward is exceedingly great." And Abram said: "O Lord, God, what can You give me, seeing that I go childless, and the one in charge of my household is Eliezer of Damascus?" And Abram said: "Since you have given me no offspring, my steward will **inherit** me." And, suddenly, the word of God came to him, saying: "That one will not **inherit** you; but your very own issue shall **inherit** you." And He took him outside, and said: "Please look heavenwards and count the stars, if you are able to count them;" and He said to him: "So will your offspring be" And he trusted in God; and He reckoned it to him as righteousness (15:1-6).*

> *Part 2. And He said to him: "I am God (Y-H-V-H) Who brought you out of Ur of the Chaldees, to give you this land to **inherit**." And he said: "My Master God, whereby (in Hebrew bamah) shall I know that I shall **inherit** it?" And He said to him: "Bring Me three heifers, three she-goats, and three rams, and a turtle-dove, and a young pigeon." He brought Him all these, and he divided them in the middle and placed each piece against its counterpart; but*

the birds he did not cut up. Birds of prey descended upon the carcasses, and Abram drove them away. As the sun was about to set, a deep sleep fell upon Abram; and, lo, a great dark dread fell upon him. And He said to Abram: "Know with certainty that your offspring shall be sojourners in a land that is not theirs, and they shall be enslaved and oppressed for 400 years; and also that nation that they shall serve, I shall judge; and afterwards they will leave with great wealth. As for you, you shall go to your ancestors in peace; you shall be buried at a ripe old age. And the fourth generation shall return here; for the iniquity of the Amorite is not yet full." And it came to pass, when the sun set and it was very dark, there appeared a smoky furnace and a flaming torch that passed between these pieces. On that day God made a covenant with Abram, saying: "To your descendants have I given this land, from the river of Egypt to the great river, the Euphrates River; the Kennites, the Kenizzites, the Kadmonites, the Hittites, the Perizzites, and the Rephaim, the Amorites, the Canaanites, the Girgashite, and the Jebusites" (15:7-21).

The first part of the passage opens by God telling Abraham that he has no reason to fear and that He will be his *"shield."* After defeating the Mesopotamian kings, Abraham could well be concerned that they will avenge his attack.[10] Another of Abraham's concerns was that his servant Eliezer *"will inherit"* him. Abraham and Sarah had no children. Abraham had previously assumed that his legacy would be perpetuated through Lot. But Lot chose another direction in life by moving to Sodom, and Abraham's next-in-line heir was now his servant Eliezer.[11] However, God interrupted Abraham and told him that Eliezer *"will not inherit"* him. Only a true biological descendant will do so.

At the beginning of the second part of this vision, Abraham asked: *"My Master God (Y-H-V-H), whereby shall I know that I shall inherit it?"* This could imply that Abraham had doubts about God's promise. Yet only two sentences previously the Torah had said: *"And he trusted in God; and He reckoned it to him as righteousness."* It is doubtful, therefore, that Abraham was seeking re-assurance. It is more likely that the Hebrew word *bamah* (literally *in what*)

---

10   The explanation I have offered is one of several interpretations of this phrase and is the most literal with respect to the text. Midrashic explanations, on the other hand, and this is the direction followed by Rashi, suggest that he was concerned that he might already have received all the reward due to him for his righteousness (Bereishit Rabba 44:4). He might even have anticipated punishment for the lives he had taken (Rashi). Nachmanides suggests that he feared he might die without children.

11   The ancient Mesopotamian Nuzi tablets explained that if a man died without offspring, his servant was considered his heir.

should be understood as: How will this come about that I will inherit, or how will I know when the time has come for me to inherit?[12]

These details are now forthcoming in the form of a highly allegorical vision. Contrary to what he might previously have anticipated, only after a long and harsh exile will his descendants actualize their inheritance.

God also sealed His promise in the form of a contract. This contract was performed in the way that contracts were commonly formalized in those days: an animal was cut up, and one or both of the parties *"passed between these pieces."* The usual Hebrew verb for making a contract is to cut a contract.

In the final sentence of this passage this contract is called a covenant. The proceedings of this covenant are highly symbolic. The *"birds of prey descended upon the carcasses"* represent external forces attempting to destroy the realization of the covenant between God and the Jewish people, or even attempting to destroy the Jewish people themselves.[13] Yet with resolve, Abraham (and in the future the Jewish people) are able to drive these vultures away.

The threesome of each animal is then cut up.[14] There is probably no particular symbolism regarding the kinds of animals and birds used, which were commonly available kosher animals and birds. The number three likely represents the three generations that will be enslaved. Hence, only *"the fourth generation"* will return to the land after 400 years have passed.[15] The intact

---

12   Other explanations have also been given. There is a view in the Talmud (TB Nedarim 32a) that Abraham's question was improper and it is because of this that the Egyptian servitude ensued. Others suggest that Abraham was asking through what merit he would inherit the land. Rashi explains that Abraham was asking by what merit would his offspring be able to sustain themselves in the land, and he was answered *"through the merit of the sacrificial offerings"* (Rashi on Genesis 15:6).

13   The second suggestion I have provided is that of the Radak on Genesis 15:11, who points out that this confirms the prediction of Leviticus 26:44 that even during our darkest hours *"I will not despise you and allow you to be wiped out completely."*

14   The details of the covenantal ceremony that I and many others have translated as *"Bring Me three heifers, three she-goats and three rams, and a turtle-dove and a young pigeon"* (Genesis 15:9) is the clearest way to signify the three-generational aspect of this contract. However, the precise translation of the Hebrew word *meshulash* is unclear. It is clearly related to the word three. Radak translates it as a 3-year-old animal, others as a 3-year-old from the womb.

15   The correspondence between *"400 years"* and *"three generations"* has been discussed by Jewish commentators. One way of looking at this sentence is to consider part of it as being in brackets, and this is the explanation of Nachmanides on Genesis 15:13. Hence, *'Know with certainty that your offspring shall be aliens in a land that is not theirs, (and they will serve them; and they will oppress them) 400 years* (Genesis 15:13). In other words, the Israelites will be aliens for 400 years but will not be in servitude all this time. Rashi on Genesis 15:13, based on the midrashic work *Seder Olam*, suggests that the 400 years started from the

"turtle dove" and *"young pigeon"* could represent a younger fourth generation that will leave Egypt.[16]

As the sun is about to set, Abraham viscerally felt the full impact of the Egyptian exile as *"a dread, a great darkness fell upon him"* (15:12). Rabbi Soloveitchik explains:

> *The bondage of Israel in Egypt was not only predicted but also illustrated and visualized. Abraham came in contact with the future sorrows and miseries of his children. He was overwhelmed by a vivid, sensuous aware-ness, which reached the intensity of real pain and suffering; a horror or great darkness fell upon him. The woes and agony of many years were condensed into a single moment. . . . Sympathetic coexistence with count-less future generations, confederacy with the unborn and anticipation of the wholeness of historical realization are the basic traits of the charis-matic historical personality.[17]*

God's commitment to this covenant is presented in two ways. First, He passed between the animal pieces as a *"smoky furnace and flaming torch."* He also made a verbal commitment that Abraham's offspring will inherit the land.

An element common to the two parts of this passage is Abraham's faith and *"trust"* that his descendants would indeed receive their inheritance, even though the birth of his child will not occur until he is elderly, and even though the actualization of this inheritance will be delayed for hundreds of years. Abraham's trust and God's fulfilment of His promise were mentioned by Nehemiah in his book, and his words were used by the Levites as a prayer in the Temple:

> *And You found his [Abraham's] heart faithful before You, and You made*
> *the covenant with him to give the land of the Canaanites, the Amorites,*

---

birth of Abraham's biological son Isaac, and not from the time of entry of Jacob's family to Egypt, since Isaac was also an alien in a land not his. Hence, the comment *"And the fourth generation shall return here"* means that only three generations will actually live in Egypt. Commentators such as Rashbam, Seforno and Rabbeinu Chananel agree with this. Following the midrashic work *Seder Olam*, Rashi's chronology is that Isaac was 60 years old when Jacob was born (Genesis 25:26), and Jacob was 130 years old when he went down to Egypt (Genesis 47:9). The Israelites were therefore in Egypt for only 210 years. The Torah does state in Exodus that the Israelites were in Egypt for 430 years (Exodus 12:40). The *Mechilta* and Talmud (TB Megilla 9a) understand this verse to be interpreted with the ad-dition *"and in other lands. . ."*

16   "The Covenant between the Pieces (7-21)" in *Abram to Abraham. A Literary Analysis of the Abraham Narrative* by Jonathan Grossman, 180. Peter Lang AG, Bern Switzerland.

17   *Chumash with commentary based on the teachings of Rabbi Joseph B. Solovitchick*, 184. OU Press, New York NY, 2013.

the Perizzites, the Jebusites, and the Girgashites, to give to his seed and You kept Your words, for You are righteous (Nehemiah 9:8-9).

Rabbi Soloveitchik points out the significance of this particular covenant/prophecy not only with respect to the redemption from Egypt but also for future redemptions:

There were many, and there are still, birds of prey that swoop down on us [the Jewish people]. And it is not only the concrete Abraham who lived thousands of years ago who chased them away. It is also Abraham the symbol. It is the Abraham who could wait and patiently expect a son at the age of one hundred. Here, he received a prophecy, a message of suffering, of martyrdom and frustration, and of endless waiting, 400 years to redemption from slavery and oppression. The Covenant between the Pieces conveys a message not so much of redemption as of spiritual survival, of being able to wait endlessly until the final day arrives.[17]

There is a question, though, that could well be asked: Why did the Israelites in Egypt warrant oppression and enslavement? Moreover, Abraham will soon rush to the defense of the inhabitants of Sodom. Why did he not do so for his own descendants?

One answer must be that this exile was God's immutable decree and He decided that it be accompanied by servitude and oppression. Abraham was not privy to the details of God's justice, so there was nothing for him to discuss. God also provided no opening for Abraham to negotiate about the justice of His decree as He would later do regarding the city of Sodom.

God controls history. History is neither a series of random events nor the result of dialectic processes. History is what God decrees it to be. And Jewish history required a preparatory period of 400 years before the Israelites would be redeemed. This does not mean, though, that there was no reason. It may be that the Jewish people had to experience the emptiness of servitude to Pharaoh to be ready to bind themselves to a new Master. They had to experience being treated harshly as strangers in a foreign land in order to appreciate how strangers needed to be treated in their own land (Exodus 22:20).[18] They would likely have rapidly assimilated into Egyptian culture in the absence of discrimination and enforced servitude. The exile also had to last for hundreds of years since the ethical behavior of the Canaanites did not yet justify their expulsion; for *"the iniquity of the Amorite shall not yet be full until then"* (Genesis 15:16).

---

18   *"You shall not taunt or oppress a stranger, for you were strangers in the land of Egypt"* (Exodus 22:20). Also, Exodus 23:9.

Abraham could have opted out. He felt *"the dread, a great darkness"* even before the covenant was sealed. He could have told God that he had had second thoughts about this entire venture. But he did not do so. Nor did the majority of Jews throughout their thousands of years of exile. This was because they, like Abraham, trusted in a future redemption even if they themselves would not witness it. They had also bound themselves to God forever, just as God had bound Himself eternally to the Jewish people. How this is so is detailed in the next blessing.

The fifth blessing: prophecies about eternity

The fifth blessing contains the second covenant made by God to the Jewish people, the Covenant of Circumcision. The themes of this covenant are the eternity of the Jewish people, the eternity of God's relationship with the Jewish people and the eternity of the relationship of the Jewish people with the Land of Israel.

The context of this fifth blessing is that the issue of descendants had been weighing on the minds of Sarah and Abraham. Abraham listened to Sarah's advice and had a child with her servant Hagar. When this son, Ishmael, was 13 years old, God again appeared to Abraham, revealing Himself through the names El Shaddai and Elohim, although the majority of this blessing is through the name Elohim. This may be because like Elohim's covenant with Noah its implications will involve all humanity. The entire blessing reads as follows:

> *When Abram was 99 years old, Y-H-V-H appeared to Abram, and said to him: "I am El Shaddai; walk before Me, and be wholehearted. I will place My **covenant** between Me and you, and will multiply you greatly." Abram fell upon his face; and Elohim spoke with him, saying: "As for Me, behold, this is My **covenant** with you. You shall be the father of a multitude of nations; you shall no longer be called Abram, but your name shall be Abraham; for I have made you the father of a multitude of nations. I will make you exceeding fertile, and I will make nations of you, and kings shall come forth from you. And I will establish My covenant between Me and you and your offspring after you throughout their generations as an everlasting covenant, to be a God to you and to your offspring after you; and I will give to you and to your offspring after you the land you sojourn in, all the land of Canaan, for an everlasting possession; I will be their God." And God said to Abraham: "As for you, you shalt keep My covenant, you and your offspring after you throughout their generations. Such shall be*

My covenant between Me and you and your offspring after you which you shall keep: every male among you shall be circumcised. You shall circumcise the flesh of your foreskin; and that shall be the sign of the covenant between Me and you. Every male among you throughout your generations shall be circumcised at the age of eight days, he who is born in the household, or purchased with money from any foreigner who is not of your offspring. Homeborn and purchased alike must be circumcised. Thus shall My covenant be in your flesh for an everlasting covenant. And if any male who is uncircumcised fails to circumcise the flesh of his foreskin, that soul shall be cut off from its people; he has broken My covenant" (17:1-14).

The word *"covenant"* (*bris*) is a keyword in this passage, and it defines the theme of this section, which is a covenant between Elohim and Abraham. In contrast to Elohim's previous covenant with Noah (9:8-17), Abraham is not to be passive but is given two instructions. The first of these is revealed at the very beginning of this passage: *"Walk before Me and be wholehearted"* (17:1).[19] God is saying: "You, Abraham, are to walk *in front of me* and be my representative to the world." This is in contrast to Noah who only walked with God (6:9).[20] How Abraham will walk before God is not yet described, but the Torah will do so after Abraham and his household have performed his second task, which is to become circumcised.

The first part of this covenant contains seven promises made by Elohim, which for convenience I have labelled #1 to #7:

#1 - You shall be the father of a multitude of nations

#2 - you shall no longer be called Abram, but your name shall be Abraham; for I have made you the father of a multitude of nations.

#3 - I will make you exceeding fertile,

#4 - And I will make nations of you,

#5 - And kings shall come forth from you.

---

19 A number of interpretations of the phrase *"wholehearted"* (*tamim*) have been proposed. Rashi commenting on this phrase suggests that Abraham should be wholehearted in the trials to which he will be subjected. Nachmanides relates it to a similar use of this word in Deuteronomy when the Bible discusses forbidden magical practices and which concludes with the phrase *"You shall be wholehearted with Y-H-V-H your God"* (Deuteronomy 18:13). Hence, just as you are to avoid magical practices and retain your trust in Me, so are you to walk before Me and maintain your belief in Me. The Radak suggests that the fulfillment of the command of circumcision will itself make Abraham perfect.

20 Rashi on Genesis 6:9 makes this comparison between Noah and Abraham.

*#6 - And I will establish My **covenant** between Me and you and your off-spring after you throughout their generations as an everlasting **covenant**, to be a God to you and to your offspring after you;*

#7 - and I will give to you, and to your offspring after you the land you so-journ in all the land of Canaan, for an everlasting possession; I will be their God (17:5-7).

The first (#1) of these seven promises is that Abraham will become *"a father of a multitude of nations."* Which nations the Bible is referring is unclear from the text. Many Jewish commentators assume that these nations are the descendants of Isaac and that the Bible is talking about the Jewish people.[21] Another possibility is that they are the nations that Abraham will sire through his concubines (25:1 and 25:5). However, Abraham's family can be considered even larger than this in that a convert to Judaism is called *"a child of Abraham."* Muslims and Christians also consider themselves spiritual heirs to Abraham's legacy. The Qur'an establishes its Abrahamic lineage through Ishmael. Christianity views Abraham as an exemplar of faith and a spiritual and possibly physical ancestor of Jesus.[22] In the theology of Paul of Tarsus, all who believe in God are considered spiritual descendants of Abraham.

To emphasize this broad aspect of his parenthood, Abraham's name underwent a change (#2). Until now he had been called Avram, meaning a father of Aram. He will now be called Avraham, a father of *a "multitude of nations."*[23]

Abraham was also promised that this covenant will bring in its wake fertility (#3) which is why the fertility aspect of God, El Shaddai, is mentioned in the first sentence of this passage. Under His aspect of Y-H-V-H, God pointed out in His fourth blessing that his seed will be as many as *"the stars in the heaven"* (15:5). In that particular Y-H-V-H blessing, Abraham's descendants will become a large nation in order to populate the land of Canaan. In this covenant promised by El Shaddai and Elohim, the universal aspect of God, they will become fruitful so they can fulfill their universal mission.

---

21 Rashi suggests that it includes the Jewish people plus the tribe of Edom (Rashi to Genesis 17:6). Nachmanides disagrees that Edom is included here and brings examples in which the Jewish people are called *nations* and *peoples* (Nachmanides on Genesis 17:6). Targum Onkelos translates the word as tribes. The Radak suggests that the reference is to the descendants of Keturah, who married Abraham after Sarah died.

22 New Testament, Romans 4:9-12.

23 The word "*riham*" in Arabic means a multitude. This word is not currently used in Hebrew, but Luzzatto suggests that it may once have been part of the Jewish lexicon. *The Book of Genesis. A Commentary by ShaDal (S.D. Luzzatto).* Translated by Daniel A Klein, 155. Jason Aronson Inc, NJ, 1998.

Abraham will also become the progenitor of kings (#5). The term kings implies sovereignty and power. Hence, his offspring will not be a small and insignificant people tucked away in a remote corner of the globe, but a major and powerful actor on the world scene in one of the central locations of the world between the two great superpowers, Mesopotamia and Egypt.

These seven promises are written in a crescendo form building up to two promises related to eternity, namely for Elohim *"throughout their genera-tions . . . to be a God to you and to your offspring after you," (17:7) (#6)*, and for Elohim to be a God eternally in *"all the land of Canaan for an everlasting pos-session"* (17:8) (#7).

In these two final sentences Elohim promised to forge a special relation-ship with Abraham and his descendants by being a God to them forever.[24] In the next-to-last sentence (#6), Elohim promised that His covenant will be *"an everlasting covenant"* and that He will be a God to Abraham and his seed for-ever. This will include periods of exile. In the last sentence (#7), God promised that the land of Canaan will belong to the Jewish people *"for an everlasting possession"* and that He will be their eternal God in the land of Canaan. Thus, an eternal people, the Jewish people, has been allotted a specific country, the Land of Israel, forever. Moreover, just as God has bonded Himself eternally to the Jewish people, so too has the Jewish nation bonded itself to God forever.[25] This is apparent with Abraham's, and thus the Jewish people's, second contri-bution to the covenant, circumcision.

Circumcision is to be *"a sign of a covenant between Me and you."* Because it is performed on every Jewish male, it also becomes an aspect of the cov-enant itself to *"be in your flesh for an everlasting covenant."* A Jewish male who is not circumcised denies that he is part of the mission of the Jewish people: *"That soul shall be cut off from its people; he has broken My covenant."*

Circumcision is performed on the eighth day after birth (17:12). As

---

24 The Be'ir Yitzchak, a super-commentator on Rashi, points out regarding Rashi's commen-tary to Genesis 17:7 that this verse does not mean *"I will uphold My covenant in order to be a God to you."* Rather, *"to be a God to you"* is the content of the covenant, so that the verse then reads *"I will uphold My covenant which is to be a God to you."*

25 There are several indications in the Torah that these promises work both ways, and at least on a national level the eternal covenant between the Jewish people and God cannot be broken. This relates particularly to the blessings and curses found in Leviticus 26:3-45 and Deuteronomy 28:1-69. It has also been suggested that the covenant established in Moab, 40 years after the Ten Commandments, was not just a repetition of the prior covenant but was meant to emphasize the eternal nature of the commitment of the people and their collec-tive fate. The Inquisition and the Holocaust are but two examples of how even those Jews who had rejected the covenant could not escape from the fate of the Jewish nation.

pointed out, the number eight in the Torah has the meaning of being a level above regular holiness – super-holiness, as it were. This is because the act of circumcision binds the Jew in the strongest way possible to a holy purpose.

There is discussion among Jewish commentators as to the symbolic meaning of circumcision. Most agree that it is a means of distinguishing the Jewish people from the rest of humanity.[26] It is clearly not an overt symbol, although every Jewish male knows that he has the circumcision engraved on his genital organ and that his connection to God has been signed in a blood ceremony. By this he is marked for one of the mission statements of the Jewish people: to stand before God as His representative to the world. It is also a sign of eternity through the aspect of procreation.

Circumcision was practiced in the ancient world well before the Jewish people performed it. It was practiced in ancient Egypt and may have been a mark of distinction of the elite. The priestly caste of that country also practiced circumcision.[27] Perhaps related to this, the Jewish people were later marked for a priestly function to the nations of the world. The Torah will be explicit about this by calling on the Israelites to become a nation of priests: *"You will be for me a kingdom of priests"* (Exodus 19.6).

The seventh blessing: the Jewish people will bring blessing to the world

The first of the seven blessings, which has the potential of bestowing blessing on the entire world was given to Abraham alone. One might assume that this would pertain also to his descendants, although until now the Torah has not explicitly stated this. In this seventh and last blessing it will do so.

In the story of the Binding of Isaac, Abraham was instructed by God to take his son Isaac and sacrifice him on one of the mountains that God will show him. One of the issues many people have with this story is understanding how an ethical God could have made such an unethical request, even if He never intended that Abraham carry it out. However, this becomes a non-issue once one appreciates that the aspect of God making this request is Elohim, the God of all mankind, and not Y-H-V-H, the God of the Jewish people. A notion espoused particularly by Canaanite society was that child sacrifice was

---

26   Sefer Hachinuch 2.

27   *The Book of Genesis. A Commentary by Shadal (S.D. Luzzatto)* translated by Daniel A. Klein, 156-157. James Aronson Inc. to Genesis 17.9. Also, "History of Circumcision" in Wikipedia (https://en.wikipedia.org/wiki/History_of_circumcision#:~:text=Herodotus% 2C%20writing%20in%20the%205th%20century%20BCE%2C%20wrote%20that%20 the,passage%20from%20childhood%20to%20adulthood).

the ultimate means of influencing the gods. The Book of Kings records two Judean kings sacrificing their children in imitation of Canaanite practices.[28] Hence, during the period in which Abraham lived, a divine instruction to sacrifice a son would not have been an unethical request; to the contrary, it would have been considered highly desirable. Judaism was then, and continues to be, a religion of protest against paganism and unethical ideas prevalent in society, and the Torah will fight relentlessly against child sacrifice (Deuteronomy 12:31). This story is the opening salvo in this protest.

As Abraham lifted up his knife to kill his son, an angel of Y-H-V-H (and not Elohim) told him to desist. Abraham then offered a ram caught in a thicket instead of his son. From this time on, this type of substitute sacrifice will become the accepted Torah way for certain types of sacrifices, with the killing of the animal being a substitute for the sacrifice of the person himself.[29]

Abraham now received a final blessing from the angel of God (Y-H-V-H) in the form of an irrevocable oath. Because Abraham was prepared to offer his son, his offspring will achieve victory in battle and the whole of humanity will bless themselves by the Jewish people:[30]

> *The angel of God (Y-H-V-H) called to Abraham a second time from heaven. And he said: "By Myself I swear – the word of God – that because you have done this thing, and have not withheld your son, your only one, that I shall surely bless you and surely increase your offspring like the stars of the heavens and like the sand on the seashore; and your offspring shall inherit the gate of its enemy. And all the nations of the earth shall bless themselves by your offspring, because you hearkened to My voice"* (Genesis 22:15-18).

---

28 King Manasseh erected altars for Baal and burnt his son as an offering (2 Kings 21:6), as did King Ahaz (2 Kings 16:3).

29 Explanation of Nachmanides of Leviticus 1:9.

30 The Hebrew verb *vehitbarachu* is in the reflexive form, meaning that the sentence reads and *"all the nations of the earth will bless themselves by your offspring."* See *The Book of Genesis. A Commentary by Shadal (S.D. Luzzatto)* translated by Daniel A. Klein, 125. James Aronson Inc. This is also how Rashi interprets this phrase in this, the last blessing in Genesis 22:18. Similarly, the verb *venivrechu* found in the part of the last sentence #7 of the first of the blessings given to Abraham (Genesis 12:3) could be either a reflexive or passive form of the verb (*shall be blessed*). Rashi is consistent and explains the end of verse Genesis 12:3 in a reflexive mode – *"A man says to his son – Be like Abraham."* However, this means that the conclusion of the verse is similar to its beginning. Nevertheless, many commentators, namely Onkelos, Ibn Ezra, Kimchi and Hirsch, view at least 18:8 and 12:3 as being in the passive form: the nations will be blessed. Onkelos translates all three verses in the passive. I use a reflexive form of the verb only for the seventh blessing.

That the nations of the world will bless themselves by the Jewish people (and not just be blessed by them) emphasizes that these blessings will be obtained through acknowledging the beliefs of the descendants of Abraham, admiring their holy behavior and imitating their ethical ways.

In sum, within these seven blessings and promises bestowed upon Abraham are the entirety of Jewish history: the survival of an eternal people, prolonged and bitter exiles and eventually redemption to a land that has been patiently waiting for them. The number seven is found throughout these passages, signifying that nothing in this blueprint of Jewish history has occurred, or will occur, by chance, but is all part of the Divine plan.

These blessings are prophecies. No other 3,500-year-old religious book contains prophecies of this nature that have been fulfilled. This is strong support for the Divine authorship of the Torah.

These blessings also contain the mission statement for Abraham and his descendants — to bring blessing to all humanity. This blessing is situated firmly in this world and not in a heavenly eschatological future and will have both material and spiritual sequelae.[31] It is introduced in the Torah by aspects of God relating specifically to the Jewish people (Y-H-V-H) and by aspects of God relating to all humanity (Elohim). It encompasses all the nations of the world as *"families"* (Genesis 12:3), and the Jewish people as God's *"firstborn son"* (Exodus 4:22). The Jews are also to be *"a kingdom of priests"* to the rest of the world in carrying out this mission (19:6).

The means by which by which they will accomplish this mission is described in the very next chapter.

---

31 Maimonides in his *halachic* work the *Mishna Torah* discusses the question as to why the Torah discusses reward for the Jewish people in material terms when the ultimate reward is in the World to Come. His answer is that material benefits in this world will enable an individual to spend more time in spiritual pursuits and thus derive the benefits of both worlds. He writes: *"Thus, these blessings and curses can be interpreted as follows. If you serve God with happiness and observe His way, He will grant you these blessings and remove these curses from you in order that you may be free to gain wisdom from the Torah and involve yourselves in it so that you will merit the life of the World to Come"* (*Mishna Torah*, Hilchos Teshuva 9:1). One could say that a similar reasoning could be used here with respect to the Torah's very material vision for humanity. Nevertheless, more leisure time can also mean more hedonic pursuits, which is why the blessing to the nations is also accompanied by their admiration of basic Jewish concepts and way of life.

Chapter 2

ABRAHAM'S BELIEFS AND VALUES AS THE FOUNDATIONS OF AN IDEAL SOCIETY

O ne of the missions of Abraham and his offspring is to bring *"blessing"* to humanity.

But how will they do this?

The Torah's answer is for the Jewish people to create a society whose beliefs, values and practices will ensure God's blessing. These can then be adopted by the rest of the world.

These beliefs and values were fully developed by Abraham at the beginning of his life in Canaan and included the following:

(i). Belief in One God

Many Jewish commentators have ascribed Abraham's greatness to his recognition that it is God who is the Creator of the universe and not the pantheons of the pagan world. Hence, the Book of Joshua emphasizes Abraham's merit in separating from the paganism of his family:

> *On the other side of the river, your father dwelt of old, Terach, father of Abraham and father of Nachor, and they served other gods. And I took your father Abraham from the other side of the river and led him throughout the whole land of Canaan (Joshua 24:2-3).*

Maimonides, the influential Jewish philosopher and *halachic* authority, elaborates on this in his monumental *halachic* work, the *Mishna Torah*:

> *He [Abraham] grasped the way of the truth and understood the just cause by his true perception. And he knew there is only one God who rules the world and He created all, and there is no other God except for Him. And he knew that the entire world erred and what caused them to err was that they worshiped the stars and other forms until they totally forgot the truth.*[1]

1   Maimonides, *Mishna Torah*, Laws of Idol Worship 1:3.

But was Abraham the originator of the idea that One God created the universe? The Torah mentions other monotheists who lived prior to the time of Abraham, such as Cain, Abel, Seth, Enoch, Noah, and Shem. The Torah also relates that following Abraham's victory over the forces of King Chedorlaomer and his Mesopotamian coalition and rescuing his nephew Lot from Sodom, Abraham was greeted by Malchizedek, king of Salem, who *"was a priest of El Elyon (God, the Most High)"* (Genesis 14:18). Says Malchizedek: *"Blessed is Abram of El Elyon (God the Most High), Acquirer of heaven and earth"* (14:19). It would seem, therefore, that at the time of Abraham there were other individuals, even in Canaan, who believed in a Supreme God who had created the universe.[2] There must have been more to Abraham than just his monotheism. One midrashic idea is that Abraham's greatness was his willingness to go through 10 trials to demonstrate his allegiance to God. An aggadic midrash is a piece of oral tradition written to fill in gaps in the Torah text, to interpret the text and enrich it with meaning. One midrash describes Abraham being thrown into a burning furnace and being saved by God after his father handed him over to the Mesopotamian ruler Nimrod for smashing the idols in his idol store.[3] Muhammad also used this midrash in his Qur'an. This midrash is likely based on an analogy with the story of Gideon in the Book of Judges, in that Gideon also smashed his father's idols (Judges 6:25-32). Nevertheless, there is no mention in the Torah of such a trial. Nor is there any mention of Abraham engaging in similar destructive activities when in Canaan. On the contrary, Abraham purposely lived in harmony with the pagans around him, as did his son and grandson.

---

2   There is a rabbinic tradition that Malchizedek is to be identified with Shem, the son of Noah. This tradition would make him extremely old (TB Nedarim 32b, *Midrash Tehillim* 76:3, *Targum Yonasan*, and Rashi to 14:18). Whether or not this is the case, there is a Biblical tradition that monotheism was known to other Semites through Noah and his son Shem.

3   Commenting on the phrase *"Haran [the brother of Abraham] died in the presence of Terach his father,"* (Genesis 11:28) another midrashic explanation (Genesis Rabba 38:13) is that Haran died as a result of his father's actions. In this version of the midrash, Terach accused his son Abram before the king Nimrod of having smashed his idols, and the king therefore cast Abram into a fiery furnace. *"Haran waited and said to himself, 'If Abram proves triumphant, I will be on his side; if Nimrod wins, I shall be on his.' When Abram was saved they said to Haran, 'Whose side are you on?' Haran replied, 'I am on Abram's side.' They therefore cast him into the fiery furnace and he was burnt to death. It is to this that the name of the place Ur-Kasdim alludes."* Ur Kasdim is interpreted here as Fire of the Chaldees. This and similar midrashim are popular in Jewish educational institutions. I have long argued, however, that stressing midrashim that emphasize only Abraham's monotheism detracts from other important aspects of Abraham's faith and mission.

Unique about Abraham, however, was his outreach in promoting belief in God. When outside the main cities of Canaan, he would offer a sacrifice and then he *"called in the name of God (Y-H-V-H)."*[4] People would come from the city to listen to his preaching. He also moved to the south of the country, rather than remain in the hill country, since the main trade routes were where he could engage with more people.

(ii). The concepts of general and individual providence

The gods of the pagan world were forces of nature. It would have been distant from the pagan mindset to imagine that a force of nature was interested in the welfare of the world and interested in establishing relationships with His created beings.[5] The Torah was the first text to promote the concepts of general and individual providence.

Commenting on the first blessing given to Abraham when he was asked to leave his homeland, a midrash says:

> *Rabbi Yitzchak said: this is analogous to someone who was passing from place to place and saw a certain palace ablaze. He said: "Can it be that this palace is without a supervisor?" The owner of the palace peered out at him and said to him: "I am the master of the palace." So too, because our forefather Abraham said: "Shall you say that this world is without a supervisor?" Therefore, the Holy One, blessed is He, peeked out at him and said to him "I am the Master of the world!"*[6]

Abraham looked at the natural world about him and asked: Is it possible for the world to function without Someone controlling it? A Supreme Being must be overseeing it.

The Talmud points out that Abraham was the first person to call God *"Adonai" (*Hebrew for *my Master) (Genesis 15:8).*[7]

---

4   Abraham called on the name of God between Beth El and Ai twice (Genesis 12:8 and 13:4) and once in Beersheba (Genesis 21:33). Promoting knowledge of God is the explanation of Nachmanides, Ibn Ezra and the Radak for his sacrificing outside the cities. Rashi, on the other hand, considers his sacrifices outside the city to be a supplication.

5   In the Noah story, God spoke freely to Noah. However, in the very similar Gilgamesh myth, the god Ea was only able to communicate with Upnapishtim about building an ark by speaking to the brick wall of his reed hut. "Gilgamesh Tablet XI" in *Myths from Mesopotamia. Creation, The Flood, Gilgamesh, and Others* in by Stephanie Dalley, i, 110. Oxford University Press, Revised edition 2000.

6   *Midrash Rabba* 39:1.

7   TB Berachot 7b.

Commenting on this, Rabbi Soleveitchick says:

Abraham's most significant spiritual discovery was the understanding that the Master of the Universe runs the world. The greatness of Abraham was not the discovery of God's omnipresence, represented by the Tetragrammaton, but rather the discovery of God's dominion. . . . The importance of the Name Adonai (my Master) lies in its lending the Tetragrammaton practical significance, connecting God as an abstract concept to His relationship with the world on a practical level.[8]

The forefathers, particularly Abraham's grandson Jacob who perceived angels moving between heaven and earth, were very cognizant of God's influence over everything that happens on earth. He also appreciated that God wished to have a relationship with him (28:12-15 and 28:20-22).

(iii). "*The way of God*" as the basis of Jewish ethics

In the following two sentences, the Torah mentions three fundamental values that Abraham promoted and passed on to his children:

And Abraham will surely become a great and mighty nation and all the nations of the earth will be blessed though him. For I have known him because he commands his children and his household after him to keep the way of God (Y-H-V-H), doing righteousness (tzedaka) and justice (mishpat), so that God might bring upon Abraham that which He had spoken of him (18:18-19).[9]

The 19th-century Biblical commentator Rabbi Samson Raphael Hirsch explains that the phrase "*to keep the way of God*" has a dual connotation: it is both the way that God Himself practices and the way He wishes everyone

---

8   *The Koren Mesorat Harav Siddur, with Commentary based upon the Teachings of Rabbi Joseph Soloveitchik*, 160-161. OU Press, Koren Publishers, Jerusalem. Also, *Chumash with Commentary based on the Teachings of Rabbi Joseph B. Soloveitchik*, Bereishis,95. The Neuwirth Edition, OU Press, NY 2013.

9   There is discussion among Jewish commentators as to the correct translation of this verse and in particular the awkward expression "*I know him in order that which.*" Nachmanides cites four explanations. He quotes the opinion of Rashi that it is a form of endearment, but admits that this leaves the Hebrew word *lema'an* (in order that) redundant. His other suggestions are that the world *yodati*, which I have translated as *to know*, actually means *to elevate*, i.e., God will elevate Abraham. Alternatively, it means *I know of him*. Nevertheless, even with these explanations one is still left with the double *that that*. The fourth explanation, and that favored by Nachmanides, is that *to know* means to intimately know and this verse is talking about Divine providence.

to tread.[10] It is often termed *Imitatio Dei*, or the imitation of God, and is the basis of Jewish ethics. It encompasses not only righteousness and justice, but every aspect of what is called in Hebrew *chesed*, translated as loving kindness, generosity, grace or mercy.

God runs His world through loving kindness. All people are to imitate this and base their lives on bestowing kindness to others. Just as practicing *tzedakah*, or charity, recognizes God's sovereignty over one's wealth and property, *chesed* or loving kindness recognizes that everything about a person – his or her body, possessions, and even the ability to emote, such as bestowing love — come from God.[11]

As distinct from righteousness/charity and justice, there is no prescribed measure or Torah mandate for a specific act of loving kindness other than the general mandate to walk in God's ways. Moreover, whereas the Torah's mandate regarding righteousness and justice applies only to interactions between one Jew and another, an overflow of *chesed*, or loving kindness, pertains to a Jew's relations with all humanity.

(iv). The ways of God are those of righteousness and justice

Two fundamental aspects of Abraham's ethics are righteousness (*tzedakah* in Hebrew) and justice *(mishpat)*. But what exactly do these terms mean?

The Hebrew word for righteousness, *tzedakah*, is often considered to mean a charitable contribution and it is discussed in the Talmud in this way. However, its Biblical usage includes more than this. Rabbi Samson Raphael Hirsch defines righteousness as *"something that no man has the right to demand from another, but which God has given everyone the justification to expect."*[10]

Rabbi Hirsch's definition of righteousness is an attempt to distinguish between the obligatory nature of justice versus what is usually regarded as the voluntary aspect of righteousness, but which in many instances the Torah mandates as being obligatory for Jews.

A simpler definition of *tzedakah* might therefore be social justice, as proposed by Rabbi Jonathan Sacks.[12] Other definitions could be the morally right

---

10 *The Pentateuch. Translation and Commentary* by Samson Raphael Hirsch Commentary to Genesis 19:19, 320. Judaica Press Ltd, Gateshead, 1989.

11 "Tzedakah: Brotherhood and Fellowship" in *Halakhic Morality. Essays on Ethics and Masorah* by Rabbi Joseph B. Soloveitchik, 177. Maggid Books, Jerusalem, 2017.

12 "Compassion: The Idea of Tzedaka" in *"The Dignity of Difference. How to Avoid the Clash of*

thing to do or compassion, although none of these definitions emphasizes the obligatory nature of many acts of righteousness.[13]

That the Torah regards certain acts of righteousness as being obligatory and more than being just good deeds is evident from the following passage:

> *When you lend your neighbor any manner of loan, you shall not go into his house to fetch his pledge. You shall stand outside, and the man to whom you are lending shall bring the security to you outside. And if he be a poor man, you shall not sleep with his pledge; you shall surely restore to him the pledge when the sun goes down, that he may sleep in his garment, and bless you; and for you it shall be an act of righteousness (tzedakah) before the Lord (Y-H-V-H) your God (Deuteronomy 24:10-13).[14]*

There is a spectrum in terms of the seriousness of unrighteousness. Giving a charitable donation to one's favored charitable organization is not mandated in Jewish law, and the failure to receive such a contribution may lead to no more than disappointment by its administrators. At the other end of the spectrum a victim may be in anguish because of the unrighteousness around him/her. At this point, the individual may *"cry out"* to God (in Hebrew *tze'aka*). Preventing such crying out is mandated in the Torah:

> *If you take your neighbor's garment as security, until sunset you shall re-store it unto him; for it alone is his covering, it is his garment for his skin; in what shall he lie down? So that it will be, if he cries out (yitzak) to Me, I shall listen; for I am compassionate (Exodus 22:25-26).*

There is a wordplay here between the two Hebrew words *tze'aka (crying out)* and *tzedakah* (righteousness), in that the two words sound somewhat similar but differ by a single letter. Nevertheless, the fact that this is a play on words should not detract from the seriousness of the situation. When the crying out of humanity reaches to the portals of heaven, God cannot remain indifferent:

Civilizations" by Jonathan Sacks, 105. Bloomsbury Publishing Plc, 2003.

13   "Tzedakah: Brotherhood and Fellowship" in *Halakhic Morality. Essays on Ethics and Masorah* by Rabbi Joseph B. Soloveitchik, 129. Maggid Books, Jerusalem, 2017.

14   This passage is discussing a past-due loan or other financial obligation in which the credi-tor is entitled to approach the court for the collateral. However, neither the creditor nor the court are entitled to enter the debtor's home and the collateral must be returned if it is required by the debtor. See *The Stone Edition. The Torah, Haftaros and Five Megillos with a Commentary Anthologized from the Rabbinic Writings*, 1061. Artscroll Series.

You shall not taunt or oppress a stranger; for you were strangers in the land of Egypt. You shall not cause pain to any widow or orphan. If you cause him pain — for if he shall surely cry out (tza'ok yitzak) to Me I will surely hear (shamo'a eshma) his outcry (tza'akaso). My wrath shall blaze and I shall kill you by the sword and your wives will be widows and your children orphans (22:20-23).

The verb repetitions here emphasize how seriously God considers this situation. If the stranger, widow or orphan *"surely cries out"* (literally: *crying out he will cry out) (tza'ok yitzak),* then *"I shall surely hear"* (literally: *hearing I will hear).*

Mishpat or Biblical justice is defined by Rabbi Hirsch as *"something that a person has the right to demand from another."*[10] It is a societal right to be able to demand equitable justice. Whether engrained in law or convention, justice is designed to provide the framework for an equitable and law-abiding society. *Mishpatim,* or the laws of justice, are laws that any law-abiding society, Jewish or non-Jewish, needs to institute to prevent anarchy.

To practice justice on a societal level means that a judicial system needs to be in place. On an individual level it means that the rules and regulations set up by this judicial system have to be adhered to. An example of this discussed in the Torah is the use of honest measures in trade:

You shall not commit a perversion in justice (bamishpat) in measures of length, weight or volume (Leviticus 19: 35).

The combination of righteousness and justice constitutes the full spectrum of obligatory moral behavior within Jewish society. Justice or *mishpat* is often framed in the Torah as a negative prohibition –- do not break the law by doing such and such, while righteousness or *tzedaka* is often discussed as a positive command aimed at preventing an act of unrighteousness.

Righteousness and justice are often linked together in the Bible because they need to be practiced together. Righteousness without justice is a Robin Hood situation; justice without righteousness is a cruel society.

As is often its way, the Torah illustrates these principles, the loving kindness exemplified by Abraham and the concepts of righteousness, justice and the way of God, by means of a story.

RIGHTEOUSNESS, JUSTICE AND THE WAY OF GOD IN A STORY ABOUT SODOM AND GOMORRAH

The English word story is perhaps an unfortunate one for describing the Biblical Sodom and Gomorrah account since this word implies that this is nothing more than a simple tale. However, it is anything but this. It is deep and multi-layered. One of its features is the use of contrasts, such as Abraham's concern for righteousness and justice compared to the people of Sodom's lack of these practices.

This story illustrates the following points:

- How Abraham followed the *"way of God"* with respect to hospitality and escorted his guests as they left his home.

- That *"God's ways"* in relation to the destruction of Sodom incorporated both righteousness and justice.

- Why the Canaanites forfeited their right to live in the land of Canaan.

- Why the descendants of Lot, namely the Moabites and Ammonites, could not remain in the land of Canaan but would need to move to Transjordan.

Some of these points are touched upon indirectly and become apparent only after delving deeply into the implications of this story.

Some words about the Canaanites. A discussion about the moral failures of the Canaanites does not resonate with readers of the Bible in the 21st century. However, it needs to be recalled that from the time of Moses and for hundreds of years thereafter the right of the Jewish people to displace the Canaanites was a very valid question. The Torah makes it clear that the Canaanites were being displaced on moral grounds, and the presumption has to be that the Israelites were taking their place on moral grounds (Genesis 15:16).

The story:

Abraham provided some visiting angels with a sumptuous repast, assuming they were travelers in need, and he then accompanied them a short distance in the direction of Sodom. When they had left, God informed him that He was about to scrutinize Sodom and Gomorrah because of the outcry (za'akat) coming from these cities and likely destroy them.[15] The angels who

---

15   The relationship between God and the three angels in Chapter 18 is complex. God appeared to Abraham in Genesis 18:1, but then disappeared until Genesis 18:7, when He

had just eaten in his home are on their way to Sodom to investigate the situation:

> *And God (Y-H-V-H) said: "Shall I conceal from Abraham what I do, and Abraham will surely become a great and mighty nation, and all the nations of the earth will be blessed through him?"* . . . *And God said: "Because the outcry of (za'akat) Sodom and Gomorrah has become great, and because their sin has been very grave, I will descend and see. If they acted in accordance with its outcry (ketza'akato) which came to me then destruction! And if not, I will know"* (18:17, 20-21).

Abraham was stunned. God was the model for righteousness and justice. How was it possible for a God of justice to destroy a city such as Sodom which undoubtedly contained within it many innocent people? If He did destroy this city, was He any different from the multitude of pagan deities that brought chaos to the world through their alleged control of nature? At this moment, Abraham's entire belief system in a God-given ethic hung in the balance. One can almost feel his anguish as he asked:

> *Far be it from You to do such a thing, to bring death upon the righteous (tzadik) as well as the guilty, so that righteous (ketzadik) and guilty fare alike. Far be it from You! Shall not the Judge (hashofet, i.e., the one who administers justice) of all the earth deal justly (mishpat)?* (18:25).

However, Abraham was mistaken in his conclusions. Abraham and God will now negotiate about God's decision to sweep away the innocent with the wicked, and Abraham will discover that God does indeed operate within the parameters of righteousness combined with justice.

In modern usage, the Hebrew word *tzadik* (a righteous person) is often thought of as someone who possesses considerable piety. However, this incorrect translation of Biblical Hebrew distorts our understanding of these negotiations since it implies that only someone truly pious warranted

---

had a conversation with Abraham regarding how many people were necessary to save Sodom and Gomorrah. Rashi suggests, based on TB Sotah 14a and *Tanchuma Yashan* 1, that Abraham had just been circumcised and God came to pay him a sick call. There is an ethical message here. Even God can be pushed aside, as it were, when acts of righteousness must be performed and visitors in need have to be cared for. A more literal explanation is that of the Biblical commentator Rashbam. He suggests that the first verse of Chapter 18 constitutes an introduction to the three angels visiting Abraham's tent, and the text is pointing out that God and his messengers, namely the three angels, can be considered to be functioning as one. There are other examples in the Torah of a merging of angel and Divine identities. For example, Jacob wrestled with a man but perceived the face of God (Genesis 32:31). Similarly, Exodus 3:2 and 3:4 and Exodus 23:21.

being saved. But this word has shifted in its meaning since the Bible was written. The word "*tzadik*" in the sentence above means someone in a state of innocence or who is not evil. This is evident from the following passage from Deuteronomy: "*When there will be a grievance between people and they approach the court and they judge them, and they vindicate the tzadik (innocent/ righteous one) and find the wicked one guilty*" (Deuteronomy 25:1-2).[16]

Similarly, King David asked about the murderers of Ishboshet, the son of Saul and his rival to the throne of Israel: "*How much more, when wicked men slew a righteous person (tzadik) in his own house, upon his bed, shall I not now require his blood of your hand, and take you away from the earth?*" (2 Samuel 4:11). David was not implying that Ishboshet possessed considerable piety; he meant only that he was innocent of any crime that would justify the death penalty.

Abraham began his plea for the innocent (*tzadikim* – plural of *tzadik*) of Sodom with two requests: one was that the innocent not be swept away with the wicked; the second was that Sodom be spared if there were 50 or more righteous people in the city. Surely, for the sake of so many innocent people, did not justice demand that the city be saved?

> *Abraham drew near and said: "Will You indeed sweep away the righteous together with the wicked? What if there are 50 righteous people within the city; Will You then wipe out and not spare the place for the sake of (lema'an) the 50 righteous within it?" . . . And God said: "If I find in Sodom 50 righteous people in the midst (betoch) of the city, then I would spare the entire place on their account (ba'avuram)." Abraham spoke up saying: "Behold, now, I venture to speak to my Lord although I am but dust and ash. What if the 50 righteous people lack five. Will you destroy the entire city for want of the five?" And He said: "I will not destroy if I find there 45." He spoke up again and said: "What if 40 should be found there?" And He said: "I will not do it on account of (ba'avur) the 40." And he said: "Let my Lord not be angry that I still speak: What if 30 should be found there?" And He said: "I will not act if I find there 30." So he said: "I venture again to speak to my Lord. What if 20 should be found there?" And He said: "I will not destroy on account of (ba'avur) the 20." So he said: "Let not my Lord be angry if I speak but this last time. What if 10 should be found there?" And He said: "I will not destroy on account of (ba'avur) the 10." And God departed when He had finished speaking to Abraham, and Abraham returned to his place* (Genesis 18:23-24, 26-33).

---

16 Lashes are not given because of a dispute between two people. The Talmud points out that this is a situation of conspiring witnesses (TB Makkos 13b).

A careful reading of this passage shows that God redirected the focus of Abraham's questions. God's emphasis was on the fate of the city rather than on the righteous who will be swept away. This was because if there were sufficient righteous people within it, they had the potential to change its propensity to do evil.[17]

A number of stylistic indicators justify this explanation:

- Abraham's initial focus was on the number of righteous people about to be destroyed. What if there are five fewer than 50 people, he asked. However, God's concern was not about how many fewer innocent people would suffice for the city to be saved, but about how many innocent people there needed to be inside the city for it to be saved. After the first verbal exchange, Abraham will accept this.

- In the first verbal exchange, Abraham used the Hebrew word *lemaʾan*, which has the connotation of purpose and means in order to or for the sake of the 50 righteous within it, whereas in His reply God used the Hebrew word *baʾavur*. *Baʾavuram* can have the same meaning as *lemaʾan* (*for their sake*) but can also mean on their account or because of them.[18] From this point on, Abraham will accept God's emphasis rather than his own. The conversation was now on account of the number of innocent people remaining in the city.

- The strongest support for this interpretation is that when the negotiations reached the number 10, the conversation was terminated. The presumption must be that both parties were satisfied with the results of their negotiations. Nevertheless, one can certainly ask: Why was it that fewer than 10 innocent people did not justify saving the city, whereas 10 or more did? This number seems quite arbitrary. In fact, any number is arbitrary!

An answer is that the number 10 represents a congregation of people. These 10 non-wicked people provide hope that the city can yet change its

---

17   That God's focus was on the entire city as much as its righteous inhabitants is developed in an insightful essay by R' Yaakov Beasley, and the points raised in this chapter are from his essay "Abraham's Prayer for Sodom" in The Israel Koschitzky Virtual Beit Midrash, Tanakh, Parsha, Introduction to Parashat HaShavua, Bereishit, Vayera (http://etzion.org.il/en/avrahams-prayer-sodom).

18   Another example of this is "*I will not continue to curse again the ground because (baʾavur) of man, since the imagery of man's heart is evil*" (Genesis 8:21). The cessation of cursing the ground is not for the sake of man, but secondary to man's character. Also, "*They provoked at the Waters of Strife and Moses suffered because of them (baʾavuram)*" (Psalms 106:32). In this instance, as well, Moses did not suffer for their sake but because of their actions. However, there are many times in the Bible where *baʾavur* does mean *for their sake*.

ways. Unless there are at least 10 innocent people ensconced within the city, there is no hope.

With these negotiations, God demonstrated to Abraham that He did indeed run the world with justice. But more than this. By showing that He was prepared to save the city for the sake of a congregation of 10 (and in order to save Lot as well), He also demonstrated His attribute of righteousness (*tzedaka*). Thus, God runs the world with the combined attributes of justice and righteousness. With this, Abraham's faith remained intact. And because God is the model for all human behavior, it follows that Abraham and his descendants should also engage with the world with righteousness combined with justice.

There is, of course, a question remaining. If there were still innocent people in the city but fewer than 10, what of their fate? God did not provide an answer to this question. One has to accept that He has His own calculations. Since He has the capability of saving an entire evil city, it needs to be taken on faith that He also has the ability to save the righteous/innocent within it. It may be that in certain situations God's attribute of justice does justify sweeping them away together with the wicked. However, it will soon become apparent that there was not a single innocent person in Sodom. Even Lot was not entirely blameless, although because of the merit of Abraham and the future role of his offspring in the history of Israel he also will be saved.

THE CONTRAST BETWEEN THE VALUES OF ABRAHAM AND THE PEOPLE OF SODOM

Abraham was sitting at the entrance to his tent during the heat of the day:

> *And God (Y-H-V-H) appeared to him by the terebinths of Mamre and he was sitting at the entrance of the tent in the heat of the day. Looking up, he saw three men standing near him; And when he saw them, he ran to meet them from the tent entrance, and prostrating himself to the ground he said: "My lords, if now I have found favor in your sight, please do not go on past your servant. Let a little water be brought, please, bathe your feet, and recline under the tree. And let me fetch you a morsel of bread that you may refresh yourselves; after that you shall pass on, seeing that you have come your servant's way." And they said: "So do as you have said." So, Abraham hastened into the tent to Sarah, and said: "Hurry! Make ready three se'ahs of choice flour, knead it, and make cakes." Then Abraham ran to the herd,*

took a calf, tender and good, and gave it to a servant boy who hastened to prepare it. He took curds and milk and the calf that had been prepared and set these before them; and he waited on them beneath the tree and they ate. . . . And the men arose from there and looked out toward Sodom; and Abraham walked with them to see them off (18:1-8, 16).

A suggestion made by Rashi is that Abraham was sitting at the entrance to his tent searching for passing visitors to whom he could extend hospitality.[19] However, this is by no means obvious from the text. Rather, the Bible says that the three men he noticed *"were standing before him."* This suggests an element of need. The men were travelling in the heat of the day and were likely in the groves of Mamre because of the shade they provided. It was therefore an act of *chesed* or loving kindness for Abraham to invite them into his tent so they could refresh themselves and partake of some refreshments. The text now emphasizes that Abraham not only performed a fitting act of kindness but embellished it.

All his efforts displayed his consideration for the comfort of his guests and his demonstrating how special they were to him. He initially downplayed what he was about to do for them (*"a little water, a morsel of bread"*) but then did the very opposite of this. (Common practice is to impress everyone about how much one intends doing but in actuality to do very little). He mobilized his entire household, namely his wife and his servants, to provide for his guests. The word *"hastened"* is mentioned twice in the text and *"ran"* twice. He served them himself, rather than leaving it to his servants. And as they were leaving, he personally escorted them from his tent.

Abraham had no ulterior motive for doing all this. He had had no prior interactions with his guests and was unlikely to ever meet them again. They would also have been pagans. He could have argued that since he was recently circumcised and now had a deeper relationship with God, his acts of kindness should be confined to members of his own household. Yet nothing was further from his mind. His *chesed* or kindness was for everyone in need who came within his orbit.

An obvious contrast with this were the people of Sodom. Lot was at the gate of the city and he noticed two men (in actuality angels). It was evening, and he promptly offered them hospitality for the night. The angels initially refused, but on his urging entered his home. This immediately aroused the ire of the inhabitants of Sodom:

---

19   Rashi to Genesis 18:1.

Before they had yet laid down, when the townspeople, the people of Sodom, converged upon the house, both young and old, all the people from every quarter. And they called to Lot, and said to him: "Where are the men that came to you tonight? Bring them out to us that we may know them". . . . And they [the men of Sodom] said: "Stand back." Then they [the men of Sodom] said: "This one came to sojourn, and he acts as a judge! Now we will deal worse with you than with them." And they pressed hardy upon the man, upon Lot, and moved forward to break the door (19:4-5, 9).

Abraham had been concerned that there might be innocent people in Sodom who would be swept away. However, the Bible makes it very clear that there was not one righteous person in the city! "*All*" the males of the city, young and old, had converged upon Lot's house to protest his inviting these people into his home.

But what were they protesting about? The people of Sodom were affluent. They lived in a rich and fertile plain. Nevertheless, they saw it as their civic duty to keep strangers out of their city to preserve the quality of their lives. If they encouraged hospitality or helped out the poor, even more indigents would come to Sodom. Therefore, anyone seeking assistance was immediately turned away and if, despite this, they succeeded in entering the city they were molested. No wonder that the cry from Sodom had come to God's attention.

However, it was not only righteousness that was in short supply in Sodom, but there was an impending breakdown of civic order and justice.

The men of Sodom complained that Lot "*is now acting like a judge.*" This was a reaction to Lot's comment to them to "*not act wickedly*" (19:7). It could also be that Lot had been providing judicial services for the city. The Bible mentions that "*Lot was sitting at the gate of Sodom*" (19:1) when he saw the two strangers/angels and invited them to his home. In ancient times, the gate was the place where communal activities of the city, including judicial ones, took place.

The men of Sodom were about to abuse Lot's guests. They demanded from Lot that he "*bring them [his guests] out to us, that we may know them*" (19:5). To "*know them*" is to have sexual relations with them. They wanted to sodomize his guests. But why would they want to do this? Could it be they wanted to use his guests for their own sexual gratification? Yet when Lot offers his daughters to them, they rejected his offer. In any case, it is difficult to see how an entire city could satisfy its sexual lusts using two men or two women. The matter must be deeper than this.

It is more likely that their demand to sodomize Lot's guests was not for their sexual gratification, but as a means of domination. In effect they were saying to his guests: Now that you have come unwanted into our city, we will take over your bodies and do with them as we wish.

There have been societies that have elevated the intimacy between two males as the highest form of love. This was not the homosexuality of Sodom. Rather, this was a form of sexual perversion unique to the Canaanites. It was mentioned previously in Genesis when describing the beginnings of the Canaanite civilization:

> And Noah, man of the earth, began and planted a vineyard. And he drank of the wine and became drunk; and he uncovered himself within his tent. And Ham, the father of Canaan, saw his father's nakedness, and told his two brethren outside. And Shem and Japheth took a garment, laid it upon both their shoulders, and the walked backward, and covered their father's nakedness; and their faces were turned backwards, and they saw not their father's nakedness. And Noah awoke from his wine, and knew what his youngest son had done unto him. And he said: "Cursed is Canaan; a slave of slaves shall he be to his brothers" (9:20-25).

This is a puzzling passage since it is far from clear who did what to whom. It would seem that Ham, the youngest of the sons of Noah, perpetrated some disgraceful act on their father and yet Ham's son Canaan was cursed. But Ham seems to have done no more that gaze upon his father's nakedness. Why then did Noah place a curse on Ham's son?

Rabbinic sources have suggested that Ham had homosexual relations with his father or even castrated him.[20] Cassuto agrees that Ham could have sodomized his father, but proposes that it was not Ham's son Canaan who was cursed by Noah but the Canaanite people of whom Canaan was the ancestor.[21] The Torah is suggesting that the values of a nation are often present at its beginnings and are carried through the generations. This will be true for Canaan with respect to sexual perversion and will also be true for Abraham's son Isaac with respect to righteousness, justice and loving kindness.

---

20   Rashi to Genesis 9:23 based on TB Sanhedrin 70a. Rashi does not regard Ham as being the youngest son but reinterprets "*small*" as meaning defective and disgraceful. Hence, he suggests that it was Ham who was cursed. However, according to the chronology of Nachmanides, Ham was indeed the youngest son.

21   "The Story of Noah's Intoxication" in *A Commentary on the Book of Genesis. Part Two. From Noah to Abraham* by U. Cassuto, 154. The Magnes Press, The Hebrew University, Jerusalem.

WHY SODOM AND GOMORRAH?

The question is an obvious one. Why did God choose to destroy Sodom and Gomorrah? Were they really the only wicked cities in the world at that time?

Perhaps they were or, at the very least, represented the worst cases of unrighteousness. However, Nachmanides makes another suggestion which will have significant implications for Jewish history: the fate of Sodom and Gomorrah was bound up with their location:

> *Know that the judgment of Sodom was due to the spiritual superiority of the Land of Israel since Sodom is part of "the inheritance of the Eternal" (II Samuel 20:19) and it does not suffer people who commit abominations. And just as this land would later vomit out a whole nation on account of their abominations (see Leviticus 18:25), it proceeded this by disgorging the Sodomites, for this entire people behaved worse than all of [the other Canaanite nations] both towards Heaven and mankind. It thus laid waste heaven and earth for them, and the land was destroyed forever, never to be restored, because they became haughty on account of their prosperity. The Holy One, blessed be He, thus made Sodom "a warning sign for rebellious people" (Numbers 17:25), namely for the children of Israel who were destined to inherit it, even as He warned them: "The whole land thereof is brimstone, and salt, and a burning... like the overthrow of Sodom and Gomorrah, Admah and Zeboiim, which God overthrew in His anger, and in His wrath" (Deuteronomy 29:22). For there have been among nations those who were exceedingly wicked and sinful, and yet God did not do to them as He did to Sodom. However, it was all because of the lofty spiritual level of this land that all this happened for there is "the Temple of God" (Jeremiah 7:4).[22]*

Nachmanides also points out that if Israel is forced to go into exile because of its failure to adhere to the covenant, the desolation of the land will be a reminder of the destruction of Sodom and its neighbors and why this destruction occurred. As the Torah says:

> *The later generation will say, "Your children who will arise after you and the foreigner who will come from a distant land when they will see the plagues of that land and its illnesses with which God has afflicted it. Sulfur and salt, a conflagration of the entire land, it cannot be sown and it cannot sprout, and no grass shall rise upon it; like the upheaval of Sodom and*

---

22   Nachmanides, *Commentary to the Torah*, Genesis 19:5.

Gomorrah, Admah and Zeboiim, which God overturned in His anger and wrath." And all the nations will say: "For what reason did God do so to this land; why this wrathfulness of great anger?" (Deuteronomy 29:21-23).[23]

The Land of Israel has an intrinsic holiness and cannot abide social injustice, sexual perversion and idolatry, whether their source be Canaanite or Israelite. Nations that perpetrate such evils when living on this land will eventually be ejected.[24]

This is why the prophets of old, such as Micah, Isaiah and Jeremiah, admonished the people not only about idolatry but also about their deficiencies of righteousness and justice. This is also why the practice of righteousness and justice will become essential features of many of the prophets' messianic prophecies.

ACTS OF LOVING KINDNESS AND LIVING LIVES OF HOLINESS

A hallmark of Abraham's life was doing acts of kindness to others. Maimonides links acts of kindness to the Torah command to love one's fellow man:

It is a positive commandment ordained by the Rabbis to visit the sick, comfort the mourners, join a funeral procession, dower a bride, escort departing guests, perform for the dead the last tender offices, act as pallbearer, go before the bier, make lamentation [for the dead], dig a grave and bury the body, as well as to cause the bride and bridegroom to rejoice and provide

---

23 Mark Twain wrote in his book *The Innocents Abroad*, describing his brief visit to Palestine in 1867 at a time that the country was under Ottoman rule: *"A desolate country whose soil is rich enough, but is given over wholly to weeds. . . . A silent mournful expanse. . . . a desolation. . . . We never saw a human being on the whole route. . . . hardly a tree or shrub anywhere. Even the olive tree and the cactus, those fast friends of a worthless soil, had almost deserted the country."* However, it has been pointed out that Mark Twain visited Palestine during the middle of the summer when the country usually looks arid because there is no rainfall then, and he was probably making comparisons to the United States which has a different type of climate. In addition, he viewed only a small part of the country, namely that with Biblical connotations. Nevertheless, it is the case that no nation that has colonized this country has been able to make it bloom as have the Jews. It is as if the land had been waiting for the return of the Jewish people to reveal its fertility.

24 Nachmanides similarly comments on the Biblical verse *"For the inhabitants of the land who were before you committed all these abominations and the land became contaminated. Let not the land disgorge you for having contaminated it, as it disgorged the nation that was before you"* (Leviticus 18:27-28), that this land will disgorge anyone who contaminates it, and it is unable to tolerate those who worship idols or engage in sexual immorality (See also *Sifra*, Kedoshim, Parshesa 4, Perek 12:14).

them with all their needs [for the wedding]. These constitute deeds of loving kindness performed in person and for which no fixed limit is prescribed. Although all these commands are only on rabbinic authority, they are implied in the precept "And you shall love your fellow as yourself" (Leviticus 19:18). That is, what you would have others do to you, do to him who is your brother in the law and in the performance of the commandments."[25]

To create its ideal society, the Torah wants more than just avoidance of acts of unrighteousness and injustice and occasional acts of righteousness or *tzedakah*. It wants a nation in which every Jew expresses love for all other Jews. Rabbi Akiva considered this to be a foundational principle of the Torah since so many other commands are based upon it.[26]

The first step in the love of another is the removal of all hatred one feels to someone who has wronged one. This can be accomplished by reproving that individual. It could be that the perpetrator was misunderstood; or, when confronted, he may admit his guilt and apologize.

You shall not hate your brother in your heart; you shall reprove your fellow and you shall not bear a sin because of him. You shall not take revenge and you shall not bear a grudge against the members of your people; you shall love to your fellow as yourself – I am God (Y-H-V-H) (Leviticus 19:17-18).

But is it really possible to love another person as one loves oneself? The authoritative medieval *halachist* and philosopher Maimonides thinks it is. In two places in his *Mishna Torah* he adopts a positive formulation as the way to carry out this command:

It is incumbent on every person to love each individual Israelite as himself, as it said: "And you shall love your fellow as yourself" (Leviticus 19:18). Hence, a person ought to speak in his praise and be careful of his property as he is careful of his own property and solicitous about his own honor. Whosoever glorifies himself by humiliating another person has no portion in the World to Come.[27]

Maimonides is suggesting that all Jews should have an emotional sympathy for all other Jews. Just as you love yourself and are concerned about

---

25   Maimonides *Mishna Torah*, Hilchot Avel (Mourning) 14:1.
26   TY Nedarim 4:9. Also, Rashi on Leviticus 19:18 quoting *Toras Kohanim* 4:12. It is foundational because many other principles of interpersonal relations are derived from it. The *Sefer HaHinnuch* (#243) explains: "*Thus, a person who loves another as himself will not steal from him, will not commit adultery with his wife, will not cheat him of goods or oppress him with words, will not move his boundary, and will not harm him in any way.*"
27   Maimonides *Mishna Torah*, Hilchot De'ot 6:13.

your own welfare, so should you be concerned about the welfare of others.[28] Nevertheless when it comes to actions one undertakes for one's neighbor, Maimonides does not place oneself and one's neighbor on the same level since this is neither possible nor *halachically* required. Rather, his guiding principle is what one would expect others to do for oneself. *"That is, what you would have others do to you, do to him who is your brother in the law and in the performance of the commandments."*[25]

Nachmanides and Rabbi Hirsch accept Maimonides' positive formulation but note that the Torah does not say love your neighbor but *"love to your neighbor."* He feels that it is unnatural to have an emotional attachment to the person of one's neighbor. Rather, Nachmanides suggests that one should not envy what one's neighbor has in terms of his "*wealth, property, honor, knowledge and wisdo*m" and should harbor no jealousy towards him.[29] Similarly, Rabbi Hirsch explains one should act in a loving manner towards everything that pertains to one's neighbor, and *"rejoice in his good fortune and grieve over his misfortune as if were our own."*[30]

The great sage Hillel also recognized that this command should be expressed in terms of what one does for one's neighbor rather placing him on the same emotional level as oneself, but he formulated the command in a different way: *"What is hateful to you, do not do to others."*[31]

But is this not changing around the Torah's words? A way of reconciling this negative formulation of the command with the positive formulation written in the Torah is the suggestion that to love one's fellow as oneself is the overarching concept, but its practical application can be the way of Hillel.[32]

In conclusion, Abraham discovered the formula for God-guaranteed prosperity and happiness for himself, his family, his future nation, and all of mankind: practicing righteousness and justice and adhering to the way of God by doing acts of kindness. The latter is expressed by loving one's neighbors. This is the Torah's masterplan for the creation of a holy, utopian society. To promote these ideas, Abraham was promised a land from which to

---

28 "Tzedakah: Brotherhood and Fellowship" in *Halakhic Morality. Essays on Ethics and Masorah* by Rabbi Joseph B. Soloveitchik, 168. Maggid Books, Jerusalem, 2017.

29 Nachmanides, *Commentary to the Torah*, Leviticus 19:17-18.

30 *The Pentateuch. Translation and Commentary* by Samson Raphael Hirsch, commentary to Leviticus 19:18.

31 TB Shabbat 31a.

32 "Birkhat Ya'avetz" by R. David Cohen, volume 1, 45-52, Mesorah Publications, 1986. Quoted in "The Love-Hate Relationship: Love and Hatred" in *The Right and the Good. Halakhah and Human Relations* by Daniel Z. Feldman, 169-183. Yashar Books, 2005. This book offers an excellent analysis of the issues involved in this command.

promulgate them and a son who would continue to disseminate them. This is hardly the totality of Judaism, but it is a large part. This is why the prophet Micah said: "*He has told you, O man, what is good and what God demands of you; but to do justice, to love loving kindness, and to walk humbly with your God*" (Micah 6:8).[33]

To carry out their role the Jewish people will need to be redeemed from Egypt following an exile of hundreds of years. The theological ramifications of this will be the next topic of discussion.

33　Judaism does not advocate that gentiles should convert to Judaism. According to Jewish tradition seven Laws of Noah or Noahide laws were given by God as a binding set of universal moral laws to all humanity. These include prohibitions against worshipping idols, cursing God, murder, adultery, sexual immorality, theft, and eating flesh torn from a living animal, and the obligation to set up courts of justice (TB Sanhedrin 59a). Although essential fundamentals, I would argue that these laws are not necessarily sufficient to lead to the establishment of a utopian society.

Chapter 3

MOSES AS THE AGENT OF REDEMPTION

The Exodus from Egypt was a watershed in human history. During this one-time event God demonstrated to the Israelites and Egyptians His ability to manipulate the natural world and influence world history according to His will. By liberating the Israelite slaves from Egypt, He also demonstrated to the Israelites that He had more right to their allegiance and service than a human master such as Pharaoh.

These are crucial theological concepts. Hence, the Ten Commandments given at Mount Sinai opens with the words "*I am Y-H-V-H your God who brought you out of the land of Egypt from the house of bondage*" (Exodus 20:2). This statement is God's claim to authority. The covenant given at Mount Sinai also presented the outline of an ideal egalitarian society to be created in the Land of Israel under God's sovereignty.

There have been social revolutions since the Israelite exodus from Egypt, particularly from the 18th century on, but they had nothing to do with God. They were therefore unable to create true freedom but merely exchanged one form of oppression for another.

The person who initiated this religious and political revolution was an individual with a history of social activism and a long-standing identity problem called Moses.

A REVELATION AT THE BURNING BUSH

All this began at a burning bush.

The closer Moses approached the bush in front of him the stranger it appeared. There were flames within the center of the bush and yet it was not consumed:

An angel of God (Y-H-V-H) appeared to him in a blazing fire from within a bush. He gazed and behold! The bush was ablaze in fire, yet the bush was not consumed. Moses said: "I must turn aside to look at this wondrous site – why the bush does not burn up." And when God saw that he turned aside to look, God (Elohim) called out to him from the midst of the bush and said: "Moses, Moses," and he replied: "Here I am!" And He [Elohim] said: "Do not come closer! Take your shoes from off your feet, for the place upon which you stand is holy ground" (3:2-5).[1]

Even more to his surprise, Moses found that not only was he beholding a vision of God but that God was now attempting to recruit him for a mission!

*And He [Y-H-V-H] said: "I am the God of your father, the God of Abraham, the God of Isaac, and the God of Jacob . . ." God said: "I have surely seen the **affliction** of My people that is in Egypt and have heeded its **outcry** because of its taskmasters, for I know its **pain**. I have come down to rescue it from the hand of Egypt and to bring it up from that land to a good and spacious land, to a land flowing with milk and honey, to the place of the Canaanite, the Hittites, the Amorites, the Perizzites, the Hivites, and the Jebusites. And now, behold, the **outcry** of the Children of Israel has reached Me; moreover, I have seen the **oppression** wherewith the Egyptians **oppress** them. Now go and I will send you to Pharaoh and you shall take My people, the Children of Israel, from Egypt" (3:6, 7-10).*

This passage shouts out the oppression of the Jewish people. God heard their *"outcry,"* their *"pain,"* their *"oppression,"* their being *"oppressed."* All these are words that would resonate with someone who feels strongly about injustice.[2]

---

1 Jewish commentators see symbolism in the Burning Bush. It could, for example, represent the lowly position of an eternal Jewish people being burnt, but not consumed, by Egyptian oppression. This is the explanation of *Midrash Shemos*, Hizkuni and Rabbeinu Bachya. The *Midrash Shemos Rabba* 1:9 explains that no place, not even a bush, is devoid of the Divine Presence. Rashi, Rashbam and Ibn Ezra viewed the Burning Bush as *"the sign for you that I have sent you"* (Exodus 3:12). Another idea is that it is linked to God's further revelation to Moses. The Burning Bush is a reflection of aspects of God Himself. A bush that burns but is not consumed is not fettered by the dimension of time. Its past, its present and its future have merged into one. This is also seen in the name of God Y-H-V-H (see reference 7).

2 "The Two Consecrations of Moses" by Rav Yonatan Grossman in *Torah Mietzion, New Readings in Tanach. Shemot*, 23, Editors Rav Ezra Bick and Rav Yaakov Beasley. Maggid Books, Yeshivat Har Etzion. In this insightful essay, the author points out that the nature of God's recruitment speech at the Burning Bush fits in with the notion that God was addressing Himself at this stage primarily to an individual with a strong sense of moral rectitude, but not necessarily a strong sense of Jewish identity.

Nevertheless, Moses had doubts he was the right person for the job (Exodus 3:11).[3] He also wished to know God's name since in the ancient world the name of a god reflected its attributes. He needed this not only for his own understanding but to convey this information to the Israelite slaves.

In responding to Moses' question, God signed off, so to speak, on His name Elohim and provided information about a new name, Y-H-V-H:

Moses said to God (Elohim): "Behold, when I come to the children of Israel and say to them: 'The God of your forefathers has sent me to you, and they ask me "What is His name?" what shall I say to them?" And God (Y-H-V-H) said to Moses: "I Shall Be What I Shall Be." And He said: "So shall you say to the Children of Israel: 'I Shall Be has sent me to you.' " God (Elohim) said further to Moses: "So shall you say to the Children of Israel; 'Y-H-V-H the God of your forefathers, the God of Abraham, the God of Isaac and the God of Jacob has sent me to you. This shall be My name forever, and this shall be My appellation from generation to generation'" (3:13-15).

The first chapter of this book discussed the Torah's use of the two main names for God, Elohim and Y-H-V-H. Each of these names describes different attributes of God. The name Elohim, first mentioned in the first chapter of Genesis, reflects the transcendent aspect of the One God who created the universe and who is concerned with the general providence of all mankind. The name Y-H-V-H describes the immanent aspect of God and a God concerned with individual providence.

The forefathers of the Jewish people, Abraham, Isaac and Jacob, were familiar with the Y-H-V-H aspect of God and brought their relationship with Him to new heights of trust and intimacy. However, this knowledge became distant to Jacob and his family when they left Laban's home in Mesopotamia and returned to the land of Canaan. Jacob's sons never referred to God by the name Y-H-V-H. When Joseph spoke about God to the Egyptians and his family (which he did frequently), he mentioned only the name Elohim. Nevertheless, the Torah makes it clear that Y-H-V-H continued to work behind the scenes while Joseph was in Egypt to further His plans for Jacob's descendants.[4]

---

3   Commenting on Exodus 4:1, Maimonides views Moses' hesitation as reflecting his concern that signs alone would be inadequate to further the belief of the people in his mission (*Mishna Torah*, Hilchos Yesodei Hatorah 8:2). Other commentators view Moses' hesitation and his concern that Pharaoh and the people would not believe in him as an inappropriate response to God's request (*Ve'Eilleh Shemos Rabba*, Abarbanel, Sforno, and Nachmanides).

4   The name of God Y-H-V-H was mentioned by Jacob in Genesis 32:10 just before he reentered Israel and while he was still on the other side of the Jordan, and once more towards

The episode at the Burning Bush was unique in that this was the only instance in history in which a Divinity named Himself in a way that reflected His own attributes, rather than being named by humans.[5] The name Elohim, for example, reflects human perception of the powers of God.

God now revealed to Moses that His name Y-H-V-H was based on the future tense of the verb "to be."[6] Y-H-V-H was the God of relationships who revealed Himself to Abraham, Isaac and Jacob, and who was now forging a relationship with Moses and who *"will be"* with Moses throughout this mission for which he was being recruited.[7] It is also noteworthy that God specifically referred to the Israelites as *"My people."* Y-H-V-H was therefore identifying Himself as the future tribal God of the Israelite people. As such, He also *"will be"* with the Israelite nation as they tread their way through history.

Moses was promised God's assistance in this mission. He was provided with *"signs"* he could use to convince the Israelites of the authenticity of his revelation from God and as an indicator of His role within nature and history, and was offered the assistance of his brother, Aaron, as his spokesman. Moses

---

the end of Genesis (49:18) when he blessed his sons. Nevertheless, despite such infrequent mention, the Book of Genesis indicates that the aspect of God Y-H-V-H was still involved behind the scenes with Jacob's family. For example, Genesis 38:7, 39:2: *"And God (Y-H-V-H) was with Joseph, and he became a successful man. . . "* and Genesis 39:21: "God *(Y-H-V-H) was with Joseph."*

5   This name of God possesses special reverence both when written and in speech. However, its exact pronunciation has been lost through the generations, as it was only uttered in the Tabernacle and Holy Temple.

6   To anyone but God, the tense of the verb to be should be in the third person: *"He Will Be"* *(yihiye)*. However, if this were the case, the Hebrew spelling of YHVH should be YH**Y**H, with the Hebrew letter *yud* (y in English) that indicates the future tense being the third letter of His name instead of *vov* (v in English). This suggests that the letter *vov* indicates that God's name also contains within it aspects of the present tense since the present tense of the verb *to be* is *hava* (הוה) containing a *vav*. Also within this name is the past tense of the verb to be, *haya* (היה). The combination of all tenses of the verb to be in His name indicates God's complete independence from time and His complete mastery over the past, present and all aspects of the future. This explanation is based on "First Paragraph. The Theophany on Mount Horeb" in *A Commentary on the Book of Exodus* by Umberto David Cassuto, 37. Vara Books, Skokie IL, USA.

7   Based on a midrash (*Shemos Rabba* 3:6) and the Talmud (TB Berachos 9b), Rashi explains this name as indicating that God will be with the Jewish people during the difficulties of the Exodus and also during future hard times. Onkelos sees in this name a promise that God will show mercy and favor to whomever He wishes. Rabbi Samson Raphael Hirsch suggests that the name Y-H-V-H describes the nature of God in relation to the universe He has created. Everything in the universe is the product of the laws of nature. Only God can *"be"* (and can do) whatever He wishes *"to be"* (and do) since He is not bound by the constraints of causality (Rabbi Samson Raphael Hirsch, *Commentary to the Pentateuch* on Exodus 3:14).

acquiesced to God's request and returned home to Midian to prepare his family for returning to Egypt.

Moses was again a social activist, as he was when younger.

WHY MOSES?

God needed a leader who would work with Him to redeem the Israelites from Egypt and lead them to the land of Canaan.

What type of person was He looking for?

One requisite would be someone who was familiar with the inner workings of the Egyptian court, who could present himself as an equal to the Egyptian royalty and who had sufficient presence to obtain their respect.

However, this alone would be insufficient. The CEO of an organization must reflect the values of that organization, especially when this organization was formed by God! Moses needed to exemplify the values that God wished imprinted on His people. He also needed to feel a strong identity and empathy with the people he was about to redeem.

Having been being brought up in the Egyptian court, there would have been no concern as to how Moses would present himself to Pharaoh. However, having spent much of his adult life as a shepherd in Midian, it was far from obvious that he exemplified Jewish values and identified strongly with the Jewish people.

Nevertheless, the Torah goes out of its way to emphasize that Moses possessed a foundational aspect of Judaism, in that he was a self-made person with strong feelings about social justice.

The Bible relates Moses' birth in the following way: *"A man went from the house of Levi and he took a daughter of Levi. The woman conceived and gave birth to a son"* (2:1)

This all seems so anonymous. In fact, it will be several more chapters before the Torah tells us that Moses' father was called Amram and his mother Yochebed (Exodus 6:20). The Torah may be emphasizing in this way that Moses' confidence was reflective of someone brought up in the Egyptian court but independent in his thinking. He was not completely Egyptian, but neither did he have the slave mentality of the Israelites.[8]

---

8   The Abarbanel writes: *"He was first exiled to Pharaoh's palace so that he could learn the tactics of leadership and monarchy which would cause him to develop courage and spiritual greatness."* Nachshoni makes the point that the Bible wishes to make a contrast with pagan literature, which attributes leadership to descent from the gods. (Y. Nachshoni, *Studies*

By the time he reached maturity, he was displaying the assertiveness of an Egyptian noble and a passion for social justice:

And it was in those days that Moses grew up and went out to his breth-
ren and witnessed their burdens: and he saw an Egyptian man beating a
Hebrew man, one of his brothers. He turned this way and that and saw
that there was no man, and he struck the Egyptian and hid him in the
sand (2:11-12).[9]

These are pivotal sentences. Despite his unusual upbringing in the Egyptian palace, raised by a princess, Moses was clearly aware of his Jewish background. Twice this passage emphasizes the words "*his broth-*
ers." Hence, he "*went out to his brothers*," and the slave being beaten was not only a "*Hebrew man*" but also "*one of his brothers*." It could be that the palace had made no effort to hide his ethnic background. He may even have experienced teasing from his Egyptian playmates. Whatever the reason, Moses was drawn towards the Israelite slaves and the injustices being perpetrated against them.

Moses' killing of the Egyptian was an extremely bold step. It consti-
tuted an act of rebellion against the entire institution of Egyptian slavery and the enslavement and harsh treatment of the Israelites in particular. He was also declaring his identification with their suffering. However, from a political perspective it was not a particularly smart move. In the absence of a practical plan, it would have no effect whatsoever on Israelite servitude. Moreover, if the death of the Egyptian taskmaster were discovered, the blame would automatically fall on the Israelites. This could only be pre-
vented by their denouncing Moses. The Israelite slaves would have had no compunction about doing this since it is doubtful they recognized Moses as being one of their tribe.

The next day Moses continued his social activism in the belief that injustice needs to be righted, whatever its source:

He went out the next day and behold two Hebrew men were fighting. He
said to the offender: "Why do you strike your fellow?" He replied: "Who

---

in the *Weekly Parsha; Sh'mos,* 323. Artscroll Judaica Classics, Mesorah Publications Ltd,
Brooklyn, NY.). My explanation is contrary to that of Abarbanel, who feels that Moses
would have developed an attachment to his biological mother and nursemaid Yocheved
during the very early years of his life.

9   Rashi to Exodus 2:11 follows *Shemos Rabbah* 1:27 that notes that the Torah says that he
saw "*into*" their burdens. In other words, this made an impression on him. Nachmanides
has a similar explanation.

made you a man, a ruler and a judge over us? Are you going to kill me as you killed the Egyptian?" (2:14.)

His killing of the Egyptian had become generally known, and it would not be long before *"Pharaoh heard about this matter and sought to kill Moses"* (2:15).

Moses' attempt at combating injustice had failed dismally, and there was no alternative for him but to flee Egypt.

Despite this setback, Moses' feelings about moral rectitude remained unabated. On arriving in Midian, he saw that the seven daughters of the priest of Midian were driven away by shepherds when they began drawing water from a well for their father's sheep. This aroused Moses' ire: *"Moses got up and saved them and watered their flock"* (2:17).

To these young women, Moses looked like an Egyptian and acted like one. He was invited into the home of Reuel, the priest of Midian, and married one of his daughters. Nevertheless, Jewish by birth and culturally an Egyptian aristocrat, Moses was unable to relate to being a Midianite any more than to his two other identities. This rootlessness could explain his naming his new son Gershon: *"He named him Gershom, for he said, 'I have been a stranger in a strange land' "* (2:22).[10]

Rabbi Samson Raphael Hirsch provides another reason why Moses was such an appropriate leader for redeeming the Jewish people.[11] God was not seeking an individual with an ego who would jump at the opportunity for leadership. In response to God's recruitment speech, Moses expressed considerable doubt he was the right person for this mission since he felt it beyond his capabilities. He also pointed out his lack of oratory skills. Such humility was precisely what God was looking for since Moses was not undertaking his own mission but rather God's.

God's second recruitment speech to Moses

When Moses arrived in Egypt, the people were much heartened by his message:

---

10   Rabbi Samson Raphael Hirsch, *Commentary to the Pentateuch* on Exodus 3:12.

11   The name *"Gershom"* comes from the Hebrew word *"ger,"* meaning a stranger. Another possible meaning to this name, besides Moses feeling distant from Midianite society, is that the root letters g-r-sh mean to drive out or expel (*legaresh*). In other words, he regretted being forced out of Egypt.

And the people believed and they heard that God (Y-H-V-H) had remembered the Children of Israel and that He saw their affliction, and they bowed their heads and prostrated themselves (4:31).

However, as God had previously warned him would happen, Moses' first encounter with Pharaoh failed abysmally. Pharaoh not only refused permission for his Israelite slaves to leave Egypt for a three-day festival, but they were now charged with finding their own straw for brick-making. The Israelites were devastated and understandably blamed Moses for this reversal. Moses in turn questioned God as to why this had happened: *"My Master,"* Moses complained, *"why have You harmed this people, why have You sent me? From the time I came to Pharaoh to speak in Your name, he has harmed this people, but You have not rescued Your people"* (5:22-23).

The situation had reached rock bottom for the Hebrew slaves. This occasioned a second speech by God to persuade Moses to continue with his mission. The analysis of this recruitment speech is of interest. It is in two sections which I label section 1 and section 2:

[Introduction] And Elohim spoke to Moses and said to him, **"I am God (Y-H-V-H).**

[Section 1] And I appeared to Abraham, to Isaac, and to Jacob as El Shaddai, and My name Y-H-V-H was not known to them.

And I also established My covenant with them, to give them the land of Canaan, the land of their sojourning, where they sojourned.

And I have also heard the wail of the Children of Israel whom Egypt enslaves, and I have remembered My covenant. Therefore, say to the Children of Israel: 'I am God **(Y-H-V-H).**

[Section 2] And I shall take you out from under the burdens of Egypt. And I shall rescue you from their service, I shall redeem you with an outstretched arm and with great judgments. I shall take you to Me for a people, and I shall be a God to you, and you shall know that I am Y-H-V-H your God Who takes you out from under the burdens of Egypt.

I shall bring you to the land about which I have raised My hand [i.e., I swore] to give it to Abraham, to Isaac and to Jacob, and I shall give it to you as a heritage. **I am God (Y-H-V-H)'** *"* (6:2-8).

This speech has a very precise literary format consisting of an introduction emphasizing that the spokesperson is God, followed by two sections, each of which is framed at its end by the phrase *"I am God (Y-H-V-H)."* The first section of the speech consists of a summary of what God has done until now for the Israelites, while the second section summarizes what God is about to do regarding each of these points. This second section is also directed at "*you*," the Children of Israel.

The equivalence between the first section containing God's promises and the second section containing God's plan for redemption is indicated in an interesting way. From the beginning of the first section beginning with the sentence "*And I appeared to Abraham . . . .*" until the end of the first paragraph, which ends with "*Therefore, say to the Children of Israel: I am God (Y-H-V-H) (6:8)*" there are 50 Hebrew words. From this point until the end of the second section there are also 50 Hebrew words. The equivalence between God's actions in the past and His promises for the future will be fulfilled to His very last word!

Unlike numbers seven and eight (and also 40 which I have not discussed), the use of the number 50 is uncommon in the Torah. It is found only once, when describing the *Yovel* or Jubilee year. After seven repetitions of the seven-year Sabbatical cycle in which the land is at rest for one year in seven, the 50th year is also a year of rest for the land and is called the *Yovel* year. The *Yovel* is the year in which you shall "*proclaim freedom throughout the land for all its inhabitants*" and everyone will return to their "*ancestral inheritance*" (Leviticus 25:10). It is also a time of social justice during which those in slavery are able to regain their freedom, return to their ancestral possession and become servants only to God. These are the very same themes that are evident in the Exodus, when God bestowed liberty upon the Israelites so they could serve Him in freedom in their own land.

The Exodus from Egypt will be entirely God's show, and the people will be almost passive in their redemption. Here, too, equivalence is apparent. The Israelites were passive in becoming slaves to Pharaoh, and they will now be passive in their transfer to God's service. Their sole involvement will be to demonstrate their allegiance to Him before the Plague of the Firstborn, by smearing blood on the doorposts of their homes from the blood of the Paschal lamb and eating this roasted lamb while dressed, ready to leave Egypt.

God's exclusive involvement in Israel's deliverance described in the second section of the above quotation is emphasized by seven expressions of delivery with seven verbs. The use of the number seven again indicates the sole involvement of God.[12] The expressions of deliverance are as follows:

---

12   Jewish tradition identifies four expressions of deliverance, and these are toasted with four cups of wine at the Passover eve *seder* service. The phrases "*I shall take you to Me for a*

"I shall take you out from under the burdens of Egypt."

"I shall rescue you from their service."

"I shall redeem you with an outstretched arm and with great judgments."

"I shall take you to Me for a people."

"And I shall be a God to you."

"I shall bring you to the land."

"And I shall give it you as a heritage."

The second sentence of the first section of this speech warrants discussion as it is somewhat enigmatic:

"And I appeared to Abraham, to Isaac, and to Jacob as El Shaddai, but I was not known to them by my name [of God] Y-H-V-H" (Exodus 6:2-3).

The question is an obvious one. How could the Torah say that the forefathers did not know the name of God, Y-H-V-H, when there are many references in Genesis indicating that they did know this name?[13]

Jewish commentators are in agreement that knowledge of God's name means something other than just knowing that this name exists. One direction in interpretation is that this new aspect of God relates to actions He will perform in the future that were heretofore unknown to the forefathers.[14]

---

people" and *"And I shall be a God to you"* are joined together as one, and the last two expressions are left for messianic times. Nevertheless, a division into seven expressions of deliverance is compatible with Biblical style of writing.

13 These are some examples: At the Covenant between the Pieces, God said to Abraham: *"I am Y-H-V-H who brought you out of Ur Kasdim to give you this land to inherit it"* (Genesis 15:7). Isaac was also familiar with the name Y-H-V-H and prayed to Him to relieve the infertility of his wife: *"Isaac entreated Y-H-V-H opposite his wife because she was barren, and Y-H-V-H allowed himself to be entreated by him, and his wife Rebecca conceived"* (Exodus 25:21). And when awakening from his vision of a ladder extending to heaven Jacob exclaimed: *"Surely, Y-H-V-H is in this place and I did not know"* (Genesis 28:16).

14 Rashi sees in this name God's assurance that He would remain faithful to his word and fulfill the promises He made to the forefathers (Rashi on Exodus 6:3). Nachmanides and Ibn Ezra suggest that this new aspect of Y-H-V-H expresses the ability of God to function above the natural order of the world. Abarbanel disagrees with Nachmanides and Ibn Ezra and feels that the forefathers also experienced supernatural events: e.g., the plague that afflicted the Egyptian pharaoh because of his conduct with Sarah, the overturning of Sodom and Gomorrah, the rescue of Lot, and the turning of Lot's wife into a pillar of salt. He suggests that the name Y-H-V-H expresses the open revelation of God, as manifested, for

Another approach is that the Torah is discussing an attribute of God contained within the name Y-H-V-H that was unknown to Abraham, Isaac and Jacob. Y-H-V-H previously encompassed God's providence to the forefathers as individuals. It will now encompass His providence to their descendants as a national God. The forefathers had no experience of this.

Finally, the third sentence of this passage makes reference to God's covenant. As discussed in the first chapter, God made two contracts with Abraham; the Covenant between the Pieces under His name Y-H-V-H, and the Covenant of Circumcision under His name Elohim. In this speech in the Book of Exodus, God referred back to the Covenant between the Pieces made by Y-H-V-H in which the theme of the heritage promised to Abraham was central (Genesis 15:1-21). As a consequence of the Exodus, this heritage will now be bestowed upon the Children of Israel:

> *I shall bring you to the land about which I have raised My hand to give it to Abraham, Isaac and Jacob, and I shall give it to you as a* **heritage**. *I am God (Y-H-V-H)* (Exodus 6:8).

One might think that after thousands of years of studying the same Five Books of Moses new methods of interpretation of the text would be unlikely. However, a new direction within Orthodoxy, the main promoter of this method, is literary analysis of the Torah text. That this is revealing many gems should not surprise us since the Torah is more than an ordinary text; it is replete with messages waiting to be revealed. The Torah is also a carefully-woven book with interlinking stories and passages. The search for harmony within the Pentateuch represents a sea change within academia, which in the past focused on searching for disharmony as a consequence of its presumed multiple authorship.

THE TEN PLAGUES

The Ten Plagues were not just 10 natural devastations that happened to affect Egypt at a time opportune for the Israelites but were part of a planned sequence brought about entirely by the agency of God. This message is emphasized in the Torah in a number of ways:

- God was able to turn the plagues on and off at will.

  Hence, when Moses asked Pharaoh when he would like the plague of

---

example, in the splitting of the Red Sea and at Mount Sinai. However, none of these suggestions relate specifically to the meaning of the word Y-H-V-H as a form of the verb *to be*.

frogs removed, Pharaoh brazenly tested Moses by asking *"for tomorrow"* (8:6). Moses obliged: *"As you say – so that you will know there is none like the Lord (Y-H-V-H) our God"* (8:6). *"Tomorrow"* now became a feature of other plagues as well, namely the removal of the mixed beasts (8:25) and the pestilence affecting the livestock (9:5).

- God made a separation between the Egyptians and the Israelites for the plagues of mixed beasts, the plague of darkness and the Plague of the Firstborn:

  And on that day I shall distinguish the land of Goshen upon which My people stands, that there be no mixture of wild beasts there; so that you will know that I am God (Y-H-V-H) in the midst of the land (8:18).

- With their incantations, Pharaoh's magician advisors were able to replicate plagues that already existed, namely the plagues of blood and frogs. However, by the third plague, the plague of lice, they were forced to admit that this plague was beyond their ability to reproduce: *"And the lice-infestation was on man and beast. The sorcerers said to Pharaoh, 'It is the finger of Elohim!' "* (8:15).

A finger, of course, is part of the hand of God. Unwittingly, they had announced that seven out of the 10 plagues were yet to come!

There have been attempts by Jewish commentators to subdivide the plagues into different groups.[15] A division proposed by Rabbi Moshe Lichtenstein looks not so much at the details of the plagues but their purpose.[16] On this basis, he divides the plagues into two groups: the first group being

---

15 The best-known grouping is that of Rabbi Yehuda described in the *seder* service of the Passover evening that divides the plagues into a first group of the first three plagues, a second group of the next three plagues, and a final grouping of the last four plagues. The first three plagues were brought about by Moses' staff; Moses used no object for bringing on plagues four to six; and plagues seven to nine involved Moses' hands, with or without the use of his staff. ("Chapter 7: The Education of Pharaoh. Recognizing Literary Patterns" in *Between the Lines of the Bible. Exodus. A Study from the New School of Orthodox Torah Commentary* by Yitzchak Etshalom, 84. Urim Publications, Jerusalem and New York, 2012). While useful for summarizing a system within the plagues it is difficult to see within Rabbi Yehuda's grouping any profound meaning. Another logical grouping divides the plagues into a group of five and then four. In the first five plagues Pharaoh hardened his own heart, while in the next four God hardened Pharaoh's heart. The Plague of the Firstborn is obviously outside this grouping.

16 "Between Va'era and Bo" by Rabbi Moshe Lichtenstein in *Torah Mietzion, New Readings in Tanach. Shemot,* Editors Rav Ezra Bick and Rav Yaakov Beasley, 101. Maggid Books, Yeshivat Har Etzion.

the first seven plagues and the second group the last three plagues of locusts, darkness and the Plague of the Firstborn.

The purpose of the first seven plagues was to instill in Pharaoh and his people recognition of the existence of God and His sovereignty over the universe. Hence, before the onset of the plagues, Moses and Aaron requested permission from Pharaoh for the Israelites to go into the wilderness to celebrate to their God Y-H-V-H (5:1), to which Pharaoh exclaimed: *"Who is God (Y-H-V-H) that I should listen to His voice to send out Israel? I do not know God, nor will I send out Israel"* (5:2).

In reference to this, God announced before the first plague: *"Through this [the first plague] shall you [Pharaoh] know that I am God"* (7:17).

Similarly, when introducing the seventh plague of hail, God told Moses to inform Pharaoh:

> *For this time, I [God] shall send my plagues against your [Pharoah's] heart, and upon your servants and your people, so that you should know that there is none like Me in all the world. . . . On account of this I have left you [Pharaoh] standing, in order to show you My power and so that My Name may be declared throughout the world* (9:14, 16).

This same point was also emphasized by Moses when he dispersed this plague: *"Moses said to him [Pharaoh]: 'When I leave the city, I shall spread out my hands to God, the thunder will cease and the hail will no longer be, so that you shall know that the earth is God's' "* (9:29).

Because the purpose of the first seven plagues was for Pharaoh to appreciate God's existence and control over nature, Pharaoh's necromancers or magicians were his advisors since they were the ones considered by the Egyptians to have a direct line to the spiritual world. Nevertheless, the Torah subtly pokes fun at their inability to impact on the spiritual forces they professed to control: *"The necromancers could not stand before Moses because of the boils, because the boils were on the necromancers and all of Egypt"* (9:7).

By the end of the seventh plague, Pharaoh was prepared to acknowledge God's omnipotence and release the Israelite slaves: *"Pharaoh sent and called to Moses and Aaron and said to them: 'This time I have sinned, God is the righteous One, and I and my people are the wicked ones. Entreat God. The thunder of God and hail has been much. I shall send you out, and you shall stay no longer' "* (9:27-28).

Pharaoh had come a long way in his education. Nevertheless, he still could not bring himself to issue the order that would bring about the slaves' release. Despite his words, an extra push was needed.

Rabbi Lichtenstein argues that as distinct from the first seven plagues, the aim of the last three was to persuade Pharaoh to finally give permission for the Israelites to leave Egypt, as well as to buttress the Israelites' faith in the omnipotence of God. This is explained in God's speech to Moses prior to the eighth plague of hail:

> *God said to Moses: 'Come to Pharaoh, for I have hardened his heart and the heart of his servants in order to place these signs of Mine in his midst; and so that you may relate in the ears of your son and your son's son how I made a mockery of the Egyptians and [that you tell of] My signs that I placed among them – that you may know that I am God (10:1-2).*

God will now make sport with Pharaoh and his courtiers, to teach the Israelites that it was the power of God that was bringing about their release. This information will be relayed by the Jewish people to future generations. This leads to a number of differences in this last group of plagues compared to the previous seven:

- Until now the plagues had constituted a severe nuisance factor. They now became devastating. The plague of locusts covered the entire land of Egypt and destroyed its agriculture. The three-day plague of darkness brought Egypt to a standstill. It was a darkness described as being darker than dark. Finally, the Plague of the Firstborn completely broke the will of the Egyptian people.

- Because God's power was no longer a theological issue for the Egyptians, the nature of Pharoah's advisors changed after the sixth plague of boils. From the eighth plague on, his advisors were no longer his magicians but his "*servants,*" namely his counselors and civil servants. The plagues were leading to grave economic consequences for Egypt, and it was only fitting that his civil servants be involved in the decision-making process of the state.

- An additional aspect to the 10th plague, the Plague of the Firstborn, was the need for Pharaoh to recognize the Israelites as God's firstborn children. Early on, while Moses was on his way to Egypt from Midian, God told him:

> *When you go to return to Egypt, see all the wonders that I have put in your hand and perform them before Pharaoh; but I shall strengthen his heart and he will not send out the people. So shall you say to Pharaoh: "So said God, My firstborn son is Israel. So I say to you: 'Send out My son that he*

may serve Me but you have refused to send him out; behold, I shall kill your firstborn son'" (4:21-23).

At this point I want to raise two questions related to the Ten Plagues. First, why it was it so important for Pharaoh to acknowledge the supremacy of God during the first seven plagues? Was it God's intention to convert Egypt to monotheism? The resistance against this from Egyptian society would have been immense. There is also no evidence from Egyptian writings that such a mass conversion ever took place.

One answer given by commentators is that in reality all the plagues were for the sake of the Jewish people, but that the lessons of the Exodus would impress themselves more on them if they were also accepted by Pharaoh. Another answer that seems close to a literal understanding of the text is that the Ten Plagues were part of a struggle between Moses and Pharaoh for ownership of the Israelite slaves. Pharaoh, as leader of Egypt, assumed he could do with his slaves as he wished since he owned them. But Y-H-V-H, the God who will walk with the Israelites through history, claimed that all power resided with Him, that the Israelites belonged to Him as His people, and that they should be permitted to leave Egypt to worship Him. Release of the slaves could only occur once Pharaoh had acknowledged the omnipotence of God and transferred ownership of his slaves to Him. Pharaoh would do this by the end of the seventh plague of hail, although further prodding would be necessary before he actually released them.

This also relates to Moses' (although in reality God's) disingenuous request at his first meeting with Pharaoh that the Israelites leave Egypt for three days in the wilderness to sacrifice to their God (5:3). Whom was he trying to fool? It would have been clear to everyone that once the slaves left with all their possessions they would never return. However, by requesting that the slaves leave for a journey of three days, Moses was proposing a clear separation of ownership. If the slaves were only allowed to worship God within the boundaries of Egypt, even with their families and even with all their possessions, then to all intents and purposes the slaves were still under Pharaoh's jurisdiction. They needed to leave Egypt for at least a three-day journey and to pass beyond the borders of Egypt and *"in the wilderness"* to be considered free servants of God.

And the second question why did God called the Israelites His *firstborn son?* Rabbi Joseph Soloveitchik explains:

This phrase [My firstborn son is Israel] implies that God had other children. Every nation is a child of God, for every human being was created in the divine image. At the moment that God revealed Himself to the Jewish people and gave us the Torah, we were chosen as a "treasured nation;" but God did not abandon the rest of the world. We [the Jewish people] are God's firstborn – and a critical task of a firstborn child is to be a role model and an effective teacher for the other children. This is accomplished not only through learning, but by setting an example in our daily lives of sanctifying the Divine Name. . . . This is what God had in mind when He gave Moses the task of redeeming the Israelites from slavery.[17]

God's control of chance and history

Until the 1920s the notion that God controlled the natural world would have been difficult to accept since there seemed to be no place for Him in the world He created, except as an observer. Until that time it was held that the universe functions like a pool table. Every action leads to a further reaction, all of which follow the laws of Newtonian physics. If God wished to control nature, He would have to break the laws of nature. However, this was not the message of the Ten Plagues[18] and we now know that this was not the laws of physics either.

Quantum physics tells us that the subatomic world is a very strange place indeed, in that the position and momentum of subatomic particles can never be precisely determined (Heisenberg's Uncertainty Principle). This means that the positions of electrons in an atom can only be described in terms of probabilities. Potentially, electrons can be found at any distance from the nucleus, although depending on their energy level they exist more frequently in certain regions around the nucleus than others. In other words, the quantum world is not a precise, deterministic world, but a fuzziness of probabilities. God operates within this subatomic fuzziness to do with nature as He wills. Or put in another way – God controls chance.

A biochemistry researcher can spend his or her entire life looking at a single reaction within nature, and to all intents and purposes the mechanism for producing that reaction came about solely by chance. However, if that single aspect of nature is viewed as part of an integrated system it becomes clear that it could never have arisen randomly. Most systems within the

---

17   "My firstborn son is Israel" in *Chumash with commentary based on the teachings of Rabbi Joseph B. Soloveitchik. Shemos*, 39. OU Press, New York. 2014.

18   Nachmanides covers these and other points that can be learned from the Exodus from Egypt, such as the truth of prophecy and the hidden miracles of everyday life, in his commentary on Exodus 13:16. According to the Torah, commandments such as phylacteries, fringes and *mezuzot* are also intended to be reminders of the Exodus from Egypt.

biological world, whether it be the production and control of a hormone, the development of an organ, the function of an organ or organelle, the reproduction of an organism, and so on and so on, involve so many complex interlocking steps that they can only be part of a designed system. These came about in a natural way because God controls chance.

A similar type of question is: Can God really claim to control history as the Torah claims, and is He really able to fulfill His promise to Moses that He *"will be"* with the Jewish people throughout history? It is an axiom of Judaism that everyone has free will. History results from the interplay of individual free wills. How then can there be room in history for God? Nevertheless, the Ten Plagues, the redemption of the Israelites from Egypt and the fulfillment of all the prophecies made in the Torah, including the eternal nature of the Jewish people, tell us that the situation is otherwise and that God is very much involved in human history.[19]

There is no psychology research which demonstrates how God can interfere with the human decision-making process, and it is unlikely there ever will be. However, when the Torah relates that *"I have hardened his [Pharaoh's] heart and that of his servants"* (Exodus 10:1) it is telling us that God does have this capability. It is also saying that God steers history by influencing the movers and shakers of this world. As the Book of Psalms says: *"Like streams of water is the heart of a king in the hands of God, whatever He wishes, so He directs it"* (Psalms 21:1).

Jewish philosophers debate how God could have hardened the heart of Pharaoh.[20] Almost all agree that Pharaoh was not persuaded to do something he did not want to do. In fact, it was the very opposite; God enabled him to accomplish what he had already decided to do. The commentator Sforno

---

19 An interesting question raised by philosophers is whether God knows the future. The difficulty is an obvious one. If the future is determined, then one has no freewill. Most Jewish philosophers are in agreement that God has foreknowledge of one's freewill choices before they are made and even while they are being decided, and philosophers such as Maimonides provide explanations as to how this could be possible (none of which are completely satisfactory). Nevertheless, there are orthodox philosophers such as the Ralbag (Gersonides) and the Shlah who limit God's foreknowledge. See "Chapter 14. The Problem of Foreknowledge" in *Illuminating Jewish Thought. Exploration of Free Will, the Afterlife, and the Messianic Era* by Rabbi Netanel Wiederblank, 67-176. Maggid Books, 2018. The Torah also seems to imply in several places that God did not know the future, as for example when He regretted having made man (Genesis 6:6) or when he wished to test Abraham (Genesis 22:1). One way of reconciling these seemingly irreconcilable positions is to say that God knows what a person is likely to decide based on that person's character and previous choices. He can also either directly or indirectly affect a person's choices and thereby bring about a predetermined future. This relates to God hardening Pharoah's heart.

20 Nachmanides, *Commentary to the Torah*, Exodus 7:3, 232-233.

suggests that God made it possible for Pharaoh to ignore the evidence that was blatantly obvious to everyone else. In a similar vein, Nachmanides proposes that God gave Pharaoh the ability to withstand the pain of the plagues so that he could continue to resist sending out the slaves. In all these explanations, Pharaoh's free will remained intact, and he still had the ability to choose between good and evil.[21]

By contrast, the Ralbag, following the Book of Psalms, sees kings as pawns in God's hands. He writes:

> *Behold, the king's heart and will are in the hands of God like streams of water that can be directed according to their need. So too, God directs the heart of the king wherever He desires. Here, we see that the acts of and thoughts of a king are limited by God, with the king being like an agent of God concerning matters of the state. This is just and wise, for if acts of a king were left to his total freedom, there could be great danger to that nation.*[22]

THE CREATION OF AN EGALITARIAN SOCIETY

The Exodus was intended to bring the people to Mount Sinai and from there to the Land of Israel. At Mount Sinai the Israelites received the blueprint for becoming a holy people that would create an ideal society based on justice, righteousness and concern for one's neighbor.

Each Jew is to become holy and the Jewish people a holy people, a "*kingdom of priests and a holy nation* (Exodus 19,5-6), because God Himself is holy (Leviticus 19:1). Holiness can be achieved by attention to the dietary and sexual laws of the Torah, its rituals and its ethics, including "*love your fellow as yourself.*"

An important point raised by Joshua Berman is that the Torah was the first attempt in history to create an egalitarian society in which the exploitation of one class over another was curtailed.[23] This was a radical departure from the ancient world, which believed that societal differences in wealth and

---

21 For a fuller discussion of this topic see "Chapter 16, Hardening the Heart and other Instances Where God Seems to Remove Free Will" in ibid., 223-246.

22 Ralbag on Proverbs 21:1. Quoted and translation from ibid., 236.

23 *Created Equal. How the Bible Broke with Ancient Political Thought* by Joshua A. Berman. Oxford University Press, 2008. Also, "Chapter 7. But is it Divine? How the Torah Broke with Ancient Political Thought" in *Ani Maamin. Biblical Criticism, Historical Truth, and the Thirteen Principles of Faith* by Joshua Berman, 167-179. Maggid Books, 2020. This chapter contains many of the arguments made in his previous book.

power were necessary for the stability of society. The first manifestation of this concept was when the Israelite slaves left Egypt as equals.

There are numerous other examples of this egalitarian direction in the Torah. For example, the ancient world believed that the gods could communicate with a king but never with the common people, since this would undermine the authority of the ruler. All the Israelites, on the other hand, received the Torah at Mount Sinai as equals. Whereas in other societies the ruler was above the law, the Torah was the first to describe equality under the law (Deuteronomy 17:18-20). The judiciary and even the king were appointed by the nation, rather than by a powerful group (16:18 and 17:15). The *Yovel* or Jubilee year, with its requisite that land be returned to its ancestral owners (Leviticus 25:10), ensured that economic power did not accumulate in the hands of the wealthy but that the common man always had the means of livelihood. The Torah also contains agricultural laws and laws of tithing that guaranteed that the disadvantaged never became destitute. As Berman writes: "*It is in the five books of the Torah that we find the birthplace of egalitarian thought.*"[24]

In conclusion, the theological principles demonstrated by the Exodus will become engraved in the consciousness of the Jewish people by their observance of the Jewish holidays, and particularly the symbols of the Passover night: the Paschal sacrifice, the *seder* service, the *matzah* (unleavened bread) and the bitter herbs; as well as the observance of other rituals such as phylacteries, *mezuzot*, and fringes on their garments (*tzizit*) that are linked by the Torah to the Exodus from Egypt.[18]

However, it could be asked: What evidence is there that the Exodus from Egypt really happened? Could it be that the Exodus as told in the Torah is no more than a Jewish myth, or at the very least a highly exaggerated account?

Because of the importance of the Exodus with respect to Jewish theology and the veracity of the Torah, the historicity of the Exodus and the subsequent conquest of Canaan will be examined in the next chapter.

---

24 "But is it Divine? How the Torah Broke with Ancient Political Thought" in *Ani Maamin. Biblical Criticism, Historical Truth, and the Thirteen Principles of Faith* by Joshua Berman, 168. Maggid Books, 2020.

Chapter 4

THE EXODUS FROM EGYPT AND CANAANITE CONQUEST – FACTS OR FICTION?

The Exodus from Egypt was *the* seminal event in Jewish history. This was when the Israelites became a nation, when they achieved their freedom by exchanging servitude to Pharaoh to the service of God, when they proceeded to Mount Sinai to become a holy people under God that would create a model society, and when they began their journey to inherit the Land of Canaan. This was also the first and only time in history that God announced His control of nature and his ability to manipulate world history.

Jewish tradition has ensured that this event has remained engraved in Jewish memory. The months of the Jewish year are based on the Exodus with the month of Nisan, when the Exodus occurred, being the first month of the year. On the Passover festival, Jews relate the Passover narrative while eating bitter herbs and unleavened bread to immortalize their time in slavery and commemorate their release. In Sanctuary and Temple times, participation in the Paschal sacrifice was obligatory for all members of the covenant. Important Jewish rituals also revolve around the memory of the Exodus, such as redeeming the firstborn son of the family, the use of phylacteries and putting fringes on the sides of garments (Exodus 13:9). The Sabbath is also linked in the Torah to the Exodus, and not only to the creation of the universe (13:12-13).

But did it really happen? If the Exodus did not occur, or if the Bible describes a highly exaggerated account, then the veracity of the entire Torah becomes suspect and Judaism becomes a culture and not a God-directed mission.

It needs to be said at the outset that there is no unassailable proof that the Israelites lived in Egypt and left during an Exodus. Slaves do not build monuments. The water level in the Nile Delta has risen, making archeology in this area difficult. In any case, it would be impossible to differentiate Israelite homes from Egyptian ones since the Israelites in Egypt were highly assimilated. The buildings they erected as slaves were Egyptian temples and not Jewish constructions. Only their enslavement kept them a distinct people.[1]

There is also no definite proof that Joshua conquered the land of Canaan 40 years thereafter. Furthermore, the commonly accepted dating for the Exodus as being during the 13th century BCE does not fit well into either Egyptian history or the archeology of Israel. There is some irony in this. It is primarily archeologists who came up with a dating of the 1200's BCE for the Exodus, and it is often archeologists who are skeptical that it actually happened!

Since conclusive proof of an Egyptian Exodus is unlikely ever to be obtained and evidence of the conquest has been difficult to establish, these issues have to be approached from a different perspective. We have to first look again at the dating for the Exodus. We can then ask what is the likelihood that these two events occurred at a proposed time? This can be examined by looking at the history of ancient Egypt and archeology in Israel at a particular period. If both of these are compatible with the words of the Torah, it can be said that these events present no challenge to faith. Moreover, the more suggestive this evidence is, the stronger is the possibility that the Biblical story is authentic. Admittedly, this is not the type of evidence that would be acceptable in verifying a scientific hypothesis. But this is not a scientific experiment.

DATING THE EXODUS FROM BIBLICAL SOURCES

A helpful first step is to attempt to date the Exodus from Biblical sources.

> *The Book of Kings relates: "In the 480th year after the Children of Israel's exodus from the land of Egypt, in the fourth year of Solomon's reign over Israel, in the month of Ziv, which is the second month, he built the Temple for God"* (1 Kings 6:1).

Based on the works of Greek historians and Babylonian and Persian records, the destruction of the First Temple by the Babylonians can be reliably dated to 587 BCE. From the reigns of the kings of Judah and the Northern Kingdom described in the Bible, Solomon's ascension to the throne can be dated to 970 BCE. Solomon began constructing his temple four years into his reign, in 966 BCE. Thus, the date of the Exodus should be 480 years before this, in 1446 BCE.

---

1   According to a midrash, the *Mechilta*, the Jews remained distinctive from the Egyptians in their language and names, in not engaging in Egyptian immorality and in not harboring informers in their midst. Others add that they also were distinct in their attire.

To what extent can this figure of 480 years from the Exodus to the building of Solomon's Temple be relied upon? Is it possible, for example, that this number has symbolic meaning since assigning symbolic meaning to numbers was common practice in the Torah? This question has been discussed in scholarly circles, and to date no symbolism related to this number has been suggested.

Another way to assess the historicity of this date is to examine whether it is chronologically consistent with other events related in the Bible.

During the time of the Judges, the tribe of Manasseh was experiencing military pressure from the Ammonites on the eastern side of the Jordan, and an individual named Yiftah was called upon to save his tribe. Yiftah had been previously thrown out of his home by his siblings because he was the son of a concubine or harlot. However, his military prowess was now needed. The Book of Judges records a speech he made to the Ammonites before engaging with them militarily, in which he asked the Ammonites why it had taken them so long to make the claim that the Israelites stole their land when this happened so long ago at the time of Moses.[2] This speech tells us incidentally that it was 300 years since they were conquered. Part of his speech reads as follows:

> *While Israel dwelt in Heshbon and its towns, and in Aror and its towns, and in all the cities that are along by the side of the Arnon, 300 years, why did you not recover them within that time? (Judges 11:26).*

It could be argued that Yiftah was a non-erudite military leader who was unlikely to have had access to reliable historic data. Nevertheless, this was a diplomatic message, and it is unlikely that he would have conjured up the number 300, although he might have done some rounding off.

There are good reasons why reliable chronological records would have been kept during the times of the judges and monarchy. The Exodus was the event that preceded the conquest of Canaan and which would lead eventually to the establishment of an independent Jewish kingdom. It was therefore an important date for the Israelites, just as a date of independence is an important date for many countries in the world today.

---

2   Shortly before the Exodus, the Amorites west of the River Jordan, under King Sihon, invaded and occupied a large portion of the territory of Moab and Ammon. The Ammonites were driven from their rich lands near the River Jordan and retreated to the mountains and valleys to the east. The territories of the Amorites, which included the former territory of the Ammonites, were taken over by the Israelites at the beginning of the conquest (Numbers 21:22-32).

There was also adequate time from the account in the Book of Judges to accommodate 180 years from the time of Yiftah to the time of King Solomon, accepting that there may have been overlap of some of the judges, that the Book of Judges was not intended to account for every single year and that 40 years needs to be added for the Israelite wanderings in the desert following the Exodus. Hence, from the time of Yiftah to the beginning of the reign of Solomon, the following judges, prophets and kings were yet to come: the judges Ibzan (seven years), Elon (10 years), Abdon, and Samson (years unknown); the prophets Eli (40 years) and Samuel (years unknown); and the kings Saul (two years) and David (forty years), a total of more than 99 years.

The Book of Chronicles records 18 generations from Korach, who perished in the wilderness after the Exodus, until Heman, who sang in Solomon's Temple (1 Chronicles 6:18-22). Using the figure of 480 years this would mean 27 years per generation, which is a realistic figure. The Book of Chronicles also records 12 generations of priests from Pinhas (the zealous priest in the desert with Moses) until the priest Azariah who served in Solomon's temple, which was 40 years per generation (5:30-37).

Problematic, however, is a statement in Chronicles that there were seven generations of Levites from Gershom (a son of Levi) to Jeathrai, who served as a Levite in Solomon's Temple (6:1-6). The end of the Book of Ruth also relates that David was the fifth generation from Nachshon, a leader of the tribe of Judah who lived at the time of Exodus (Ruth 4:20-21). Although Boaz was old when he married Ruth (3:10), it is difficult to see how five generations could be accommodated into the 440 years from the time of the Exodus to the birth of David. There is no explanation for these difficult passages, although one can postulate that these particular genealogical lines were unreliable and individuals were left out.

WHO WAS THE PHARAOH OF THE EXODUS?

A helpful exercise is to ascertain how well the date of 1446 BCE for the Exodus fits into Egyptian history. One can also ascertain who was the pharaoh at this date and examine whether his history is compatible with the Exodus story.

Two dating systems are used by scholars to determine the reigns of the pharaohs, a low chronology and high chronology. These dates are based on an astronomic observation, the heliacal rising of Sothis, which was recorded on papyrus in the ninth year of the reign of Amenhotep I, an early pharaoh of the 18th dynasty. Astronomers have been able to pinpoint precisely the year in which this event occurred by charting the positions of stars in antiquity. However, the precision of this dating depends on the latitude at which this observation was made. Therein lies the problem. The papyrus was found in Thebes, but the observation could equally have been made in Thebes, Memphis, Heliopolis, or any other Egyptian city, leading to a range of uncertainty of 25 years. The earlier dating (assuming the rising was observed at Memphis) constitutes the so-called "low chronology," and the later dating (with the observation being made at Thebes) is the "high chronology."

Which of these two systems is more accurate has been a matter of debate for many years. However, a recent study using radiocarbon dating of biological specimens obtained from museums favors the low chronology for the Middle Kingdom and the high chronology for the later New Kingdom, which includes the 18th dynasty, the dynasty of most interest to us.[3] Having said this, I find the low chronology somewhat more helpful for fitting ancient Egyptian history into Biblical dating. Nevertheless, the dates in Table 1 should not be regarded as being precise, particularly as one goes back earlier than the reign of Amenhotep I.

Table 1. The early pharaohs of the 18th dynasty with the approximate dates of their rule

Ahmose 1	1570 to 1546 or 1551 to 1527 BCE
Amenhotep 1	1546 to 1526 or 1525 to 1504 BCE
Thutmose 1	1526 to 1513 or 1506 to 1493 BCE
Thutmose II	1513 to 1499 or 1493 to 1479 BCE
Hatshepsut	1512 to 1490 or 1479 to 1457 BCE
Thutmose III	1504 to 1450 or 1479 to 1425 BCE
Amenhotep II	1453 to 1419 or 1427 to 1397 BCE

There is considerable uncertainty as to the dates of the early pharaohs of the 18th dynasty. The dates given are those commonly found in the literature, with the earlier dates reflecting the low chronology and the later dates the high chronology.

Accepting 1446 BCE as the date of the Exodus and depending on whether one uses the low or high chronology, then the Exodus would have been either towards the end of the approximately 54-year rule of Thutmose III

---

3   Ramsey CB et al. "Radiocarbon-based chronology for dynastic Egypt." Science 2010; 328: 1554-1557.

or the beginning of the 26-year reign of his son Amenhotep II. The ascension of Amenhotep II is usually dated to 1453 BCE using the low chronology or 1427 BCE by the high chronology (see table 1).

From the words of the Bible, it seems more likely that the Exodus occurred towards the beginning of the reign of Amenhotep II rather than during the reign of Thutmose III:

> *During those many days, it happened that the king of Egypt died and the Children of Israel groaned because of the work and they cried out. Their outcry because of the work went up to God. And God heard their moaning. . . . (Exodus 2:23-24).*

The ruler preceding Thutmose III was a woman named Hatshepsut. If Thutmose III were the pharaoh of the Exodus, the Bible should have referred to Hatshepsut as the pharaoh or queen that died rather than "*king of Egypt.*" Hatshepsut often regarded herself as king rather than queen of Egypt, and many of her statues show her with the false beard typical of the pharaohs. However, her own view of the matter should not have changed the emphasis of the Bible.

Moreover, there is no record of any large gaps in Thutmose III's history that suggests a decrease in military or construction projects as a result of his losing his chariot force and slaves at the Reed Sea. The pharaohs did not engage in colonizing activities but had periodic campaigns outside of Egypt to collect tribute, and this tribute was brought to their temples as gifts for the gods. Egypt was a rich country and could afford a large standing army, and the chariot force was a critical component of this. If the pharaoh's chariots had been destroyed, the army would have been rendered impotent for a number of years, and this would have been reflected in fewer military campaigns. The pharaohs also engaged in extensive temple building, and these building projects were recorded on the walls of their temples. Loss of a large number of slaves would have been reflected in a decrease in recorded state-building activity.

All of this makes it difficult to fit the Exodus into the reign of Thutmose III, as we know that he was an extremely powerful and successful pharaoh. He engaged in 16 foreign military campaigns and built up the most formidable army in the Middle East. We also know (because he told us) that he was a great builder, constructing over 50 temples, including massive additions to Egypt's chief temple in Karnak. The Egyptian construction industry reached its pinnacle in design and style at this time, never again to be equaled.

Moreover, if Thutmose III were the pharaoh of the Exodus, the Exodus in 1446 BCE would have been towards the end of his rule and well after the death of Hatshepsut. However, the Torah verse previously quoted implies that the Exodus took place shortly after the death of the new pharaoh's father and hence at the beginning of his reign. The crying out of the Israelites and God's listening to them could have extended over many years, but it is more in keeping with the sense of the verse that the crying and listening occurred within a relatively short time. Rabbinic exegesis picks up on this. A midrash points out that unlike false gods who have no ability to listen, when God listens He answers quickly.[4]

All this points to Thutmose III's son Amenhotep II as the most likely candidate for the Pharaoh of the Exodus.

Amenhotep II was 18 years old when he became pharaoh. For the first two years of his reign he ruled as a co-regent with his father, and the Israelites would have been familiar with his policies even before his father died. Amenhotep would almost certainly have wished to continue the building endeavors of his father, and for this he needed slaves. For the Israelites the future portended harsh labor without respite. This would have been good reason that they *"cried out"* when Amenhotep II took over the full reins of power. Amenhotep II's wish to emulate the building accomplishments of his father could also have accounted for his stubbornness in his dealings with Moses.

Amenhotep II did engage in building activities but never on the scale of his father, and his building projects largely focused on enlarging smaller temples all over Egypt.[5] This is surprising since a large body of Israelite workers should have been available to him from the time of his father – unless most of them had left Egypt early in his reign.

Moreover, unlike his father, Amenhotep II led only two or three campaigns during his more than 29-year rule, with his last campaign being in the ninth year of his rule.[5] This also is unexpected since in theory his father should have bequeathed him a large standing army. According to scholars, cracks were beginning to appear in the power of the Egyptian

---

4   *Yalkut Shemoni*, Parshat Shemos 169.
5   D. Petrovich D in an essay entitled "Amenhotep II and the historicity of the Exodus-Pharaoh", TMSJ 17/1 (Spring 2006), 81-110, writes that Amenhotep II's last campaign in the ninth year of his rule was quite atypical. It went no further than Palestine and brought back 101,128 slaves and 1,032 wooden chariots. This author suggests that his capture of so many slaves and chariots was needed to fill the void left by the loss of his Hebrew slaves and his chariots.

Empire during his reign.[6] One scholar has this to say about the reign of Amenhotep II:

> *It seems possible to consider this reign as unsuccessful, a time of decline; a few exploits abroad, a few preserved memorials, an almost complete absence of [self-documented] sources after the ninth year of the reign.*[7]

It is also noteworthy that Amenhotep's successor, Thutmose IV, was his son, but not his firstborn or heir apparent. This also fits into the Biblical story since Amenhotep II's firstborn would have died during the plague of the firstborn.

One further issue needs clarifying. The kings of the 18th dynasty were mummified and their mummies placed in tombs in the Valley of the Kings in Thebes. This included Amenhotep II, whose mummy was discovered in 1898 in the Valley of the Kings in its original sarcophagus.[8] However, according to the Bible, the pharaoh of the Exodus drowned in the Sea of Reeds.

Or did he?

Jewish tradition is inconclusive on the matter. The author of Psalm 136 was clearly of the opinion that he did:

> *And [He] overthrew Pharaoh and his host in the Reed Sea, for His mercy endures forever* (Psalms 136:15).

However, although Pharaoh's army was totally destroyed by drowning, there is no verse in Exodus stating explicitly that he died at that time, and there are midrashim that pick up on this point. They conclude that Pharoah remained alive after this debacle to be a witness to this event.[9] The Biblical verse is as follow:

---

6   *The Macmillan Bible Atlas* by Yohanan Aharoni and Michael Avi-Yonah, 35. New York, Macmillan, 1977.

7   Vandersleyen, L'Egypte 2:341.

8   "Amenhotep II" in Wikipedia. (https://en.wikipedia.org/wiki/Amenhotep_II).

9   The midrashic literature is divided on this matter. The midrashic work *Yalkut Shimoni (Yalkut Shemoni* 238) states the following: "*The water came back and covered the chariots and the horsemen*" – this includes even Pharaoh; this is the opinion of Rabbi Yehuda who quotes the verse 'Pharaoh's chariots and army.' Rabbi Natan says: 'Except for Pharaoh, about whom it says: 'On account of this I have left you standing [in order to show you My power and so that My name may be declared throughout the world' "] (Exodus 9:16). The point bothering Rabbi Natan is that according to the Bible, Pharaoh's role was to be a living witness to God's power, "*so that My name may be declared throughout the world*", a role he obviously could not fulfill if he perished. Another midrash (*Midrash Aggadah Shemos* 14:28) picks up on the Bible's words that "*there did not remain of them up to one.*" The expression up to one is a Biblical idiom that usually means no one. However, the midrash concludes that there was indeed up to one person who survived the splitting of the Reed Sea, and this was Pharaoh himself.

He [Pharaoh] harnessed his chariot and took his people with him. He took 600 elite chariots and all the chariots of Egypt with officers on them all. . . . The water came back and covered the chariots and the horsemen of the entire army of Pharaoh who were coming behind them in the sea – not one of them remained (literally: there did not remain of them up to one). . . . Pharaoh's chariots and army He cast in the sea and the select of his officers were sunk in the Sea of Reeds" (Exodus 14:6-7, 14:28, 15:4).

The Egyptian oppression

Having postulated a date for the Exodus of 1446 BCE and suggested that this could have been during the reign of the 18th dynasty pharaoh, Amenhotep II, one can examine the beginning of the Israelite exile in Egypt as related by the Torah to see if this also fits into this time period.

The Bible begins the story of the Israelite oppression with the following verses:

A new king arose over Egypt who did not know of Joseph. He said to his people, "Behold! The people, the Children of Israel are more numerous and stronger than we. Come let us deal wisely with them lest they become numerous and it may be that if a war will occur, they, too, may join our enemies and wage war against us and go up from the land" (Exodus 1:8-10).

These verses seem to indicate that this succession was different from previous ones. This was a king who not only did not know of Joseph but who was a *"new king."* But do not all successions bring a new king?

Egyptian history may provide an answer to this question.

The pharaoh in question may have been Ahmose I, who was from the southern kingdom of Egypt and succeeded in uniting northern and southern Egypt by expelling the Hyksos from the Nile Delta. This struggle was begun by his grandfather, who likely lost his life in the attempt, was continued unsuccessfully by Ahmose I's father and was finally completed by Ahmose I. The rule of Ahmose I over a united Egyptian kingdom began somewhere between 1570 BCE to 1551 BCE (see Table 1).

The unification of Egypt by Ahmose I was a highly significant event in Egyptian history, and his 18th dynasty would become one of the most powerful and successful in Egyptian history. This unification would also have serious implications for the Israelite people.

Scholars still debate who were the Hyksos that Ahmose I defeated. The most accepted theory is that they were a Semitic people who invaded northern Egypt during a period of political instability in Egypt. The beginning of their 15th dynasty is usually dated to between 1663 to 1648 BCE, and they ruled during what is called the Second Intermediate Period of the Middle Kingdom. They established themselves in the Nile Delta and Middle Egypt and also ruled over southern Egypt for a time.

The Jewish Roman historian Josephus, quoting from the work of the Egyptian Manetho, describes the Hyksos invasion of Egypt:

> *By main force they easily seized it without striking a blow; and having overpowered the rulers of the land, they then burned our cities ruthlessly, razed to the ground the temples of gods. . . . Finally, they appointed as king one of their number whose name was Salitis.*[10]

Some scholars question this description and suggest that the Hyksos could have infiltrated into Egypt more peacefully before seizing power, although this seems a less likely scenario. The Hyksos are credited with bringing chariots and improved bows and maces into Egypt, a new technology that gave them an advantage in warfare. Chariots would subsequently become the tanks of the ancient world.

The Hyksos established their administrative capital in Avaris in the northeast region of the Nile Delta.[11] They also adopted Egyptian ways to make themselves accepted by their Egyptian subjects. Nevertheless, they were always regarded by the Egyptians as foreigners. The name Hyksos comes from two Egyptian words *hekau khasut* meaning foreign rulers.

Could it be that the pharaoh who related his dreams to Joseph was a Hyksos king? If this is the case, then the Egyptian exile probably lasted just over 200 years (see note 15 to chapter 1). Moreover, if Joseph worked for the Hyksos, it is not surprising that Ahmose I "*did not know of Joseph*" and would have had no interest in finding out what Joseph had done for the country.

Unfortunately, there is very little archeological evidence from the Hyksos period. As mentioned, the high water table has made archeology in this area difficult. In addition, when the Egyptians succeeded in expelling the

---

10   Quoted in *History of Egypt from the Earliest Time to the Persian Conquest*, James Henry Breasted, 216. Republished in 2003.

11   Avaris was located near the modern Tell el-Dab'a. It was then a busy port, a trade and administrative center on the eastern-most branch of the Nile. It was abandoned during the 18th dynasty, but the area was rebuilt by Rameses II as his administrative capital, Pi Rameses.

Hyksos from Egypt they erased all traces of their occupation since this was not a period of which they were particularly proud. It is not surprising, therefore, that no mention of Joseph has ever been found in Egyptian historic records.

Whether or not Joseph and the Hyksos were contemporaries, the Israelites and Hyksos probably lived in close proximity since the Israelites also settled in the Nile Delta.

The children of Jacob were herdsmen rather than farmers. The Nile River overflows its banks during the summer months and deposits silt on the sides of the river. This increases the fertility of the fields and makes them suitable for growing grains and vegetable gardens. However, these fields are surrounded by desert, so that Middle and Lower Egypt would have been unsuitable for herdsmen. The Nile Delta area, on the other hand, would have been excellent terrain for sheep and cattle grazing, and the Bible tells us that the land of Goshen in the Nile Delta was where they settled.

If Joseph had worked for the Hyksos, it is likely that the Israelites had a very close relationship with these people. The Israelites may even have been a favored population in the Delta area. However, when Ahmose I took over the country the Israelites would have suddenly found themselves in a very different situation. Like the Hyksos who had just been expelled, they were a foreign people. They may have also been too numerous, powerful and entrenched in the country to be evicted. However, in Ahmose's eyes they were a potential threat. If they were to join a counter-coup, they could have reversed the gains he had made for the Egyptian people. It needed the cunning of a person like Ahmose I to figure out how this problem could be resolved. His solution was persecution and enforced labor:

> So they appointed tax collectors over it in order to afflict it with their burdens; they built storehouses (miskenot) for Pharaoh, Pithom and Ra'amses. . . . They embittered their lives with hard work, with mortar and with bricks and with every labor of the field, all their labors that they performed with them was crushing labor (Exodus 1:11-14).

The Hebrew word *Pithom* probably comes from the words *Pi-Atum* which means the house of Athum and *Ra'amses* means born to Ra. Both Athum and Ra were gods of the Nile Delta. It is very possible, therefore, that the Israelites were building administrative and storage facilities for temples of worship for the sun gods and not storage cities to benefit the populace. The building of such temples was typical of the activities of the 18th dynasty pharaohs.

Their building of these temples would have had a significant consequence for the Israelites. The role of religion was extremely pervasive in Egyptian society. If the Egyptians would have invited the Israelites to join their pagan worship, they may well have been attracted to it. However, building pagan temples in conditions of enforced labor was a different matter entirely and would have given the Israelites a very different perspective on paganism. This could explain why, despite a sojourn of hundreds of years, the Hebrews brought nothing of Egyptian mythology and very little of Egyptian culture with them into the desert and into their new country.

Who was the pharaoh who issued the directive that all male Israelite children be killed? From the wording of the Bible it could have been the same "*new king*" who initially enslaved the Israelites. It could also have been a later pharaoh, and this would not contradict the words of the Torah. This leader initiated a new policy when he realized that forced labor had been unsuccessful in achieving Israelite population control.

One way of determining the identity of this pharaoh is from the date of Moses' birth, since his family was directly affected by this decree.

The Book of Exodus relates that "*Moses was 80 years old and Aaron was 83 years old when they spoke to Pharaoh*" (Exodus 7:7). The period of the Ten Plagues would have been quite brief, probably lasting less than a year. This is evident from the fact that Moses first spoke to Pharaoh when he was 80, that he led the Israelites for 40 years in the wilderness and died when he was 120 (Exodus 1:11). One can conclude, therefore, that Moses was born in about 1527 BCE.

Depending on whether one uses the high or low chronology, the date of 1527 BCE is compatible with either Ahmose I, Amenhotep I or Thutmose I being the pharaoh who initiated this cruel decree. As explained previously, I find the low chronology to be more helpful in fitting the story of the Exodus into the events of the Egyptian exile, and Thutmose I may well have been the pharaoh responsible.

There is another good reason for focusing on Thutmose I. Until the time of Thutmose I, Thebes was the main administrative center for the Egyptian kingdom. However, Thutmose I moved his administrative center northwards to Memphis together with his army. Memphis was on the Nile and close to the Nile Delta. From now on the Israelites and the pharaohs will be in much closer proximity to each other – and it will not be a happy relationship.

The fact that Thutmose I moved close to the Delta could also explain how Pharaoh could so easily have spoken to the Hebrew midwives. If the pharaohs had been living in Thebes, it would have been a one-and-a-half-week journey by donkey to relay a message. It could also explain how Moses could be rescued by the daughter of Pharaoh when he was sent down the Nile in a reed basket.

Who was this daughter of Pharaoh who rescued Moses from the Nile? This might seem an impossible question to answer since Pharaoh likely had a number of wives. He would have had a primary wife who was his queen, as well as secondary wives. However, an intriguing possibility is that the stepmother of Moses was the daughter of Thutmose I's primary wife. This daughter's name was Hatshepsut.

Thutmose I's primary wife was Ahmes, and she had only a single child, a daughter called Hatshepsut. Hatshepsut married a stepbrother from a secondary wife, Mutneferet, to solidify the succession. This husband was Thutmose II. Thutmose II might have been young when he ascended to the throne and he died young after being pharaoh for 13 years. Hatsheput now found herself a regent for a very young stepson. Hatshepsut had no sons, only a daughter, and her stepson had been born to a secondary wife of Thutmose II. Although initially a regent, it is generally agreed that she assumed the position of pharaoh and was quite successful at it. She was so successful, in fact, that she began thinking of herself in a rather manly way and, as previously mentioned, some of her monuments show her with the typical beard sported by the pharaohs. She did all the things that a pharaoh of the 18th dynasty was supposed to do: she built temples throughout the country, engaged in military campaigns and recorded her triumphs with statues and other monuments. When she passed away, she was succeeded by her stepson Thutmose III.

And then something strange happened. Decades after her death many of her cartouches and monuments were smashed. The damage is too extensive to have been carried out randomly by vandals and must have been officially sanctioned. It could have been authorized by her stepson or by the pharaoh after him, Amenhotep II. Historians are at a loss to explain why it happened. One suggestion is that Hatshepsut was seen as an affront to the pharaohs' masculinity; but this is a rather lame reason and does not explain why the damage was perpetrated years after her death. If Thutmose III had wanted to be nasty to his stepmother, he had plenty of opportunity to do so soon after her death.

However, there is another suggestion that fits rather nicely into the Exodus story. Hatshepsut was the daughter of Thutmose I. Could she have been the foster mother of Moses? She had only one daughter and may already have been scheming to avoid just the type of succession problem that did in fact transpire. If Moses had kept to the script, he might have been directed to marry Hatshepsut's daughter and become pharaoh of Egypt!

This may be taking speculation too far. Nevertheless, it is possible that Hatshepsut was recognized by the Egyptians as the person who had saved Moses and brought him into the royal palace. When Moses destroyed the agriculture of Egypt, devastated the Egyptian army and released Pharaoh's slaves, there was only one way for the pharaoh of the Exodus, Amenhotep II, to get back at his stepmother, and this was to destroy her images. This action was more than symbolic. These images were intended to help ease her descent into the underworld.

There are clearly no proofs here and much speculation. Nevertheless, Biblical history and the history of the 18th Egyptian dynasty do seem to match up with each other rather nicely.

THE ARCHEOLOGY OF THE CONQUEST

The Exodus from Egypt and Joshua's conquest of Canaan are, of course, two sides of the same coin. If the Exodus took place in 1446 BCE and the Israelites wandered in the desert for 40 years, then the conquest should have begun in about 1406 BCE.

There are respected archeologists who support a conquest at the end of the 15th century and beginning of the 14th century BCE.[12] However, many archeologists disagree with this, and they postulate that if the Israelites arrived in Canaan at all, they came at the end of the 13th century BCE, which would be the end of the Late Bronze Age. However, this presents a host of problems in trying to relate archeological findings, or lack of findings, to the Biblical story. There is, for example, no evidence of destruction in Jericho during this period.

It needs to be appreciated that there are ideological overtones to this debate. The early days of archeology in Palestine during the late 19th century were directed at verifying the historicity of the Bible. This was how archaeologists obtained their funding, and this was what people were interested in. More recently, many Israeli archeologists in particular have attempted to sever the connection between archeology and the Bible, a text they regard as

---

12   For a list of scholars who accept this approach see "Classical Models for the Appearance of Israel in Palestine" by Paul J. Ray Jr. in *Critical Issues in Early Israelite History*, eds Richard S. Hess, Gerald A. Klingbeil and Paul J Ray, Jr. Bulletin for Biblical Research Supplement 3, 79. Winona Lake, Indiana. 2008.

having no more significance than any another Near Eastern text (and some would quip having even less significance).[13] There are Biblical minimalists who even question whether there was an Israelite conquest at all, especially since evidence for a 13th-century BCE conquest is almost non-existent; they suggest that mountain ridge settlement in Canaan came not from the east but from disgruntled breakaway Canaanite tribes from the west.

Having said this, most archeologists are in agreement that by the 12th century BCE, in Iron Age I, there was a substantial Israelite population in the central mountain range that was dissimilar to the Canaanite population in a number of ways. Their pottery was different (and archeological identification is very much about pottery); Israelite vessels were roughly-made vessels, whereas the Canaanite population used typical Iron Age collared-rim cooking pots and storage jars (i.e., jars with a slightly inset collar close to the rim of the vessel) and they also imported vessels typical of the Middle Bronze Age.

The Israelites built four-room homes and this may even have been an Israelite innovation. These houses were typically rectangular with three rooms parallel to the longitudinal axis and a fourth space parallel to its short axis that had the same length as the other three rooms. The enclosed courtyard in this fourth space provided a place for a cistern, cooking and storage. Stone pillars or walls served as room dividers and provided support for a second story.[14] Israelite settlements used agricultural terracing on the hillsides. Evidence of literacy and use of a proto-Canaanite script has also been found in a few Israelite villages (although the name "proto-Canaanite" is a misnomer since this writing had nothing to do with the Canaanites and may even have been invented by the Israelites while in Egypt). Their settlements also contained no pig bones because of Jewish dietary laws, while these are typically found in Canaanite and Philistine settlements.

The Book of Joshua describes short, blitzkrieg-type campaigns against the major Canaanite cities, and this would have eliminated any subsequent resistance to an Israelite presence in the country. This was followed by a second stage of settlement. However, the Israelites were unable to remove the Canaanite presence in the plains and valleys and were forced to settle in

---

13 "Agendas on the Right and Agendas on the Left" in *Ani Maamin. Biblical Criticism, Historical Truth and the Thirteen Principles of Faith* by Joshua Berman, 72. Maggid Books, Koren Publishers, Jerusalem, 2020.

14 "The Appearance of Israel in Canaan in Recent Scholarship" by Patrick Mazani in Critical Issues in Early Israelite History, eds Richard S. Hess, Gerald A. Klingbeil and Paul J Ray, Jr. Bulletin for Biblical Research Supplement 3, 101. Winona Lake, Indiana. 2008.

the more sparsely-populated central mountain range.[15] This means that for a period of time there were two cultures present in the country. The question is when this began.

The archeologist Yitzhak Meitlis provides considerable evidence that two cultures existed in Canaan from the end of the Middle Bronze Age (which he conveniently proposes ended in 1400 BCE), and that there were features of an Iron Age culture present in Canaan from as early as the Middle Bronze Age.[16]

Table 2. Archeological periods

Period	Accepted dating	Characteristics	Alternate dating system (Meitlis)	As reflected in the Bible
Middle Bronze Age II	1800-1550	Development of urbanization and fortifications. Violent destruction at the end of this period.	1800-1400 BCE	Patriarchal period. Exile in Egypt. Exodus, desert encampments
Late Bronze Age	1550– 1150 BCE	Egyptian rule of Israel. Large number of imported vessels.	1400 -1150 BCE	Israelite conquest of Canaan by Joshua. Period of the judges
Iron Age I	From 1150- 1000 BCE	Spread of use of iron. Israelite settlement in the hill country. Philistines on the coastal plain	1150-1000 BCE	Period of the judges until conquest of Jerusalem by David

(This table is taken from "Understanding Time and Place" in *Excavating the Bible. New Archeological Evidence for the Historical Reliability of Scripture* by Yitzhak Meitlis, 16-17.)

---

15   See Judges 1:19: "And God (*Y-H-V-H*) was with Judah, and they drove out the inhabitants *of the mountains; but they could not drive out the inhabitants of the valley, for they had iron chariots.*"

16   "The Conquest of the Land of Israel" in *Excavating the Bible. New Archeological Evidence for the Historical Reliability of Scripture* by Yitzhak Meitlis, 53-118. Eshel Books, Maryland, USA, 2012.

There can be no doubt that Meitlis is a Biblical maximalist. However, the beauty of his approach is that everything now fits perfectly together. The archeological findings at Jericho, for example, have always been problematic to those suggesting an Iron Age conquest since it was mainly unoccupied during the Iron Age. For a Biblical maximalist, however, lack of Iron Age findings would be expected since Joshua placed a ban on anyone settling in the city (Joshua 6:26).

Archeological excavations at Tel es-Sultan, the ancient fortified city of Jericho, have revealed a 15-foot-high stone wall at the base of an embankment that surrounded the tel. The embankment itself was formerly plastered over, and at its top was a mudbrick double-layered wall surrounding the city which was preserved to a height of eight feet. Archeologists have found red bricks from this wall heaped up beyond the stone wall at the base of the embankment that would have enabled an enemy to climb over the wall via this newly formed ramp, as related in the Book of Joshua (Joshua 6:20). The double wall on top of the tell has been dated to the Early Bronze Age. The destruction and conflagration in the city date to the Late Bronze Age. Based on the Canaanite pottery in the city reported by previous excavations, Bryant Wood has dated the destruction of Jericho to about 1400 BCE.[17] Interestingly, many full-grain storage jars were found in the city ruins, which is compatible with a sudden conquest occurring during the spring, rather than a prolonged siege during which the grain would have been consumed.[18] All this is compatible with the Biblical story.

Two extra-Biblical sources also support a Late Bronze Age arrival of the Israelites in Canaan. One is the Merneptah Stele. This is a victory stele found in the Valley of the Kings in Thebes, commemorating a successful military campaign by Merneptah, the son and successor of Rameses II, against Lybia and Canaan in the fifth year of his reign, approximately in 1209 BCE. This stele

---

17 "Did the Israelites Conquer Jericho? A New Look at the Archeological Evidence" by Bryant G. Wood in Biblical Archeology Review March/April 1990. I have summarized this article but have not included the preceding archeological excavations done by others with whom Wood disagrees. Wood's assessment from his excavations is very much based on the Canaanite pottery found within the city, including locally manufactured and imported pottery typical for the Late Bronze Age which he feels was incorrectly evaluated by Kathleen Kenyon. Radiocarbon data is not quite consistent with Wood's theory, but there may be reasons for this. An article which focuses on the disputes and includes radiocarbon dating data is "Jericho chronology dispute" in Conservapedia. (https://www.conservapedia.com/Jericho_chronology_dispute).

18 That the conquest of Jericho occurred in the early spring is evident from Joshua 2:6, 3:15, 4:9 and 5:10.

describes his victory against a number of enemies, one of which is "*Israel:*"

> *The princes are prostrate, saying: "Mercy!"*
>
> *Not one raises his head among the Nine Bows.*
>
> *Desolation is for Tehenu; Hatti is pacified;*
>
> *Plundered is the Canaan with every evil;*
>
> *Carried off is Ashkelon; seized upon is Gezer;*
>
> *Yanoam is made as that which does not exist;*
>
> *Israel is laid waste; his seed is not;*
>
> *Harru is become a widow of Egypt!*
>
> *All lands together, they are pacified.*

Reliefs of the Canaanite battles show the Canaanite city-states Ashkelon, Gezer and Yanoam, while the Israelites are pictured as trampled. If indeed the words "*Israel is laid waste*" are describing a conflict with the Israelite people, it would be difficult to fit this into an early 13th-century BCE Exodus since the Israelites would barely have arrived in the country.[19] Supporters of a late Exodus suggest that the Israel mentioned here was not the Israelite people, although it is difficult to imagine who else it could be. No Canaanite tribe had a name resembling this. It is more logical to assume that the Israelite people had been in Canaan for several hundred years and that they were established in the hill country throughout Judea and Samaria. These villages would have been difficult to conquer in their entirety since they were so spread out, and this stele inscription may have been more bluster than reality. Whatever the reason, this military action did not even merit mention in the Book of Judges.

Another important piece of evidence for an early conquest are the Tel el-Amarna letters. These letters date from the middle of the 14th century BCE and originate from the royal archives of Akhetaten, the capital city of Egypt at the time of Amenhotep IV. There are 380 tablets, and 300 of them include correspondence between Egypt and its vassal cities in Canaan and Syria. Canaan at this time was loosely controlled by the Egyptians. Eighteen of these letters contained complaints to the pharaoh about the social disorder in the country as a result of the activities of the *Habiru*. The meaning of this term is

---

19   "The Appearance of Israel in Canaan in Recent Scholarship" by Patrick Mazani in *Critical Issues in Early Israelite History*, eds Richard S. Hess, Gerald A. Klingbeil and Paul J Ray, Jr. Bulletin for Biblical Research Supplement 3, 108. Winona Lake, Indiana. 2008.

uncertain, and it could be referring derogatively to bandits, brigands or mercenaries, but it could also be referring to the Israelites.

Of considerable interest is that all the Canaanite cities writing letters of complaint were those specifically mentioned in the Book of Judges as *not* being conquered by Joshua. Meitlis comments:

> *In short, the list of major city-states found in the El-Amarna letters matches almost exactly the cities that the Bible regards as cities that survived as Canaanite cities during the period of the Judges.*[20]

Meitlis also quotes the Israeli archeologist Amihai Mazar:

> *The list of unconquered cities (Judges 1:15-35) is corroborated by archeological research. In many of the cities mentioned, especially in the Jezreel and Bet-Shean Valleys, we find continuity in the survival of Canaanite culture up until the close of the 11th century BCE.*[21]

Consider the city of Shechem. There is no mention in the Book of Joshua of this city ever being conquered by the Israelites, which is surprising since it was a large Canaanite city-state in the central highlands. The Armana letters could indicate why. We read in these letters that the king of Shechem was accused by his rivals of maintaining good relationships with the Habiru and even giving some of them land.[22] The king of Shechem wrote several letters to Amenhotep IV stating that he was Pharaoh's loyal vassal and in one letter wrote that he was handing over his son who had been collaborating with the Habiru. The king of Megiddo also complained that he was facing an attack of a coalition of Habiru and Shechemites. Interestingly, there is no mention of Jericho in any of the letters, presumably because it was no longer controlled by the Canaanites.

---

20 "The Conquest of the Land of Israel" in *Excavating the Bible. New Archeological Evidence for the Historical Reliability of Scripture* by Yitzhak Meitlis, 93. Eshel Books, Maryland, USA, 2012.

21 "The Relationship between Archeology and Historical Research" by Amihai Mazar, Lee Levine and Amihai Mazars eds. In *The Controversy over the Historical Validity of the Bible* (Heb), 107. Jerusalem, 2001.

22 "What is the Biblical date for the Exodus? A response to Bryant Wood." JETS 50/2 (June 2007) 225-247.

A 13ᵀᴴ-CENTURY BCE CONQUEST AND RAMESES II AS THE PHARAOH OF THE EXODUS

Many scholars who suggest an Israelite conquest in the 1200's BCE focus on Rameses II as being the most likely pharaoh of the Exodus.[23] His father Seti I, therefore, would have been the Pharaoh who initiated the oppression.[24]

The strongest evidence for Ramses II being the Pharaoh of the Exodus comes from Tel Hazor. This large tel is located north of the Sea of Galilee near the Hula Valley. Hazor was an extremely powerful Canaanite city that led an alliance of northern Canaanite cities against Joshua, which he defeated. It is the only city mentioned in the Book of Joshua that was burnt to the ground (Joshua 11:10-11). Interestingly, an Egyptian offering table was found in the rubble of a conflagration in Hazor with hieroglyphics indicating that it was dedicated by a high priest of Ramesses II.[23] This strongly suggests that Ramses II was the Pharaoh at the time of the Israelite conquest.

Before jumping to conclusions, however, it is worth noting that archeology shows there was only minimal occupation of the city for 150 to 200 years after this. This is inconsistent with the Book of Judge which tells us that there was another Israelite victory over the forces of Hazor at the time of the prophetess Deborah. The Israelites were then under great pressure from the Canaanites who had reestablished their city. Sisera's army was routed by Deborah's commander Barak at Mount Tabor, following which: "*And God subdued on that day Jabin the king of Canaan before the Children of Israel. And the hand of the Children of Israel prevailed constantly harder against Jabin the king of Canaan until they destroyed Jabin, king of Canaan*" (Judges 4:24). Another possibility, therefore, is that the conflagration found by archeologists was caused not by Joshua but by Devorah and Barak.[25] This makes a lot of sense, since it is otherwise difficult to see how the Canaanites at Hazor became so troublesome to the Israelites when the archeological evidence in Hazor after the conflagration indicates that there was little settlement.

---

23 "What is the Biblical date for the Exodus? A response to Bryant Wood." JETS 50/2 (June 2007) 225-247.

24 "Who Destroyed Canaanite Hazor?" by Amnon Ben-Tor in Biblical Archeology Review 39:4, July/August 2013.

25 "The Conquest of the Land of Israel" in *Excavating the Bible. New Archeological Evidence for the Historical Reliability of Scripture* by Yizhak Meitlis, 86-89. Eshel Books, Maryland, USA, 2012.

Is there any other evidence that Ramses II could have been the Pharaoh of the Exodus or the conquest? He ruled from 1279 to 1213 BCE based on the low chronology and from 1304 to 1237 BCE based on the high chronology. He was the grandson of Rameses I who was of non-royal birth and came from a noble family from the Nile Delta region. He established the city of Pi–Rameses (meaning the House of Rameses) as his new capital and his residence in the Nile Delta on the ruins of the Hyksos capital of Avaris. Assuming the Israelites were still in Egypt, this new, or more accurately rebuilt, city would have been close to Israelite settlement.

That Rameses II was born in the Nile Delta accounts for the fact that he worshipped the sun god Ra rather than Amun or Amun-Ra, the gods of pharaohs of the 18th dynasty, who lived in Thebes. The name Rameses II means the son of Ra. The gods of Egypt were sometimes associated with specific locales, and Ra was a state deity in northern Egypt from the time of the fifth dynasty.

The following verse describing the Israelites' path from Egypt during the Exodus is often taken as supporting evidence for Rameses II being the pharaoh of the Exodus: *"The children of Israel journeyed from Rameses to Succoth, about 600,000 on foot, the men, aside from the children"* (Exodus 12:37).

However, it is unlikely that this Rameses mentioned in the Bible was named after either Rameses II or his capital city, Pi-Rameses. The Torah tells us that the Israelites settled in *"the land of Rameses"* when they arrived in Egypt, and this was many years before the Exodus (Genesis 47:11). The Israelites were also recorded as building storage facilities or a temple of *"Raʿamses"* during the Egyptian oppression, and this could have been in Heliopolis or anywhere else in the Nile Delta.

Moreover, the history of Rameses II does not reflect the loss of his army or of a large body of slaves. In fact, Rameses II is often regarded as Egypt's greatest and most powerful leader. The early part of his reign was focused on building cities, temples and monuments, and he engaged in numerous military campaigns in Syria, Nubia and Libya.

In conclusion, many scholars consider the Exodus to have taken place in the 1200s BCE if it took occurred at all. However, this date fits in poorly with Egyptian history, and the pharaoh at that time, Rameses II, is an unlikely candidate for pharaoh of the Exodus based on descriptions of his temple building and his numerous military campaigns. On the other hand, the history of the Egyptian 18th dynasty fits in well with the Biblically-derived date for the Exodus of 1446 BCE.

Archeologists may well find evidence in the future that will enable them to date the conquest of Canaan more definitively. In the meantime, believers in the Exodus and conquest of Canaan as described in the Torah can be assured that there is currently no evidence that contradicts their beliefs.

Chapter 5

THE UTOPIAN PROPHECIES OF ISAIAH THE SON OF AMOZ AND MICAH

O f all the figures discussed in this book, the prophet Isaiah (*Yeshayahu*) the son of Amoz has had the most influence on the Jewish concept of messianism and, via Judaism, on that of Christianity and Islam.

- Similar to the prophet Hosea, who was an older contemporary of Isaiah, Isaiah preached that a Jewish kingdom that failed to practice justice and righteousness was doomed to destruction and exile. Prior to this time, the prophets of ancient Israel had prophesied punishment, but never exile.

- He promised that despite exile, a remnant of the Jewish people would survive and be redeemed.

- He prophesied that a time will come when the omnipotence of God will be fully revealed to all mankind, and a utopian existence will be created on earth. This period will subsequently be called the messianic age.[26]

- He wrote that in this messianic age the righteousness and justice of the Jewish people will become a light unto the nations.

- He advised a policy of non-involvement in the struggles of the great powers, whom he considered to be agents of God.

---

26 An even earlier source for the messianic idea may be the Book of Psalms, and in particular a group of psalms beginning with Psalm 90 up to Psalm 99. For example, "*for He arrives, for He arrives to judge the earth. He will judge the world with righteousness, and nations with His faithful truth*" (Psalm 96:13). These particular psalms have traditionally been ascribed to the prophet Moses, while most others are ascribed to King David. However, a psalm before this group, Psalm 89, ascribes its authorship to "*A Maskil by Eisan the Ezrachite.*" This person may have lived in First Temple times (I Chronicles 2:6). Ibn Ezra has suggested that the Book of Psalms was redacted by the Men of the Great Assembly. The Book of Psalms was certainly in use in First Temple times, and later authors besides those mentioned in the psalms themselves could have composed a few of them.

Judaism is a utopian religion. Its underlying premise is that the Jewish people should strive towards the creation of an ideal society. It is implicit in the Torah that this will serve as an example to the rest of humanity. Isaiah now stated this explicitly. The Torah also never promised that perfection would be achieved. The originality of Isaiah the son of Amoz was to assert that an earthly utopia would indeed materialize.

Isaiah's messages of consolation have been of particular comfort to the Jewish people. The Talmud has this to say about this topic:

> *The entire Book of Jeremiah is about destruction, and the beginning of the Book of Ezekiel is about destruction and its end is about consolation, and the entire book of Isaiah is about consolation.*[27]

This is, of course, an oversimplification. There is far more to the Book of Isaiah than just passages of consolation. However, the Talmud is recognizing that a major aim of Isaiah's prophecies was to provide hope and comfort to the Jewish people, and it is this aspect of his book that Jews have latched onto foremost. This is why, for example, passages of consolation are read from the Book of Isaiah in the synagogue each Sabbath for the seven weeks after Tisha B'Av, the important fast day of the year that mourns the destruction of both Temples.

However, there are at least four questions that an academic book of this nature needs to ask for a full understanding of Isaiah's prophecies. They are also interrelated.

First, should all of Isaiah's words be taken literally?

The impact of his book has been so great because of its biting critiques and beautiful soaring poetry rich in imagery and figurative expressions. But did Isaiah intend that most of his words be taken literally or figuratively?

What, for example, are we to make of the following prophecy?

> *The light of the moon will be like the light of the sun, and the light of the sun will be seven times as strong, like the light of seven days, on the day that God binds up His people's wounds and heals the injuries it has suffered* (Isaiah 30:26).

Or

> *And it shall be at the end of the days (in Hebrew "be'acharit hayomim ")
> that the mountain of the Lord's house shall be firmly established at the top*

---

27   TB Bava Basra 14b.

of the mountains, and it shall be raised above the hills, and all the nations shall stream to it (2.1).

In actuality, the nearby Mount of Olives overlooks the Temple Mount and not the other way round. Did Isaiah really believe that the Temple Mount will be raised physically above the other mountains or was he speaking symbolically? In the former instance, Isaiah was talking about a change in the nature of the world as could occur at the End of Days, while in the second instance he was describing symbolically the profound changes that will take place at some point in time.

The influential medieval *halachist* and philosopher Maimonides believed there would be no changes in nature during the messianic age, and he interpreted such expressions as metaphors.[28] Rabbi Akiva also did not anticipate a miraculous salvation during the Bar Kochba Revolt which he considered to be a messianic venture (see Chapter 10). However, there have been many Jewish scholars who did not agree with Maimonides and who anticipated a miraculous messianic age.

Second, what is the historical context for the various prophecies made by Isaiah?

For much of his book this has been difficult to determine as there are few hints within the chapters that enable his prophecies to be put into their historical context. At times when such context does appear to be present, other chapters seem to be out of chronological order. According to the Talmud, Isaiah was assassinated by Hezekiah's son Manasseh. His prophecies had not yet been collated and they were put together by Hezekiah and his assistants; some of the chronological order may have been lost during this process.[29] On

---

28 Maimonides wrote: "*Do not presume that in the messianic age the nature of the world will change or there will be innovations in the work of creation. Rather the world will continue according to its pattern. Though Isaiah [11.6] states: 'And a wolf will dwell with the lamb, the leopard will lie down with the young goat,' these words are a metaphor and a parable. . . . Similarly, other Messianic prophecies of this nature are metaphors. In the messianic era everyone will realize which matters were implied by these metaphors and which allusions they contained*" (Maimonides, *Mishna Torah*, The Laws of Kings and their Wars 12:1). The medieval debate as to the nature of messianic times can be traced to a talmudic debate between Rabbi Yochanan and Samuel (TB Berachot 34b). Samuel held that there will no difference in messianic times to the current age while Rabbi Yochanan accepted the plain meaning of the prophets' prophecies. Maimonides accepted the opinion of Samuel, while his contemporary the Ra'avad accepted Rabbi Yochanan's opinion. A compromise position is that of the Shelah (23b) who suggested that initially the messianic age will follow the natural order of the world. This will be followed by a more miraculous period.

29 TB Baba Basra 15a, TB Yevamot 49b.

the other hand, the chapters do not seem randomly arranged, and many of the first 39 chapters, in particular, show a sequence.

The first words of the opening chapter provide a good example of the contextual puzzles presented by this book. It opens with the sentence: *"The vision of Isaiah the son of Amoz which he saw concerning Judah and Jerusalem, in the days of Uzziah, Jotham, Ahaz, [and] Hezekiah, kings of Judah"* (Isaiah 1:1), and then goes on to relate that *"the land is desolate; your cities burnt with fire"* (1:7). However, the end of this chapter and the subsequent one discuss messianic times. Is this first chapter (which happens to be written in the present tense) the introduction to a prophetic consolation at a time of desolation of the land that occurred to parts of the country during the invasion of Rezin and Pekach, or to most of the country during the invasion of the Assyrian king Sennacherib? Or could it be that Isaiah was prophesying about a future destruction at the End of Time? Various explanations for this passage have been proposed by the classic medieval Jewish commentators based on different historical contexts.[30]

Let us take another example. Chapter 6 relates that Isaiah received a vision of God surrounded by angels and that this occurred at the time of the death of King Uzziah, the ninth king of Judah, which would have been in approximately 742 BCE. During this vision Isaiah was given the mission of warning the people about the impending destruction of their country and exile. This vision would also have established Isaiah's prophetic credentials for his subsequent prophecies. It reads as follows:

> *Then I heard the voice of the Lord saying: "Whom shall I send, and who will go for us?" And I said: "Here I am, send me!" . . . And I said: "How long, my Lord?" And He said: "Until cities become desolate without inhabitant and houses without people, and the land becomes waste and desolate. And God will banish the people far away, and abandoned places will be many in the midst of the land"* (6:8, 11-12).

But when did this vision occur in relation to his other prophecies? Rashi suggested that this passage truly belongs at the beginning of the Book of Isaiah and this was Isaiah's first prophecy.[31] Other commentators have proposed that Isaiah was already prophesying earlier in Uzziah's reign, at

---

30 Ibn Ezra and Radak explain that this prophecy is about the future destruction of Judah by Assyria with Jerusalem being unscathed. Rashi suggests it is a prophecy about the future exile of Judah. Abarbanel and Malbim explain that this is the type of prophecy that Isaiah made throughout the reigns of these four kings.

31 Rashi to Isaiah 1:1.

the time when his son Jotham had taken over from his father when Uzziah developed leprosy.[32]

Of relevance to this second question is a statement at the beginning of the 11th chapter of Isaiah that "*a shoot shall spring from the stump of Jesse*" (11:1) and which continues with a messianic narrative. An opinion in the Talmud suggests that this passage is referring to King Hezekiah, and that God considered Hezekiah to have messianic potential at the beginning of his reign.[33] If one accepts this opinion, there could be an historical context to at least one of Isaiah's utopian prophecies.

Third, and perhaps the most contentious of all issues regarding the Book of Isaiah – who wrote it?

Only one author, Isaiah the son of Amoz, is mentioned in the book, and the opening chapter informs us that he began prophesying during the reign of King Uzziah. Jewish tradition, therefore, usually considers there to be only one author of the Book of Isaiah.[34]

An issue arises because of prophecies in Chapter 45 and onwards that suggest that the prophet was prophesying at a time *after* the conquest of Babylon by Persia. These are the opening sentences of Chapter 45, whose first words are in the past tense:

Thus said God to His anointed one, to Cyrus, whose right hand I grasped, to subdue nations before him, ungirding the loins of kings, opening portals

---

32　Radak suggests that the time of Uzziah's death was not necessarily the beginning of his prophetic career.

33　Ibn Ezra and the Malbim suggest that these sentences could refer to King Hezekiah. The Talmud also states: "*Rabbi Tanhum says that bar Kapara taught in Tzippori. . . . the Holy One, Blessed be He, sought to designate King Hezekiah as the Messiah and to designate Sennacherib and Assyria, respectively, as Gog and Magog, [all from the prophecy of Ezekiel with regard to the end of days (Ezekiel, chapter 38), and the confrontation between them would culminate in the final redemption]. The attribute of justice said before the Holy One, Blessed be He: Master of the Universe, and if with regard to David, king of Israel, who re-cited several songs and praises before You, You did not designate him as the Messiah, then with regard to Hezekiah, for whom You performed all these miracles, [delivering him from Sennacherib and healing his illness], and he did not recite praise before You, will You desig-nate him as the Messiah?*" (TB Sanhedrin 94a). Another passage on the same page relates that God was not prepared to reveal why He did not make Hezekiah the Messiah since the time of the messianic redemption is known only to Him. Nevertheless, other Jewish com-mentators, such as Rashi and Radak, assume that Isaiah is talking about a messianic era much further into Jewish history.

34　There were traditional Jewish commentators, such as Ibn Ezra, prepared to take the histori-cal evidence into consideration. Nevertheless, he did not regard the matter as being of any great consequence.

before him and letting no gate stay shut: "I will go before you, and I will straighten out crooked paths; I will smash copper doors and cut down bars of iron. And I will grant you treasures of darkness and hidden riches of secret places so that you may know that it is I the Lord, the God of Israel, Who calls [you] by your name" (45:1-3).

Three chapters later Isaiah even took it upon himself to persuade the exiles that the time of redemption was at hand: "*Leave Babylon, flee from the Chaldeans; with a voice of singing declare, declare this, publicize it to the end of the earth; say 'God has redeemed His servant Jacob'* " (48:20).

The Persian ruler Cyrus defeated the Babylonians in 539 BCE, and soon after encouraged the Jewish exiles to return to Judea. However, there was an interval of about 200 years between the death of King Uzziah and Cyrus' proclamation. For this reason, many Biblical scholars assume that there must have been an additional author of the Book of Isaiah. This presumed author is called the Second Isaiah or Deutero-Isaiah. The existence of a Second Isaiah could also explain minor differences in emphasis apparent from Chapters 40 and onwards compared to the previous chapters.

In actuality, the situation may be even more complicated than this. Two chapters from the end of the book, we read: "*Your holy cities have become a desert, Zion has become a desert, Jerusalem a desolation. Our sanctuary and our glory wherein our forefathers praised You is burnt with fire, and all our coveted places have become a waste*" (64:9-10). There then follows a description of the sinfulness of that generation. This sounds like a description of the destruction of the First Temple by the Babylonians in 586 BCE. The so-called Second Isaiah may have been alive at this time, although Isaiah the son of Amoz would definitely have not. These prophecies also seem nonchronological if one postulates the existence of a Second Isaiah, since they would have been irrelevant to the generation leaving Babylon whose sins had already been whitewashed and who were in the main no longer inclined to paganism (40:2). This leads some scholars to suggest that there were even more authors of these prophecies than the Second Isaiah.

Two highly respected modern orthodox scholars who discuss this topic are Yoel Bin-Nun and Binyamin Lau.[35] Like most traditional Jewish commentators before him, Bin-Nun is not prepared to accept that there was more than one Isaiah, and he suggests that even the prophecies about Cyrus were made by one prophet. This is not an impossible claim. The role of a prophet is to

---

35 "Isaiah and his disciples" in *Isaiah. Prophet of Righteousness and Justice* by Yoel Bin-Nun and Binyamin Lau, 218. Maggid Books, 2019.

foresee the future, and Isaiah the son of Amoz was able to foretell the destruction of the Temple, the defeat of Babylon, the rise of the Persian Empire, the role and even the name of its first leader Cyrus, and that Cyrus would support a Jewish return to Zion. Others would say that this suggestion stretches credibility.

In defense of there being one Isaiah, it has been pointed out that a presumed Second Isaiah would have lived at about the same time as the Men of the Great Assembly were canonizing the Bible. They would therefore have known about him and would have had ample opportunity to mention his name in the text. It is also the case that in the modern period, the notion of multiple authorship of a Biblical book has a threatening ring to many traditional Jews because of the ideas of Biblical criticism and its proposition that the Torah itself had multiple authors.

An alternative and plausible suggestion is that the Book of Isaiah reflects the work of a school of Isaiah's students or followers. These followers agreed with many of the ideas of their mentor and delivered their prophecies in the same literary style. Those living during the lifetime of Isaiah the son of Amoz may have even studied in the same study hall with him, or at the very least met up with him occasionally to exchange ideas and manuscripts. During his lifetime, the prophets Amos and Hosea were prophesying in the Northern Kingdom, and Micah, who lived in the Shefela in the hill country between the coastal plain and the highlands, was prophesying in Judah (Micah 1:1). The prophet Micah, in particular, may have belonged to this school since his book contains a prophecy with almost the same wording as a prophecy of Isaiah although, as will be shortly discussed, Micah may not have agreed with all of his mentor's ideas.[36]

And the fourth question. Was Isaiah prophesying allegorically about the immediate future or literally about messianic times and the End of Days?

The former idea has much to support it, particularly with respect to Isaiah's prophecies following Cyrus' proclamation. The Babylonian Jews at that time would have been fully aware of the situation in Judea. Doubtless, they had sent people to scout out the land. Homes and agricultural land had been deserted for two generations and would require considerable repair.

---

36   The issue as to who prophesied first is discussed in scholarly circles. Micah was probably younger than Isaiah the son of Amoz in that he prophesied during the reigns of Jotham, Ahaz and Hezekiah (Micah 1:1), whereas Isaiah also prophesied during the end of the reign of Uzziah. Bin-Nun suggests from subtle textual hints in their books that the other prophets who prophesied at this time were part of his school, and there were certainly later prophets who continued his prophetic tradition (see ibid, pxxviii).

They were, moreover, living comfortable lives in Babylon. Agriculture was different in Babylon than in Judea in that there were dependable sources of water from the rivers and canals of Babylon. Many were leading fulfilling religious lives in their country of exile. It would have been obvious to them that Isaiah's "*Every valley shall be raised, and every mountain and hill shall be lowered, and the crooked terrain shall be made level and the closed mountains a plain*" (41:4) describing their impending journey to Zion would not happen in this way, nor would their buildings be filled with precious stones (54:11-12). Hence, it is possible that the Second Isaiah was not talking about the End of Days but was providing words of encouragement wrapped in beautiful but highly metaphorical language designed to engage the people – just as it engages us today.

He was also making important points that the people needed to internalize. Despite their being in exile, God would never forsake His people (49:14-16). The return to Zion would be a true redemption. Cyrus could be considered an agent of God (45:1), a point that will be reiterated in the Book of Ezra (Ezra 1:1). The returnees would be helped by God in their efforts to establish a Jewish homeland in Zion. And despite the inability of the Jewish people to establish an ideal society during the monarchy, this was still a feasible project if they practiced justice and righteousness. These were all issues that would have concerned the exiles in Babylon. And finally, their practice of Judaism had universal implications that could only be realized in Zion, and not in Babylon.

An interesting although speculative idea is that the Second Isaiah's prophecies were part of a debate that was consuming Jewish Babylonia at that time as to whether Cyrus' proclamation should truly be considered an announcement of redemption. But how could a gentile proclaim Jewish redemption? As we shall see, the timing of Cyrus' announcement was also well before the end of the 70-year period of exile prophesied by Jeremiah. Despite these reservations, the Second Isaiah was of the opinion that this definitely was the beginning of redemption and that Cyrus should be considered the "*savior*" of the Jewish people. His allegorical speeches were his attempt to persuade the Jews of Babylon to pack their bags and move to Judea. Many Jews, however, and particularly the large number who did not immigrate, were not convinced.

It should be noted that the Hebrew expression *be'acharit hayomim* mentioned in the prophecy that begins "*And it shall be at the end of the days (in Hebrew be'acharit hayomim) that the mountain of the Lord's house shall be firmly established at the top of the mountains and it shall be raised above the hills, and all the nations shall stream to it"* (2.1) does not mean necessarily the End of Days, but could denote sometime in the future. Jacob, for example, used these same words when talking about the future of his children, and it was not his intent that his words be fulfilled only at the End of Time (Genesis 49:1).

From an academic viewpoint these are all fascinating points. From an historical perspective, however, their relevance is quite limited. From the standpoint of Jewish history, more important than what modern scholars speculated Isaiah might have said is what Jewish tradition thought he did say. The Men of the Great Assembly that canonized his book, the sages of the Jewish oral tradition, the kabbalists of later periods, and the generations of Jews that listened to his words of consolation on the Sabbaths following Tisha B'Av believed the Jewish tradition that there would eventually be a messianic future at the End of Days. It must be, therefore, that there was only one Isaiah and that this prophet was talking about a glorious messianic future. Since this is a book about the interaction of Jewish history and Jewish ideas, this is the perspective I will adopt for the remainder of this chapter.

THE HISTORIC BACKGROUND TO ISAIAH'S PROPHECIES

An historical review of this period will be helpful in understanding the momentous issues that faced the Jewish people and Isaiah in this period and how these may have influenced Isaiah's prophecies.

The Israelite kingdom split during the reign of King Solomon's son, Rehoboam, in about 930 BCE. The tribe of Benjamin joined with the tribe of Judah to form the Southern Kingdom, while the other 10 tribes living in Samaria and Transjordan became part of the Northern Kingdom.

From the time of Jotham, the 11th king of Judah, the Southern and Northern Kingdom were faced with the rising power of the Assyrian Empire. This was centered in Nineveh in Upper Mesopotamia (close to the present-day city of Mosul in northern Iraq) and it would dominate the Near East. At the height of its power, it stretched through the Fertile Crescent as far as Egypt. It had the most formidable and technologically advanced army of its time. Vassal countries provided tribute, and the assumption must be that this was onerous.

The Assyrian Empire did not require vassal states to adopt Assyrian gods, but worshiping the gods they favored would have been regarded as a strong gesture of fealty. The impotence of Judah in relation to this great power may also have persuaded some Jews that the gods of Assyria were more powerful than their own invisible God. Suffice it to say that paganism was widespread in the Jewish kingdoms.

The popularity of paganism in Jerusalem during the First Temple period has been corroborated by archeological digs. Within the borders of the city as it existed then, including in the City of David, literally thousands of small idols and talismans have been found. The pagan ceremony of sacrificing one's child to Molech took place in the Valley of Hinnom outside, but adjacent to, the city walls and but a short distance from the Temple Mount. In the ancient village of Motza, only a few kilometers from Jerusalem, archeologists have found a complete pagan temple.[37] Much of Israel's paganism may have been in the form of syncretism. People followed many of the cultural aspects of Judaism but also engaged in pagan worship. Culturally they were Jewish, but religiously they were open to the cultures around them. This ambivalence towards monotheism was associated with radical swings in state policy between monotheism and paganism.

The Bible considered Uzziah and his son Jotham as being *"good kings."* However, Jotham's son Ahaz garnered no such compliment by the Book of Kings:

> *And he [Ahaz] did not do what was proper in the eyes of the Lord His God like David his father. He went in the ways of the kings of Israel, and he also passed his son through fire in the abominable manner of the nations whom God had driven out from before the children of Israel. And he slaughtered sacrifices and burnt incense on the high places and on the hills and every green tree* (2 Kings 16:2-4).

Passing a *"son through fire"* is, of course, an explicit prohibition in the Torah and is regarded as the depths of despicable pagan practice (Leviticus 18:21, 20:2-5).

The history of Judah is very much intertwined with that of the Northern Kingdom, in that both were subject to the same political and, probably, social forces too. The next-to-last king of the Northern Kingdom was Pekah son of Remaliah who came to power during the last year of Uzziah's reign and reigned for 20 years.

A major issue for the Northern and Southern Kingdoms was whether to remain compliant vassal states of the Assyrian Empire or to build alliances and rebel. The risks of rebellion were considerable. Assyrian policy was to exile rebellious populations and replace them with people from other countries,

---

37 "Another temple in Judah! The Tale of Tel Moza" in Biblical Archeological Review January/ February 2020, volume 46, number 1.

both as a punishment and as a means of preventing further uprisings. Despite this, King Pekah decided to rebel, and he made an alliance with King Rezin of Aram, a former enemy state. Together they invaded Judah with the intent of seizing territory, deposing Ahaz and installing a king willing to join an alliance against the Assyrians. It appears to have been a devastating attack. One hundred and twenty thousand Judean males were killed and 200,000 women and children enslaved (2 Chronicles 28:5-18). Jerusalem was also besieged. At this desperate time for the Kingdom of Judah, the Assyrian monarch Tiglath-Pileser was marching southwards towards Gaza on a military campaign.[38]

The prophet Isaiah arrived at the palace and advised Ahaz that the Northern Kingdom's alliance with Rezin would fail and that the Northern Kingdom would be destroyed (Isaiah, Chapters 7 and 8). He also advised Ahaz not to seek help from the Assyrians but to do nothing. This was unacceptable to Ahaz, and he called on the Assyrians to save him. Tiglath-Pileser was only too happy to oblige. The Assyrians were paid off with money from the Temple treasury. It is unclear if this was part of the deal, but Ahaz also visited Tiglath-Pileser and brought pagan worship into his kingdom while discontinuing the burning of incense and sacrifices in God's Temple:

> And he sacrificed to the gods of the kings of Aram who had smitten him and he said: "For the gods of the kings of Aram – they are helping them. To them I shall sacrifice and they will help me," but they caused him to stumble, as well as all Israel. And Ahaz gathered the vessels of the House of the Lord, and he cut the vessels of the House of God, and he closed the doors of the House of God, and he made himself altars in every corner in Jerusalem. And in every city of Judah, he made high places to burn incense to strange gods; and he angered God, the God of his fathers (2 Chronicles 28:23-25).[39]

Tiglath-Pileser now turned his attention to the Northern Kingdom. He captured the territory of Naphtali in the Galilee and Israel's territory in

---

38   These campaigns are summarized in "Isaiah before King Ahaz of Judah (734-732 BCE)" in *Isaiah. Prophet of Righteousness and Justice* by Yoel Bin-Nun and Binyamin Lau, 55-79. Maggid Books, 2019.

39   This first sentence could in theory reveal why Ahaz adopted idolatry in preference to monotheistic worship. However, it is a confusing sentence. It is unclear, for example, why Ahaz would want to adopt the pagan worship of the defeated nation Aram. It is difficult to conceive that their gods had helped Aram against Assyria. A suggestion is that Aram had already adopted the idolatry of Assyria, and this is the type of worship Ahaz wished for his kingdom. In other words, Ahaz was choosing the most successful gods. This would also be a strong symbol of fealty to Assyria.

northern Transjordan belonging to the tribes of Reuben, Gad and Manasseh. These people were exiled to Assyria and other places (2 Kings 15:29 and 1 Chronicles 5:26). This would be the first of two exiles of the Northern Kingdom.

Pekah was eventually assassinated, and his now-diminished Northern Kingdom was taken over by Hosea, a captain in Pekah's army and self-appointed head of the country's Assyrian party. He became a vassal of Assyria and paid it tribute. However, Shalmaneser, then king of Assyria, suspected him of insurrection. In 722 BCE the king successfully besieged Samaria, the capital of Israel, exiled its population, and brought other nations into the country in their place (2 Kings 17:6 and 17:24). This was effectively the end of Jewish rule in the territory of the Northern Kingdom.

Back to the kingdom of Judah.

Hezekiah (*Chizkiyahu*) became king upon the death of his father Ahaz and ruled for the next 25 to 29 years, from about 715 to 686 BCE. The Book of Kings enthuses about him, as does Isaiah, since his ascension to the throne resulted in a major change in the religious orientation of the kingdom. The Book of Kings explains:

> *And he did right in the eyes of God, like all that his father David had done. He abolished the high places and smashed the monuments, and cut down the asherah, and crushed the copper serpent that Moses had made, for until those days the children of Israel were burning incense to it, and he called it Nehushtan (2 Kings 18:3-5).*

The Book of Chronicles elaborates further on his campaign against pagan worship in Judah and the Northern Kingdom:

> *And when they completed all this, all the Israelites who were present went out to the cities of Judah and they smashed the monuments and cut down the asherim, and they demolished the high places and the altars from all Judah and Benjamin and in Ephraim and Manasseh until they had completely destroyed [them], and all the Children of Israel returned, each man to his inheritance, to their cities (2 Chronicles 31:1).[40]*

---

40   There is archeological evidence supporting Hezekiah's attempt to centralize monotheistic worship in Jerusalem. In Tel Arad in the Negev, which is not far from the modern city of Arad, a small Temple to God has been unearthed in this Judean fortress. It had an inner sanctum, or Holy of Holies, containing a smooth standing stone that was probably a *massebah* and two altars for incense. Hezekiah would not have wanted to destroy a Temple of God, and instead he buried the entire structure. The cooperation of the Northern Kingdom in this religious revival suggested to the Malbim that Hosea, the king of Israel at that time,

The Book of Chronicles describes Hezekiah's sanctification of the Temple during the first year of his reign. The Temple was purified during an eight-day ceremony, and everything unclean was dumped into the nearby Kidron Valley. During this ceremony, many sin offerings were slaughtered as atonement for the people's transgressions. A musical ceremony was held, followed by peace offerings and thanksgiving offerings in the hundreds. Notices were also sent throughout the Jewish kingdoms, north and south, to gather in the House of God for the Festival of Passover. This attempt to unify the people of the two Jewish kingdoms was only partially successful (2 Chronicles 30:5-11).

The second exile of the Northern Kingdom occurred in the sixth year of Hezekiah's reign. A consequence of this for Hezekiah's kingdom was that a sizable number of Jews managed to escape the Assyrian conquest and made their way to Judah. Because of this, Jerusalem experienced a large population increase. Some Jews may also have been able to remain in the country despite a new population being brought in.

Hezekiah eventually felt strong enough to gather an alliance to rebel against Assyria. However, his ally Egypt was defeated, and other allies were either defeated or surrendered. This left Hezekiah alone to face the wrath of the Assyrian Empire in the 14th year of his reign.

Sennacherib now advanced against the fortified cities of Judah and proceeded to destroy them. Hezekiah sent him silver and gold procured by stripping his palace and the Temple, but this failed to halt the Assyrian advance against Jerusalem. An influential peace party in the city advised surrender. In this perilous situation Hezekiah consulted Isaiah who prophesied that Jerusalem would not be captured, that Assyria would hear a rumor and retreat, and that Sennacherib would die (2 Kings 19:2):

> And King Hezekiah's servants came to Isaiah. And Isaiah said to them, "So shall you say to your master. So has the Lord said: 'Have no fear of the words that you have heard, that the servants of the king Assyria blasphemed Me. Behold I will imbue him with a desire; and he will hear a rumor and return to his land, and I will cause him to fall by the sword in his land' " (2 Kings 19:5-7).

This is exactly what happened. That night there was a great slaughter in the Assyrian camp from a cause not defined in the Bible (nor by the Assyrian

---

had abolished the calves for worship that had previously been set up in Beth El and Dan by Jeroboam, the first king of the Northern Kingdom.

records that otherwise confirm Sennacherib's withdrawal), and the Assyrians withdrew from their siege of Jerusalem, leaving much spoil behind. Sennacherib was subsequently assassinated by his two sons, as Isaiah had prophesied:

> *Therefore, so has God said concerning the king of Assyria: "He shall not come into this city, nor shoot an arrow there, nor shall he advance before it with a shield, nor pile up a siege mound against it. He shall go back by the same way he came. He shall not enter this city." says God. "And I will protect this city to save it, for My sake and for the sake of My servant David." And it came to pass on that night that an angel of God went out and slew 85,000 in the Assyrian camp. And when they arose in the morning, behold, they were all dead corpses. And Sennacherib, the king of Assyria, retreated and stayed in Nineveh. While he was worshipping in the temple of Nisroch his god, Adramelech and Sharezer his sons slew him with the sword, and they fled to the land of Ararat, and Esarhaddon his son reigned in his stead* (2 Kings 19:32-37).

That Jerusalem was never captured and Hezekiah remained king is also confirmed by Assyrian records. However, Judah's territory was much diminished by this conflict, many of its cities had been destroyed, and a heavy tribute was imposed on the country.

King Hezekiah died in 687 BCE. The throne now passed to his 12-year-old son Manasseh, who strongly aligned himself with the Assyrian Empire. He wanted nothing to do with religious reform and reversed the religious policies of his father.

The events surrounding the eventual destruction of Jerusalem and the Temple by the Babylonians are summarized in the next chapter. During this period there were two large waves of Judean exile to Babylon. Following the death of the Babylonian monarch Nebuchadnezzar, the Babylonian Empire began to weaken. The Persian Cyrus succeeded in taking over Media and began building his own empire. He fought against Babylon, and in 539 BCE captured the city of Babylon and, with it, its empire.

WHAT BOTHERED ISAIAH THE SON OF AMOZ AND HIS DISCIPLES?

The prophets of this time, namely Isaiah and Micah in the Southern Kingdom and Amos and Hosea in the Northern Kingdom, prophesied about destruction. Why did they do this?

Before answering this question, it will be helpful to discuss the Torah's approach in general to prophets and their prophesying.

The ancient world believed that there existed a spiritual realm and that it was possible to tap into it through astrologers, witchcraft, magic, and superstitious practices such as the use of talismans, and thereby to predict and even influence the future. The Bible does not deny the existence of this realm (since it is also the realm of God) but is strongly opposed to the use of magic and superstitious practices. How then could the Jewish people approach this realm once the prophet Moses had passed away? The Book of Deuteronomy explains:

For these nations that you are possessing – they listen to astrologers and diviners; but as for you – not so has the Lord your God given for you. The Lord your God will raise up for you a prophet from among your brethren, like myself [i.e., Moses]; to him you shall heed" (Deuteronomy 18:14-15).

Thus, the Torah seems to view the prophet's primary role as being a fortune teller to the leaders and to the people. This could, of course, encourage charlatans who would falsely direct the people. To guard against this the Torah warns:

When you will say in your heart, "How can we know the word that God has not spoken?" What the prophet will speak in the name of God and that thing will not occur and not come about - that is the word that God has not spoken; with willfulness has the prophet spoken it, you shall have no fear of him (Deuteronomy 18:21-22).

For earlier prophets such as Elijah and Elisha, their main issue was the idolatrous practices of the people. However, Isaiah and his colleagues also felt it necessary to point out the social ills of their societies. They saw their role as explaining the relevance of important Torah concepts such as justice and righteousness to their generation, and explaining why events in history had happened or were about to happen as a consequence of their behavior.[41] They also believed they could shape Jewish history by changing the behavior of the Jewish people.

These prophets saw was that the two kingdoms had drifted far from the egalitarian society described by the Torah. The rich were exploiting the

---

41   "*The Prophets and Psalmists as Exegetes (Part 1)*" by Rabbi Menachem Leibtag on YouTube. (https://www.youtube.com/watch?v=LHePbYb9gIU). The familiarity of the prophets with the books of the Torah is evidence against an evolutionary approach to the composition of the Torah as adopted by higher Biblical criticism.

disadvantaged, corruption was rife in the justice system in support of the privileged class, and no provisions were being made for the disadvantaged of society, such as the widow and orphan. As Isaiah rebuked:

> *Your silver has become dross; your wine diluted with water. Your princes are rebellious and companions of thieves; Each of them loves bribery and pursues payments; they do not judge the cause of the orphan, and the widow's grievance never comes to them* (Isaiah 1:22-23).

Isaiah was well aware that righteousness and justice were no longer on the pedestal the Torah had assigned for them:

> *For the vineyard of the Lord of Hosts is the House of Israel and the people of Judah are the seedlings He lovingly tended: and He hoped for justice, but behold there was injustice; for righteousness, but behold an outcry (tze'aka in Hebrew)* (5:7).

Moreover, not only was idol worship tolerated in the kingdoms, but the rulers had accumulated wealth and had imported many horses for their chariots. There is an explicit prohibition in the Book of Deuteronomy about a king accumulating too much wealth and going down to Egypt to buy horses for a large chariot force (Deuteronomy 17:16-17). Not surprisingly, the kings of this period had conveniently forgotten about these prohibitions. Not so Isaiah:[42]

> *For You [God] have abandoned Your people, the house of Jacob, because they were full of [witchcraft] from the East and soothsayers like the Philistines, and they pleased themselves with children of foreigners. And its land became full of silver and gold, without end to its treasures; its land became full of horses, with no end to its chariots* (2:6-7).

These prophets understood that remaining in the Land of Israel was based on a contract; allegiance to God and His covenant would bring blessing. The Torah also warns in stark terms about destruction and exile if the Jewish

---

42 According to commentators such as Nachmanides (see his commentary to this verse), the issue in this Biblical command is lacking sufficient trust in God. Isaiah himself says this: "*Woe to those who go down to Egypt for aid, and who rely on horses and trust in chariots, and they do not rely on the Holy One of Israel and God they did not seek*" (Isaiah 31:1). Rabbi Samson Raphael Hirsch also raises the point that this command is to prevent an inappropriate reliance on Egypt to provide a continual supply of horses. This explanation is also compatible with Isaiah's words. Of interest is that Isaiah was familiar with the Book of Deuteronomy and his prophecies sometimes constitute a commentary on this book. This is evidence against the view of Biblical critics who propose that the discovery of the Book of Deuteronomy at the time of King Josiah was that of a newly written book.

people fail to adhere to the provisions of the covenant: "*God will scatter you among all the peoples, from the end of the earth to the end of the earth, and there you will work for gods of others, whom you did not know – you or your forefathers – of wood and of stone*" (Deuteronomy 28:64).

Unlike in previous generations, exile of the population had now become a very real possibility. The Assyrians exiled populations that resisted their hegemony (and the Babylonians would later do this as well). It is estimated that the Assyrians displaced as many as 4½ million people between 745 to 612 BCE. The Judeans during the reign of Ahaz were witness to the first exile of the Northern Kingdom, and this kingdom was completely dismembered during the reign of Hezekiah.

Isaiah also pointed out to the people that practicing the cult alone without attention to the social injustice within the country was self-defeating. The Book of Jeremiah also contains such sentiments (Jeremiah 7:21-23). In the following passage Isaiah likens the characteristics of the Israelites to the people of Sodom and Gomorrah as described in the Book of Genesis, the obvious implication being that their fate will be similar:

> *Had not the Lord of Hosts left us a very small remnant [who were loyal to the Torah], we would have been like Sodom, we would have resembled Gomorrah. Hear the word of God you rulers of Sodom, give ear to the teaching of our God, you people of Gomorrah: "Why do I need your many sacrifices?" says the Lord. "I am sated with elevation offerings of rams and suet of fatlings; and the blood of bull, sheep and goats I do not want. When you come to appear before Me, who requested this of you, to trample My courtyards? No longer should you bring a worthless meal-offering, it is incense of abomination to Me; New Moon and Sabbath, your calling of convocations, I cannot endure iniquity along with solemn assembly. Your New Moons and your appointed seasons My soul hates, they have become a burden to Me, I am weary of bearing [them]. And when you spread out your hands [in prayer], I will hide My eyes from you, even though you pray at length I will not listen; your hands are full of blood*" (1:9-15).

There have been religious reformers who have attempted to read into these sentences their own views about the primacy of social justice versus ritual. However, it is most unlikely that Isaiah would have advocated abandoning the sacrificial cult or religious holidays. Later prophets and even later chapters in the Book of Isaiah never considered this possibility (Jeremiah 17:26 and Isaiah 56:7). The major project of the returnees to Zion was rebuilding the Temple and resuming the sacrificial cult. Rather, Isaiah was saying that attempting to develop a relationship with God via the cult and religious ritual are meaningless if accompanied by widespread social injustice.

During the reign of Ahaz, Judah was steeped in idolatry, and even the Temple was no longer functioning as a Temple to God. Hezekiah would later destroy places of pagan worship, but social injustice was a more difficult problem to tackle. The admonitions of the prophets were a heartfelt plea to the people to take action lest the Torah's warnings be fulfilled.

THE MESSIANIC IDEAS AND FOREIGN POLICY OF ISAIAH

Through the eyes of the prophets the future looked gloomy for the Jewish people, and it seemed almost inevitable to them that unless there was a change in the nature of society there would be a day of reckoning. Nevertheless, Isaiah also believed that a utopian existence would be realized after this, at a time that has traditionally been interpreted as being the messianic era.

He also felt that the role of the Jewish people will be to broadcast the praise of God among the nations: *"This people which I formed for Myself that they might declare My praise"* (43:21). This was hardly an original idea. The Book of Deuteronomy describes the universal dimensions of Judaism in that *"all the peoples of the earth shall see that the name of God is called upon you [the Jewish people]"* (Deuteronomy 28:10) and that the laws of the Torah are *"your wisdom and your discernment in the eyes of the peoples"* (ibid., 4:6). Hence, Isaiah's messianic era will be nothing but universal. This will be a time when the nations of the world will discard their idols, acknowledge the omnipotence of God and beg to learn of God's ways. These eschatological ideas have been extremely influential in Judaism and via Judaism have entered into Christianity and Islam.

Hence, Isaiah described a day of judgment for mankind when idolatry would be abandoned and the omnipotence of God would be recognized:

> *None but God will be exalted on that day. . . . Mankind's haughtiness will be humbled and men's arrogance will be brought down, and God alone shall be exalted on that day. And the idols will completely disappear. And they [idolaters] will go into caves in the rocks and holes in the ground because of the fear of God and because of the glory of His majesty when He rises to shake the earth* (Isaiah 2:11, 17-19).

As discussed in the Book of Deuteronomy, on that day God will avenge Himself on the enemies of the Jewish people (Deuteronomy 32:41) and purify the people (ibid., 30:6):

"Therefore," says the Master, the God of Hosts, the Mighty One of Israel, "Oh, I will be appeased of My adversaries, and I shall avenge Myself of My enemies. And I will turn My hand against you [the Jewish people] and purge away your dross as with lye and remove all your slag" (Isaiah 1:24-25).

No mention is made by Isaiah of a messianic superman who will organize this messianic era. Rather, everything will be engineered by God. However, he does mention that a descendent of David will be His representative in coordinating society's improvement.

As did Solomon at the dedication of his Temple (1 Kings 8:41), Isaiah envisaged the Temple in Jerusalem as becoming the focus for the universal recognition of God. As one of the most famous passages in the Book of Isaiah tells us, this recognition will be followed by universal peace:

The word that Isaiah son of Amoz prophesied concerning Judah and Jerusalem. And it shall be eventually (literally: at the end of the days), that the mountain of the Lord's house shall be firmly established at the top of the mountains, and it shall be raised above the hills, and all the nations shall stream to it. And many peoples shall go, and they shall say, "Come, let us go up to the Lord's house, to the house of the God of Jacob, and let Him teach us of His ways, and we will go in His paths," for out of Zion shall the Torah come forth, and the word of the Lord from Jerusalem. And He shall judge between the nations and reprove many peoples, and they shall beat their swords into plowshares and their spears into pruning hooks; nations shall not lift the sword against nation, neither shall they learn war anymore. "O house of Jacob, come and let us go in the light of God" (2:1-5).

Isaiah's ideas about the messianic era are elaborated more in the 11th chapter of the book. He described a descendant of David judging the people and reorganizing society for the practice of justice and righteousness. This in turn will herald an era of universal peace such that even carnivorous animals will give up their meat-eating instincts. About this, he may be speaking figuratively. However, he may also be taking us back to the pristine vegetarian state of the world that existed from the time of the Garden of Eden to the time of Noah (Genesis 1:30 and 9:3:

And a shoot will grow from the stump of Jesse, and a twig will sprout from his roots. And the spirit of God will rest upon him, a spirit of wisdom and understanding, a spirit of counsel and might, a spirit of knowledge and fear of God. He will be animated by the fear of God. He will not judge by what his eyes perceive nor decide by what his ears hear. He will judge the poor justly, and rebuke with fairness the humble of the earth, and he will smite the earth with the rod of his mouth and with the breath of his lips he will slay the wicked. And righteousness will be the girdle of his loins and faith the girdle of his loins. And a wolf will live with a lamb, and a leopard will lie down with a kid; and a calf, a lion cub and a fatling together, and a young child will lead them. And a cow and a bear will graze and their young ones will lie down together; and a lion, like cattle, will eat hay. And a suckling child will play over a viper's hole and the weaned child will stretch out his hand over an adder's den. They will neither harm nor destroy on all My holy mountain, for the land will be full of the knowledge of God as water covers the sea bed. And it will be on that day, that the root of Jesse which stands as a banner for peoples, nations will seek him, and his resting place will be glorious (11:1-10).

The return of the exiles from Judah and the former Northern Kingdom will be part of the messianic era. As we shall see in the next chapter, the Torah's notion of an ingathering of the exiles (Deuteronomy 30:3-4) will also be taken up by the prophet Jeremiah:

And it shall be on that day that the Lord will once again apply His hand to recover the remnant of His people who will have remained from Assyria and from Egypt and from Pathros and from Cush and from Elam and from Sumeria and from Hath and from the islands of the sea. And He will raise a banner for the nations, and assemble the banished of Israel and gather the dispersed of Judah from the four corners of the earth. . . . And there shall be a highway for the remnant of His people who remain from Syria, as there was for Israel on the day they went up from the land of Egypt (11:11-12, 16).

Towards the end of the book, Isaiah described non-Jews desiring to become proselytes and participate in His Covenant. In this way the Temple will become a house of prayer for all people:

And the foreigners who join themselves to God to serve Him and to love the name of God, to be His servants, all who guard the Sabbath against desecration and hold fast to my Covenant. I will bring them to My holy mountain and I will cause them to rejoice in My house of prayer, their elevation-offerings and their feast-offerings will find favor upon My altar, for My House shall be called a house of prayer for all peoples (56:6-7).

In this new ideal world, the Jewish people will become a *"light"* to mankind because of their practice of justice and righteousness. In the following passage the words *"My servant"* have been interpreted as referring either to the entire Jewish nation, the Messiah or even to Cyrus:

Behold My servant whom I uphold, My chosen one, whom My soul desired; I have placed My spirit upon him, he shall promulgate justice to the nations. He shall not shout out nor raise [his voice]; nor cause his voice to be heard in the street [in order for people to respect his rulings]. Even a bruised reed he shall not break or snuff out even a flickering flaxen wick; but with truth shall he execute justice. He will not slacken nor tire until he establishes justice in the land and islands will long for his teaching. . . . I, God, have called you with righteousness; I will strengthen your hand; I formed you for a covenant to the people, for a light to the nations (42:1-4, 6).

This theme of the light of Zion's righteousness being recognized by humanity is repeated in a subsequent chapter:

For Zion's sake I will not be silent, and for Jerusalem's sake I will not rest until her righteousness emanates like a bright light, and her salvation blazes like a torch. And nations shall see your righteousness, and all kings your glory, and you shall be called a new name that the mouth of God will pronounce. Then you will be a crown of glory in the hand of God and a royal diadem in the palm of your God. No more shall you be called "forsaken," nor shall your land be called "desolate," but you shall be called "Hefziba (I delight in her)" and your land "Beual (inhabited)" for God takes delight in you, and your land shall be inhabited (62:1-4).

In the next-to-last chapter, Isaiah again discussed the peace that is destined to pervade his utopian world, and he included in this section his previous pristine vision of animals at peace with each other, this time specifically on the Temple Mount in Jerusalem:

For behold, I am creating new heavens and a new earth, and the former [events] will no longer be remembered and shall never come to mind. But be glad and rejoice forever in what I am creating, for behold I am creating Jerusalem as a joy and My people as a delight; for I will rejoice over Jerusalem and exult in My people, and no longer will be heard there a sound of weeping or a sound of crying. No longer shall be heard from there a youth or an old man who will not fill his days; he who dies at 100 years shall be reckoned a youth, and he who fails to reach 100 years shall be reckoned accursed. And they shall build houses and inhabit them, and they shall plant vineyards and eat their fruit. . . . A wolf and a lamb shall graze together; and a lion, like cattle, will eat straw, and the serpent's food shall be earth; they will not inflict harm nor destroy on all My holy mount; says God (65:17-21, 25).

Of interest is how much of Isaiah's foreign-policy advice was aligned philosophically with his prophetic visions. According to rabbinic tradition, Isaiah's father was a brother of King Amaziah, the father of King Uzziah, and Isaiah was therefore related to the kings of Judah.[43] He had political influence and was sometimes consulted by royalty about important domestic and foreign policy decisions; although more often than not his advice was not heeded.

Isaiah regarded the great powers as being tools in the hands of God: "*And He shall raise an ensign to far-off nations, and He shall whistle to him [the enemy] from the end of the earth, and behold, quickly, swiftly, he shall come*" (5:26). As mentioned, he was also convinced that a righteous remnant of Judah would survive the machinations of these powers. All this led him to a very passive approach with respect to his foreign policy advice. Hence, he advised King Ahaz to neither ally with Pekach and Rezin, nor to submit to the Assyrians, but to stay above the fray. Ahaz ignored his advice and called on the Assyrians for help. Similarly, at the time of Hezekiah, Isaiah was against war preparations for an alliance against Assyria, especially one that relied on the Egyptians. He opposed strengthening the defensive Broad Wall of Jerusalem and diverting Jerusalem's water supply to inside the city (22:9-11). This advice was also ignored by Hezekiah. As we shall now see, the prophet Micah was also against Hezekiah's trust in an Egyptian alliance, although he was not in accord with Isaiah's passivism. Nevertheless, Isaiah was probably justified in his opposition to Hezekiah's attempt to break loose from Assyria since it led to the destruction of much of Judah.

THE NEW IDEAS OF THE PROPHET MICAH

It is not always recognized that one of the most well-known and inspiring of Isaiah's messianic prophesies is also found in the Book of Micah word for word except for some minor differences. It reads as follows:

---

43   TB Megilla 10b.

And it shall be eventually (lit: at the end of the days), that the mountain of God's house shall be firmly established at the top of the mountains, and it shall be raised above the hills, and peoples shall stream upon it. And many nations shall go, and they shall say, "Come, let us go to God's mount and to the house of the God of Jacob, and let Him teach us of His ways," and we will go in His paths, for out of Zion shall the Torah come forth and the word of God from Jerusalem. And He shall judge between many peoples and reprove mighty nations afar off; and they shall beat their swords into plowshares, and their spears into pruning hooks; nation shall not lift the sword against nation; neither shall they learn war anymore. And they shall dwell each man under his vine and under his fig tree, and no one shall make them move, for the mouth of the God of Hosts has spoken. For all peoples shall go, each one in the name of his god, but we will go in the name of God, our God, forever and ever. "On that day," says God, "I will heal the limping one and the lost one I will gather, and those whom I harmed. And I will make the limping one into a remnant, and the scattered one into a mighty nation, and God shall reign over them on Mount Zion from now and forever" (Micah 4:1-7).

As distinct from the prophecy in the Book of Isaiah, this version can be placed in its historic context in that the previous chapter of his book ends with the words: "*Therefore, because of you, Zion shall be plowed as a field, Jerusalem shall become heaps, and the Temple Mount like the high places of a forest*" (Micah 3:12). In other words, this prophecy is Micah's consolation for the destruction of Judah and Jerusalem.

But when were these words of Micah spoken since it will be many years before Jerusalem and Judah are destroyed and the people of Judah exiled? Some sentences in the Book of Jeremiah help us here. When Jeremiah was threatened with death for prophesying the end of Judah and the exile of its inhabitants, the elders mentioned that the prophet Micah also prophesied about the end of the Jewish state, and he was not sentenced to death. Ergo, Jeremiah should not be put to death for making the same prophesy:

Then some of the elders of the land arose and said to the entire assemblage of the people, saying: "Micah the Morashtite prophesied in the days of Hezekiah the king of Judah, saying: 'Thus said the Lord of Hosts: "Zion shall be plowed as a field, Jerusalem shall become ruins, and the Temple Mount shall become like heaps in the forest." ' "Did Hezekiah and all of Judah put him to death? Did he not fear God? And he entreated God and

God relented of the evil which He had pronounced against them. But we are about to bring great evil on ourselves [by putting Jeremiah to death]" (Jeremiah 26:17-19).

These verses place Micah's prophecy during the reign of Hezekiah. There is no indication in the Book of Jeremiah when exactly Micah made this prophecy, but the Book of Micah may help us. Micah lived in the Lowlands some distance from Jerusalem. When Sennacherib attacked Judah, he devastated the Lowlands, including the important fortress of Lachish, and Micah may be describing this in the first chapter of his book:

For the one dwelling in disobedience hoped for good, yet disaster descended from God to the gate of Jerusalem. Hitch the chariots to the swift steeds, you inhabitants of Lachish; it is the beginning of sin for the daughter of Zion, for in you were found the transgressions of Israel (Micah 1:12-13).

There is discussion among scholars as to who first enunciated a messianic vision of a world totally at peace. Was it Micah or Isaiah? Based on the passages I have quoted it is possible to make the following speculation. Isaiah, who was older than Micah, first made this prophecy early in Hezekiah's reign to encourage him to continue with his religious reforms.[44] Micah, who was present in the countryside during the attack of Sennacherib, saw the devastation from this and prophesied the end of the Judean kingdom. Like Isaiah, he was aware of the destruction of the Northern Kingdom and the exile of its population, and he reasoned it was now the turn of Judah. He also believed that Isaiah had been premature in prophesying about a utopian world during the reign of Hezekiah, although this did not negate his vision of messianic times.

Of considerable interest because of its implications for later Jewish history, is that Isaiah and Micah appear to have had different approaches to political activism in their own time, and perhaps even with respect to messianic times. I have mentioned that Isaiah had a very passivist approach to foreign policy due to his belief that the events of history were being engineered by God according to His will. Micah, on the other hand, had a far more interventionist approach, since he believed that Israel would also have a role in determining its future.[45] He wrote:

---

44 An age difference is assumed because Isaiah prophesied "*in the days of Uzziah, Jotham, Ahaz, [and] Hezekiah, kings of Judah*" *(1:1)* whereas Micah prophesied "*in the days of Jotham, Ahaz [and] Hezekiah, the kings of Judah*" (1:1), although this cannot be regarded as definitive.

45 These ideas are discussed in "Micah vs. Isaiah: For and Against the Rebellion" in *Isaiah.*

And the remnant of Jacob shall be among the nations, in the midst of many peoples – like a lion among the beasts of the forest, like a fierce lion among the flocks of sheep, which, if it passes through, treads down and tears in pieces, with none to deliver. Your hand shall prevail over your oppressors, and all your enemies shall be cut down (Micah 5:7-8).

Moreover, in Micah's visions, the Messiah from the stock of David will not just be someone inspired by God to judge the people and act as the rallying person for appreciating His wonders, but also a leader of the people against the enemies of Israel. Only when he has succeeded will peace prevail in the land:

But you, Bethlehem Ephrathah – you should have been the lowest of the clans of the Judah – from you shall one emerge for Me, to be a ruler in Israel; one whose origin is from of old, from ancient times. . . . And he shall stand and lead by the might of God, with the pride of the Lord his God; and they shall dwell [securely], for then he shall become great to the ends of the earth. . . . And they [his other appointees] shall lay waste the land of Assyria with the sword, and the land of Nimrod at its gates; and he [the Messiah] shall deliver us from Assyria should it invade our land and trample within our border (Micah 5:1, 3, 5).

In conclusion, the elaboration of what will become classic messianic ideas can be traced to Isaiah and his school. He and Micah assumed that the people of Judah would eventually be exiled (which they were), and that their redemption would be a messianic one (which it was not). As delineated by Isaiah (but not by Micah), the Jewish people will have a passive role on "*that day*" as manifestations of the omnipotence of God unfold.

At a time in history when Judah was relatively powerless against the surrounding great powers, Isaiah's advice was very appropriate, even though it was rarely heeded. Messianic passivism and waiting for "*that day*" will subsequently become the trend in Jewish history following the debacle of the Bar Kochba Revolt, although kabbala will provide a non-violent means of hastening the appearance of messianic times.

It seems likely that the prophets Ezekiel and Zechariah were highly influenced by the tradition of Isaiah's school of prophecy, particularly as regards to a Day of Judgment and revelation of God, as were the Essenes of Qumran, John the Baptist, and Jesus of Nazareth. Through Jesus and early

---

Prophet of Righteousness and Justice by Yoel Bin-Nun and Binyamin Lau, 167-181. Maggid Books, 2019.

Jewish Christians, the essential core of this tradition will make its way into the eschatology of Christianity, although it will be significantly altered along the way by Paul of Tarsus and later Christian theologians. Islam borrowed many of its World to Come ideas from Christianity and Judaism, and in this way the ideas of Isaiah also entered into Islamic eschatology.

Jeremiah is the next major prophet we will meet. He does not tread completely in the footsteps of Isaiah's prophetic tradition and may not even have known about it. Nevertheless, since his words were based on Torah ideas there will be many similarities. What then did he preach? This will be our next topic for discussion.

Chapter 6

REDEMPTION ACCORDING TO THE PROPHET JEREMIAH

J eremiah can be considered a tragic figure. In the early part of his life he prophesied about a destruction and exile he knew could occur and which he desperately tried to prevent. Only when destruction was almost inevitable did the people begin listening to him; by then it was too late to change the course of history.

Jeremiah lived at the chaotic end of the First Temple monarchial period and he prophesied during the reign of King Josiah until the final exile of the Southern Kingdom of Judah. Unlike Isaiah, his advice to the people was very practical and down-to-earth and he more than anyone else provided guidance to the Jewish nation as it approached the new situation of exile.

- Like Isaiah, his evaluation of the religious and ethical status of the Southern Kingdom of Judah was based on fundamental Torah principles.

- He wrote a letter to the Jews of Babylon from the first exile outlining how they should live in exile. This advice would continue to be relevant to the Jewish people for thousands of years.

- He emphasized that despite the destruction of Jerusalem and the Temple the Jews were still God's people; exile did not mean the termination of God's covenant.

- He prophesied that the exile would be of short duration and he advanced a period of 70 years.

- A plain reading of the text suggests that He did not prophecy that the future redemption would be associated with a utopian world, although he did prophesy that the Jewish people would change their behavior as a result of the lessons they had learnt.

A previously quoted talmudic sentence explains:

The entire Book of Jeremiah is about destruction, and the beginning of the Book of Ezekiel is about destruction and its end is about consolation, and the entire book of Isaiah is about consolation.[1]

Destruction summarizes well what the Jewish people have taken away from Jeremiah's writings. A reading from the Book of Lamentations (which according to Jewish tradition was also written by Jeremiah) is part of the synagogue service during Tisha Be'Av, the fast day commemorating the destruction of both Temples.

Nevertheless, this quotation is somewhat of a simplification. While most of Jeremiah's prophecies do concern the future destruction of the kingdom of Judah, his book also contains several chapters of consolation that discuss the future renewal of Jewish life in Israel, and these will be more the focus of this chapter.

Before going further, some history about the Kingdom of Judah is needed to understand the historical context to Jeremiah's prophecies. We will continue from where we left off in the previous chapter.

MORE HISTORY ABOUT THE KINGDOM OF JUDAH

Manasseh, the 14th king of Judah (reigned 698 to 642 BCE) assumed the throne on the death of his father Hezekiah when he was 12 years old, and he reigned for 55 years. The story is already a familiar one. He reversed the religious orientation of Judah from monotheism to paganism in a throwback to his grandfather Ahaz, and this was associated with defilement of the Holy Temple. This was all part and parcel of being a loyal vassal of Assyria. As the Book of Kings relates:

And he [Manasseh] did that which was evil in the eyes of God; like the abominations of the nations whom God had driven out from before the children of Israel. For he rebuilt the high places that Hezekiah his father had destroyed, and he erected altars for Baal, and made an asherah as Ahab the king of Israel had done, and bowed down to all the host of the heaven, and worshipped them. And he built altars in the House of God, concerning which God had said: "In Jerusalem I will establish My name." And he built altars for all the host of Heaven in the two courts of the House

---

1   TB Bava Basra 14b. The context of this statement is that the Talmud questioned the position of the Book of Isaiah in the order of the books of the Prophets, and concluded that books about destruction are placed next to those about destruction and those about consolation are placed next to those about consolation rather than being in the order in which these prophets lived.

of God. And he passed his son through fire; he practiced soothsaying and divination, and he consulted necromancers and familiar spirits; he did much that was evil in the eyes of God to provoke [Him] (2 Kings 21:1-6).[2]

The Book of Kings also tells us that at this time the prophets of God began prophesying about the destruction of Judah, indicating that a prophetic tradition was developing that the actions of Manasseh had sealed the fate of the Judean kingdom:[3]

And God spoke through His servants the prophets, saying: "Because Manasseh has committed these abominations, has done more wickedly than all the Amorites who were before him, and has caused Judah to sin with his idols. Therefore," the Lord, the God of Israel, has said, "Behold, I am bringing such calamity on Jerusalem and Judah that whoever hears of it both his ears will tingle. And I will stretch over Jerusalem the measuring line of Samaria and the plumb line of the house of Ahab, and I will wipe Jerusalem as one wipes a dish, wiping it and turning it upside down. And I will cast off the remnant of My inheritance and deliver them into the hands of their enemies, and they shall become plunder and prey for all their enemies" (21:10-14).

Manasseh's son Amon became king after the death of his father, and he continued the policies of his father that included cooperation with the Assyrians and debasement of the religious rites in the Temple. He was assassinated after two years by his noblemen, but they too were murdered, and Amon's 8-year-old son Josiah (*Yoshiyohu*) was installed on the throne.

Josiah (reigned 640-609 BCE) was of a completely different mindset from his father and grandfather, and beginning in the 12th year of his reign, he initiated a policy of religious reform that included purging the country and Jerusalem of idolatry. He also destroyed all vestiges of idolatry in Samaria. This territory was now only loosely ruled over by Assyria, and Josiah seems to have had some degree of control over it. He also attempted to persuade Jews still remaining there to worship in the Temple in Jerusalem:

And in the eighth year of his reign, while he was still a youth, he began to seek after the God of David his father, and in the 12th year he began to

---

2   Manasseh's kingdom was prosperous and experienced peace during his entire 55-year reign, and this may have been due in no small measure to his positive relationship with the Assyrian Empire. However, as the prophets pointed out, there was a price to pay for this. Mitigating factors for his paganism are discussed in Mishna Sanhedrin 10:2 and TB Sanhedrin 102b. According to 2 Chronicles 33:12-13, Manasseh repented at the end of his life when brought before the king of Assyria for suspected treason.

3   According to *Midrash Seder Olam*, these prophets were Nahum and Habakkuk.

purge Judah and Jerusalem of the high places, the asherim [sacred trees or poles that honored the goddess Asherah, consort of El], the graven images and the molten images. And they demolished the altars of the Baalim in his presence, and the sun images that were above them he cut down, and the asherim, the graven images, and the molten images he broke in pieces, ground them into dust, and strewed it on the graves of those who had sacrificed to them. And the bones of the priests he burned on their altars, and he purged Judah and Jerusalem. And he did so in the cities of Manasseh and Ephraim and Simeon as far as Naphtali with their ruins of destruction all around (2 Chronicles 34:3-6).

Six years later, in the 18th year of Josiah's reign, repairs were begun on the Temple and "*a scroll of the Law (*In Hebrew *sefer haTorah) of God by the hand of Moses*" was discovered.[4] It was read before the king, and he rent his clothes because of its contents (2 Chronicle 34:14-33 and 2 Kings 22:8). The prophetess Hulda was consulted and had little to say of comfort. She prophesied that Jerusalem would indeed be destroyed as the curses in the scroll indicated, although Josiah would merit not witnessing any of this destruction. Not discouraged, the king called the people of Judah to the Temple for a public reading of the scroll and enacted a covenant with them to keep the commandments. With this the people returned to God (2 Chronicles 34:33 and 2 Kings 23:3). Nevertheless, the Bible makes clear that their repentance was far from complete (Jeremiah 3:6-10).

Josiah died in battle in the 31st year of his reign. In 612 BCE, the Medes allied with the Babylonians against a weakening Assyrian Empire, and its capital, Nineveh, fell to their combined forces. Three years later, Pharaoh Necho of Egypt, who was an ally of the Assyrians, marched up the coast to battle the Babylonians. Josiah engaged the Egyptians at Megiddo but was killed by Egyptian archers.[5] Pharaoh Necho, meanwhile, continued to the north to do battle with the Babylonians.

---

4   It is unclear from the text what book was discovered in the Temple precincts. It may have been the Book of Deuteronomy or even the entire Torah. Radak conjectures that the Torah was forgotten during Manasseh's reign. The references in Isaiah to ideas from Deuteronomy would discount the suggestion that this book was newly created in late First Temple times (see chapter 5, reference 17).

5   This engagement is described in 2 Chronicles 35:20-24, where it is related that Pharaoh Necho told Josiah in the name of God to stop opposing him. *Lamentations Rabba* 1:18 suggests that what Pharaoh Necho said "*from the mouth of God*" were actually Jeremiah's words. One might surmise from this that the opinion of the sages was that Jeremiah thought that Josiah should not have got involved in a great power struggle between Egypt and Babylon.

Josiah had three sons – Johoahaz, Jehoiakim and Zedekiah. Jehoahaz became king, but the Egyptians, who now controlled Judah, deposed him after only three months on the throne and replaced him with his half-brother Jehoiakim, whom they felt would be more supportive of an Egyptian-Assyrian alliance against Babylon (2 Kings 23:30-35). They also helped themselves to a heavy tribute. Neither the Book of Chronicles nor the rabbinic literature are complimentary about Jehoiakim (reigned 609-598 BCE), whom they regarded as a godless tyrant.[6]

The story continues its tumultuous course that will end in two Judean exiles. In 605 BCE the Babylonian king Nebuchadnezzar defeated the Egyptians and the remnant of the Assyrian army at the Battle of Carchemish. He then marched to Jerusalem and besieged the city. This was good reason for Jehoiakim to change his allegiance from the Egyptians to the Babylonians, and he remained a vassal of Babylon for three years. However, sensing weakness of the Babylonians when they failed in an invasion of Egypt, he switched sides. Nebuchadnezzar then sent a large force to besiege Jerusalem and restore order, but Jehoiakim died before the siege ended. Jeremiah had prophesied that Jehoiakim would *be buried with the burial of a donkey, dragged and cast out beyond the gates of Jerusalem,* and this is exactly what happened (Jeremiah 22:18-19).[7] Jehoiakim's son Jehoiachin (also called Jeconiah), who had just been appointed king, surrendered to the Babylonians.

Jehoiachin's surrender saved Nebuchadnezzar from having to conquer Jerusalem, and he treated the city relatively mildly. He sacked the riches of the Temple, deported Jehoiachin to Babylon as a royal guest, and in 597 BCE exiled some 10,000 of Jerusalem's leading citizens to Babylon, leaving only the poorest of the population in Judah (2 Kings 24:12-16). Among those exiled was a young priest called Ezekiel.

That it was the prominent citizens of Jerusalem who were exiled and not the lower classes would have important consequences for the continuity of Judaism, since it ensured that the Jews in Babylon remained a distinct faith-bound community. The Jewish infrastructure they established would also serve well the next Jewish exile when Jerusalem was destroyed 10 years later. The Jews settled near the city of Nippur, near the Kebar River, between the Euphrates and Tigris Rivers and not far from Babylon. They were given a reasonable amount of autonomy and fared well financially. Jeremiah called

---

6   2 Chronicles 36:8 and TB Sanhedrin 103b.
7   According to the Roman Jewish historian Josephus, Nebuchadnezzar killed Jehoiakim and his body was disposed of as Jeremiah had prophesied. (*Antiquities of the Jews*, Book X, chapter 6, part 3).

this group the "*good figs*," a remnant of Israel that would survive the exile, and he prophesied that everyone else in Jerusalem would be destroyed by "s*word, famine and pestilence*" (Jeremiah 24:9).

In the meantime, the Babylonians appointed Zedekiah, a puppet king and uncle of Jehoiachin, as ruler of Judah. Zedekiah (reigned 597 to 586 BCE) visited Babylon and swore loyalty to Nebuchadnezzar. However, many of influence in his kingdom advised rebellion, although Jeremiah counselled continuing subjugation to the Babylonians, whom he regarded as agents of God. Despite this, Zedekiah broke his oath to Nebuchadnezzar and rebelled against the Babylonians on the assumption he would receive support from Egypt. Jeremiah realized that the Jewish kingdom was now doomed.

The final bitter siege of Jerusalem took place in 586 BCE and lasted three months. The city and the Temple were burnt to the ground and its residents killed or deported to Babylon. Zedekiah and his followers attempted to escape but were captured. Zedekiah's sons were killed before his eyes, and he was then blinded and imprisoned in Babylon.

Following the destruction of Jerusalem, Gedaliah was made governor of the area around Jerusalem, which was now a Babylonian province. He was the head of a household that had supported both Josiah's religious reforms and the prophet Jeremiah. However, he was assassinated soon after by those who disagreed with his policies, and the Jews remaining in the country fled (2 Kings 25:25). This was the end of Jewish life in Judah.

There were thus three waves of Judean exile to Babylon. The first was in 597 BCE at the time of King Jehoiachin and involved about 8,000 people. The second and largest was after the destruction of Jerusalem in 586 BCE and probably involved about 75,000 people. There may have been a third, smaller emigration after the assassination of the governor Gedaliah in about 582 BCE, although most Jews emigrated to Egypt, including the prophet Jeremiah.

JEREMIAH'S PROPHECIES OF DOOM AND DESTRUCTION

Jeremiah was born to a priestly family in the village of Anatot in the Judean Desert a few miles northeast of Jerusalem.[8]

Jewish tradition holds that Jeremiah wrote the Book of Jeremiah as well as the Book of Kings and Lamentations assisted by his scribe and disciple, Baruch ben Neriya. His book does not always follow chronological order, and

---

8   Anatot was in the location of the present-day Arab village of Anata, close to the Ein Prat Nature Reserve.

as for the Book of Isaiah it is often difficult to place its chapters in their historic context.

Jeremiah wrote that in the 13th year of King Josiah's reign, in 626 BCE, when he was still young, he experienced a vision from God. This would determine the direction of his life and also his future prophecies:

> *And the word of God came to me saying: "What do you see, Jeremiah?" And I said, "I see a rod of an almond tree." And God said to me: "You have seen well, for I hasten to fulfill My word." And the word of God came to me a second time, saying: "What do you see?" And I said: "I see a bubbling pot and its spout is facing north." And God said to me: "From the north the evil will break forth upon all the inhabitants of the land. For behold, I am summoning all the families of the kingdoms of the north, says God, and they will come and each one will set his throne at the entrance of the gates of Jerusalem and by its walls roundabout and against all the cities of Judah. And I will pronounce My judgments against them [the inhabitants of Judah] for all their evil, for thy have forsaken Me and have offered unto other gods and prostrated themselves to the work of their hands. And you therefore gird your loins and arise and speak to them all that I command you; do not be frightened of them, lest I let you be broken before them. . . . And they shall fight against you but will be unable to defeat you, for I am with you, says God, to rescue you"* (1:11-17, 19).[9]

At the time of this prophecy, it would have been unclear to Jeremiah which nations would descend on Judah from "*towards the north.*"

Jeremiah was well aware that while some of the people had returned to monotheism and Temple worship during Josiah's reforms, paganism and social injustice were still rife among the population.[10] Also, contrary to the words of false prophets, the physical presence of the Temple would be

---

9   The significance of the bubbling pot is clear. The significance of the almond tree is that just as it blossoms before all other trees, so God will hasten to perform his word (Rashi). Radak points out that an almond is called *shaked* in Hebrew because of its quick ripening period.

10   There is a rabbinic tradition that the people did not significantly change their ways, but Josiah was unaware of this. The text itself says: "*And God said to me [Jeremiah] in the days of King Josiah: Have you seen what the backsliding Israel has done? . . . . And yet for all this, her treacherous sister Judah did not return to Me with all her heart but falsely, says the Lord.*" (Jeremiah 6:6,10). Hence, the Talmud says: "*Josiah, however, did not know that his generation found but little favor [in the eyes of God]*" (TB Taanit 22b). See also *Lamentations Rabba* 1:18 – "*Josiah did not know that his entire generation worshipped idols. . . . [Josiah] would send two wise men to purge their homes from idols. They would enter, but find nothing. As they left [the scoffers] would have them close the door, so that, on the inside, the idols would be reattached.*"

insufficient in and of itself to prevent destruction and exile if the people continued to transgress the Ten Commandments and the principles of justice and righteousness:

> *The word that came to Jeremiah from God saying: "Stand in the gateway of God's house and proclaim there this word and say: 'Hear the word of God, all you of Judah who enter these gates to prostrate yourselves before God. So said the Lord of Hosts, the God of Israel; Improve your ways and your deeds and I will allow you to dwell in this place. Do not trust the false words that say: "The Temple of God, the Temple of God, the Temple of God are these [buildings]." Only if you truly improve your ways and your deeds, if you truly perform judgment between one man and his fellow; do not oppress a stranger, an orphan, or a widow, and do not shed innocent blood in this place, neither follow after other gods for your detriment, then I will allow you to dwell in this place in the land that I gave to your forefathers, for ever and ever. . . . Can one steal, murder and commit adultery and swear falsely and burn incense to the Baal and go after the gods of others that you never knew and then come and stand before me in this Temple, upon which my Name is pronounced and say, "We are saved – in order to continue committing all these abominations. . . . Therefore, so says the Lord God, behold My anger and wrath will be poured out on this place, upon man and upon beast, upon the trees of the field and upon the produce of the soil; it shall burn and not be extinguished" (7:1-7, 9-10, 20).*[11]

In Chapter 3 of his book, we read that Jeremiah encouraged Jews exiled from the Northern Kingdom, or perhaps Israelites still living in the former territory of the Northern Kingdom, to return to Temple worship in Jerusalem. This could have been during Josiah's reforms.[12] Reuniting the tribes was

---

11 In his book, Rabbi Lau attempts to provide an historic context for much of Jeremiah's words. This entails some rearranging of the chapters of his book. Although placed early in the Book of Jeremiah in Chapter 7, he suggests that this particular prophecy was made later during the reign of Jehoiakim. See "Jeremiah's Prophecies of Doom" in *Jeremiah. The Fate of a Prophet* by Binyamin Lau, 89. Maggid Books, Jerusalem, 2013. Other commentators do not attempt to date it.

12 In "Prophesying Reunification" in *Jeremiah. The Fate of a Prophet* by Binyamin Lau, 17. Maggid Books, Jerusalem 2013, Rabbi Lau recognizes that chapters in this book are not always chronologically arranged and suggests that this chapter took place during Josiah's reforms and was directed at Jews still remaining in the former Northern Kingdom. A refutation of his suggestion is that Jeremiah calls their territory "*the north*" (Jeremiah 3:12) rather than Samaria and the Galilee. In addition, the part of the sentence "*and they will come together from the north land to the land that I caused your forefathers to inherit*" (ibid., 3:18) indicates that these Jews were then living further north than the Land of Israel. Rashi,

consistently in Jeremiah's thoughts, and he would return to this topic in his prophecies of consolation regarding a future redemption.

In this same chapter, he made the northern tribes a surprising offer regarding the Ark of the Covenant by proposing that it be removed from the Holy of Holies. The cherubim over the Ark were thought to represent God's footstool, and Jeremiah now suggested that all Jerusalem should be considered the throne of God:[13]

> *Return, O rebellious children, says God, for I possessed you, and I will take you [i.e., the Jews from the northern tribes], one from a city and two from a family, and I will bring you to Zion. And I shall appoint shepherds for you according to My own heart who will care for you with knowledge and understanding. And it shall be, when you multiply and are fruitful in the land in those days, says God, they will no longer say "The Ark of God's Covenant," neither shall it come to mind, neither shall they mention it, nor shall they remember it, nor shall it be done anymore. At that time people will call Jerusalem "The Throne of God," and all nations shall gather to it in the name of God, to Jerusalem, and they will no longer follow the visions of their evil heart (3:14-17).*

By the 25th chapter of his book, Jeremiah admits that despite preaching repentance for 23 years, the people had failed to listen to him or other prophets. Now, in the fourth year of the reign of Jehoiakim, he prophesied irrevocable destruction by the hands of Babylon:

> *Therefore, so said the God of Hosts: Because you did not heed My words, behold I am going to send for all the peoples of the north, declares the Lord, and for My servant, King Nebuchadnezzar of Babylon, and I shall bring them against this land and its inhabitants, and against all these surrounding nations, and I will destroy them and make them a desolation, an object of whistling and eternal ruin. And I will cause to cease from them the sound of mirth and the sound of gladness, the sound of the bridegroom and*

---

based on TB Megilla 14b, suggests that Jeremiah went to the places of residence of most of the Ten Tribes, which would have been outside of Israel.

13 The Ark of the Covenant was initially in Shilo in Samaria, but after it was retrieved from the Philistines who had captured it, it became the symbol of the glory of the House of David. It was subsequently hidden during the reign of Manasseh (2 Chronicles 35:3) but brought into the Temple again during the reign of Josiah. The Talmud suggests that Josiah hid it again (TB Yoma 52b). Jeremiah may be suggesting that Jerusalem would become a city for all Jews and not just the nation attached to the dynasty of David. Other commentators suggest that the Ark of the Covenant would no longer be taken out to battle as in the past as peace will reign (Rashi and Radak).

the sound of the bride, the sound of a mill and the light of a candle. And this whole land shall become a desolate ruin. And those nations shall serve the king of Babylon for 70 years. And when these 70 years are over, I will punish the king of Babylon and that nation and the land of the Chaldeans for their sins, declares God, and I will make it for everlasting desolation. (25:8-12).

JEREMIAH'S PROPHECIES OF CONSOLATION

Now that God's decision for destruction and exile was final, Jeremiah began making prophecies of consolation and these are found in the later chapters of his book. These include a letter of encouragement he wrote to the exiles in Babylon after the first exile during the time of Jehoiachin/ Jeconiah which out-lines how the people should adjust to their new situation. He also mentioned again that in 70 years they will be redeemed:

Thus said the God of Hosts, the God of Israel, to the whole community that I exiled from Jerusalem to Babylon: Build houses and settle, plant gardens and eat their produce. Take wives and beget sons and daughters; take wives for your sons, and give your daughters to husbands, and they shall bear sons and daughters. Multiply there; do not [let your numbers] diminish. Seek the welfare of the city to which I have exiled you and pray to God on its behalf; for in its prosperity you shall prosper. . . . When Babylon's seventy years are completed, I will remember you, and I will fulfill to you My favor-able promise to return you to this place. For I know the thoughts that I am thinking about you, says God, thoughts of peace and not evil, to give you a future and hope. You will then call out to Me, and come and pray to Me, and I will hearken unto you. . . . And I will gather you in from all the na-tions and from all the places where I dispersed you, declares God, and I will return you to the place from which I have exiled you (29:1-7, 10-12, 14)

While Nebuchadnezzar was besieging Jerusalem, Jeremiah was impris-oned by Zedekiah because of his defeatism with respect to Babylon. While in incarceration he received a directive from God to redeem a field in his native town of Anatot. Given the situation, this made little sense, but its purpose was to demonstrate publicly the certainty of a future redemption. Witnesses to the sale were gathered, and the documents from the sale were placed for preser-vation in an earthen vessel:

And Jeremiah said: The word of God came to me saying: "Behold, Hanamel, the son of Shallum your uncle is coming to you saying "Buy my field that is in Anatot, for the right of redemption is yours to buy it." Then Hanamel, my uncle's son, came to me in the prison yard, according to the word of God and said to me: "Please buy my field that is in Anatot, that is in the territory of Benjamin, for the right of inheritance is yours, and you have the right of redemption; buy it for yourself." And I knew that it was the word of God. So, I bought the field in Anatot from Hanamel, my cousin, and weighed him the money, seven shekels and 10 pieces of silver. And I wrote out the deed and signed it, and I designated witnesses, and weighed the money on a scale. . . . And I charged Baruch in their presence, saying: "Thus said the Lord of Hosts, the God of Israel: Take these documents, this deed of purchase, the sealed one and this open scroll and put them in an earthen vessel so they will endure for many years. For thus says the Lord of Hosts, the God of Israel: Houses and fields and vineyards shall be purchased again in this land (32:6-10, 13-15).

Beginning in chapter 30, the Book of Jeremiah contains several chapters of consolation regarding this future redemption. Its significance will be confined to the Jewish people, and none of the universalism of Isaiah is found in these chapters:

This is the word that came to Jeremiah from God saying: Thus said the Lord, God of Israel, saying: "Write down for yourself the words I have spoken to you in a scroll. For behold, days are coming, says God, when I will return the captivity of My people Israel and Judah, says God, and I will return them to the land that I gave their forefathers and they shall possess it." . . . And it shall be on that day, declares the Lord of Hosts, that I will break the yoke from off your neck, and I will break your thongs, and foreigners will no longer enslave them. And they will serve the Lord their God and David their king, whom I will establish over them" (30:1-3, 8-9).

Measure for measure, those who inflicted harm on the Jewish people will themselves be destroyed, Jerusalem will be rebuilt and the relationship between God and the Jewish people restored. The Jews are an eternal people and a return to their former strength and number is assured:

Therefore, all who devoured you will themselves be devoured; all who oppressed you will go into captivity; who plundered you will be plundered; and all who preyed upon you I will give for prey. For I will bring healing to you and I will heal you of your wounds, says God, though they called you an outcast, that is Zion whom no one seeks out. Thus said God: Behold, I am returning the captivity of the tents of Jacob, and I will have mercy on its dwellings, and the city will be built on its mound and the palace established in its proper place. And thanksgiving and the sound of merrymakers will emanate from them, and I will multiply them, and they shall not be diminished, and I will increase them, and they will not dwindle away. . . . And their prince shall be from them, and their ruler shall emerge from their midst, and I will bring him close, and then he will be able to approach Me, for who would otherwise dare approach Me? says God. And you shall be My people, and I will be your God (30:16-19, 21-22).

The prophecies in Chapter 31 are directed specifically at those from the former Northern Kingdom.[14] Jeremiah tells them that God's love for them has not diminished, and they will return to their former lands in Samaria:

From long ago, God appeared to me: With everlasting love have I loved you: Therefore, have I drawn you to Me with loving kindness. I shall yet rebuild you, and you shall be built, O virgin of Israel; again you shall take up your timbrels, and go out with the dances of merrymakers. You will again plant vineyards on the mountains of Samaria, indeed planters will plant and redeem. For there will be a day when watchmen will call out on the mountains of Ephraim: Rise! Let us go up to Zion, to the Lord our God. . . . Behold, I will bring them from the land of the north and gather them from the ends of the earth, and with them the blind and the lame, the pregnant and the birthing mother together; a great company will return here. With weeping they will come, and with supplications will I lead them; I will guide them along brooks of water, upon a straight road on which they will not stumble, for I am ever a Father to Israel, and Ephraim is My firstborn (31:2-5, 7-8).

In what may be a deliberate contrast to the gloom of his previous prophecies, the joy of the forthcoming redemption emanates from his words:

Then shall the virgin rejoice with dance, and young men and old men together, and I will transform their mourning into joy, and I will comfort them and cheer them in their sorrow (31:12).

The returnees will form an independent kingdom in Judea and Samaria

---

14   Rabbi Lau suggests that this chapter should be placed much earlier in the Book of Jeremiah in conjunction with Chapter 3. See "Chapter 31: Children shall return to their borders" in ibid., 22-28. However, it seems equally appropriate to place Chapter 31 among later prophecies of consolation after the fate of Judah had been almost sealed by the siege of Jerusalem.

under the dynasty of David. This king will rule securely with righteousness and justice, his security will be assured and his dynasty will never be broken:

> *In those days, and at that time, I will cause a sprout of righteousness to grow for David, and he will administer justice and righteousness in the land. In those days, Judah will be saved, and Jerusalem will dwell in security, and this is what people will call it [Jerusalem]: "God is our righteousness." For thus says God: There shall not be cut off from David a man who sits on the throne of the house of Israel (33:15-17).*

Earlier in his book Jeremiah prophesied that the manifestations of God in His seeking the dispersed exiles from the northern tribes will even exceed those seen during His redeeming the Israelites from Egypt:

> *Assuredly, days are coming, declares God, when it will no longer be said: As God lives Who brought up the children of Israel from the land of Egypt, but as God lives Who brought up the children of Israel from the land of the North and from all the lands where He had scattered them. . . . Behold, I shall send many fishermen, says God, and they will fish them out, and afterwards I shall send many trappers and they will hunt them from upon every mountain and every hill and out of the clefts of the rocks (16:14-16).*

But will not this future redemption be part of an ever-recurring cycle of sin, exile and redemption? Not so, stated Jeremiah, who envisaged a permanent change in the relationship between God and His people. The chastisement that the Jewish people suffered will bring about an enduring return to God (31:17). He also projected his listeners to a time when a *"new covenant"* will be established and everyone from Judah and Israel will be aware of the presence of God:

> *Behold days are coming, says God, that I will make a new covenant with the house of Israel and with the house of Judah. Not like the covenant that I sealed with their forefathers on the day I took hold of them by the hand to bring them out of the land of Egypt, forasmuch as they broke My covenant, although I was Lord over them, says God. But this is the covenant that I will make with the house of Israel after those days, says God. I will place My law within them and I will inscribe it upon their heart, and I will be their God and they shall be My people. And no longer shall one teach his neighbor, each man his brother, saying: "Know God!" for they shall all know Me from the least of them to the greatest, says God, for I will forgive*

their iniquity and their sin I will no longer recall (31:30-33).

By the term *"new covenant,"* Jeremiah certainly did not mean the abrogation of the covenant made by God at Mount Sinai and its replacement by a new one, as the Christian tradition understands it. More acceptable explanations from a Jewish perspective include a new and permanent increase in Jewish commitment, or a covenant that will never again be broken. Since Israel will never again break the covenant, God will no more think of retracting His blessings for Israel than the sun will cease to illuminate the day.[15]

INTERPRETATIONS OF THE PROPHECIES OF JEREMIAH

The prophesies of Jeremiah present some penetrating questions regarding the messianic era and the prophecies of prophets in general.

First, did Jeremiah assume that the future redemption he was prophesying about would be a natural one or a messianic one at the End of Days, as could be implied by the utopian prophecies of Isaiah?

---

15 There have been a number of explanations for Jeremiah's idea of a *"new covenant."* The traditionally accepted explanation is that Jeremiah was referring to the messianic period. Radak suggests that the covenant will then never again be broken. Nachmanides envisions a change in human behavior in the messianic era (Nachmanides, Deuteronomy 36:6). The Shelah understands that in the messianic period there will be a deeper and more fundamental understanding of the Torah. (See "The Meaning of Brit Chadash" in *Illuminating Jewish Thought. Explorations of Free Will, the Afterlife, and the Messianic Era* by Rabbi Netanel Wiederblank, 572-576. Maggid Books). There could also be a non-miraculous, non-messianic explanation. Jeremiah may well be providing an interpretation of the verse from Deuteronomy that at the end of the exile "*The Lord your God will circumcise your heart and the heart of your offspring, to love the Lord your God with all your heart and with all your soul that you may live*" (Deuteronomy 30:6). Loss of the people's desire for idolatry while in Babylon could have led to a stronger relationship to God's covenant. The loss of desire for idolatry in the Persian period is discussed in the following talmudic passage: "[*The verse states]: And they cried with a loud voice to the Lord their God* (Nehemiah 9:4). *What was said? Rav said, and some say it was Rabbi Yohanan who said: Woe, woe. It is this, [i.e., the evil inclination for idol worship], that destroyed the Temple, and burned its Sanctuary, and murdered all the righteous ones, and caused the Jewish people to be exiled from their land. And it still dances among us, [i.e., it still affects us]. Didn't You give it to us solely for the purpose of our receiving reward [for overcoming it]? We do not want it, and we do not want its reward. [We are prepared to forgo the potential rewards for overcoming the evil inclination as long as it departs from us. In response to their prayer] a note fell to them from the heavens upon which was written: Truth, [indicating that God accepted their request]*" (TB Yoma 69b). This allegorical talmudic passage implies that the people's desire for idolatry did not disappear until they returned to Zion. However, it could also be that their repentance and distaste for idolatry had already occurred in Babylon. This change in thinking hardly created utopia, but it did create the potential for a more steadfast relationship between God and the Jewish people.

The opinion of the Talmud and traditional medieval Jewish commentators such as Rashi, Ibn Ezra and Radak are that Jeremiah's prophecies, like those of the prophets Isaiah, Zephaniah, Zechariah and Malachi, were directed towards a messianic era.[16]

Nevertheless, the Book of Jeremiah does imply that Jeremiah's prophecies were accepted by those awaiting redemption as indicating a natural redemption, and there was no anticipation that redemption was about to herald a utopian messianic future. Daniel, the prophet Zechariah and the Book of Chronicles also accepted that the redemption Jeremiah was prophesying about would happen after 70 years of exile (Jeremiah 29:10, Daniel 9:2, Zechariah 1:12 and 7:5, II Chronicles 36:21). Why then would Jewish tradition assume that Jeremiah was thinking messianically?

One reason, perhaps, is that the redemption from Babylon did not follow exactly Jeremiah's script.

Jeremiah prophesied that the future redemption would occur 70 years after the Babylonian exile, whereas it seems to have transpired much sooner.[17] He thought that the exiled northern tribes would participate in redemption, which they did not; that the ingathering of the exiles would be more revelatory of God's power than the Exodus from Egypt (16:14), whereas it was less; that Babylon would be destroyed and the Babylonians taken into captivity (30:16), which was not the policy of Persia; that the Davidic dynasty would form an independent Jewish state, whereas David's descendent Zerubbabel disappeared from the Bible; and that the future redemption would be one of

---

16 The following statement is found in TB Berakhot 34b: "*And Rabbi Chiya bar Abba said in the name of Rabbi Yochanan: 'All the prophets prophesied only about the messianic period, but as for olam-haba [the World to Come], [the prophet Isaiah said]: "No eye besides Yours has seen [the World to Come]" [literally: "that which He will do for one who awaits Him" (Isaiah 64:3)]." '*

17 The Book of Chronicles explains that the number 70 corresponds to the number of Sabbaths (Sabbatical and Jubilee years) that were not previously kept and this number in years would therefore appease the land during the exilic period (II Chronicles 6:21). This is based on the Book of Leviticus: "*Then the land will be appeased regarding its Sabbaths*" (Leviticus 26:34). Daniel, speaking during the reign of Darius, assumed that the period of 70 years began from the destruction of the Temple, but seemed puzzled as to when the end point would be (Daniel 9:2). Counting from the destruction of Jerusalem to the decree of Cyrus, the period of the Babylonian exile was 48 years. From the time of the first Babylonian exile at the time of Jehoiachin it was 58 years (597 BCE to 539 BCE). One way of making it accord more with 70 years is to count from the time that Nebuchadnezzar came to the throne in 605 BCE, which was 66 years. Alternatively, it could be the time from the destruction of the First Temple (587/586 BCE) to the completion of the building of the Second Temple in 515 BCE, which was 70 years. However, this does not fit exactly with Jeremiah's words which imply that the end of the exile would be in 70 years.

joy. The exiles' initial return may well have been joyous, but this would soon give way to the realities of their situation.

A number of suggestions have been made within an orthodox framework to explain these loose ends.

One explanation given is that the messianic-like prophecies of the prophets represent messianic potential. Everything the prophets prophesied will occur, but not necessarily in the era about which the prophecy was made. This explanation is favored by Rabbi Hayyim Angel in his writings and is discussed in his book *Haggai, Zechariah and Malachi* in relation to the lack of actualization of the prophecies of these prophets at the beginning of the redemption from Babylon.[18] Rabbi Angel also points out that this explanation is favored by the Malbim, a respected rabbi and Biblical commentator from the early 19th century. This is why the Malbim was prepared to interpret the prophetic books in a more literal way than the medieval Jewish commentators.[19] As mentioned in the last chapter, there is discussion in the Talmud as to why Hezekiah did not become the Messiah. One could similarly say that Jeremiah thought that all his prophecies would be realized in 70 years, but the people were unworthy of a complete messianic redemption.

Another possibility is that there was evolution in the development of the messianic concept. The prophets of ancient Israel were convinced that the Torah's ideal society would eventually be realized and this is why they prophesied about it. They also appreciated that God would need to intervene in a more open way to bring about this perfect world, so that the messianic era could herald the end of the world we know. Nevertheless, the precise details of the messianic idea were unclear in their minds. Despite this, their confidence about a future messianic era will be accepted by the Men of the Great Assembly and the sages of the Mishna and the Jerusalem and Babylonian Talmud and will become a fundamental belief of Judaism.

However, it is well-recognized that a belief in messianism does have the potential for negative consequences. It can lead to inappropriate messianic activism and the notion that one can double-guess God's plans for Jewish history, since one's actions appear to be in accord with His will. This will be discussed in greater detail in relation to Rabbi Akiva (see Chapter 10). It can also lead to inappropriate messianic passivism and the belief that only God can resolve the internal problems or halachic dilemmas of the Jewish people.

---

18   Prophecy as Potential" in *Haggai, Zechariah, and Malachi: Prophecy in an Age of Uncertainty*, xviii-xx. Maggid Books, 2016. See also Tosafot to TB Yevamot 50a and TB Berakhot 4a.

19   For details on the approach of the Malbim, see his commentary to Haggai 1:1.

There is no reason, therefore, to tackle them. This will be discussed in chapter 14 in the chapter about Theodor Herzl. Messianism has also led to the appearance of false messiahs and an individual such as Shabtai Zvi who led to considerable damage within the Jewish world (see chapter 13).

Another explanation is that proposed by Rabbi Jonathan Sacks (although not specifically in relation to Jeremiah) that the utopian words of the prophets should be viewed as the light at the end of the tunnel.[20] This light is something to strive towards — an inspiration to that generation and all future generations. Thus, the writings of the prophets should not be regarded as prophecies that are definitely bound to occur but as visions of hope for the future that might eventually be realized.

This explanation has advantages. It recognizes that prophetic visions reflect the perspective of a particular prophet and the historic period in which he lived, and this can lead to differences in their visions. It also resolves the problem of inaccurate predictions. Nevertheless, it does not diminish in any way the value of these visions, since it stresses the prophetic idea that the Jewish people and humanity in general should be directing themselves towards creating a more perfect world. The visions of the prophets were something to aspire to, a final destination. Their stirring words also provided consolation and hope to the Jewish people throughout their 2,000 years of exile.

The visions of the prophets also contained important messages that needed to be conveyed in the manner they did. Thus, Jeremiah stressed that the destruction of Jerusalem and the exile from Judah did not indicate the termination of God's relationship with the Jewish people. As he proposed in the Book of Lamentations (which he wrote): *"And I [either Jeremiah or the people] said: 'My strength and my hope are perished from God' "* (Lamentations 3:18). But this was not so: *"The grace of God has not ceased, and His compassion does not fail"* (ibid., 3:22). The impending exile will also be limited in duration, and he uses the number 70 to emphasize this point.

---

20 "Time as a Narrative of Hope" in *Haggadah. Hebrew and English Text with New Essays and Commentary* by Rabbi Jonathan Sacks, 75-83. The Continuum International Publishing Group Inc, New York, 2010. Rabbi Sacks writes: *"My own interpretation of the messianic idea, however, is that it stands in relation to Jewish history as the stars did to ancient navigation."* He quotes Kenneth Minogue (political theorist 1930-2013) as saying: *"When you steer by a star you don't aim to arrive there."* Rabbi Sacks continues *"The perfect world – the world we rehearse every Shabbat – is beyond history; but history itself is the attempt, never wholly successful, but marked none the less by real and significant advance, to come ever close to that ideal. God alone can bring about a world of perfect justice, but we are not wrong to keep that vision constantly before us as we seek to create a society less random and cruel than those in the past."*

In conclusion, it was the Torah that introduced the idea of hope into the world, and this idea was expanded upon by the prophets of ancient Israel. As Rabbi Sacks explains, man in the ancient world viewed history as cyclical just as the phases of nature.[20] What had been in the past would be so in the future. It was the Torah that introduced the notion that history is not circular but linear. God controls history and through redemption moves Jewish history forward towards freedom and the potential for the creation of a better society based on justice, righteousness and the ways of God. This is the basis of Jewish hope, and through the dissemination of the visions of the prophets it became the model that propelled forward the moral, scientific and material progress of humanity.

Chapter 7

THE PROPHETS HAGGAI AND ZECHARIAH CONFRONT REALITY

The return to Zion from Babylon was not easy. During the 48 years since the people had been exiled from Judah, Jerusalem had become an expanse of weed-covered ruins. Nothing was left of the Holy Temple. Agricultural conditions in the countryside were difficult and the people were confronted with famine.

This return was not following exactly the prophesies of Jeremiah. There could be little joy when agricultural conditions were so difficult, the exiles from the former Northern Kingdom had not appeared, Judea was a small and insignificant part of the Persian Empire and not an independent state, and Temple-building was soon halted by Cyrus through the efforts of their enemies. Even the significance of the 70 years of exile prophesied by Jeremiah seemed unclear.

The main issue that Haggai and Zechariah, the prophets who accompanied the returnees, had to deal with in this period was persuading the people that God was with them in this venture, that they should continue building the Temple, and that a glorious future awaited the nation. In contrast to some of the prophets of previous generations, these prophets were respected and their advice was listened to and acted upon.

There is no textual evidence that the prophecies of Isaiah were well known during this period, although they would become so when the Bible was canonized. Nevertheless, it is possible that a school of prophecy continued to study Isaiah's writings during this period, and the prophet Zechariah, in particular, may have been influenced by his ideas. Isaiah had talked about the chastisement of the people, exile, the saving of a remnant by the direct intervention of God, His vengeance against the enemies of the Jewish people, and the creation of a new utopian world. This would form the kernel of a new form of prophecy we now call apocalyptic.

The word apocalypse meant initially no more than a revelation, but nowadays refers to a belief that God will intervene in a cataclysmic struggle between the forces of good and evil to save an elected faithful, leading finally to a new world order. As we shall see in subsequent chapters, this tradition will have considerable influence on Christian and Islamic eschatology.

Zechariah's later prophecies, together with the writings of Daniel and Ezekiel, marked a new direction in the messianic utopian vision. These prophecies envisaged God intervening directly in human history and bringing about cataclysmic events of a cosmic order that presaged the end of the world that we know.

This period of return was also one of transition with respect to the spiritual and political leadership of the people. Some 82 years after the return to Zion, the scribe Ezra arrived in Judea and began strengthening the foundations of Jewish life. His arrival marked the end of prophetic leadership and the beginning of a new phase of religious leadership, that of Rabbinic Judaism. Its sages will provide impetus to further development of the Oral Law. Haggai, Zechariah and Malachi were therefore the last of the prophets.[1] The prophecies of Malachi are not dated, but there is a body of opinion that he also prophesied during this period.[2] The subsequent arrival of Nehemiah also provided new political leadership, supported at the highest level of the Persian Empire.

THE HISTORY OF THE PERSIAN PERIOD

Shortly after defeating the Babylonians and taking over their empire in 539 BCE, the Persian monarch Cyrus announced to the Jewish exiles in Babylon his permission for them to return to Zion. The speech he made is quoted in the Book of Ezra:

---

1   See "Why did Prophecy Cease?" in *Haggai, Zechariah, and Malachi: Prophecy in an Age of Uncertainty* by Hayyim Angel, 145-153. Maggid Books, 2016. Angel discusses why the era of prophecy came to an end and provides the traditional Jewish approaches together with pertinent references. One explanation given is that the Jewish people no longer merited such direct communications from God because of their sinfulness (Rashi, Ibn Ezra and Radak to Amos 8:11). Alternatively (or in addition) there was lack of respect for the prophets (*Avot DeRabbi Natan B*,47), and failure to emigrate in sufficient number from Babylon to Judea (*Pesikta Rabbati 35* and Maharsha to TB Yoma 9b). There is also a midrash explaining that Haggai, Zechariah and Malachi had a reduced level of prophecy (*Pesikta DeRav Kahana* 13). A non-traditional explanation might be that a new type of religious leadership was needed for the historical period that was unfolding.

2   This issue is discussed in "Overview of Malachi" in ibid., 119. It is traditionally accepted that Malachi was the last of the prophets (*Tosefta Sota* 13:3, TB Yoma 9b, TB Sanhedrin 11a) and commentators bring internal Biblical evidence for this (Radak, Abrabanel and ZerKavod). Based on his concerns about intermarriage, it is assumed that his prophecies were made at an even later time than those of Haggai and Zechariah and when Ezra was also concerned about this issue (Ezra 9).

In the first year of Cyrus, the king of Persia, when the word of God from the mouth of Jeremiah was fulfilled, God aroused the spirit of Cyrus, the king of Persia, and he issued a proclamation throughout all his kingdom, and put it also in writing, saying: "So said Cyrus, the king of Persia: All the kingdoms of the earth the Lord God of the heavens has delivered to me, and He has charged me to build Him a house in Jerusalem, which is in Judea. Whosoever is among you of all His people may His God be with him – let him go up to Jerusalem, which is in Judea, and build the house of the Lord, God of Israel, the God Who is in Jerusalem" (Ezra 1:1-3).

But did Cyrus really make his proclamation in such monotheistic terms? It could be that someone Jewish had written his speech for him. It was also state policy that the nations of this new Persian empire be encouraged to express their religious identities. Moreover, it would not have been difficult for Cyrus to make the switch between his own creator god and that of the Jews. None of this would have negated the feeling of the Jews that everything they were witnessing was God-directed.

The religion of the Persian Empire was Zoroastrianism. This is one of the world's most ancient religions and was introduced by the Persian prophet Zoroaster in the second millennium BCE. Zoroastrians believed in a dualistic cosmology of good and evil and the prominence of a supreme creator god, Ahira Mazda, a deity of wisdom. Their beliefs encompassed free will, a day of judgment, messianism, the ultimate triumph of good over evil, heaven, hell, and the resurrection of the dead.

There are many commonalities of belief between Judaism and Zoroastrianism regarding the afterlife and End of Days, and academicians debate the degree of borrowing that could have occurred between the two religions, given that the Jewish people were now living in the Persian Empire. It is also the case that these matters were not distinctly formulated in the Bible prior to this time. Nevertheless, there is no clear answer as to whether such borrowing occurred and if it did, in which direction.

The Persians held that every nation in their empire should retain its own deities and religious practices, and Cyrus went out of his way to be helpful to those Jews contemplating immigration to this new Persian province. He retrieved the Temple vessels which Nebuchadnezzar had placed in his own temple and gave them to Sheshbazzar, a leader and prince of Judah who accompanied the returnees. He also suggested that Jews remaining in Babylon should help out financially with the return.

Responding to his encouragement to immigrate were "*the heads of the families of Judea and Benjamin and the priests and Levites*" (Ezra 1:5). According to the Book of Ezra some 42,360 people heeded Cyrus' call, which would have been about a third of the Jewish population of Babylon, although it is unclear if this number included all the women and children (ibid., 2).

When they arrived in Judea the new settlers set up an altar, began offering daily sacrifices and ordered supplies for the construction of the Temple. In their second year they laid the foundations of the Temple, and when this was completed a major ceremony was held. The loud weeping that accompanied this event was for mixed reasons. Some were crying with joy, while those older wept because of their memories of the splendor of the First Temple.

It soon became apparent that the people brought into the country at the time of the Assyrian conquests, especially the Samaritans, were not pleased with the appearance of the Jewish returnees. The Samaritans had been relocated to the north of the country by the Assyrian king Sargon II (2 Kings 17:24) as a replacement population for the northern tribes, and they had adopted the God of Israel for protection (2 Kings 17:25-33). They offered the Judeans a deal whereby they would help in the Temple-building project. It is unclear if this was a genuine proposal or one made to sabotage their efforts. In any case, their offer was rejected, probably because the Samaritans were not completely monotheistic. The Samaritans now harassed the Jews and wrote to Cyrus advising him to stop the building of the Temple on the grounds that the Jews were unlikely to pay their taxes and were a people with a history of rebellion. Cyrus accepted their counsel and the project was halted as it turned out for 18 years.

Two important leaders who immigrated to the country either at the beginning of the return, or more likely several decades later, were Zerubbabel and Jeshua. Zerubbabel was appointed as governor of Judea, or the province of Yehud as it was called by the Persians. He was the grandson of King Jehoiachin who was of the Davidic dynasty and who had been brought to Babylon by Nebuchadnezzar during the first exile. (It has been suggested that the leaders Sheshbazzar and Zerubbabel were one and the same person, although this seems unlikely given that both had Persian names). Jeshua was the High Priest of the returnees and the grandson of the High Priest Seraiah, who had been killed during the destruction of Jerusalem by Nebuchadnezzar (2 Kings 25:18-21).

In the year 520 BCE, some 19 years after the pronouncement of Cyrus and in the second year of the reign of Darius, the third ruler of the Persian

Empire, the prophets Haggai and Zechariah began prophesying and encouraging the people, their governor Zerubbabel and the priests to finish building the Temple, even without official permission, and to use local materials rather than expensive imported supplies. At this point, the Jews' enemies made a final attempt to have the Temple destroyed:

> *Now the prophets, Haggai the prophet, and Zechariah the son of Iddo, prophesied to the Jews in Judea and Jerusalem, inspired by the God of Israel. Then Zerubbabel the son of Shealtiel and Jeshua the son of Jozadak arose and began rebuilding the House of God which is in Jerusalem; with the support of the prophets of God. At that time, Tattenai, the governor of the other side of the river, and Shethar-bozena and their companies came to them and said: "Who issued you the authorization to build this House and finish this structure?" Then we [the officials] said to them: "What are the names of the men who are constructing this building?" But the eye of their God was upon the elders of the Jews, and they did not make them cease working until the matter came to Darius, and a letter was sent back in reply* (Ezra 5:1-5).

Darius examined the records of the original permission granted by Cyrus and ruled that the building of the Temple should be completed. He also provided the funding that the prophet Haggai had prophesied would be forthcoming and animals for "*pleasing sacrifices to the God of heaven, and pray for the lives of the king and his children*" (6:10). The Temple was duly completed within five years, and this was followed by a grand dedication ceremony and the celebration of the Feast of Passover.

Ezra the scribe arrived in Judea in about 457 BCE, some 82 years after the first immigration. He came with impressive credentials in Torah learning. He also brought with him a financial contribution from the king Artaxerxes, gifts from the people in Babylon, more immigrants, exemption from taxes, and almost unbelievable authority granted him by Artaxerxes to enforce Jewish law. With this authority he was able to revive sagging Jewish life:

> *Now after these things, in the reign of Artaxerxes, king of Persia . . . this Ezra went up from Babylon; and he was a scribe expert in the law of Moses, which the Lord God of Israel had given; and the king granted him his entire request, according to the hand of the Lord his God upon him. And there went up some of the Children of Israel, and of the priests, and the Levites, and the singers, and the gatekeepers, and the Nethinites to Jerusalem, in the seventh year of King Artaxerxes. . . . For Ezra had set his heart to*

*seek the law of God, and to perform and teach in Israel statutes and or-
dinances. And this is the copy of the letter that King Artaxerxes gave to
Ezra the priest, the scribe of the words of God's commandments and His
statutes to Israel. . . . "We further advise you that it is not permissible to
impose tribute, poll tax, or land tax on any priest, Levite, musician, gate-
keeper, Nethinim, or other servant of this House of God – no one shall
be empowered to levy the king's due, the head tax or the meal tax upon
them. And you, Ezra, by the divine wisdom you possess, appoint judges
and magistrates who know the laws of your God to judge all the people in
the province of Beyond the River, and teach those who do not. And whoever does not obey the law of your God and the law of the king, judgment
shall be inflicted upon him promptly, whether by execution, banishment,
confiscation of goods or imprisonment"* (7:1, 6-7, 10-11, 24-26).

Almost immediately Ezra found himself faced with a major issue, intermarriage. This had become widespread among all classes of the people and
threatened to dilute Jewish identity (9:1-2).

As noted by Rabbi Hayyim Angel, there is no general prohibition in the
Torah against intermarriage, but only against intermarriage with Canaanites.[3]
The prohibition against intermarriage with non-Canaanites was probably a
later rabbinic prohibition. Jewishness was initially patrilineal, which meant
that a man could bring a former non-Jewish woman into his home as his wife,
and the household would still be considered Jewish. This would have been
how the sons of Jacob established Jewish households, for example.

Ezra's plan was drastic. Any foreign wife was to be sent away, even if
there were children from the marriage. It is unclear from the Bible how many
men actually did this, although a public shaming ceremony would have encouraged compliance (10:17). The Talmud also relates that Ezra introduced
additional safeguards into Jewish law designed to provide inner strength to
the religious life of the community.[4]

---

3   "Battle against intermarriage" in ibid., 107-111.
4   TB Bava Kama 82a. Ezra instituted 10 regulations. Some were obviously intended to en-
    courage marital relations within a framework of modesty. Many of his decrees were not
    permanently accepted, although some were: 1. Worshippers should read from the Torah
    scroll during the afternoon service on the Sabbath; 2. They should read from the Torah
    on Monday and Thursday; 3. Courts should adjudicate on Monday and Thursday; 4. The
    people should launder on Thursday; 5. They should eat garlic on the Sabbath eve to en-
    hance marital relations; 6. A woman should arise early in the morning to bake (so as to
    make bread available for the poor); 7. A woman should wear breeches; 8. A woman should
    comb her hair and then immerse herself in the mikvah (ritual bath); 9. Peddlers should
    circulate in the towns (to make adornments available to woman); 10.There should be im-
    mersion after a seminal emission.

The prophet Haggai

Haggai began prophesying two decades after the return of the exiles and his prophecies are contained within the two chapters of his book. Haggai prophesied to a dispirited people who, given all the setbacks that had occurred, questioned whether they truly had God's support in rebuilding the Temple. Haggai's message was that God was indeed *"with you."* This message was sufficient to inspire the people and their leaders Zerubbabel and Jeshua to resume work on its rebuilding (5:1-2):

> *Then spoke Haggai, God's messenger, fulfilling God's mission to the people saying: "I am with you," says God. And God aroused the spirit of Zerubbabel the son of Shealtiel, the governor of Judea, and the spirit of Jeshua, the son of Jehozadak the High Priest, and the spirit of all the rest of the people; and they came and set to work on the House of the Lord of Hosts, their God (Haggai 1:13-14).*

Haggai also explained to the people that the drought they were experiencing was no reason to delay building. To the contrary, God had brought about the drought because of their procrastination. Their sadness about the Temple's architectural plans was also misplaced since the glory of this Temple would eventually surpass that of Solomon's:

> *Speak now to Zerubbabel the son of Shealtiel, the governor of Judea, and to Jeshua the son of Jehozadak, the High Priest and to the remnant of the people saying: "Who among you is left that saw this house in its former glory? How does it look to you now? It must seem as nothing to you. And now be strong Zerubbabel, says God, and be strong Joshua the son of Jehozadak the High Priest, and be strong all the people, says God, for I am with you. . . . And I will shake up all the nations, and they shall come with the precious things of all the nations. And I will fill this House with glory, said the Lord of Hosts. Silver is Mine and gold is Mine, says the Lord of Hosts. The glory of this last House shall be greater than the first one, declares the Lord of Hosts. And in this place I will grant peace, says the Lord of Hosts" (2:2-4, 7-9).*

In the final prophecy in his book, Haggai reported on a communication he had received from God:

> *And the word of God came to Haggai a second time on the 24th of the month saying: "Speak to Zerubbabel, the governor of Judea, saying: I will*

shake up the heaven and the earth. I will overthrow the throne of kingdoms and I will destroy the power of the kingdoms of the nations. And I will overthrow the chariots and their riders; and the horses and riders shall fall, each one by the sword of his brother. On that day, declares the Lord of Hosts, I will take you, O My servant Zerubbabel the son of Shealtiel, says God, and I will make you as a signet; for I have chosen you, says the Lord of Hosts" (2:20-23).

What should one make of this messianic prophecy? Haggai appeared to be telling the people that their governor Zerubbabel would soon establish an independent Jewish state and there would be a *"shaking up"* of the universe to make this happen. Depending on the extent to which his speech was disseminated, this could be considered a highly inflammatory prophecy, to the point of encouraging insurrection against the Persian Empire.

Classic Jewish commentators such as the Radak link this prophecy to later wars and even the defeat of the Persian Empire by the Greeks. However, it is doubtful that Haggai was looking that far into the future. More likely, he was talking about Zerubbabel and the period in which the returnees then found themselves.

The connection to this speech may be coincidental, but there is no further mention of Zerubbabel again in the Bible after the period of the rebuilding of the Temple and certainly no mention of an existing dynasty of David. Could it be that this prophecy contributed to his going underground, or even his death? If the Persians had heard about this prophecy, they could have considered Zerubbabel the potential leader of a rebellion.

Nevertheless, despite the disappearance of the last direct descendant of David, the notion that a seed of David will reestablish the Jewish kingdom will endure in Jewish eschatology.

THE PROPHECIES OF ZACHARIAH

Like those of Haggai, the prophecies of Zachariah began in the second year of the reign of Darius and are found in three sections in his book. The first section contains visions providing hope to the Jewish community, the middle section concerns a *halachic* question asked of him, and the last five chapters relate to a messianic future.[5]

---

5   Based on a literary analysis of these chapters, there is an opinion that the last section of the Book of Zechariah was written by another author, so called Deutero-Zechariah. Other than to mention this opinion, this line of speculative thought will not be pursued here.

The Talmud and Jewish commentators admit that Zachariah's prophecies are often difficult to understand in that they are highly allegorical and often abstruse.[6] Even Zachariah could not comprehend the visions he saw and they had to be explained to him by an angel.[7] Maimonides suggested that they constituted a type of prophecy inferior to that of his predecessors since he did not receive the interpretation of his visions directly.[8] However, another way of looking at them is that they were written in a highly engaging literary format. We will look at two examples.

In his first vision Zechariah saw a man riding on a red horse standing among the myrtles, followed by red, black and white horses. The angel explained to him that these horses had been sent by God to roam the earth. While doing this, they found everyone at ease except for the returnees to Zion. The angel declared that the current situation of the returnees was temporary. The Temple will be rebuilt, and although Jerusalem currently possessed none of its former glory, it will in the future become a large and prosperous metropolis:

> *Then the angel of God spoke and said: "O Lord of Hosts, how long will You not have compassion on Jerusalem and on the cities of Judah, upon whom you are wroth these threescore and 10 years?" And God answered the angel that spoke with me with good words, even consoling words; And the angel that spoke with me said unto me: "Proclaim, saying: 'So said the Lord of Hosts: I am jealous for Jerusalem and for Zion with a great jealousy; and I am very angry with the nations that are at ease; for I was only angry a little, and they helped for evil'. Therefore, so said God: 'I have returned to Jerusalem with mercy: My house shall be built there,' says the Lord of Hosts. 'A plumb line shall be stretched out over Jerusalem [to measure it].' Further, proclaim, saying: 'Thus, said the Lord of Hosts: My cities shall again spread out with prosperity; and God shall yet comfort Zion, and shall yet choose Jerusalem'" (Zechariah 1:12-17).*

See "The End of the Line" in *The Prophets. Who They Were. What They Are* by Norman Podhoretz, 291. The Free Press, 2002.

6   TB Megilla 3a and the comments of Rashi, Ibn Ezra and Radak to Zechariah 1:1.

7   His other visions related to smiths destroying the nations that harmed Israel (Zechariah 2:1-4), an angel measuring Jerusalem (Zechariah 2:5-9), Joshua being purified in the heavenly Holy of Holies (Zechariah 3), the purification of the Land of Israel of sinners and of sin itself (Zechariah 5:1-11), and finally God's power and glory throughout the world (Zechariah 6:1-8). Meyers and Meyers. *Anchor Bible*, Haggai, Zechariah 1-8, lv.

8   Maimonides *Guide to the Perplexed* II:45

His fourth vision related to the heavenly purification of the High Priest Joshua:

And He showed me Joshua, the High Priest, standing before the angel of God. And Satan was standing on his right hand to accuse him. And God said to Satan: "God shall rebuke you, O Satan; may God who has chosen Jerusalem rebuke you. For this is a brand plucked from the fire." Now Joshua was wearing filthy garments and standing before the angel. And the latter spoke up and said to his attendants, saying: "Take the filthy garments off him." And he said to him: "See, I have removed your iniquity from you, and I will clothe you with clean garments." And I [Zecharia] said: "Let them put a pure miter on his head," and they put the pure miter on his head. And they clothed him with [priestly] garments while the angel of God stood by. And the angel of God charged Joshua, saying: "So said the Lord of Hosts: If you walk in My ways, and if you keep My charge, you, too, shall rule My house and you too shall guard My courtyards and I will permit you to move about among these attendants. Hear, now, O Joshua the High Priest, you and your companions who sit before you, for these men are a sign that I am going to bring My servant the Branch. . . . On that day, says the Lord of Hosts, you shall call – each man will invite his neighbor to the shade of the vine and fig tree" (3:1-8, 10).

A number of explanations have been given as to the meaning of this vision.[9] It may relate to confirmation of Joshua's personal suitability to be High Priest. Others see it as a purification of the representative of the nation. But who is the "*Branch*" discussed at the end of this quotation? Zechariah was probably referring to Zerubbabel, as this expression was used elsewhere in his book in apparent reference to him: "*Behold, a man whose name is the Branch, who will spring up out his place and build the Temple of God*" (6:12).

In the middle section of his book, Zechariah was asked the following pointed question: Given that the Temple is being rebuilt, is there still a need to observe a public fast day decreed to commemorate the destruction of the First Temple (7:4)?

Zechariah drew out his answer. He pointed out that the Temple was destroyed because they did not practice justice, loving kindness and mercy,

---

9   "Fourth Vision: Joshua in the Heavenly Court" in *Haggai, Zechariah, and Malachi: Prophecy in an Age of Uncertainty*, 1454-153. Maggid Books, 2016. The first explanation is supported by the Talmud in TB Sanhedrin 93a.The second by Ibn Ezra and Rabbi Eliezer of Beaugency. The notion that the "*Branch*" is Zerubbabel is suggested by Rashi and Ibn Ezra.

and they oppressed the disadvantaged (7:11). He also painted a picture of the many children and elderly who would eventually be living in Jerusalem, referred to the future redemption of those still in exile and repeated Isaiah's universal message of Judaism:

> Thus said the Lord of Hosts: "Old men and women shall yet sit in the streets of Jerusalem, each man with his staff in his hand because of old age. And the streets of the city shall be filled with boys and girls playing in its streets." ... So said the God of Hosts: "Behold I will save My people from the lands of the east and from the lands of the west" (8:4-5, 7).

He then provided his answer. It was not a straight *halachic* one with a yes/ no answer, but a more prophetic one, with an answer of "not yet." If you change your behavior and:

> Speak the truth to one another, render true and perfect justice in your gates. And let no one think evil of his neighbors in your heart, nor shall you love a false oath – because all these are things I hate, says God (8:16-17).

Then, fast days commemorating the destruction of the First Temple will become days of joy and at that time fasting will no longer be necessary.[10] The messianic vision will also become a reality:

> And the word of the God of hosts came unto me, saying: Thus said the God of hosts: The fast of the fourth month, and the fast of the fifth, and the fast of the seventh, and the fast of the tenth, shall be to the house of Judah joy and gladness, and cheerful seasons; but love truth and peace. So said the Lord of Hosts: It shall yet come to pass that peoples and the inhabitants of many cities shall come. And the inhabitants of one shall go to another, saying: "Let us go and entreat the favor of the Lord of Hosts. I, too, will go." And many peoples and the multitude of nations shall come to seek the Lord of Hosts in Jerusalem, and to pray before God. So said the Lord of Hosts: In those days it shall come to pass that 10 men from nations of every tongue shall take hold of the skirt of a Jewish man, saying: "Let us go with you, for we have heard that God is with you" (8:18-23).

---

10   The question relates to the Fast of Tammuz, The Fast of Av, the Fast of Gedaliah and the Fast of Tevet. Other than the Fast of Gedaliah, all these fasts pertain to the destruction of the First Temple. Angel points out that Zechariah's answer is unclear and there is a debate as to whether the people actually continued to fast at these times during the Second Temple period. Maimonides felt that they did continue to fast (*Commentary to Mishna Rosh Hashana* 1:3), whereas Ibn Ezra suggests that they did not, since these fasts were human initiatives. See "Halakhic Question, Prophetic Response," ibid., 76.

ZECHARIAH, EZEKIEL AND THE APOCALYPTIC TRADITION

The last part of Zechariah's book contains apocalyptic messianic prophecies. In these prophecies the Jewish people will become an independent nation with a king: "*Behold, your king shall come to you. He is just and victorious; humble, and riding on an ass and a foal, the offspring of [one of] she-donkeys*" (9:9). This king will be of the Davidic dynasty (9:9, 12:10, 13:1). The northern and southern tribes will become united (9:10, 10:7). A mighty battle will be waged on Israel's soil, Israel's enemies will be destroyed, idolatry will cease, false prophets will be removed, much of the world will be destroyed (13:8-9), and Jerusalem will be plundered and ravaged. Purifying spring water will then appear miraculously from Jerusalem and flow towards the Dead Sea and the Mediterranean, and on that day God will become King over all the earth. He will be recognized as One and His name as one (14:9). Finally, all nations remaining on earth will come yearly to Jerusalem on the Feast of Tabernacles to prostrate themselves before Him (14:16):

> *Behold, a day of God is coming when your plunder shall be shared in your very midst. For I will gather all the nations against Jerusalem to wage war; and the city shall be captured, the houses plundered, the women violated, and half the city shall go into exile – but the rest of the people shall not be uprooted from the city. Then shall God go forth and fight against those nations, as He is wont to make war on a day of battle. And on that day, His feet shall stand on the Mount of Olives, which is before Jerusalem to the east, and the Mount of Olives shall split across from east to west, so that there will be a very great valley; and half of the mountain shall move towards the north, and half of it towards the south. And the Valley of the Mountains shall be stopped up; for the Valley of the Mountains shall reach only unto Azel; it shall be stopped up as during the earthquake in the days of Uzziah king of Judah; and the Lord my God shall come, and all the holy ones with you. And it shall come to pass in that day, that there shall be no sunlight, but heavy clouds. And there shall be one day which shall be known as God's, not day, and not night; but it shall come to pass at eventide there shall be light. In that day, fresh water will flow from Jerusalem: part of it towards the Dead Sea, and part of towards the Mediterranean, throughout the summer and winter. And God will be King over all the earth; in that day God will be One, and His name one*" (14:1-9).

These prophecies resemble to some extent Ezekiel's earlier apocalyptic visions of an earth-shattering struggle between Israel and the nation of Gog from Magog. Ezekiel prophesied during the Babylonian exile, and in the 38th chapter of his book he described a final reckoning with the nations of the world in a cataclysmic war on Israel's soil after their return from exile. This will be initiated by the prince Gog from the land of Magog, who will invade Israel with the armies of other nations at a time when the Jewish people are unsuspecting and unprepared:[11]

And the word of God came to me, saying: "Son of man, direct your face towards Gog of the land of Magog, the prince, leader of Meshech and Tubal, and prophesy concerning him; Say: Thus said the Lord God: Behold, I am against you, Gog, the prince, leader of Meshech and Tubal. I will turn you around, and I will place hooks into your jaws and lead you out with your entire army, horses and horsemen, all of them clothed in splendor, a great assembly with buckler and shield, all of them wielding swords. Persia, Cush and Put will be with them, all of them with shield and helmet. . . . And you will attack; coming like a storm; you will be like a cloud covering the earth, you and all your cohorts and the many nations with you. Thus said the Lord God: It shall be on that day that ideas will arise in your heart, and you will conceive a wicked design. You will say, 'I will advance against a land of open towns, I will fall against a tranquil people living securely, all of them living without [protective] walls; and having neither bars nor gates, to take spoil and seize plunder, to turn your hand against resettled ruins, against a people gathered from the nations, which possess livestock and property, that dwell upon the navel of the earth.". . . Therefore, prophesy, son of man and say to Gog: "Thus said the Lord God: Surely, on that day, when My people Israel dwells securely, shall you not know it? And you shall come from your place out of the uttermost parts of the north, you and many peoples with you, all of them mounted on horses, a vast horde,

---

11 Who is Gog from Magog? In Ezekiel's prophecy, the prince Gog is *"from the land"* of Magog (Ezekiel 39:6). Later mention of this prophecy often cites two people or nations, Gog and Magog. Magog is identified in Genesis as a descendent of Yaphet, the son of Noah, as are Mesach and Tubal (Genesis 10:2). The similarity is too close to be coincidental, but its relevance is far from clear. The following passage from the Book of Ezekiel also implies that Ezekiel was elaborating on a story already well known from the prophecies of others and was not describing something new: *"Thus said the Lord God: 'Are you the one of whom I spoke in earlier days, through My servants, the prophets of Israel who prophesized in those days, years [ago] that I would bring you against them? It shall be on that day that Gog comes against the soil of Israel – the word of the Lord God – My raging anger will flare up'"* (Ezekiel 38:17-18).

a mighty army, and you will come up against My people Israel like a cloud covering the earth. This will happen at the End of Days (b'acharit hayamim in Hebrew) that I will bring you against My land, in order that the nations may know Me, when I become sanctified through you before their eyes, O Gog" (Ezekiel 38:1-4, 9-12, 14-16).

This battle will end with miraculous happenings including a great earthquake, pestilence and a shower of large hailstones, fire and brimstone, the salvation of Israel and the complete destruction of Gog and his alliance. God's intervention will lead to His recognition among the nations (38:23, 39:7, 27-28) and the recognition that Israel's suffering in exile was not because of God's inability to save them but because of their sinful behavior (39:23).[12]

Following these happenings, the land will be purified:

Now you, son of man, prophesy against Gog, say: "Thus said the Lord God: Behold I am going to deal with you, Gog, the prince, leader of Meshech and Tubal. I will lead you astray and drive you on; I will cause you to ascend from the uttermost parts of the north and lead you to the mountains of Israel. And I will strike your bow from your left hand, and cast down your arrows from your right hand. You will fall upon the mountains of Israel, you and all your cohorts and the peoples who are with you; I will give you to carrion birds of every sort and to the beasts of the field to be devoured. You will fall upon the open field, for I have spoken it, says the Lord God. . . . Behold, it is coming and it will happen, declares the Lord God. This is the day of which I have spoken" (39:1-5, 8).

An obvious question is whether Zechariah and Ezekiel were describing the same conflict despite differences in the details. The medieval Biblical commentator Rashi suggested that they are one and the same.[13] The most obvious similarity is the recognition that achieving the utopian state cannot be accomplished by man's efforts alone, but requires the open manifestation of God to overcome Israel's enemies and bring about Judaism's universal mission.

A difference pointed out by Rav Mosheh Lichtenstein is that their aims are different. The aim of the battle against Gog from Magog is to restore God's reputation in the world which had been sullied by the Jewish exile, while

---

12 A helpful comparison of the apocalyptic prophecies of these two prophets is found in "Appendix VI. The War of Gog and Magog" in *The Ethics of Deuteronomy* by Rabbi Dr. Abba Engelberg, 349-354. Kodesh Press, New York, NY, 2021.

13 Rashi on TB Megilla 31a. Also comments of Radak on Zechariah 14:1.

Zechariah's vision is a continuation of the redemptive process.[14] Nevertheless, these aims are not necessarily mutually exclusive.

This type of vision occurred when Jewish history seemed stuck, and the people felt powerless against the historical forces arrayed against them. For Ezekiel, this was because the geopolitical forces within the Babylonian Empire offered no hope of the Jewish people achieving redemption. For Zechariah, it was because their situation in the Persian Empire suggested no likelihood that the Jewish people would ever achieve independence. Everything was now in the hands of God.

There will be no further apocalyptic prophetic visions in the Bible after Zechariah because he marked the end of the prophetic period. The Bible was also canonized. Nevertheless, this was not the end of this type of apocalyptic literature, and it continued to flourish during the Second Temple period. During the Roman occupation of the Jewish kingdom and the loss of Jewish political and religious independence the zealots felt that their only recourse was revolt. Others, however, believed that the end of the world was imminent when God's glory would become manifest. This was the case for the Essenes of Qumran and two influential individuals in the history of religion — John the Baptist and Jesus of Nazareth.

More about Qumran and these two individuals in the next chapter.

---

14 "The War of God and Magog: The Haftara of Shabbat Chol Ha-moed Sukkot" by Harav Mosheh Lichtenstein. The Israel Koschitzky Virtual Beit Midrash. Holiday, Sukkot. (https://www.etzion.org.il/en/war-god-and-magog-haftara-shabbat-chol-ha-moed-suk-kot).

Chapter 8

APOCALYPSE ACCORDING TO THE ESSENES OF QUMRAN, JOHN THE BAPTIST AND JESUS OF NAZARETH

Judaism in the Second Temple period was split into a number of factions, none of whom were cordial to each other – namely Pharisees, Sadducees and groups of apocalyptic Jews that based their ideas on the Biblical apocalyptic prophets. These apocalyptic groups included the Essenes and early Jewish Christians. The apocalyptic ideas of Jesus of Nazareth, for example, were not preached in a vacuum, but were part of the beliefs of a significant sector of Jews in Second Temple times.

An influential figure in the initiation of Jesus as a preacher was his second-cousin John the Baptist. Some scholars have suggested that John the Baptist spent time in the Essene settlement of Qumran in the Judean Desert, and this is even mentioned in the movie shown to visitors when they visit Qumran. It is not cited in the New Testament, nor in any other ancient text, but it is quite plausible. Qumran was primarily a commune for priests, and John came from a priestly family. John appreciated an ascetic existence, and this was an ascetic community. In Qumran, he would have studied Essene apocalyptic views about the End of the World and would have agreed that the conditions of the Roman occupation and the corruption of the Jewish priesthood made this scenario increasingly likely.

However, there was at least one aspect of Essene theology with which he would have disagreed and could have led him to leave Qumran. This Essene commune believed that only its members would inherit the World to Come after the forces of evil had been overcome in a final apocalyptic battle. John would have felt that the congregation of Israel was full of virtuous people. However, they needed to be alerted that the end of the world would soon be upon them so that they could increase their piety and be worthy of resurrection. This would now be his life's mission. Much sooner than either of them anticipated, this mission would be passed on to his disciple and second cousin Jesus of Nazareth when John was put to death by Herod Antipas.

THE DIFFERENT BRANCHES OF JUDAISM IN SECOND TEMPLE TIMES

More about the diversity in ideologies and religious practices within Judaism during late Second Temple times.

The Judaic movement most connected to the common people was that of the Pharisees. The Pharisees adhered to the Torah and its oral tradition, which they continued to interpret and develop. The Oral Law consists of laws accepted by tradition and rabbinic decrees designed to safeguard Torah law. The Oral Law has provided Judaism the ability to adjust its interpretations and practices throughout the centuries. The Pharisees also believed in the eternity of the soul, reward and punishment after death, and the resurrection of the body after death. Their World to Come was solidly on this earth. They did not encourage asceticism, although there were Pharisees who practiced more ascetic lifestyles. In general, Pharisaic Judaism endeavored to bring aspects of spirituality into worldly pursuits rather than to eschew life's pleasures.

Another influential group of Jews was the Sadducees. The main focus of Judaism at this time was its Temple, and much of its priesthood, including the High Priests, were Sadducees. The Maccabean leadership of the Jewish kingdom was also Sadducee, as was much of the upper class. The Sadducees accepted all the provisions of the written Torah but denied the validity of an Oral Law. There were therefore conflicts with the Pharisees over ritual, including in the Temple. They did not believe in the existence of an eternal soul or judgment after death since these were not specifically mentioned in the Torah. They also favored Hellenization.

In addition, there were two groups within Judaism in late Second Temple times with apocalyptic beliefs, the Essenes and early Christians. As previously discussed, the word apocalypse refers to the belief that God will intervene in a cataclysmic way in the struggle between the forces of good and evil and that a select faithful will be saved.

The writings of Josephus, Philo and other historians from this time indicate that there were about 4,000 Essenes living in self-contained communities in villages throughout Israel, including an Essene community in Jerusalem in the area of Mount Zion. These sources also describe a community of priestly Essenes living in Qumran, although the location of this community was not identified until the 1940s with the discovery of the Dead Sea Scrolls.

In 1947 a young Bedouin shepherd threw a stone into a cave in the Jordanian Judean Desert near the Dead Sea, and to his surprise the stone made a sound as if it had hit something solid and not the floor of a cave. He climbed up to the cave and found what were clearly ancient jugs containing manuscripts. This find would lead over time to the discovery of 10 additional caves containing almost 1,000 complete and fragmentary manuscripts, as well as exploration of the nearby ruins of Qumran.

The scrolls were written by members of the Qumran Essene community (the Yahad) who wrote and deposited them in these caves as libraries or, more likely, as places where they could be hidden from the Romans. They included books of the Bible, commentaries on the Bible written by the commune, texts that had not been included in the Bible, and scrolls defining their communal rules. Their copies of the Bible have been of considerable interest to scholars since Bible scrolls from as early as the Second Temple period had not previously been located.[1]

The Essene community in Qumran consisted mainly of priests who had left the Temple in Jerusalem and were attempting to create an alternative holy community in the desert in preparation for the End of Days. They believed that the current functioning of the Temple was corrupt. They lived as a commune, and individual monies and property were handed over to the group. Worldly pleasures were renounced for an ascetic existence. Most members were celibate males. For those married, marital relations were viewed in procreative terms, and they avoided sex, for example, during their wives' pregnancies. They purified themselves frequently in ritual baths, especially before meals, as they would do when eating food from the Temple.

They kept to the Torah rigidly, although they rejected many of the Pharisaic interpretations of the Oral Law. Their own interpretations were not based on lines of tradition. In contrast to the Pharisees, who believed that prophecy had ended with the prophets Haggai, Zechariah and Malachi, their leader, the Teacher of Righteousness, reserved the right to interpret the books of the prophets in a prophetic way. Most significantly, they followed a solar calendar, whereas the Pharisees, Sadducees and early Christians used a lunar calendar adjusted to the time of year so that the religious festivals, which were also agricultural festivals, remained in the correct season. The Essenes would therefore have celebrated Jewish holidays at different times from other Jews, and effectively cut themselves off from the religious life of the rest of the Jewish world. It also meant they were not dependent on the Pharisees for

---

1   The only extant scroll prior to this period is the priestly blessing from the Book of Numbers found as an amulet on a silver scroll in a burial cave from First Temple times in Ketef Hinnom in Jerusalem, adjacent to the Begin Museum. It was written in the seventh century BCE in Paleo-Hebrew and preceded the Dead Sea Scrolls by some 400 years.

fixing their calendar. They did not accept divorce, despite this being accepted in the Torah, and regarded someone who married after divorce as being guilty of adultery.

The admission process for novices was extremely rigorous and stretched over several years. Novices were sworn to secrecy regarding the rules of the commune and the esoteric books they studied.[2]

Their austere lifestyle is described by the Jewish historian Josephus writing in this same period:

> *Before the sun rises, they utter nothing of the mundane things, but only certain ancestral prayers to Him, as if begging Him to come up. After these things, they are dismissed by the curators to the various crafts that they have each come to know, and after they have worked strenuously until the fifth hour they are again assembled in one area, where they belt on linen covers and wash their bodies in frigid water. After this purification they gather in a private hall, into which none of those who hold different views may enter: now pure themselves, they approach the dining room as if it were some [kind of] sanctuary. After they have seated themselves in silence, the baker serves the loaves in order, whereas the cook serves each person one dish of one food. The priest offers a prayer before the food, and it is forbidden to taste anything before the prayer; when he has had his breakfast, he offers another concluding prayer. While starting and also while finishing, then, they honor God as the sponsor of life. At that, laying aside their clothes as if they were holy, they apply themselves to their labors again until evening. They dine in a similar way: when they have returned, they sit down with the visitors, if any happen to be present with them, and neither yelling nor disorder pollutes the house at any time, but they yield conversation to one another in order. And to those from outside, the silence of those inside appears as a kind of shiver-inducing mystery. The reason for this is their continuous sobriety and the rationing of food and drink among them – to the point of fullness.[2]*

This community was preparing itself for a new world era in which the forces of evil would be overcome, and virtue and peace would reign eternally. They regarded the rest of the Jewish world as sinful and doomed, and they anticipated that they alone would be the sole righteous remnants of a cosmic struggle between good and evil.

---

2   This paragraph is quoted from The Jewish War by Josephus Book II, Chapter 8. Details can also be found in the essay "Josephus on the Essenes" on the website of the Biblical Archeological Society (https://www.biblicalarchaeology.org/daily/biblical-artifacts/dead-sea-scrolls/josephus-on-the-essenes/).

The Essenes viewed the prophecies of Isaiah as describing an approaching golden age at the End of Time. They also believed in two Messianic figures who would help usher in the expected eschatological era, one a High Priest and the other a Davidic king.[3] They accepted the concepts of the immortality of the soul and divine reward and punishment. They believed in predestination, although they also acknowledged the existence of free will.

Qumran was the repository of many eschatological manuscripts, as well as being a study center for this type of literature. Much of the apocalyptic literature from this period was written anonymously because of its prophetic nature. A work found in the first cave that was relatively intact and has been extensively analyzed is *The War of the Sons of Light against the Sons of Darkness*, also known as the *War Scroll*. Many other scrolls of this genre have been found in nearby caves.[4]

This particular scroll was written during either the Seleucid or Roman periods and is a prophecy about a 40-year series of apocalyptic cosmic struggles between the Sons of Light (which would be the Yahad) and the Sons of Darkness. The Sons of Darkness are Edom, Moab, Ammon, the Amalekites, the Philistines, and violators of the covenant (namely anyone opposing the Yahad), led by the Kittim of Ashur. Each side will fight with angelic hosts and supernatural beings, and only after a 3:3 draw and during the final seventh battle will victory be achieved by the Sons of Light with the direct intervention of God. All the Sons of Darkness will be eliminated in a terrible carnage, and darkness and evil will be destroyed forever. For the Sons of Life there will be peace, blessing and glory.

In one of the Isaiah scrolls the following passage from Isaiah was given particular emphasis. This is of interest because its first sentence was also quoted in the Gospel of Mark as the calling card for John the Baptist. As did John, the Essenes saw this passage as reflecting their mission, which was to announce the imminent arrival of the Kingdom of God:

A voice calls: "In the desert, clear the way of God, straighten out in the wilderness, a highway for our God." Every valley shall be raised, and every

---

3   This idea appears in the Damascus Document. This was first found in the Geniza storeroom in a synagogue in Cairo, but its roots are from Qumran, with fragments found in caves 4 and 5.

4   "The Essenes and the Apocalyptic Literature" by K. Koher in The Jewish Quarterly Review, New Series, vol 11, No 2 (Oct 1020), 145-168. The Dead Sea Scrolls have been a treasure trove of these documents. See "Scrolls and Fragments" in Wikipedia Dead Sea Scrolls. The titles of the numerous documents and fragments found in each of the 11 caves are listed at https://en.wikipedia.org/wiki/Dead_Sea_Scrolls.

mountain and hill shall be lowered, and the crooked terrain shall be made level and the closed mountains a plain. And the glory of God shall be revealed, and all flesh together shall see that the mouth of God spoke (Isaiah 40:3-5).

Before discussing the apocalyptic messages of John the Baptist and Jesus of Nazareth, we need to review some history of this period.

A BRIEF HISTORY OF THE SECOND TEMPLE PERIOD

When the returnees left Babylon for Judea in about 539 BCE, they remained under the rule of the Persian Empire although Persian control was not particularly tight. The Persians were defeated by Alexander the Great in 331 BCE. He inherited their empire and brought Hellenism to the Near East. As did the Persians, Alexander the Great believed in religious autonomy for the nations in his kingdom. He died at a young age, and his empire was fought over by his generals. Ptolemy took over the southern part of his empire, including Egypt, while Seleucid took the northern section. Israel was initially part of the Ptolemaic Kingdom, but was subsequently conquered by the Seleucids, who promulgated very anti-Jewish laws during the rule of Antiochus. These laws were responsible for the Maccabi Revolt.

The Chanukah story celebrating the Maccabi victory can leave the impression that this revolt was short-lived and that the Temple was rapidly restored to its full function on a permanent basis. However, this was far from being the case. The struggle of the Maccabee brothers against the Seleucid Greeks continued over decades. Even the Temple could not be readily accessed, as the Greeks erected a fortress, the Accra, close to the Temple. It was not until the reign of the Maccabean king Alexander Yannai that the Jewish kingdom achieved stability and strength and was even able to extend its borders. However, a civil war between the two sons of Alexander Yannai after their father's death enabled the Roman general Pompey to invade Jerusalem in 61 BCE.

Encouraged by a semi-Jewish Idumean family, the Jewish state came under increasing control of the Roman Empire. Herod, who was from this family, was elected king of the Jews by the Roman Senate at the urging of Marc Anthony, although it took Herod three years to crush the Maccabean Antigonus and control the country. His entry into Jerusalem marked the end of the reign of the Maccabean dynasty.

Herod the Great (73-4 BCE) ruled Judea as a semi-independent kingdom. Herod's rebuilding of the Temple and its recognition as one of the wonders of the Roman world brought many Jewish and non-Jewish visitors to the country. However, together with the increased wealth coming into Jerusalem and Herod's interference in the Temple leadership came corruption of the priesthood. This corruption is recognized in the Talmud and would have been strongly felt by the Essenes. The alignment of the priesthood with the Sadducees who had no respect for the Oral Law also brought religious contention into the confines of the Temple.

After the death of Herod, his murderous non-Jewish son Archelaus reigned over Judea. However, after nine years the Romans decided to dispense with a monarchy, and Judea was now ruled directly by procurators. Many were insensitive to the religious feelings of the Jews, some were openly antisemitic, and others squeezed the Jews with taxes to their own advantage. The Jews were almost goaded into the Great Revolt, which lasted from 66 to 73 CE. Jerusalem was destroyed, although most of the country was otherwise unaffected.

WERE JOHN THE BAPTIST AND JESUS OF NAZARETH INFLUENCED BY THE ESSENES?

Much has been written by scholars as to whether Jesus and his followers were influenced by the Essene movement. This is usually linked to attempts to discover the historic Jewish preacher from late Second Temple times called Jesus of Nazareth.

There is little doubt that Jesus was not an Essene in that many of his views were contrary to theirs, such as his adherence to Pharisaic law, his identification with the entire Jewish people, and the non-exclusivity of his preaching. Like the Essenes, however, his mission was wrapped in apocalyptic terms.[5] He also held to the unacceptability of divorce, believing that the Torah's acceptance of divorce was a concession (Mark 10:2-12), and believed that living in poverty was the optimal state.

To what extent did Jesus borrow these ideas from the Essenes? Jesus would certainly have been aware of their ideas, not because he was an Essene but because the ideas of the thousands of Essenes in the Jewish kingdom would have been part of the discourse of Second Temple times and he may well have agreed with parts of their program. It has been speculated that some,

---

5   I have been much influenced on this topic by Bart Herman's book *Jesus Apocalyptic Prophet of the New Millennium*. Oxford University Press, New York, 1999. Many of the ideas about Jesus discussed in this article and also the quotations from the four gospels are discussed in his book.

or even many, of Jesus's followers were sympathetic to Essene ideas before they met Jesus and may even have been followers of the Essene movement. These people would have approved of the ascetic lifestyle of the Essenes but not necessarily their exclusivity.

Jesus may have believed that some of the practices of the Essenes, such as their ascetic lifestyles, offered the best way to personal holiness. Both Jesus and the Essenes also believed that an apocalyptic cosmic event would usher in the Kingdom of God. Both groups considered this moment to be close, although Jesus anticipated its arrival at any moment whereas the Essenes were less specific. This vagueness allowed their community to continue even when their leader, the Teacher of Righteousness, passed away. The Essenes held that only a select community trained in holiness would inherit the Kingdom of God, whereas Jesus believed it was open to everyone who repented of his or her sins and adopted a life of righteousness, including those from the lowest rungs of society. In fact, his mission often concentrated on such people. Both groups anticipated a time of judgment and assumed that most of the world would be destroyed.

Almost our only sources of information about the life of Jesus are the four gospels: Mark, Mathew, Luke, and John. Despite their titles, they were probably written anonymously. The first, the Gospel of Mark, was written between the mid-60s to early 70s CE. Mathew and Luke were written 10 or 15 years later, and the Gospel of John was probably written in about 90 to 95 CE. Assuming Jesus died in about 30 CE, there was a gap of at least 30 years between his death and the first account of his life. Thus, none of the gospel writers was an eyewitness to Jesus' ministry, and all were relying on textual information handed down to them. The Gospel of Mark is closest to the events recorded and seems the most reflective of the apocalyptic ideas of John the Baptist and Jesus of Nazareth.[6]

These four gospels contain numerous discrepancies and omissions. They were written primarily to provide their communities with information about Jesus, but their accounts also reflect their own perspectives of what Jesus was attempting to accomplish. The theology of Christianity changed after Jesus' death and before the years the gospels were written, primarily because under the influence of Paul of Tarsus it became a gentile, rather than Jewish, movement. Paul also held that belief in the person and mission of Jesus should take the place of repentance and acts of righteousness as the means of entering the Kingdom of God. The apocalyptic aspects of Jesus' ministry were also

---

6   "How did the gospels get to be this way?" (ibid., 48).

described in a progressively attenuated form from the Gospel of Mark to that of John.

According to the four gospels, the starting point of Jesus's mission was his baptism by John the Baptist, his second cousin. Little is written in the New Testament about John's ministry, although we know from the gospels that his preaching was eschatological and identical to that of Jesus.[7] He believed that the Kingdom of God was imminent, and he baptized people as part of a process of repentance and preparation for the World to Come. His use of ritual bathing was thus different from that of the Essenes at Qumran who used it as a means of maintaining spiritual purity. It was also different from the baptism promoted by Paul of Tarsus which would be accepted by Christianity and used as a means of establishing or affirming belief in Jesus.

According to the Gospels of Mark and Luke, it was John the Baptist who initiated Jesus into his own apocalyptic movement. However, John was incarcerated by Herod Antipas (according to the Jewish historian Josephus for preaching against the king's sexual affairs and divorcing his wife), and Herod had him killed while he was imprisoned in his fortress.

In the last two sentences of the following passage, Mark established a direct connection between the imprisonment and death of John and Jesus proclaiming the Kingdom of God, suggesting that Jesus had taken over John's mission:

The beginning of the good news of Jesus Christ, the Son of God. As it is written in the prophet Isaiah, "See, I am sending my messenger ahead of you, who will prepare your way; the voice of one crying out in the wilderness: "Prepare the way of the Lord, make his paths straight," "(Isaiah 40:3). John the baptizer appeared in the wilderness, proclaiming a baptism of repentance for the forgiveness of sins. And people from the whole Judean countryside and all the people of Jerusalem were going out to him, and were baptized by him in the river Jordan, confessing their sins. . . . In those days Jesus came from Nazareth of Galilee and was baptized by John in the Jordan. And just as he was coming up out of the water, he saw the heavens torn apart and the Spirit descending like a dove on him. And a voice came from heaven, "You are my Son, the Beloved; with you I am well pleased.". . . Now after John was arrested, Jesus came to Galilee, proclaiming the good news of God, and saying, "The time is fulfilled, and the kingdom of God

---

7   See Luke 3:1-23, Mark 1:1-14, Mathew 3:13-17 and John 1:29-34.

has come near; repent, and believe in the good news." (Mark 1:1-5, 9-11, 14-15).[8]

THE APOCALYPTIC VIEWS OF JESUS

Much of the textual evidence for the apocalyptic ideas of Jesus is found in the early Gospel of Mark. In the following quotation, Jesus foresaw the Temple being destroyed and a *"Son of Man"* bringing Divine judgment to a new world:

> *As he came out of the temple, one of his disciples said to him, "Look, Teacher, what large stones and what large buildings!" Then Jesus asked him, "Do you see these great buildings? Not one stone will be left here upon another; all will be thrown down." When he was sitting on the Mount of Olives opposite the temple, Peter, James, John, and Andrew asked him privately, "Tell us, when will this be, and what will be the sign that all these things are about to be accomplished?" . . . "When you hear of wars and rumors of wars, do not be alarmed; this must take place, but the end is still to come. For nation will rise against nation, and kingdom against kingdom; there will be earthquakes in various places; there will be famines. This is but the beginning of the birth pangs. . . . "But in those days, after that suffering, the sun will be darkened, and the moon will not give its light, and the stars will be falling from heaven, and the powers in the heavens will be shaken. Then they will see "the Son of Man coming in clouds' with great power and glory. Then he will send out the angels, and gather his elect from the four winds, from the ends of the earth to the ends of heaven"* (Mark 13:1-4, 7-8, 24-27).

Compared to the War Scroll studied by the Essenes, the features of apocalyptic wars between nations were subdued in these verses and in the following quotation from Luke, but they were present nevertheless. The Temple will be destroyed.[9] Jesus' words also implied physical changes in the nature of the world as in the prophesies of Isaiah, although he may have been speaking allegorically:

---

8   See also Luke 3:1-22. The Gospel of Luke downplayed the apocalyptic aspects of John and Jesus' mission, but did mention the election of Jesus from heaven. It emphasized John's insistence on repentance from sin, which would also become a vital aspect of Jesus' preaching. The sentence *"I will send my messenger ahead of you who will prepare your way"* is not found in the current version of Isaiah.

9   There is no mention in the gospels as to what, if anything, will take the Temple's place. The Essenes believed it would be rebuilt. A verse in the Book of Revelation saw no need for the Temple in God's Jerusalem at the End of Time (Revelation 21:22).

When you hear of wars and insurrections, do not be terrified; for these things must take place first, but the end will not follow immediately. Then he said to them, "Nation will rise against nation, and kingdom against kingdom; there will be great earthquakes, and in various places famines and plagues; and there will be dreadful portents and great signs from heaven. . . . When you see Jerusalem surrounded by armies, then know that its desolation has come near. . . . For there will be great distress on the earth and wrath against this people; they will fall by the edge of the sword and be taken away as captives among all nations; and Jerusalem will be trampled on by the Gentiles, until the times of the Gentiles are ful-filled. There will be signs in the sun, the moon, and the stars, and on the earth distress among nations confused by the roaring of the sea and the waves. . . . Then they will see 'the Son of Man coming in a cloud' with power and great glory. Now when these things begin to take place, stand up and raise your heads, because your redemption is drawing near" (Luke 21:9-11, 20, 23-25, 27-28).

The entry ticket into the Kingdom of God is acts of righteousness. The unrighteous are doomed to eternal punishment.

It is helpful to consider what Jesus thought righteous deeds (*tzedakah* in Hebrew) would accomplish. Such acts could have two aims: one is to im-prove the world, and the other is to elevate one's personal level of holiness. The Torah considers both aspects.[10] Jesus came down firmly on personal holiness:

As he was setting out on a journey, a man ran up and knelt before him, and asked him, "Good Teacher, what must I do to inherit eternal life?". . . You know the commandments: "You shall not murder; You shall not commit adultery; You shall not steal; You shall not bear false witness; You shall not defraud; Honor your father and mother." " He said to him, "Teacher, I have kept all these since my youth." Jesus, looking at him, loved him and said, "You lack one thing; go, sell what you own, and give the money to the poor, and you will have treasure in heaven; then come, follow me." When he heard this, he was shocked and went away grieving, for he had many possessions. Then Jesus looked around and said to his disciples, "How hard it will be for those who have wealth to enter the kingdom of God!" (Mark 10:17, 19-23).

---

10   The command to *"love your fellow as yourself"* is written in the Book of Leviticus (19:17-19), a book about individual and communal holiness.

Jesus could have advised this individual to use some of his wealth to improve society, but this was not his goal. Wealth was of no importance because the world everyone was familiar with was about to come to an end. This could explain why Jesus regarded wealth as having no purpose other than to be given away, and lowliness and humbleness to be virtues. All that mattered was personal virtue:

> *Jesus said to his disciples, "Therefore I tell you, do not worry about your life, what you will eat, or about your body, what you will wear. For life is more than food, and the body more than clothing. . . . Do not be afraid, little flock, for it is your Father's good pleasure to give you the kingdom. Sell your possessions, and give alms. Make purses for yourselves that do not wear out, an unfailing treasure in heaven, where no thief comes near and no moth destroys. For where your treasure is, there your heart will be also."* (Luke 12:22-23, 32-34).

Maintaining family harmony for its own sake was also pointless. In fact, he almost anticipated its breakup by those following his teachings:

> *"Do you think that I have come to bring peace to the earth? No, I tell you, but rather division! From now on five in one household will be divided, three against two and two against three; they will be divided: father against son and son against father, mother against daughter and daughter against mother, mother-in-law against her daughter-in-law and daughter-in-law against mother-in-law"* (Luke 12:51-53).[11]

> *"Brother will betray brother to death, and a father his child, and children will rise against parents and have them put to death; and you will be hated by all because of my name. But the one who endures to the end will be saved"* (Mark 13:12-13).

Conceptually, these are difficult messages. Judaism sees considerable value in family harmony. Poverty is also not an ideal in Judaism. These could be reasons why people in the main towns around the Sea of Galilee, such as Chorazin, Bethsaida, Capernaum, and Decapolis, which is where he did most of his preaching, were not prepared to accept his ideas.

Finally, Jesus stressed that the Kingdom of God was imminent and would occur during his and his followers' lifetimes:

---

11   See "The family and the kingdom" in *Jesus Apocalyptic Prophet of the New Millennium* by Bart Herman, 134. Oxford University Press, New York, 1999.

"Truly I tell you, this generation will not pass away until all these things have taken place. Heaven and earth will pass away, but my words will not pass away. But about that day or hour no one knows, neither the angels in heaven, nor the Son, but only the Father. Beware, keep alert; for you do not know when the time will come. . . . or else he may find you asleep when he comes suddenly. And what I say to you I say to all: Keep awake." (Mark 13:30-33, 36-37).

What will Jesus' role be at the End of Days?

Who is the *"Son of Man"* mentioned so frequently by Jesus? The earlier gospels recorded Jesus as saying that he was a human figure appointed by God to judge mankind:

"Be on guard so that your hearts are not weighed down with dissipation and drunkenness and the worries of this life, and that day does not catch you unexpectedly, like a trap. For it will come upon all who live on the face of the whole earth. Be alert at all times, praying that you may have the strength to escape all these things that will take place, and to stand before the Son of Man" (Luke 21:34-36).

A possible source for this individual is the Book of Daniel, which is also an apocalyptic work. Daniel described a vision in which four beasts arose one after the other and caused devastation on earth, and interpreted these as representing four powerful nations that will finally be destroyed. Then the following will occur:

"I was looking until thrones were set up, and the Ancient of Days took His seat; His raiment was as white snow, and the hair of his head like clean wool. His throne was tongues of fire, its wheels were a burning fire. A river of fire was flowing and emerging from before Him; a thousand thousands served Him, and ten thousand times ten thousands stood before him. Justice was established and the books were opened. . . . I saw in the visions of the night, and behold with the clouds of the heaven, one like a son of man was coming. He came up to the Ancient of Days and was presented to Him. And He gave him dominion, glory and kingship, that all peoples, nations and tongues should serve him. His dominion is an eternal dominion which shall not pass away, and his kingdom one that shall not be destroyed" (Daniel 7:9-10, 13-14).

The Jewish commentator Rashi interprets the *"Ancient of Days"* as being God Himself who will establish justice in the world and then appoint a human agent to bring about a utopian world. Similarly, Jesus believed that the Kingdom of God would be established by a human figure appointed by God.

It is doubtful that Jesus thought he would be this *"Son of Man."* Rather, he saw his role, as did John, as a *messenger*, a savior figure.[12] Both Mark and Luke introduced this idea by quoting a passage from the Book of Isaiah:

> *"The spirit of the Lord God was upon me because God anointed me to bring good tidings to the humble; He sent me to bind up the broken-hearted, to declare freedom for the captives, and for the prisoners to free from captivity"* (Isaiah 61:1).

At his crucifixion, the title of King of the Jews was placed above Jesus' cross (Mark 15:26 and John 19:19). This could have been an expression of derision by the Romans, but it could also suggest that either he and/or his followers considered his role to be more than just a messenger but a messianic figure.[13] This would accord with the passage in Luke describing an angel appearing to the Virgin Mary and announcing his birth, although this may also reflect later ideas:

> *"Do not be afraid, Mary, for you have found favor with God. And now, you will conceive in your womb and bear a son, and you will name him Jesus. He will be great, and will be called the Son of the Most High, and the Lord God will give to him the throne of his ancestor David. He will reign over the house of Jacob forever, and of his kingdom there will be no end"* (Luke 1:30-33).

It is of interest that the notion of a *"son of God"* or *"son of the Most High,"* a human figure who will judge the world with righteousness, was also found in one of the Dead Sea Scrolls:[14]

> *He will be called great and he will be called Son of God, and they will call*

---

12 Mark 1:2 and Luke 4:16-19.

13 The issue of what role Jesus considered himself to have is obviously an important one in the development of Christianity. The matter is discussed in "Jesus' trial before Pilate" in *Jesus Apocalyptic Prophet of the New Millennium* by Bart Herman, 221. Oxford University Press, New York, 1999.

14 This interesting association is mentioned in an essay "The Essenes and the origins of Christianity" by Moshe Dann from the Jerusalem Post in July 13, 2018 (https://www.jpost.com/jerusalem-report/the-essenes-and-the-origins-of-christianity-562442).

him Son of the Most High. . . . He will judge the earth in righteousness. . . . and every nation will bow down to him.[15]

God also calls the Jewish people "*My son*" in the Torah (Exodus 4:22). In this context it means no more than being appointed by God for a specific role and is not indicative of any Divine status.

In conclusion, the Essenes in Qumran believed that an apocalyptic end to the world was imminent, leading to the dawn of the Kingdom of God, and they copied and studied apocalyptic texts describing this era. The notion of a new world era followed from the prophecies of Isaiah, Ezekiel, Zechariah, Joel and Daniel. John the Baptist also believed in an imminent, messianic new world and he urged his followers to repent so as to be among the privileged to inherit this new kingdom on earth. Jesus took over John's program after John was murdered by Herod Antipas. It seems likely that both John and Jesus regarded themselves as messengers of God, announcing that this era would soon be upon them.

One wonders how the Jews could have survived as a single people with a single faith with this multitude of antagonistic factions – Pharisees, Sadducees, Essenes and Jewish early Christians. The answer could well be that they would not. Judaism survived because these factions disappeared. The event that caused this was the Great Revolt (66-73 CE). With the loss of the Temple the Sadducees became irrelevant. The Essenes fought in the Great Revolt and they were killed by the Romans. The Zealots, or messianic branch of the Pharisees, were also killed by the Romans. The Pharisee leadership was in the peace camp and survived, thus ensuring the survival of a single people with a single faith. The challenge of the Pharisees will now be to attract the population to their branch of Judaism. This will be covered in chapter 10 when discussing Rabbi Akiva. It is worth noting that Judaism was the only monotheistic faith that contracted to less factions. This never happened within Christianity or Islam. It is suggested that this ensured its survival after the destruction of its Temple.

The Jewish Christians also survived the Great Revolt. It is doubtful that Jesus' theology would have become the basis of a world religion were it not for Paul of Tarsus, who developed doctrines more appealing to the gentile world. To do this, he directed the messianism of his new religion towards a spiritual, rather than earthly World to Come and dispensed with most of the laws of Judaism. More about Paul in the next chapter.

_____

15   This manuscript is 4Q 246.

Chapter 9

PAUL OF TARSUS AND CHRISTIAN MESSIANISM

Sha'ul (Saul) from the city of Tarsus, usually known by his Greek name Paul, took upon himself the mission of making Jesus' mission relevant to the gentiles of the Roman Empire. In doing this, he can be considered one of the most innovative theologians in the history of religion by providing new meaning to the terms resurrection, salvation and messianism.

Resurrection is a fundamental belief of Judaism. Paul's innovation was to describe a resurrection in which the human body would be recreated afresh as an immortal spiritual body rather than a physical one. Paul also believed that all humanity was inherently sinful and that no law, not even that of Moses, could remedy this. However, by dying on the cross, Christ became the savior of mankind by absolving believers of sin. Everyone could now receive expiation from sin by believing in Christ, and he or she would be resurrected together with Christ at the time of the Kingdom of God. At this time, Christ the Messiah would bring the entire earth under his aegis in a new age of universal harmony (Acts 3:19-21). Like Jesus, Paul believed that these events, namely the Kingdom of God and resurrection, were very imminent.

A late gospel, the Gospel of Luke, would subsequently introduce the idea that believers in Christ would not have to wait for an apocalyptic event for their entry to the World to Come (although this event would still occur), but could enter the heavenly Kingdom of God at the time of death. This would also be a time of judgment leading to reward and punishment in paradise or hell. This gospel thereby joined together Jewish and Pauline ideas with Greek concepts of the afterlife and the soul.

These ideas were quite distant from those of the ancient prophets of Israel who spoke of a very physical Messiah (the Hebrew word for an anointed one) of the Davidic dynasty who would bring peace and material benefit to the Jewish people and facilitate the universal recognition of God by the nations of the world. They were also distant from the beliefs of Jesus of Nazareth and the early Jewish Christians who still existed as a movement after Jesus' death.

By dint of extraordinary effort, Paul was able to disseminate his ideas among gentiles in the Roman Empire, and his version of Christianity, not that of the early Jewish Christians in Jerusalem, would become the accepted one in the Roman Empire. The Christianity practiced today is Pauline Christianity, and much of the New Testament is a forum for his ideas.

However, also within Paul's ideas were the seeds of Christian hatred towards Jews and this hatred would only grow after his death. His supersession theology, including the notion that Christianity had now taken over the messianic role of Judaism, would be developed further by the early Church fathers and its consequences for Jews would play itself out in world history over the next two millennia.

This all began on a journey that Paul made to Damascus.

PAUL'S VISION OF CHRIST

Paul was a citizen of the Roman Empire, born to a practicing Jewish family in the city of Tarsus in present-day Turkey between 5 BCE and 5 CE (Phili 3.5). When young he was sent to Jerusalem to learn at the rabbinic school of Rabban Gamaliel the Elder, one of the most prominent rabbis of that time, so that his knowledge of the Jewish tradition would have been very comprehensive (Acts 22:3).

We know far more about Paul and his thoughts than we do about the ideas of Jesus. This is because Paul wrote letters to the communities he established in the Roman Empire providing advice and encouragement, and these letters elaborated on his philosophical ideas. Many of these letters made their way into the New Testament. Pauls' authorship of six of them is undisputed, although there is debate as to the authorship of the remaining seven. The Acts of the Apostles, often known just as Acts, is a history of the early Christian church, and 21 of its 28 chapters describe the conversion and activities of Paul. It is a continuation of the Gospel of Luke and was written by an anonymous author in about 80 to 90 CE, at least 13 years after Paul's death.

According to Paul's own words, while on the road to Damascus he experienced a vision of Christ in Paradise (2 Corinthians 12:2-4). This would have been sometime between 31 to 35 CE. In this vision, Christ revealed to him the gospel he would subsequently teach to the Roman world (Galatians 1:11-12). Unlike the other twelve apostles, Paul never saw Jesus in the flesh, nor had he had previous contact with the Jewish Christians in Jerusalem. It was not until three years later that he met James the brother of Jesus, who was then leader of Jewish Christians who had remained together as a group following Jesus' death (Galatian 1:18-24). Paul's proselytizing was therefore his own initiative, and he considered himself a free agent with respect to the ideas he promoted during his thousands of miles of travelling.

Paul lived at a time when there was considerable interest in the Roman Empire in conversion to Judaism. Many pagans saw the worship of Roman gods and sometimes of the Caesars themselves as bankrupt, and righteous gentiles could be found in many of the synagogues of the large cities in the Roman Empire.

One of Paul's novel ideas was that Jew and gentile alike could enter into a new community of Christ without the need to adhere to Jewish law. A consequence of this was that Paul would be involved in conflict wherever he went: for encouraging Jews to forsake their covenant, for encouraging gentiles interested in conversion to dispense with circumcision and other Jewish practices, and for being involved in a movement that was illegal under Roman law and was sometimes persecuted. These conflicts are reflected in the New Testament. In the end, they would lead to his death.

Some background into Jewish and Greek ideas of the afterlife will be helpful in understanding the novelty of Paul's teachings.

THE AFTERLIFE IN JEWISH AND GREEK THOUGHT

The Torah has next to nothing to say about the soul and life after death. The Hebrew words *nefesh* and *ruach* found in the Torah are often translated as soul, but in actuality they mean more in the way of a life-giving force than anything spiritual (for example, Leviticus 17:11). However, during the creation of man in the second creation account, the Torah does speak about the *neshoma* (also translated as soul) as an aspect of God that is infused into man: *"And the Lord God (Y-H-V-H Elohim) formed man of dust from the ground, and He breathed into his nostrils the neshoma (soul) of life, and man became a living nefesh (soul)"* (Genesis 2:7).

At the time of the Bible people believed that the body descended at death to a pit in the earth called *sheol*. The existence of *sheol* is mentioned many times in the Bible, particularly in the Book of Psalms, although never in the context of anything spiritual. Psalm 115, for example, says the following about death:

"As for the heavens – the heavens are God's (Y-H-V-H's), but the earth He has given to mankind. Neither the dead can praise God, nor any who descend into silence. But we will praise God henceforth and forever. Praise God!" (Psalm 115:16-17).[1]

In the witch of Endor story in the Book of Samuel in which a necromanceress makes Samuel appear to King Saul it is also mentioned that she *"brought up"* the figure of Samuel from the dead (I Samuel 28:7-19). Samuel also questions *"Why have you roused me, to bring me up?"* (I Samuel 28:15) suggesting that he existed within the earth.

The Garden of Eden story does leave open the possibility of something spiritual beyond this world. Death is one of the main topics of this story. Man was called Adam because he came from and will return to the earth (*adama* in Hebrew). After eating of the fruit of the Tree of Knowledge of Good and Evil, he was expelled from the Garden of Eden and *"cherubim and the blade of the flaming sword"* (Genesis 3:24) were placed at the eastern entrance to the Garden of Eden to guard the way to the Tree of Life. The implication is that eternal life is closed to man in this world. Nevertheless, this does not rule out the possibility of a spiritual existence beyond this world of toil and pain, although this is far from explicit:

> *The Book of Ecclesiastes, written by King Solomon, does mention an aspect of spirituality after death:[2] "And the dust returns to the earth as it was, and the spirit returns to God who gave it"* (Ecclesiastes 12:7).

And that's about it.

Why is the Torah so silent about what happens after death? It could be a reaction to the Egyptian obsession with death which the Israelites would have experienced firsthand during their exile in Egypt. Because of this, Judaism made great efforts to distance itself from anything connected to death. Everyone,

---

1   Radak interprets the *"we"* who continue praising God forever as being everyone in the world of souls. Another explanation is that even though we have failed previously, we will continue from now on to praise him (Beis Avraham). The most literal interpretation would seem to be everyone who is still alive.

2   For the sake of completeness, it should be mentioned that scholars have argued that, based on its language, the Book of Ecclesiastes was written much later than the early Israelite monarchy, possibly in the Persian period or even as late as the Hellenistic period. The use of pseudonyms was very common in later Jewish religious literature. Thus, this book was written from the perspective of a Jewish monarch with an entire kingdom at his disposal. Somewhat contradicting this idea is the mention of judgment in Ecclesiastes but not resurrection, which probably would have been mentioned at least in the Hellenistic period. But all this is highly speculative.

including priests, became spiritually impure if there were physical contact with such things as a corpse, certain insects and dead animals and would be forbidden from entering the Temple until rendered ritually pure. Unlike the Egyptians, the Israelites built no large mausoleums for the dead, such as the pyramids, since the focus of the Torah is about living, not preparing for death.

Because they were not explicitly mentioned in the Torah, the Sadducees in the Second Temple period did not believe in a final judgment or World to Come and held that all existence ceased after death.[3] However, after the Great Revolt against the Romans the Sadducees ceased to exist as a party, and the ideas of the Pharisees became those most prevalent in the Jewish world.

The Pharisees believed in an afterlife in which there was reward and punishment. The possibility of there being no recompense for goodness or evil would have been unimaginable to them. They also believed that the body would be resurrected as an initial stage of the World to Come. Hence, the World to Come was firmly on this planet and not in the heavenly realms. The sages felt so strongly about the belief in resurrection that the Mishna records the following measure for measure statement:

> *"Every Jew has a share in the World to Come . . . . and the following people do not have a share in the World to Come; one who says that the resurrection is not stated in the Torah . . . ."*[4]

This statement may seem very uncompromising. However, it is worth recalling that belief options related to the afterlife for a Jew in the Second Temple period were limited to resurrection or non-existence. Hence, a lack of belief in resurrection would be akin to not believing in an afterlife.

The only definite mention of resurrection in the Bible is found in the final chapter of the apocalyptic work the Book of Daniel, although the Rabbis find allusions to resurrection in other places in the Bible.[5] This is the quotation from Daniel:

---

3   This is not to say that the Sadducees believed that life should be reserved for hedonism. The Greek philosopher Epicurus, for example, despite his later reputation, believed that the happiest life was one that avoided pain and promoted pleasure, but not necessarily dissipated pleasure.

4   Mishna Sanhedrin 10:1.

5   An example of a hint of resurrection mentioned in the Torah is: "*See now, that I, I am He – and no god is with Me. I cause death and life. I struck down and I will heal*" (Deuteronomy 32:39). A phrase in Psalms could indicate that resurrection was a later belief than the beginning of the monarchy: "*For He [God] remembered that they [the Israelites at the time of the Exodus] were but flesh, a fleeting breath, not returning*" (Psalms 78:39). Nevertheless, Radak points out that this does not contradict a belief in resurrection, which is outside the realm of nature.

And it will be a time of distress the like of which has never been since the nation came into being, and at that time your people will be delivered, all who are inscribed in the book. And many who sleep in the dust of the earth will awaken – some to eternal life, others to reproaches and everlasting abhorrence. And the wise will be radiant like the brightness of the sky, and those who lead the many to righteousness will be like the stars forever and ever (Daniel 12:1-3).

An indication that resurrection was an established belief among Jews by the Hasmonean period comes from the Book of Maccabees (which is not part of the Jewish canon), which records the following retort made by a victim being tortured for his beliefs: "*You accursed wretch, you dismiss us from this present life, but the King of the universe will raise us up to an everlasting renewal of life because we have died for His laws*" (2 Maccabees 7:9).

The Greeks did not believe in resurrection, but they did have the concept of eternal souls, the existence of which even preceded the creation of the world. The first detailed discussion of the soul is not found in Jewish sources but in the writings of the Greek pagan philosopher Plato in the Phaedo when he reported on the ideas of his teacher Socrates.[6] The soul described by Plato is released from being trapped in the body at death and goes to a place called Hades where there is judgment.[7] Eventually it reaches even higher celestial realms. The soul has substance, although considerably less than matter or air. Having said this, Plato admitted that this was all speculation, and death may well result in dreamless non-existence. A cross-pollination of ideas between Greek, Persian and Jewish cultures cannot be excluded, although who borrowed from whom is impossible to know.

By the talmudic period, the idea of a soul joined to the human body was well established. As the Talmud says: "*Just as the Holy One, Blessed is He, is pure, so too is the soul pure.*"[8] The Greek idea of a soul residing permanently in heaven would not enter Judaism until the writings of Maimonides in the Middle Ages. The concept of resurrection was introduced to Western civilization through Pauline Christianity.

---

6 "Will Justice be Done? The Rise of Postmortem Rewards and Punishments" in *Heaven and Hell. A history of the Afterlife* by Bart D. Ehrman, 60. Oneworld Publications, England, 2020. Judaism does not believe in a soul that predates Creation, although the influential Jewish philosopher Nachmanides mentions that once a soul is created it is eternal.

7 Hades is the god of the soul and ruler of the underworld in the Greek religion and mythology. His name became synonymous with the underworld.

8 TB Berokhot 10a.

Paul's theology[9]

Paul brought a number of new ideas to Christianity that were different from Jewish beliefs and even from those of the early Jewish Christians:

(i). The spiritual nature of resurrection:
The resurrection of Jesus and his sighting by the apostles, Paul himself and others indicated to Paul that the reincarnation of Christ was the first proto-type, so to speak, of the future resurrection of mankind. The spiritual nature of the reincarnated body was described in a letter Paul sent to his congregants in Corinth, the largest city in ancient Greece:

> But in fact Christ has been raised from the dead, the first fruits of those who have died. For since death came through a human being, the resur-rection of the dead has also come through a human being. . . . But some-one will ask, "How are the dead raised? With what kind of body do they come?" . . . Not all flesh is alike, but there is one flesh for human beings, another for animals, another for birds, and another for fish. There are both heavenly bodies and earthly bodies, but the glory of the heavenly is one thing, and that of the earthly is another. . . . So it is with the resurrection of the dead. What is sown is perishable, what is raised is imperishable. It is sown in dishonor, it is raised in glory. It is sown in weakness, it is raised in power. It is sown a physical body, it is raised a spiritual body. If there is a physical body, there is also a spiritual body. Thus, it is written, "The first man, Adam, became a living being"; the last Adam became a life-giving spirit. But it is not the spiritual that is first, but the physical, and then the spiritual. The first man was from the earth, a man of dust; the second man is from heaven (1 Corinthians 15:20-21, 35, 39-40, 42-47).

(ii). Christ as the son of God:
Paul believed that Jesus was the son of God. He was also a scion of David and was thus linked to the traditional Jewish idea of a Messiah of the Davidic

---

9   For this section I have relied heavily on James D. Tabor's book *Paul and Jesus. How the Apostle transformed Christianity*. Simon and Schuster Paperbacks, 2012. Many of the New Testament quotations in this section are those included in his book. Tabor also points out that Paul did not talk much about Jesus' messages to his own followers. What was impor-tant to him was what Jesus had become. He also notes that the heavenly aspect of Jesus is called Christ, the Lord, Jesus Christ, or the Lord Jesus Christ, and only occasionally Jesus. The world Christ means savior in Greek. I follow this convention and use the name Christ in this chapter for the resurrected Jesus.

dynasty. In a letter to the Christian community in Rome Paul explained:

> *Paul, a servant of Jesus Christ, called to be an apostle, set apart for the gospel of God, which he promised beforehand through his prophets in the holy scriptures, the gospel concerning his Son, who was descended from David according to the flesh and was declared to be Son of God with power according to the spirit of holiness by resurrection from the dead, Jesus Christ our Lord* (Romans 1:1-4).

In a passage from Philippians, Paul urged this community to be humble and to look out for the welfare of each other just as Jesus did in his equality with God:

> *Do nothing from selfish ambition or conceit, but in humility regard others as better than yourselves. Let each of you look not to your own interests, but to the interests of others. Let the same mind be in you that was in Christ Jesus, who, though he was in the form of God, did not regard equality with God as something to be exploited, but emptied himself, taking the form of a slave, being born in human likeness. And being found in human form, he humbled himself and became obedient to the point of death — even death on a cross. Therefore, God also highly exalted him and gave him the name that is above every name, so that at the name of Jesus every knee should bend, in heaven and on earth and under the earth, and every tongue should confess that Jesus Christ is Lord, to the glory of God the Father* (Philippians 2:3-11).

(iii). Believers in Christ become children of God together with Christ:

In Paul's mystical ideas, believers in Jesus have joined, like Paul himself, a select and privileged group of individuals who have received the spirit of God and become children of God together with Christ, the firstborn son of God.[10] In this way, even the lowliest in society could become a co-heir with Christ and could call God his Father:

> *For all who are led by the Spirit of God are children of God. For you did not receive a spirit of slavery to fall back into fear, but you have received a spirit of adoption. When we cry, "Abba! Father!" it is that very Spirit bearing witness with our spirit that we are children of God, and if children, then heirs, heirs of God and joint heirs with Christ — if, in fact, we suffer with him so that we may also be glorified with him* (Romans 8:14-17).

---

10   "A Cosmic Family and a Heavenly Kingdom," ibid., 108.

(iv). Joining with the cosmic spirit of Christ:

As participants in the spirit of Christ, his followers will have equal privileges with him in judging the future cosmic order, including judging the angels. Paul mentioned this in the context of his advice to the congregation in Corinth not to take their disputes to outside parties:

> *When any of you has a grievance against another, do you dare to take it to court before the unrighteous, instead of taking it before the saints? Do you not know that the saints will judge the world? And if the world is to be judged by you, are you incompetent to try trivial cases? Do you not know that we are to judge angels — to say nothing of ordinary matters?* (1 Corinthians 6:1-3).

An important concept for Paul was that of being *"in Christ"* and he used this phrase many times in his letters. In an admonition against sexual immorality, for example, Paul pointed out that during resurrection his followers' bodies will become one in Christ:

> *And God raised the Lord and will also raise us by his power. Do you not know that your bodies are members of Christ? Should I therefore take the members of Christ and make them members of a prostitute? Never! Do you not know that whoever is united to a prostitute becomes one body with her? For it is said, "The two shall be one flesh." But anyone united to the Lord becomes one spirit with him* (1 Corinthians 6:14-17).

This mystical attachment to Christ is maintained by two rituals that Paul brought to Christianity. One is baptism. Baptism was practiced by John the Baptist and Jesus as a *"baptism of forgiveness"* once their followers had repented of their sins in preparation for the Kingdom of God (Mark 1:4-5). For Paul, however, becoming *"baptized into Christ"* was a means of becoming joined together with the cosmic spirit of Christ and thereby forming a single body with all believers in Christ. This ritual was probably accompanied by a declaration:

> *If you confess with your lips that Jesus is Lord and believe in your heart that God raised him from the dead, you will be saved. For one believes with the heart and so is justified, and one confesses with the mouth and so is saved* (Romans 10:9-10).

Another ritual for maintaining connection with Christ was the Eucharist, or Holy Communion, in which participants ate the flesh of Christ and drank his blood through bread and wine. This would likely have been done in a group session in a secret location. During these sessions, the participants would verbalize their free thoughts inspired by the spirit of Christ. These could include the following:

> *To each is given the manifestation of the Spirit for the common good. To one is given through the Spirit the utterance of wisdom, and to another the utterance of knowledge according to the same Spirit, to another faith by the same Spirit, to another gifts of healing by the one Spirit, to another the working of miracles, to another prophecy, to another the discernment of spirits, to another various kinds of tongues, to another the interpretation of tongues. All these are activated by one and the same Spirit, who allots to each one individually just as the Spirit chooses* (1 Corinthians 12:7-11).

(v). Expiation from sin through belief in Christ:
Another important aspect of Paul's theology was that Christ's death and subsequent resurrection would bring expiation from sin for all those who believed in Christ and were mystically joined with him:

> *But now, apart from law, the righteousness of God has been disclosed, and is attested by the law and the prophets, the righteousness of God through faith in Jesus Christ for all who believe. For there is no distinction, since all have sinned and fall short of the glory of God; they are now justified by his grace as a gift, through the redemption that is in Christ Jesus, whom God put forward as a sacrifice of atonement by his blood, effective through faith. He did this to show his righteousness, because in his divine forbearance he had passed over the sins previously committed; it was to prove at the present time that he himself is righteous and that he justifies the one who has faith in Jesus. Then what becomes of boasting? It is excluded. By what law? By that of works? No, but by the law of faith* (Romans 3:21-27).

Since absolution from sin was obtained by belief, there was no longer need for the revealed Law of Moses. Instead, believers in Jesus would inherit "*the Torah of Christ.*" This new form of the Torah was mentioned twice by Paul in his letters in Galatians and Corinthians:

> *Now before faith came, we were imprisoned and guarded under the law until faith would be revealed. Therefore, the law was our disciplinarian until Christ came, so that we might be justified by faith. But now that faith has come, we are no longer subject to a disciplinarian, for in Christ Jesus you are all children of God through faith. As many of you as were baptized into Christ have clothed yourselves with Christ. There is no longer Jew or Greek, there is no longer slave or free, there is no longer male and female;*

168

for all of you are one in Christ Jesus. And if you belong to Christ, then you are Abraham's offspring, heirs according to the promise (Galatians 3:23-29).

Paul was attempting here to break down all barriers between Jew and gentile. He saw his community in Christ as a single body in which all were equal as a new Israel. Neither Jew nor gentile had any obligation to keep the Mosaic Law. There are also indications from his letters in the New Testament that Paul himself was no longer Torah-abiding:

We ourselves are Jews by birth and not Gentile sinners; yet we know that a person is justified not by the works of the law but through faith in Jesus Christ. And we have come to believe in Christ Jesus, so that we might be justified by faith in Christ, and not by doing the works of the law, because no one will be justified by the works of the law (Galatians 2:15-16).

For neither circumcision nor uncircumcision is anything; but a new creation is everything! As for those who will follow this rule—peace be upon them, and mercy, and upon the Israel of God (Galations 6:15-16).

It goes without saying that righteous gentiles attending synagogues in preparation for conversion to Judaism should reconsider circumcision since this would be an alienation from Christ:

For freedom Christ has set us free. Stand firm, therefore, and do not submit again to a yoke of slavery. Listen! I, Paul, am telling you that if you let yourselves be circumcised, Christ will be of no benefit to you. Once again, I testify to every man who lets himself be circumcised that he is obliged to obey the entire law. You who want to be justified by the law have cut yourselves off from Christ; you have fallen away from grace. For through the Spirit, by faith, we eagerly wait for the hope of righteousness. For in Christ Jesus neither circumcision nor uncircumcision counts for anything; the only thing that counts is faith working through love (Galatians 5:1-6).

(vi). The rule of God in the World to Come:

Finally, Paul provided a glimpse of the World to Come when all evil will have been extirpated, death overcome and God's rule will be unopposed:

Then comes the end, when he hands over the kingdom to God the Father, after he has destroyed every ruler and every authority and power. For he must reign until he has put all his enemies under his feet. The last enemy to be destroyed is death. For "God has put all things in subjection under his feet." But when it says, "All things are put in subjection," it is plain that this does not include the one who put all things in subjection under him. When all things are subjected to him, then the Son himself will also be subjected to the one who put all things in subjection under him, so that God may be all in all (1 Corinthians 15:24-28).

Ehrman points out two other ideas that entered into Christian theology through the later Gospel of Luke.[11] One was that the Kingdom of God can be in the heavenly realm. Luke did not negate the notion of an apocalypse but diminished its importance in favor of Greek ideas. He thereby pushed Christian theology further into heaven from its Jewish base on earth. Luke also emphasized the notion of punishment at death. In the following quotation from a parable about a rich man and a poor man called Lazarus in the Gospel of Luke, the rich man goes to purgatory (in Greek hades) for not sharing his wealth:

In Hades [hell], where he was being tormented, he looked up and saw Abraham far away with Lazarus by his side. He called out, "Father Abraham, have mercy on me, and send Lazarus to dip the tip of his finger in water and cool my tongue; for I am in agony in these flames" (Luke 16:23-24).

Luke's ideas of a heavenly Kingdom of God and heavenly punishment in hell owed much to Greek thought, and they would have a major influence on Christian theology following Paul's death.

HEADFIRST INTO CONFLICT

Paul's theology was a carefully crafted one. Nevertheless, from a Jewish perspective, almost all his ideas were heretical. This almost guaranteed conflict with the Jewish communities he visited.

Judaism could never accept that God could split Himself into parts and that one of these parts could become corporeal. One of the basic tenets of Judaism is that God is a unity. This concept is mentioned in the opening sentence of one of the most important prayers of Judaism, the Shema: "*Hear O Israel, Y-H-V-H is our God, Y-H-V-H is One.*"[12]

---

11   "The Beginnings of Postmortem Rewards and Punishments" in *Heaven and Hell. A History of the Afterlife* by Bart D. Ehrman, 193. Oneworld Publications, London, England, 2020, and "Glory and Torment After Death in Luke," 197.

12   One does find in the Torah the concept of angels as messengers of God that function on earth in human form. They return to Heaven when they have completed their mission and

The notion that God would abrogate His covenant with the Jewish people was also completely unacceptable to Jews. Jews believe that the covenant binding the Jewish people to God is eternal.

Judaism would also strongly disagree with Paul's proposition that there was no recourse to obtaining atonement from sin other than by believing and identifying with Jesus. Judaism would agree that man is inherently sinful. After all, the Torah does say this: "*Since the design of man's heart is evil from his youth*" (Genesis 8:21). Nevertheless, the entire thrust of the Bible is to show how sin can be prevented by adherence to the commandments of the Torah.

This is why the Torah described a series of choices being made – Noah was selected from all mankind, Seth from Noah's children and Abraham from all Semites, leading eventually to the formation of closely-knit tribes and then to a nation with the potential for directing mankind towards ethical behavior. Practicing the laws handed down through Moses at Mount Sinai is an essential part of this and can never be replaced just by faith alone, even in God.

A merciful God also provides mechanisms for obtaining forgiveness from sin: through guilt sacrifices made in the Temple through which one vicariously offers oneself up to God; and through the festival of Yom Kippur (Day of Atonement), in which sacrificial rites and prayer lead to forgiveness from sin for individuals and for the community.[13] In this way, Jews can start afresh without feeling overwhelmed by unexpiated sin.

Finally, the Jewish concept of the Messiah has always been that of an individual who will obtain political and religious freedom for the Jewish people in the Land of Israel and who will facilitate a gentile revival towards God. Utopia will be firmly on this earth, although prophetic visions could imply that this will be a new type of world. The Christian notion that the Messiah is a godly figure whose purpose is to save those who believe in him so that they can eventually inherit a spiritual World to Come but who leaves Jewish suffering on earth unresolved, would have been impossible for any Jew to take seriously.

It is therefore not surprising that Jews reacted in a strongly negative way to Paul's proselytizing in their synagogues. Paul admitted as such. He described his life as a Christian as being one of tribulations and suffering and recounted: "*Five times I received from the Jews the 40 lashes minus one*"

---

can be thought of as robotic extensions of God.

13   Nachmanides *Commentary to the Torah* to Leviticus 1:9.

(2 Corinthians 11:24). Lashes were a Biblical punishment for transgressing Torah law. Jews subsequently made great efforts to identify and ban Jewish Christians from their midst.[14]

After Jesus' death, his Jewish followers in Judea continued to exist as a Christian group under the leadership of Jesus' brother James. Paul's disagreement with them did not come into the open until the end of his life. Paul met James twice in Jerusalem.[15] At his first meeting with the apostles and elders they agreed that non-Jews should not be discouraged from joining their movement since Jesus himself believed that the Kingdom of God would include gentiles. James also made the decision at that time that gentiles would not have to be circumcised but that they should abstain from eating food polluted by idols, from engaging in sexual immorality, from eating the meat of strangled animals, and from eating blood (Acts 15: 20). Other than this, Paul was given a free hand to continue his work among the gentiles.

It seems likely that until his second and final meeting with James, the Jewish Christians in Jerusalem were unaware that Paul was no longer a practicing Jew. They also did not realize that he was encouraging potential converts to Judaism, and even Jews, to reject the Mosaic covenant. The New Testament indicates that he was not always completely honest with the Jewish communities in which he was proselytizing:

> *For though I am free with respect to all, I have made myself a slave to all, so that I might win more of them. To the Jews I became as a Jew, in order to win Jews. To those under the law I became as one under the law (though I myself am not under the law) so that I might win those under the law. To those outside the law I became as one outside the law (though I am not free from God's law but am under Christ's law) so that I might win those outside the law. To the weak I became weak, so that I might win the weak. I have become all things to all people, that I might by all means save some. I do it all for the sake of the gospel, so that I may share in its blessings* (1 Corinthians 9:19-23).

During his final visit to Jerusalem and while undergoing a test of his Jewish practice, Paul was denounced by diaspora Jews, and there was an uproar in the Temple (Acts 21:18-36). He was arrested. As a Roman citizen, he

---

14 TB Berakhot 28b-29a. A curse against heretics was added to an important communal prayer, the Eighteen Benedictions. If a congregant was called upon to lead this prayer and he refused, it was assumed he was a secret Christian. This was one way that Jewish Christians were separated from the Jewish community.

15 Galations 1:18-19, Galations 2:9 and 2:12.

demanded his right to be judged only by the Caesar and he was transported to Rome where he spent two years under house arrest. He was finally beheaded by Nero as part of a wave of persecution of Christians.

Understandably, a theological conflict between Paul and the Jewish Christians in Jerusalem is not mentioned in the New Testament. Nevertheless, it is apparent from many sources that Paul's theology held no traction with them. Included in the New Testament is a letter composed by James the brother of Jesus.16 This letter contains none of Paul's doctrines, such as Jesus being the son of God in human form and dying as a savior on the cross for the world's sins. In its 108 verses there is much mention of God but nothing about Jesus being a Messiah or savior figure.

In this letter, James adopted the normative Jewish view that faith without virtuous deeds was "*useless*." Could this have been directed at the ideas of Paul? This is certainly a possibility:

> *Do you want to be shown, you senseless person, that faith apart from works is barren? Was not our ancestor Abraham justified by works when he offered his son Isaac on the altar? You see that faith was active along with his works, and faith was brought to completion by the works. Thus, the scripture was fulfilled that says, "Abraham believed God, and it was reckoned to him as righteousness," and he was called the friend of God. You see that a person is justified by works and not by faith alone. Likewise, was not Rahab the prostitute also justified by works when she welcomed the messengers and sent them out by another road? For just as the body without the spirit is dead, so faith without works is also dead* (James 2:20-26).

Most of James' admonitions were ethical. He reminded his readers that loving your neighbor as yourself was an important principle of the Torah (as it was in Jesus' teachings). In addition, he emphasized that the Torah needed to be kept in its entirety and that its components were not subject to choice (although most Jews nowadays would not necessarily agree that breaking one law is akin to breaking them all, although James may have been talking about such commands as the Ten Commandments):

> *You do well if you really fulfill the royal law according to the scripture, "You shall love your neighbor as yourself." But if you show partiality, you commit sin and are convicted by the law as transgressors. For whoever*

---

16 It would seem that the decision to include this letter in the Christian canon was a controversial one. "Christianity before Paul" in *Paul and Jesus. How the Apostle transformed Christianity* by James D. Tabor, 23. Simon and Schuster Paperbacks, 2012.

keeps the whole law but fails in one point has become accountable for all of it. For the one who said, "You shall not commit adultery," also said, "You shall not murder." Now if you do not commit adultery but if you murder, you have become a transgressor of the law (James 2:8-11).

His letter also expressed the apocalyptic idea promoted by Jesus that the Kingdom of God would soon be upon them:

Be patient, therefore, beloved, until the coming of the Lord. The farmer waits for the precious crop from the earth, being patient with it until it receives the early and the late rains. You also must be patient. Strengthen your hearts, for the coming of the Lord is near. Beloved, do not grumble against one another, so that you may not be judged. See, the Judge is standing at the doors! (James 5:7-9).

Of interest, because of its similarities to James' letter, is a text called the *Didache* (meaning *teaching* in Greek), discovered in 1873 in a library in Constantinople.[17] Its title is "The Teaching of the Lord through the Twelve Apostles to the Nations," and it is a guide from about the first century CE for converts to Christianity. It contains ethical messages, some of which are found in the gospels. Missing are any of the ideas of Paul. It also contains nothing about Jesus' resurrection from the dead, and the only emphasis on Jesus, who is called "*the servant*" of the Father, is his message.

What happened to the Jewish Christians from Jerusalem? There is a tradition that they fled to Transjordan before the destruction of Jerusalem by Vespasian. There were also non-Pauline Jewish Christian groups dispersed in the Jewish diaspora. Persecuted by Jews and Christians alike, they had no long-term future. There was also a limit to which the notion of an imminent apocalypse could be maintained.

A group that could have been a remnant of the original Jerusalem Jewish Christians were the Ebionites.[18] Little is known about them other than from the polemics of the Church fathers who regarded them as heretical. They kept the Torah, repudiated the teachings of Paul, used only the Gospel of Matthew, and believed that Jesus was solely human and a prophet of the messianic age. They continued to exist until at least the seventh century CE.

---

17   Didache in Wikipedia (https://en.wikipedia.org/wiki/Didache).
18   Against Heresies 1.26.2 by Irenaeus. Also, Ebonites in Wikipedia (https://en.wikipedia.org/wiki/Ebionites#:~:text=Ebionites%20(Greek%3A%20E1%BC%98%CE%B2%CE%B9%CF%89%CE%BD%CE%B1%E1%BF%96%CE%BF%CE%B9%2C%20Ebionaioi,centuries%20of%20the%20Common%20Era).

The roots of Christian antisemitism

Why did Christianity turn against the faith of its founders?

Rabbi Jonathan Sacks, one of the great religious thinkers of our times, lists the numerous reasons often given for antisemitism and provides his own explanation — that Jews have always been different from the prevailing culture:

Some have seen it [antisemitism] in psychological terms: displaced fear, externalization of inner conflict, projected guilt, the creation of a scape-goat. Others have given it a socio-political explanation: Jews were a group who could conveniently be blamed for economic resentments, social unrest, class conflict, or destabilizing change. Yet others view it through the prism of culture and identity: Jews were the stereotyped against whom a group could define itself. There have been voices within the Jewish tradition that see hostility as inevitable. "Esau hates Jacob," or "From Sinai, hate (sinah in Hebrew) descended into the world." Yet others, noting the concentration of antisemitism among the very faiths – Christianity and Islam – that trace their descent to Abrahamic monotheism, favor a Freudian explanation in terms of the myth of Oedipus: we seek to kill those who gave us birth. It would be strange indeed if so complex a phenomenon did not give rise to multiple explanations.[19]

All these reasons may have validity in explaining dislike of Jews. However, it is questionable whether they adequately explain the visceral hatred felt towards Jews by many Christians, which erupted as murderous pogroms throughout the centuries and led eventually to the Holocaust. The Holocaust had nothing to do with Christianity, but the Christian hate for Jews permeating Europe was the necessary backdrop for the Nazis' Final Solution.

James Carrol, in his book *Constantine's Sword*, considers four reasons for Christianity's antagonism to Jews:[20]

- The anti-Jewish sentiments expressed in the New Testament.
- Christianity's ascent to a position of power within the Roman Empire.
- Emperor Constantine's emphasis on the cross and the subsequent focus of Christianity on Jesus's suffering and death and Jewish culpability for this.

19 "Not One Alone" in *Rabbi Jonathan Sacks's Haggadah* by Jonathan Sacks, 38. Continuum, New York, 2010.
20 "Parting of the Ways" in *Constantine's Sword. The Church and the Jews. A History* by James Carrol, 144. Mariner Books, New York 2001.

- The theologian Augustine's response to the theological dilemma of Judaism's existence.

Paul planted the seeds of a world religion, a fellowship of Jews and gentiles united in their attachment to Jesus. However, most Jews were not interested in his program and strongly resisted his proselytizing. They also did their best to prevent Jewish Christians from bringing Christian ideas into their midst, particularly into their synagogues. The gospels were written in the first century CE, and their anti-Jewish polemic reflected the antagonism between early Pauline Christians and Jews. The canonization of the New Testament between 393 and 397 CE would canonize this anti-Jewish sentiment.

The Gospel of Matthew, for example, contains a long diatribe against Pharisaic (rabbinic) Jews that includes the following sentence: "*You snakes! You brood of vipers! How will you escape being condemned to hell?*" (Matthew 23:33).

The Gospel of John, a later gospel written from a Pauline perspective, mentions Jews 61 times and of these 31 can be considered derogatory. In the following speech by Jesus, Jews were condemned as being from the devil:

> *Jesus said to them [Pharisee Jews], "If God were your Father, you would love me, for I came from God and now I am here. I did not come on my own, but He sent me. . . . You are from your father the devil, and you choose to do your father's desires. He was a murderer from the beginning and does not stand in the truth, because there is no truth in him. When he lies, he speaks according to his own nature, for he is a liar and the father of lies. . . . Whoever is from God hears the words of God. The reason you do not hear them is that you are not from God*" (John 8:42, 44, 47).

It seems highly unlikely that a practicing, albeit liberal, Pharisee such as Jesus would really have said this about other practicing Jews, especially given his emphasis on love of one's fellow man.

Until the time of Constantine, Christians constituted about 10% of the Roman Empire, and Christianity was an underground, and sometimes persecuted, religion while Judaism was an accepted faith. Constantine did not become emperor of the entire Roman Empire until 324 CE, but his Edict of Milan of 313 CE provided official tolerance for Christianity prior to this. Constantine's mother Helena was Christian, although her son was not baptized until shortly before his death. Constantine realized that Christianity could become a unifying force for his empire, and with its hierarchal structure and other-worldly focus he could control it. Its disunity with respect to dogma was an immediate issue, and he resolved this by convening the First Council of Nicaea in 325 CE which established the Nicaea Creed and affirmed the divine nature of Christ as the son of God. All these efforts would put Christianity on an equal footing with Judaism in the Roman Empire and soon on an even higher footing.

Constantine attributed his vision of Jesus' cross as being responsible for his victory at the Milvian Bridge. Subsequently, while preparing for the building of the Church of the Holy Sepulchre in Jerusalem, Helena's workmen discovered the very cross on which Jesus was crucified. The symbol of the cross and Jesus' suffering on it would now become a focus for Christianity. This would result over the millennia in repeated accusations and violence against Jews as having collective guilt in killing Christ.[21] Melito of Sardis (died in 180 CE), a Bishop and highly reputed theologian, proposed that Christ was God and a perfect man at one and the same time. Over the centuries, this has led to Jews being held responsible for attempting to kill God, putting them in the same league as the devil.

Another idea. Hatred of the Jew has arisen not only because of vitriolic texts and the perceived Jewish guilt for the death of Jesus, but also because Christianity and Judaism (and also Islam) have competing messianic goals. These eschatological concepts are not peripheral to these religions' theologies but fundamental to them.

Probably unintentionally, Paul of Tarsus had cooked up a toxic brew in the relationship between Christians and Jews by suggesting that believers in Christ had replaced the Jews as the chosen of God and were participating in a new *Torah of Christ* that would enable them to reach the spiritual Kingdom of God. According to this supersession or replacement theology, the Old Testament had been replaced by the New Testament and had no role in Christianity other than to indicate the roots of God's new covenant with the Christians. Following the destruction of the Jewish Temple, the Bar Kochba Revolt and the Christianization of the Roman Empire, the Jewish Holy Land became a Byzantine Christian country and their former capital

---

21 The Christian accusation against Jews of deicide is usually based on the following statement in the Gospel of Matthew: "*So when Pilate saw that he was gaining nothing, but rather that a riot was beginning, he took water and washed his hands before the crowd, saying, "I am innocent of this man's blood; see to it yourselves." And all the people answered, "His blood be on us and on our children!*" (Matthew 27:24–25). The Second Vatican Council (1962-1965) of the Catholic Church under Pope Paul VI repudiated the collective, multigenerational guilt of Jews in *Nostra aetate*. The Evangelical Lutheran Church in America has similarly negated the guilt of the Jewish people for the death of Jesus.

city a Christian center of worship, all of which confirmed God's choice of the gentile over the Jew.

Despite this, there remained about three million Jews in the Roman Empire who still practiced the very faith deemed irrelevant by Paul and the later gospels. Their faith also remained an attractive alternative to many pagans in the Empire. This left the Church with a theological dilemma: What did the continuing presence of this people rejected by God mean to Christianity, and what should be done about them?

In effect, Christianity had defined itself in reference to Judaism. This meant that Christianity could only feel secure in its role as the chosen of God if Jews remained rejected by God and occupied an inferior position in society. Hence, the answer of the influential bishop, philosopher and theologian Augustine (354–430 CE) was that the Jews should not be exterminated (!), but left to wander the world in a degraded state as witnesses to God's new covenant with Christianity. Since it is not in the nature of Jews to act in this way, this almost guaranteed continuing conflict throughout the centuries. Moreover, this theological dilemma for Christianity has come to a head with the creation of the State of Israel and the apparent announcement by God that He has not forgotten His people.

Nevertheless, to totally understand the full dimensions of the eschatological clash between Judaism and Christianity and their messianic roles in this world, we need to turn to the last book in the New Testament, the Book of Revelation, and the different ways it has been interpreted by Christianity.

THE ESCHATOLOGICAL IMPLICATIONS OF THE BOOK OF REVELATION

The Book of Revelation is the only exclusively eschatological and apocalyptic text in the New Testament, and it has had a considerable influence on Christian eschatology, Christianity's relationship to Judaism and even on the foreign policy of the United States.

Revelation is the last book in the canon of the New Testament for most branches of Christianity. It is not read in the Divine Liturgy of the Eastern Orthodox Church, but is quoted by many of its churches. It uses extravagant and obscure imagery, much of it derived from the Old Testament, such as the books of Daniel, Ezekiel, Psalms and Isaiah, although these books are never directly quoted. From clues within the book, it is commonly dated to the reign of the Roman emperor Domitian (81 to 96 CE). It is thought to have been written by a Jewish Christian prophet named John to comfort other Christians suffering persecution and to critique the emperor worship within the Roman Empire, although this is by no means its only interpretation.[22]

The book opens with a series of visions in which Jesus revealed the future to the author who was a prophet. The prophet then ascended to heaven, saw there the throne of God and was informed about disastrous apocalypses destined to occur on earth. He wrote about a seven-year period of the Great Tribulation during which the Beast or Antichrist, the devil's agent on earth, will try to consolidate his power and hold on other nations. The last three and half years of the Tribulation will be particularly onerous because of God's wrath against the Beast and his agents, who in desperation will oppose each other and the return of Christ. After this Tribulation, Christ will return in glory to earth to usher in 1,000 years of peace and blessing. This period is called the millennium (from the Greek word meaning a thousand).[23] As the Book of Revelation relates:

> Then I saw an angel coming down from heaven, holding in his hand the key to the bottomless pit and a great chain. He seized the dragon, that ancient serpent, who is the Devil and Satan, and bound him for a thousand years, and threw him into the pit, and locked and sealed it over him, so that he would deceive the nations no more, until the thousand years were ended. After that he must be let out for a little while. Then I saw thrones, and those seated on them were given authority to judge. I also saw the souls of those who had been beheaded for their testimony to Jesus and for the word of God. They had not worshiped the beast or its image and had not received its mark on their foreheads or their hands. They came to life and reigned with Christ a thousand years. (The rest of the dead did not come to life until the thousand years were ended.) This is the first resurrection. Blessed and holy are those who share in the first resurrection. Over these the second death has no power, but they will be priests of God and of Christ, and they will reign with him a thousand years (Revelation 20:1-6).

An important issue for Christianity is when and for what purpose Jesus will return to earth. From a literal understanding of these verses, this would seem to be before the 1,000-years. However, under the influence of the early

---

22   Wikipedia. Book of Revelation (https://en.wikipedia.org/wiki/Book_of_Revelation).

23   "Chapter 3, Thy Kingdom Come in Visions of Apocalypse: What Jews, Christians and Muslims Believe About the End Times, and How Those Beliefs Affect Our World" by Robert Leonhard. Strategic Assessments. National Security Analysis Department, 58-59 (https://www.jhuapl.edu/Content/documents/ApocalypseVision.pdf).

church fathers, the eschatological prophecies of the Book of Revelation were interpreted figuratively. According to this interpretation, the symbolism of Revelation relates to a spiritual conflict between heaven and hell. Christ is thought to currently reign in heaven with the saints, and the Kingdom of God represents a spiritual rather than physical or political concept. Hence, the Kingdom of God will not be physically established throughout the "millennium." The Catholic Church also holds that Jesus is currently active on earth through the agency of his Church, and this will lead to continuing improvement in the state of the world.[24] When these ideals have been realized, Christ will appear for the resurrection and final judgment. Hence, there will be no physical apocalypse or defined millennium. These beliefs are termed amillennialism.

Closely related to this is postmillennialism. This view came to the fore during the Reformation when it was held that the pope was the Beast and the prophecies of Revelation related to the struggles of the Church.[25] In this interpretation, Christ will appear after the 1,000 golden years of the millennium, which will be a time of blessing, peace and joy. World history will end with the resurrection and final judgment. These ideas were adopted by many Protestant churches. Nowadays, the differences between postmillennialism and amillennialism are not considered of great consequence, and they are often grouped together when contrasted with premillennialism.

In both amillennialism and postmillennialism, the Jews have been displaced in favor of the Church, and the Christian Church has taken over the Jewish utopian mission described by the Torah and elaborated on in the messianic visions of the prophets of ancient Israel.

In contradistinction to amillennialism and postmillennialism is premillennialism and, in particular, dispensational premillennialism. This takes literally the prophecies of the Book of Revelation and believes that Christ will appear before the millennium and at any time before the appearance of the Antichrist and the seven-year Tribulation. This will be followed by the Battle of Armageddon as foretold in Revelation 11, the resurrection of the dead, the 1,000-years of the golden millennium, and ultimately the final judgment. The dispensational aspect of this belief is its historical progression, in which there is a series of stages in God's self-revelation and plan of salvation.

Dispensational premillennialism had early roots in Christianity but was mainly discarded until more recent times, when it was adopted in the 19th

---

24 Ibid., 67.
25 Ibid., p68.

century by many evangelicals. It has a more pessimistic view of the world than postmillennialism and believes that the world is basically evil. Only the active intervention of Christ will defeat the malignant powers of the world and bring about the golden age.

Premillennialist thinking also assigns Jews a major role in Christian eschatology, by recognizing that Christians and Jews are on separate tracks towards the End of Days and that the prophecies of ancient Israel refer to the Jewish people and not the Church. This includes the notion that the ingathering of Jewish exiles is an important step in the Second Coming of Jesus and the arrival of the Kingdom of God. Dispensationalists believe that Jews are God's chosen people, and there must be Jews living in Israel and the Temple must be rebuilt before Armageddon can occur. Many also hold that Christians should treat Jews favorably in order to receive God's blessing. At the final battle of Armageddon an Antichrist will arise and temporarily occupy the Temple, but he will be defeated by Jesus. Premillennialism assumes a mass conversion to Christianity at the End of Days and believes that those who do not convert are destined for hell. Premillennial eschatology leads to much affection for Jews since Christians and Jews are working together towards common eschatological goals. At least temporarily.

Many postmillennialists, on the other hand, do not assume a mass conversion and regard Jews as doomed.[26]

MILLENNIALISM AND ITS POLITICAL IMPLICATIONS

Leonard Robert is an employee of the US National Security Analysis Department who has noted patterns in American foreign policy that seem to follow a dialectic between postmillennial and premillennial thinking. This dialectic also influences American policy towards Israel. This is because several recent American presidents have been strongly ideological in their Christianity with respect to postmillennial thinking while many in the Republican Party arc cvangclical Christians.

Robert has pointed out that a tenet of postmillennialism is that socially the world is becoming a better place to live in through the agency of the Church and that a natural evolution will lead to the eradication of war, poverty, crime, and disease. This leads to an optimism regarding social planning,

---

26   See Revelation 21:8: "*But the cowardly, the unbelieving, the vile, the murderers, the sexually immoral, those who practice magic arts, the idolaters and all liars — they will be consigned to the fiery lake of burning sulfur. This is the second death.*" Non-believers are destined for the same fate as these other sinners.

although there is awareness that temporary setbacks are inevitable. Idealists also feel that the United States has a central role in bringing democracy, human rights, economic prosperity, and peace to the world. These religious ideas were already part of the thinking of America's Founding Fathers at the beginning of the Republic. Robert summarizes their views as follows:

> *America was the Great Experiment, the last, best hope for the world, a light to all others. Having been chastened concerning religious conflict from the bloody European experience, this nation would embrace no state religion, nor tie itself too closely to any particular creed. But it would, nevertheless, be energized by its own peculiar form of missionary zeal: bringing the light of freedom to a fallen world.*[27]

This way of thinking is very evident from the words of Thomas Jefferson, a Founding Father, the principal author of the Declaration of Independence from Great Britain, and the third president of the United States:

> *The station which we occupy among the nations of the earth is honorable, but awful. Trusted with the destinies of this solitary republic of the world, the only monument of human rights, and the sole depositary of the sacred fire of freedom and self-government, whence it is to be lighted up in other regions of the earth, if other regions of the earth shall ever become suscep-tible of its benign influence.*[28]

In general, amillennial and postmillennial ideas lead to government policies supporting an interventional role in social reform, an international emphasis on human rights, and an optimistic approach to curing poverty, crime, pollution and war. This way of thinking is also highly supportive of an international approach to tackling the world's problems, whether these be global warming or nuclear proliferation. These positions are usually support-ed in America by the Democratic Party.

Premillennial thinking, on the other hand, is more pessimistic about the state of the world, since it recognizes that only Christ can resolve its social ills and create the golden age at his Second Coming. It is more prepared to confront evil, although it recognizes that this produces only a temporary re-spite for freedom. It is also suspicious of internationalism.

---

27   "Political implications, Chapter Three" in *Thy Kingdom Come in Visions of Apocalypse: What Jews, Christians and Muslims Believe about the End Times, and How Those Beliefs Affect Our World* by Robert Leonhard. Strategic Assessments. National Security Analysis Department, 76 (https://www.jhuapl.edu/Content/documents/ApocalypseVision.pdf).

28   Thomas Jefferson, R to A. Citizens of Washington, Washington ed. viii, 157 (1809).

These millennial ideas also influence the support or lack of support that Israel experiences from the American people and its government. The displacement theology of postmillennialism generally leads to no love for Israel, and in particular to a reluctance to support expansive Israeli territorial aims that could be messianic in nature. It can also lead to providing financial and diplomatic support to Israel's enemies, especially when there appear to be issues of human rights.

Premillennial Christian Zionists, on the other hand, tend to support the ingathering of Jewish exiles, control of Judea and Samaria by the Jewish state, and the rebuilding of the Temple (since Revelation 11 foresees a functioning Temple during the time of the Tribulation). Their goodwill and support have been invaluable to the State of Israel from the time of the Balfour Declaration to the present day.

The messianism of the Russian Orthodox Church

The Russian Orthodox Church is the largest of the Eastern Orthodox Churches, and as for the Catholic Church it holds amillennial beliefs. It separated from the Roman Church in the 1400s, and with the fall of Constantinople, the Grand Dukes of Moscow considered themselves heirs of the Byzantine Emperors and a "Third Rome." It claims exclusive jurisdiction over other Eastern Orthodox Christians residing in former member republics of the Soviet Union, other than in Georgia.

Basing himself on the Book of Revelation, Patriarch Krill, the present-day head of the Russian Orthodox Church, holds there is a force holding back the appearance of the antichrist into this world, and views his church as being the force saving Christianity and mankind prior to the imminent Second Coming of Christ. He regards the West as decadent because of its freedoms and liberal democracy, and particularly because of its homosexuality. He is quoted as saying *"The church keeps people from losing their bearings in life. . . . it is the Orthodox faith, living and acting in the Orthodox church – this is the force that holds back (the antichrist)."*[29]

Vladimir Putin, the president of Russia, and his immediate colleagues may hold similar views to Patriarch Krill on matters of religion. A less generous interpretation of the situation is that they are using Patriarch Krill to provide a religious veneer for their imperial aims. As does Krill, Putin bemoans

---

29 "Russian Patriarch says Orthodox faithful are holding back the antichrist," Reuters, April 7, 2022 (https://www.reuters.com/world/europe/russian-patriarch-says-orthodox-faithful-are-holding-back-antichrist-2022-04-07/).

the breakup of the Soviet Union as a result of the policies of perestroika (restructuring) and glasnost (openness) introduced by Mikhail Gorbachev when general secretary of the Communist Party of the Soviet Union and then president. Both recognize the need for a strong autocratic leader able to reverse some of the changes from the 1991 breakup of the Soviet Union. Thus was born a marriage in heaven between Krill and Putin, but hell for Ukrainians and Russian soldiers when Putin unleashed these ideas with tanks and artillery on its neighbor, a neighbor that was increasingly flirting with the West.

For Russia, this invasion has been a lesson in unintended consequences. Ukraine has been driven even deeper into the embrace of the West, while Patriarch Krill has witnessed the breakup of the relationship between his church and the Ukrainian Orthodox Church and their rejection of his messianic ideas.[30]

---

30 "Ukrainian Orthodox Church Breaks With Moscow Over War" by Neil MacFarquhar, in New York Times, May 28, 2022 (https://www.nytimes.com/2022/05/28/world/europe/ukraine-orthodox-church-moscow.html).

Chapter 10

RABBI AKIVA AND THE BAR KOCHBA REVOLT

Rabbi Akiva brought messianism and the hope associated with messianism to the forefront of the Jewish tradition after the destruction of the Second Temple.

However, one finds in Jewish texts almost two sages called Rabbi Akiva. There is the revered and beloved rabbi who systematized the Jewish oral tradition and profoundly influenced the direction of Jewish law after the destruction of the Second Temple. This was the Rabbi Akiva who gave the Jewish people the beginnings of the Mishna and a wealth of *halachic* and aggadic material. In one midrash, he is placed on the same pedestal as Ezra the Scribe, the sage credited with initiating Rabbinic Judaism when prophecy came to an end at the beginning of the Second Temple period.[1]

The other Rabbi Akiva, much less discussed in Jewish religious literature, is the messianic revolutionary. This Rabbi Akiva was the most respected rabbinic leader in Judea in the years preceding the Bar Kochba Revolt against Rome. His encouragement of this revolt and his pronouncing its military leader Shimon ben Kosiba the Messiah were significant factors in the debacle that followed. This revolt led to the decimation of the country and the first steps towards 2,000 years of Jewish exile.

However, I would like to suggest that one cannot split Rabbi Akiva in this way. His messianism, his absolute faith in God and his stretching of religious concepts to their logical limits were an integral part of his personality, his approach to Judaism and his leadership of the Jewish people.

In retrospect, there was little chance that the Bar Kochba Revolt could have succeeded without God's overt intervention. The Romans would never have permitted Judea to become an independent state. Rome was internally stable and faced no external threats, and all the might of its empire was applied to suppressing this revolt. Rome was always brutal with the rebels it defeated. In the end, the country of Judea was left decimated and without Jews.

---

1   *Sifre Deuteronomy* 48.

185

The story of Rabbi Akiva illustrates well one of the two potential hazards associated with messianism. One is inappropriate messianic passivism and the belief that God alone will solve all the problems of the Jewish world. The other is inappropriate messianic activism, exemplified by Rabbi Akiva's revolutionary zeal and his support of the Bar Kochba Revolt. This type of activism is usually associated with complete trust in God and the belief that He will resolve all problems resulting from such activism since the cause is in accord with His will. The mistake in this approach is the presumption that one knows with certainty God's will and His intended direction for Jewish history.

Rabbi Akiva's contribution to Judaism after the destruction of the Second Temple

After the destruction of the Second Temple in 70 CE, the Pharisees found themselves the winners of the dispute regarding the direction of Judaism. The Sadducees, Essenes and Zealots were gone. They had either been killed by the Romans or had become irrelevant after the destruction of the Temple. This placed considerable onus on a small group of rabbis to determine the course of Judaism.

As noted in the previous chapter, Judaism was beset with religious controversies, many of them centered on the Temple. One might even question whether the Jews would have been able to survive as a unified people in this situation since there was no room for compromise among any of these groups. Pharisaic Judaism, on the other hand, had the means of regulating its disagreements through majority rule among the sages. One could well say that there was a guiding hand to Second Temple history that ensured the survival of a single form of Judaism – although its cost was high.

During the siege of Jerusalem during the Great Revolt, the Pharisee Rabban Yochanan ben Zakhai requested permission from the Roman general Titus to leave the city and open a religious center in Yavne on the coastal plain. This city functioned almost as a refugee camp for displaced Jews. The Pharisees had split from the Zealots and Sadducees and were the peace camp during the Great Revolt. Their request was granted as Titus saw this struggle as being against extremists and not against the Jewish people. Among ben Zakhai's five main disciples were Rabbi Eliezer ben Hyrcanus and Rabbi Yehoshua ben Chananyah, and both would become major players in the subsequent strengthening of Judaism.[2]

---

2   "Five disciples" in *The Story of the Jews in the Classical Era 350 BCE-750 CE* by Berel Wein,

The challenges facing these sages were considerable. Judaism needed to be reinvented from a religion whose focus was the Temple to a religion of practice of Jewish law and Torah study. Prayer and vitalization of the synagogue would become a substitute for the sacrificial cult, although the rituals of the Temple would be documented for future generations and the memory of the Temple kept alive by new decrees. People also had to accept this program, which meant that the rabbis at Yavne had to disseminate a love of Judaism and its laws by outreach and by establishing new centers of Jewish learning.

After two years, Rabban Gamaliel II was brought to Yavne as head of its Sanhedrin (the supreme religious body). He was a descendent of the great sage Hillel and had the prestige necessary for making the Sanhedrin at Yavne the definitive voice for the direction of halacha. The path was not an easy one, and *halachic* and even personal disputes (although all for the sake of heaven) are recorded in the *halachic* and midrashic literature.

Rabbi Akiva was born in about 50 CE, approximately 20 years before the destruction of Jerusalem.[3] It can be surmised from midrashic sources that his parents were poor and uneducated. He received no traditional religious education. However, living in Lod, not far from Yavne, he was exposed to the programs of the sages and was attracted to them. His initiation into Torah learning is described in a midrash:

> *What were Rabbi Akiva's beginnings? It is said: When he was 40 years old he had not yet studied a thing. One time he stood by the mouth of a well. "Who hollowed out this stone?" he wondered. He was told: "It is the water which falls upon it every day continually." . . . Thereupon Rabbi Akiva drew an inference with regard to himself: "If that which is soft wears down that which is hard, then all the more so shall words of Torah which are as hard as iron hollow out my heart which is flesh and blood!" Thereupon he turned to the study of Torah. He went with his son and they appeared before an elementary teacher. Rabbi Akiva said to him: "Master, teach me Torah." Rabbi Akiva took hold of one end of the tablet and his son took the other end. The teacher wrote aleph bet [the beginning of the Hebrew alphabet] and he learned it; aleph tav [the letter tav being the end of the*

181. Shaar Press 1996.

3   "Akiva's Early Life" in *Akiva. Life, Legend, Legacy* by Reuven Hammer. The Jewish Publication Society, University of Nebraska Press, Lincoln, 2015. The author makes this estimation based on the approximate year that Rabbi Akiva died and about how old he would have been when he died.

alphabet] and he learned it; the Book of Leviticus and he learnt it. He continued studying until he learnt the whole Torah.[4]

Akiva's primary teachers were the two distinguished disciples of Rabban Yochanan ben Zakhai, Rabbi Eliezer ben Hyrcanus and Rabbi Yehoshua ben Chananyah. The former was now the head of the Beis HaVaad in Yavne that formulated policy and *halachic* decisions.[5] Akiva also studied under Rabban Gamaliel II when Rabban Yochanan ben Zakhai left Yavne and Rabban Gamaliel II took over as head of the Sanhedrin. Rabbi Akiva remained especially close to Rabbi Yehoshua who ordained him and introduced him to mystical teachings.[6] Following his ordination, Rabbi Akiva established his own yeshiva in Bnei Brak, not far from his home town.

Rabbi Akiva produced no written systematic theology. However, in his mind he undoubtedly had one and it is possible to piece it together from his sayings as cited in the Jerusalem and Babylonian Talmud and midrashim, recognizing that with the passage of time some of these stories may have become embellished with additional and not necessarily accurate layers of detail and interpretation. The Babylonian Talmud was completed almost 400 years after Rabbi Akiva's death.

Ideas that influenced his approach to Torah interpretation as well as his messianism included the following:

(i). The Torah is from heaven

The expression "Torah from heaven" (in Hebrew - *Torah min hashomayim*) usually signifies the notion that the Torah is God-given. However, Rabbi Akiva took this a step further by suggesting that Moses reached into the heavens to receive the Torah, implying that the Torah already existed in heaven before it was handed over on Mount Sinai. This meant to Rabbi Akiva that not a word or letter of the Torah is extraneous and each has meaning. Not all his colleagues accepted this. Rabbi Ishmael, the author of the midrash *Mechilta d'Rabbi Ishmael* and with whom Rabbi Akiva had many debates, was of the opinion that the Torah speaks in the language of man and there needs to be leeway in interpreting its language. Jewish tradition recorded both views, although the interpretations of Rabbi Akiva gained more traction in the *halachic*

---

4   *Avot deRabbi Natan, recension A*, Chapter 6. Quoted in "Rabbi Akiva's Early Years" in *The Sages: Character, Context and Creativity. Volume II: from Yavneh to the Bar Kokhba Revolt*, by Binyamin Lau, 191. Maggid Books, Koren Publishers Jerusalem, 2011.

5   "The Leadership in Yavne" in *The Story of the Jews in the Classical Era 350 BCE-750 CE* by Berel Wein, 184. Shaar Press, 1996.

6   TY Sanhedrin 1:2.

and aggadic literature. The fact that he and his students were responsible for collecting much of the material that made its way into the Mishna and midrashim could be partially responsible for this.

(ii). The importance of the Oral Law

An important stance of the sages was that the Oral Law has equal standing with the Written Torah. Because he began his Torah learning late in life, Rabbi Akiva appreciated the challenges involved in assimilating all the material comprising the Oral Law, which at that time existed mainly as oral bites of information. He therefore spent considerable time collecting and systematically arranging this material. As the Jerusalem Talmud informs us:

> It is Rabbi Akiva who systemized the midrash, laws and aggadot [non-legal material]. There are those who say this was done by the men of the Great Assembly. What Rabbi Akiva did was to institute general and specific rules.[7]

How he did this is related in the following talmudic passage:

> When Rabbi Akiva would systemize laws for his students, he would say: "If anyone has heard some reasonable argument against his fellow student, let him come forth and tell it."[8]

Rabbi Akiva's principal disciples did much of the work of collecting and arranging this material, although it was reviewed by him before being included in his volumes. Arranged by topic, it constituted an early form of the Mishna and *Tosefta* (a source of supplementary *halachic* and aggadic traditions), and this was used by Rabbi Yehuda HaNasi when he arranged the final form of the Mishna.[9] When arranged according to the order of the Biblical text, it formed the *halachic* midrashim, the *Sifra* and *Sifrei*.

> For Rabbi Yochanan said: An anonymous Mishna [generally reflects the view of] Rabbi Meir, and anonymous Tosefta R' Nechemia, and anonymous Sifra Rabbi' Yehuda, and anonymous Sifrei Rabbi Shimon, and all these [Tannaim stated their opinions] based on Rabbi Akiva.[10]

---

7   TY Shekalim 5:1.
8   *Tosefta Zavim* 1:5. Quoted in "The Organizer of Torah" in *Akiva. Life, Legend, Legacy* by Reuven Hammer, 79. The Jewish Publication Society, University of Nebraska Press, Lincoln, 2015.
9   The Mishna was completed by Rabbi Yehuda HaNassi. The *Tosefta* is a compilation of Oral Law that was not included in the Mishna.
10   TB Sanhedrin 86a.

(iii). Everything that God does is for the good

One facet of Rabbi Akiva's awareness of the immanence of God was his belief that everything God does is for the best, a concept he absorbed from one of his teachers, Nachum Ish Gamzu. This is illustrated in the Talmud with the following well-known story told within the context of a discussion about accepting misfortunes with recognition of the goodness of God:

> *Rav Huna said that Rav said that Rabbi Meir said; and so it was taught in a baraita in the name of Rabbi Akiva: One must always accustom oneself to say: Everything that God does, He does for the best. [The Gemara relates]: Like this incident, when Rabbi Akiva was walking along the road and came to a certain city, he inquired about lodging and they did not give him any. He said: "Everything that God does, He does for the best." He went and slept in a field, and he had with him a rooster, a donkey and a candle. A gust of wind came and extinguished the candle; a cat came and ate the rooster; and a lion came and ate the donkey. He said: "Everything that God does, He does for the best". That night, an army came and took the city into captivity. [It turned out that Rabbi Akiva alone, who was not in the city and had no lit candle, noisy rooster or donkey to give away his location, was saved]. He said to them: "Didn't I tell you? Everything that God does, He does for the best."[11]*

If the lamp had been lit, the soldiers would have discovered him; likewise had the donkey brayed or the rooster crowed they would have heard the noise and made efforts to capture him. One can speculate that this episode happened when Rabbi Akiva was hiding from the Romans during the Bar Kochba Revolt. The inhabitants of the city would have been reluctant to host him because of the consequences if the Romans discovered they had concealed him.

The notion that everything God does is for the good relates to Rabbi Akiva's belief in the immanence of God, to his belief that God has a direct hand in all that transpires on earth, to his trust in God, and his conviction that Divine providence is able to overcome all obstacles. These ideas will also drive his messianic activism.

---

11   TB Berackot 60b. The basis for this discussion is the Mishna on 54a which states that *"A person is obligated to bless [God] for the bad just as he blesses [God] for the good."*

THE MYSTIC ACTIVITIES OF RABBI AKIVA AND HIS COLLEAGUES

Rabbi Akiva and a number of his colleagues engaged in mystic activities similar to those of the prophets. The forefathers had experienced visions of aspects of God. Moses, Aaron and his sons Nadab and Abihu, and the 70 elders saw "*the God of Israel*" after the Ten Commandments were given (Exodus 24:10). Moses requested to see God after the sin of the golden calf but was only permitted to catch a glimpse of the "*back of God*" (Exodus 33:23). Isaiah described a heavenly vision at the beginning of his mission, during which he saw God on His throne (Isaiah 6:1-3). Ezekiel provided an even more graphic vision of God in heaven, which is termed by the Rabbis *ma'ase merkava* (Work of the Chariot) (Ezekiel 1:4-28). This was the vision most studied by the sages.

The Talmud records that Rabbi Yochanan ben Zakhai engaged in mystical teachings and passed this knowledge on to his disciples. Rabbi Yehoshua, Rabbi Akiva's teacher and associate in Yavne, passed it on to Rabbi Akiva who in turn conveyed it to some of his students.

The first stage in a mystical experience was for the teacher to relate to an individual student the details of Ezekiel's vision. In an episode described in the Talmud, a student requested Rabban Yochanan ben Zakai to teach him a chapter from *ma'ase merkava*. The Talmud described that as he was doing this, fire descended from heaven, (presumably the same fire as in Ezekiel's vision), trees sang in praise of God, and angels from the fire confirmed that these sages were truly experiencing a *ma'ase merkava* experience.[12] Because of the nature of these experiences, these discussions were never in groups and were limited to students possessing the necessary discernment.

As mentioned, many of Rabbi Akiva's intellectual endeavors were about pushing concepts to their acceptable limits, and it is perhaps not surprising that Rabbi Akiva wished to draw as close to God as humanly possible. In the following passage, Rabbi Akiva and his colleagues attempted to enter the *pardes*. The Hebrew word *pardes* means orchard, but also has the meaning of "*Paradise*" (this is also the source of the English word). The following account is told in a number of places:

> *The Sages taught: Four entered the orchard [pardes], [i.e., dealt with the loftiest secrets of Torah], and they are as follows: Ben Azzai; and ben Zoma; Aher, [the other, a name for Elisha ben Avuya]; and Rabbi Akiva.*

---

12   TB Hagigah 14b.

Rabbi Akiva, [the senior among them], said to them: "When, upon your arrival in the upper worlds, you reach pure marble stones, do not say: Water, water, although they appear to be water, because it is stated: 'He who speaks falsehood shall not be established before My eyes'" (Psalms 101:7). [The Gemara proceeds to relate what happened to each of them]: Ben Azzai glimpsed at the Divine Presence and died. And with regard to him the verse states: "Precious in the eyes of the Lord is the death of His pious ones" (Psalms 116:15). Ben Zoma glimpsed at the Divine Presence and was harmed, [i.e., he lost his mind]. And with regard to him the verse states: "Have you found honey? Eat as much as is sufficient for you, lest you become full from it and vomit it" (Proverbs 25:16). Aher chopped down the shoots of saplings. [In other words, he became a heretic]. Rabbi Akiva came out safely.[13]

There is no doubt that the sages engaged in these mystical practices. What is not clear is why they did so, given the attendant risks. For the prophets Isaiah and Ezekiel, these visions established their prophetic credentials, but there is no suggestion from any source that Rabbi Akiva and others were attempting to engage in a prophetic experience.

A possible answer may relate to the immanence of God already felt by Rabbi Akiva and his colleagues. They perceived God's presence through His Torah, its laws and His engagement with their lives and they now wished for an even closer relationship with the Divine. It is interesting that an attempt to reach into the realm of the angels is included to this day in Jewish daily morning prayer.

RABBI AKIVA'S MESSIANISM

Rabbi Akiva was an influential figure in directing the thoughts of his colleagues towards messianism. This is evident from the following passage quoted in the Talmud and in a midrash:

On another occasion they [i.e., Rabban Gameliel, Rabbi Elazar ben Azariah, Rabbi Yehoshua and Rabbi Akiva] were ascending to Jerusalem after the destruction of the Temple. When they arrived at Mount Scopus and saw the site of the Temple, they rent their garments [in mourning, in keeping with halachic practice]. When they arrived at the Temple Mount, they saw a fox that emerged from the site of the Holy of Holies. They began

---

13   TB Hagigah 14b.

weeping, and Rabbi Akiva was laughing. They said to him: "For what reason are you laughing?" Rabbi Akiva said to them: "For what reason are you weeping?" They said to him: "This is the place concerning which it is written: 'And the non-priest who approaches shall die' (Numbers 1:51), and now foxes walk in it; and shall we not weep?" Rabbi Akiva said to them: "That is why I am laughing, as it is written, when God revealed the future to the prophet Isaiah: 'And I will take to Me faithful witnesses to attest: Uriah the priest, and Zechariah the son of Jeberechiah' (Isaiah 8:2). Now what is the connection between Uriah and Zechariah? [He clarifies the difficulty]: Uriah prophesied during the First Temple period, and Zechariah prophesied during the Second Temple period, as he was among those who returned to Zion from Babylonia. Rather, the verse established that fulfillment of the prophecy of Zechariah is dependent on fulfillment of the prophecy of Uriah. In the prophecy of Uriah it is written: 'Therefore, for your sake Zion shall be plowed as a field, and Jerusalem shall become rubble, and the Temple Mount as the high places of a forest' (Micah 3:12), [where foxes are found]. [There is a rabbinic tradition that this was prophesied by Uriah]. In the prophecy of Zechariah it is written: 'There shall yet be elderly men and elderly women sitting in the streets of Jerusalem' (Zechariah 8:4). Until the prophecy of Uriah [with regard to the destruction of the city] was fulfilled I was afraid that the prophecy of Zechariah would not be fulfilled, [as the two prophecies are linked]. Now that the prophecy of Uriah was fulfilled, it is evident that the prophecy of Zechariah remains valid." [The Gemara adds]: The Sages said to him, employing this formulation: "Akiva, you have comforted us; Akiva, you have comforted us."[14]

Another indication that Rabbi Akiva's colleagues sympathized with his messianic ideas is seen in the following *Tosefta* which discusses the requirement to recite the *Shema* at night. The *Shema* is one of the most important prayers in Judaism, and amongst other topics it contains the requirement for every individual to mention the Exodus from Egypt. The first paragraph of this *Tosefta* is also found in the Passover *Haggadah*, which is recited on the eve of Passover. Although only marginally related to Passover, it may have

---

14   TB Makkot 24b and *Sifre Deuteronomy* 43. The sages of that time knew the Bible backwards. In all of Scripture there is no such prophecy uttered by a prophet called Uriah. This prophecy was uttered by Micah. However, as Tosefos points out, in Jeremiah Chapter 26 it is mentioned that another prophet besides Micah, named Uriah, made such a prophecy. Uriah's prophecy had been fulfilled in that Jerusalem was then like heaps of rubble.

been included in the *Haggadah* because of its messianic message. The two sages mentioned in this passage are ben Zoma, who had not yet received his ordination and Rabbi Elazar ben Azarya, who had been appointed head of the Sanhedrin as a replacement for Rabban Gameliel II. Rabban Gameliel II had been deposed because of his autocratic behavior in attempting to maintain the authority of the Sanhedrin (although he would later be reinstated in a joint appointment). Rabbi Akiva would doubtless have participated in the following discussion as one of the sages:

> We mention the Exodus from Egypt at night. Rabbi Elazar ben Azarya said: "Behold I am about 70 years old and I never merited that the Exodus from Egypt should be mentioned at night, until ben Zoma explained it from a verse: 'In order that you may remember the day you left Egypt all the days of your life' (Deuteronomy 16:3). 'The days of your life' refers to the days. 'All the days of your life' refers to the nights." But the sages say: "'The days of your life' refer to this world. 'All the days of your life' refer to the messianic age."

> Ben Zoma said to them: "But does one mention [at all] the Exodus from Egypt in the messianic age? For has it not already been said: 'Assuredly the time is coming,' declares the Lord, 'when it shall be no more said: "As the Lord lives who brought out the Israelites out of the land of Egypt," but rather, 'As the Lord lives who brought the Israelites out of the northland' [Jeremiah 16:14-15).

> They said to him: "It is not that the mention of the Exodus will be removed from its place [in the liturgy], but that the Exodus from Egypt will be [mentioned] in addition to sovereignty (malchi'ot). Sovereignty (malchi'ot) will be primary, and the Exodus from Egypt will be secondary."[15]

This may have been more than just a theoretical discussion as anticipation of the approach of the messianic age could have been present among the sages. However, given the political situation, they were probably treading a fine line in their discussion of "*sovereignty.*" Did they mean Jewish sovereignty as opposed to Roman sovereignty, or the sovereignty of God versus that of the Romans? It is unclear from this passage, although it might have made little difference to the Romans, and probably to the sages as well. It will be recalled

---

15   *Tosefta,* Berakhot 1:10. The first paragraph of this passage is also mentioned in Mishna Berokhot 1:15.

that at this time the Jewish people were living in their own land but had no sovereignty and no Temple.

Another example. During the Passover service in Temple times, paschal lambs were slaughtered in the Temple during the day and roasted in groups in the evening. During this barbecue, there would have been some narrative and discussion as to the significance of this sacrifice. With the destruction of the Temple, paschal lambs were no longer part of this ritual, and it was now up to the sages to formulate a ceremony and narrative in their stead. The following *Tosefta*, which is not in the *Haggadah*, explains how Rabban Gameliel II, the head of the Sanhedrin, celebrated his Passover night and the topics he felt appropriate for discussion:

> *Once Rabban Gameliel and the elders were reclining in the house of Boethus ben Zonin in Lod, and they were occupied in studying the laws of Passover all that night, until the cock crowed. They lifted the table, made themselves ready and went to the house of study [to pray].*[16]

Rabbi Akiva's yeshiva was in Bnei Brak, where he was the chief rabbi. He also arranged a Passover service to which his colleagues were invited and, as can be seen from the following text (which is included in the *Haggada*), the themes of the evening's discussions were very different from those of Rabban Gameliel II. It is also noticeable that Rabban Gameliel was not one of his guests. One might even speculate that Rabban Gameliel might not have been enthusiastic about the topics he thought might be discussed at this gathering:

> *It happened that Rabbi Eliezer, Rabbi Joshua, Rabbi Elazar the son of Azariah, Rabbi Akiva, and Rabbi Tarfon sat all night in Bnei Brak telling*

---

16 *Tosefta Pesahim* 10:12. The practice of spending the night studying the laws of Passover and vicariously recreating the Paschal lamb meal by studying its laws has Biblical support, as the following midrash points out: *"And so we find that there are four sons: One who is wise, one who is wicked, one who is simple, and one who does not know how to ask. What does the wise child say: 'What are the testimonies, the statutes, and the laws which the Lord our God has commanded you?' (Deuteronomy 6:20). . . . . Rabbi Eliezer says: 'From where do we know that if there was a group of sages or students, they are required to engage in the study of the laws of Passover until midnight? Because it says: "What are the testimonies, the statutes, and the laws which the Lord our God has commanded you?" ' "* (Deuteronomy 6:20) (*Mechilta deRabbi Yishmael* Bo 18). This opinion is reflected in the *Haggadah* with the paragraphs before the meal that begin with the words, *"Rabban Gameliel used to say: 'Whoever does not discuss three things on Passover has not kept {the Seder) properly. They are the Passover lamb, the matzah and the bitter herbs. Our forefathers ate the Passover lamb long ago.' "*

the story of the going out from Egypt, until their students came to tell them that it was time for the recitation of the morning Shema.[17]

But what exactly did these sages talk about? It would certainly have included the Biblical narrative about the Exodus and its midrashic-like explanations, examples of which are found in the present-day *Haggadah*.[18] One explanation proposed is that they were discussing preparations for the Bar Kochba Revolt. However, this is far too speculative an explanation. There is no evidence that this was even in the planning stage at this time. Nevertheless, Rabbi Akiva's seder would have provided him a platform to discuss his view that the Passover night was an appropriate time for not only discussing the past exodus from Egypt but also the future redemption, a redemption he anticipated would be messianic.

A discussion regarding this is found in the following Mishna:

And he concluded with the redemption. Rabbi Tarfon says: "Who has redeemed us and redeemed our ancestors from Egypt," and he would not go any further. Rabbi Akiva says "So may the Lord our God and the God of our ancestors bring us to future festivals and pilgrimages."[18]

Rabbi Akiva's ideas prevailed. This is the reason that the end of the *Haggadah* narrative (the *Maggid* in Hebrew) concludes with his messianic hopes:

Blessed are you God, King of the universe, Who redeemed us and redeemed our fathers from Egypt and brought on us on this night to eat matzah and bitter herbs. So may the Lord our God and God of our fathers bring us to future festivals and holidays that may come to us in peace, when we shall rejoice in the rebuilding of Your city and shall be joyful in Your Temple service; and there we shall partake of the sacrifices and Pesach offerings.[19]

Through a passage such as this the *Haggadah* narrative has become not only a ceremony celebrating a central event in Jewish history, but also one that incorporates the certainty of a future messianic redemption.

This would have been exactly as Rabbi Akiva intended.

---

17 The Passover *Haggadah*. This section is preceded by the paragraph *"We were slave to Pharaoh in Egypt. . . . "*

18 Mishna Pesachim 10:6.

19 The Passover *Haggadah*.

RABBI AKIBA AND THE BAR KOCHBA REVOLT

The Bar Kochba Revolt began in about 132 CE, but the precipitating factors for it had been building up long before.

In 70 CE Vespasian's son Titus finished the job begun by his father and conquered Jerusalem and destroyed the Temple. He became emperor of Rome after his father, but reigned for only two years before being assassinated, probably by his brother Domitian who succeeded him as emperor. Domitian was no lover of the Jews. Nevertheless, his reign led to a period of political stability in the empire and Rabban Gameliel's leadership was able to flourish in Yavne.

Domitian's rule was followed by that of the emperor Nerva, who was far more sympathetic to the Jewish people. He relaxed decrees made against them, including the special Jew tax, and conversion to Judaism was no longer considered a crime. He reigned for only two years and was followed by the warrior Trajan, who reversed Nerva's favorable Jewish policies and attempted to crush Jewish religious life. He deposed Agrippa II, the great grandson of Herod the Great and Miriam, as ruler of the Galilee and placed this part of the country under direct Roman rule. The yeshiva at Yavne was also forcibly disbanded. Rabban Gameliel II escaped to Lod, and it is from here that he and Rabbi Tarfon, Rabbi Elazar ben Azaryah, Rabbi Yehoshua, and Rabbi Akiva led the Jewish people. Trajan also mercilessly put down Jewish uprisings in Turkey, Iraq, Syria, Egypt, Libya, and Cyprus, leading to the decimation of some of these communities and the death of hundreds of thousands of Jews.

Trajan's main general and adopted son Hadrian came to power in 117 CE. He gave the initial impression that he was prepared to relax the campaign against Judaism and even rebuild the Temple and repair the walls of Jerusalem. The Sanhedrin was able to reconvene in Usha in the Galilee at this time under the leadership of Rabbi Akiva. However, when Hadrian realized the enthusiasm he had generated for rebuilding the Temple, he reversed his position and became even tougher than Trajan had been in his persecution of Judaism.

Hadrian spent two years in Israel and during this time he banned circumcision, Sabbath observance, public prayer, ritual purity, and other rituals.[20] The straw that may have broken the camel's back for the Jews were his decisions to rebuild Jerusalem as a Roman city that would be called Aelia Capitolina and to place a temple to Jupiter in the area of the Holy Temple.

---

20   TB Bava Basra 60b. A circumcision was announced by the grinding of a millstone (TB Sanhedrin 32b).

This could have been an attempt by Hadrian to remake Jerusalem a part of his enlightened Roman empire, but the people of Judea did not perceive his decision in the same light.[21] When Hadrian left the country, the Jews prepared for guerilla warfare and began digging extensive cave systems within their settlements for hiding. These systems still exist today.

Why was there such wrath against the Jewish people and their religion throughout the Roman Empire? Historic records provide few hints. Nevertheless, a mutual hatred seems to have developed between Rome and the Jews. A number of explanations have been proposed for this. The events of the Great Revolt did not engender positive feelings on either side. The Jews of Babylon took the side of the Parthians when Trajan unsuccessfully raided Mesopotamia. The Jews refused to adopt the Roman-Hellenistic culture of the Roman Empire. There were numerous converts to Judaism within the empire, and this was regarded as a threat by the Roman leadership. The Jews were considered uncivilized by Romans. Messianic feelings were prevalent in the Jewish population. Hatred of the Jewish religion was not a feature of the pagan world since their empires were able to tolerate multiple gods, but Jewish messianism was a different matter, as its political goals were a threat to Roman interests. The Jews also despised the Romans as pagans and occupiers, and considered them as natural foes of the Jewish people as descendants of Esau.

Rabbi Akiva was now elderly. His former colleagues, Rabbi Yehoshua, Rabbi Elazar ben Azaryeh, Rabbi Tarfon, Rabbi Yishmael, and Rabban Gameliel II, who might have opposed or at least tempered his decisions were no longer alive, and there were no other sages of sufficient stature to counter his enthusiasm for revolution.

The commander of the Jewish forces was a fearless individual called Shimon ben Kosiba. Rabbi Akiva saw him as God's response to his hopes and teachings about a messianic redeemer, and he crowned him the King Messiah by renaming him Bar Kochba (Son of the Star):

> *Rabbi Shimon bar Yohai taught: Akiva, my master, would interpret the following verse "A star has arisen from Jacob." (Numbers 24:17). Rabbi Akiva, when he saw Bar Kochba would say: "This is the King Messiah."*[22]

---

21   "Jerusalem as 'Aelia Capitolinia': Historical and Political Background" in *The Sages: Character, Context and Creativity. Volume II. From Yavneh to the Bar Kokhba Revolt* by Binyamin Lau, 327. Koren Publishers Jerusalem, 2011.

22   Rabbi Binyamin Lau discusses the notion that Rabbi Akiva may have believed that there would be two messiahs, one with physical attributes and the other with more spiritual ones, and Bar Kochba would have been the physical messiah, or the Messiah Son of Joseph (TB Succah 51a), in "A Star has Arisen from Jacob: The Debate between Rabbi Akiva and the

However, it was not only Rabbi Akiva who was thinking in such terms, but much of the country was fired up with messianic fervor. Nevertheless, there was opposition to Rabbi Akiva's ideas: "*When Akiva would see Bar Kochba, he would say: 'This is the King Messiah.' [And then] Rabbi Johanan ben Torta would tell him: 'Akiva, grass shall grow from your cheeks and yet the son of David shall not appear.' "*[22] This opposition was seemingly ineffective.

However, at an early stage of this revolt Rabbi Akiva should have had concerns about the type of Messiah he had crowned: "*When he [Bar Kochba] would go to war he would say: 'Master of the Universe, do not help and do not hinder us! Is it not You, O God, who has forsaken us? Do not go forth, O God, with our legions'" (Psalm 60:12).*[23]

As during the early stages of the Great Revolt, the Roman army was unprepared for conflict, and Bar Kochba's forces were able to wipe out an entire Roman legion. For 30 months the country was independent with its own administration and even its own coinage. This was seen by Rome as a threat to the integrity of its entire empire. The might of Rome was now brought to bear on Judea, and tens of thousands of reinforcements were brought into the country. Rather than wait to be attacked by guerilla forces, Rome's tactic was to destroy each town and village one by one and to completely decimate the country of Judea. As the Roman historian Dio Cassius recorded:

> *Fifty of their most important outposts and 985 of their most famous villages were razed to the ground. 580,000 men were slain in the various raids and battles, and the number of those that perished by famine, disease and fire was past finding out. Thus, nearly the whole of Judea was made desolate.*[24]

Belatedly, Rabbi Akiva and his colleagues realized that Bar Kochba was not the Messiah they were awaiting. Bar Kochba and his forces were finally besieged in the fortified city of Beitar. The city fell on the Ninth of Av in about 135 CE, and the hundreds of thousands of people inside the city were massacred.

---

sages about the Leadership of Bar Kokhba" in *The Sages: Character, Context and Creativity. Volume II. From Yavneh to the Bar Kokhba Revolt* by Binyamin Lau, 342. Koren Publishers, Jerusalem, 2011. That there was opposition to Rabbi Akiva's position is evident from TY Ta'anit 4:5. However, no sage of that generation had the prestige and authority of Rabbi Akiva to successfully oppose him. A verse from Numbers 24:17 states that "*a star shall step forth from Jacob.*" However, this prophecy by the prophet Balaam is considered by many to refer to King David.

23 YT Ta'anit 4:5. Bar Kochba took this quotation from Psalms out of context, in that the Talmud considered it a rhetorical question (TB Gittin 57a).

24 Dio Cassius, *Roman History*, Book 69.

Rabbi Akiva was imprisoned sometime during the revolt. The sources are unclear, but it was probably at an early stage of the revolt, and he could have been incarcerated for up to three years.[25] The Romans would have found it difficult to execute him since he was not actively involved in the revolt, but they would have been aware of his influence. Twenty-four thousand of his students died in the revolt.[26] Despite being incarcerated, he continued to teach Torah and was finally condemned to death. The hour of his execution in the hippodrome in Caesarea was the time for saying the *Shema* prayer, in which Jews accept upon themselves the yoke of heaven. Rabbi Akiva drew out the word *One*, referring to God, and died a martyr's death while his flesh was being torn apart with iron combs, a particularly gruesome form of Roman torture.[27]

In conclusion, Rabbi Akiva had complete trust in God and a belief that everything that God does is for the best.[11] However, transferring this faith from an individual to the political level and dragging an entire country into the consequences of this belief was hazardous, especially when his faith transcended the limits of logic. The messianic activism of a religious leader such as Rabbi Akiva was particularly perilous because his influence over the people was so great.

The Bar Kochba Revolt was a sobering experience for the Jewish people, and this type of messianic activism will not be promoted in later Jewish texts such as the Talmud. The passivism of the Talmud is exemplified by its description of the "three oaths." According to this tradition, God imposed three oaths: two on the Jewish people not to go en masse to the Land of Israel and not to rebel against the nations of the world and one on the non-Jewish nations not to oppress Israel overmuch.[28]

From this time on, many sages will believe that the next Jewish redemption will be messianic, supernatural, and totally in God's hands. On the other

---

25 *Tosefta Sanhedrin* 2:8. This *Tosefta*, whose topic is the intercalation of the year, mentions that Rabbi Akiva was in prison for three years.

26 Rabbi Berel Wein offers the (not original) opinion in "Rabbi Akiva and the Aftermath of Bar Kochba's Defeat" in his book *The Story of the Jews in the Classical Era 350 BCE-750 CE*, 214. Shaar Press, 1996 that this is the basis for the period of semi-mourning that Jews observe between the holidays of Passover and Shavuot. This reason for their death is not explicitly mentioned in any Jewish source, but their participation in the Bar Kochba Revolt is recognized as a strong possibility.

27 TY Berachot 9:7, TY Sotah 5:7 and TB Berachot 61b.

28 TB Ketubot 111a and *Shir Hashirim Rabba* 2:7. The three oaths are based on three verses from the Song of Songs describing the intense love between God and the Jewish people that existed in earlier times and will exist again in messianic times. See also Maimonides in his *Iggeres Taiman* with reference to violation of the oaths via false messiahs.

hand, the influential medieval philosopher and *halachist* Maimonides will note Rabbi Akiva's lack of expectation of a miraculous salvation to support his view that the future messianic era will be a natural one.[29] Rabbi Akiva's messianic expectations were not for an upending of the laws of nature and the end of the world as we know it. Rather, his hopes were related primarily to achieving independence from Rome and rebuilding the Temple.

The longing for the era of redemption will continue to be part of the Jewish tradition. Because of Rabbi Akiva's students, this anticipation made its way into primary Jewish texts. The Passover night was always a celebration of the Exodus from Egypt, but because of the expectations of Rabbi Akiva and his colleagues this night also became a celebration of the hope for future redemption.

Despite the tragedy of the Bar Kochba Revolt, one might say that in the grand scheme of history all of Rabbi Akiva's efforts did turn out for the good. Rather than being a preparation for the messianic era, his efforts constructing the links in the chain of tradition were a necessary preparation for 2,000 years of exile. His development of the Oral Law kept and continues to keep Jews together as a people. His sayings expressing his hopes for redemption and religious independence were instrumental in combating despair and keeping alive the expectation of a future redemption.

---

29   Maimonides, *Mishna Torah*, the Laws of Kings and their Wars, 11:3. Maimonides writes: "*One should not presume that the Messianic King must work miracles and wonders, bring about new creations within the world, resurrect the dead, or perform similar deeds. This is [definitely] not true. [Proof may be brought from the fact] that Rabbi Akiva, one of the greatest sages of the Mishna, was one of the supporters of King Bar Kozibah [named Bar Kochba by R'Akiva] and would describe him as the Messianic King. . . . The Sages did not ask him for any signs or wonders.*"

Chapter 11

MUHAMMAD AND THE JEWS

Muhammad was in his usual cave on Mount Hira overlooking the city of Mecca and doing what he usually did in this cave – thinking and planning.

Seven years ago, he had received his first communication from Allah in this very place. This revelation conferred on him the status of prophet of God. He was now in the same league as Moses and Jesus. After further revelations, he would become convinced that the revelations he was receiving were even more authentic than those received by these other prophets.

He had been designated by Allah to bring knowledge of the one true God to his countrymen and guide them on leading ethical lives. The Arabian Peninsula would cease being a pagan country. Instead, its people would be united in serving Allah by praying to Him at fixed times, giving charity and caring for the widow and orphan. Muhammad was an orphan, and he knew what it was like to be dependent on the goodness of others.

He had made good progress in his proselytizing. He was a forceful speaker and convincing leader. He had a group of devoted followers in Mecca. Nevertheless, he could feel the antagonism of the leaders of the city. They were fearful of him: that he would take over the Kaaba, their holy shrine; that he would control the trade resulting from the annual pilgrimage; and that he would interfere with how they ran their lives. They were right of course. One day he would do all this. But not yet. He was not powerful enough.

It would only be a matter of time before he would have to leave Mecca and establish a base elsewhere. He had been planning for this. He would move to the oasis of Yathrib where he had a group of influential converts and supporters.

Eventually, he would return to Mecca.

MUHAMMAD – FROM MECCA TO MEDINA AND BACK

Muhammad (570-632 CE) was born in Mecca, the main city of the Arabian Peninsula. He was a member of a clan of the large Quraishi tribe. His father had died when he was six, and he was raised by his paternal grandfather and then by an uncle. At age 25 he married a wealthy widow, Khadijah, who recognized his spirituality and business acumen. The latter was useful for her trading business. Together they had two sons (both of whom died) and four daughters, all of whom survived.

Arabia was then a pagan country, whereas much of the Near East was monotheistic or Zoroastrian. The Arabians worshipped an ill-defined chief god called Allah and his offspring. The central shrine of the country was in Mecca and was called the Kaaba. This building contained a large black rock and statues of the Bedouin tribes' many gods. The Bedouins would come on pilgrimage once a year to worship at this holy site.

Muhammad was familiar with Judaism and Christianity, having visited their communities while travelling in the large cities of the Middle East as a camel trader. He had also befriended Jews in Mecca who explained to him about the Jewish belief in one God and about their laws. They also told him wonderful stories from their Torah: about Abraham, who almost sacrificed his son Ishmael, who would become a forefather of the Arabian people; about Adam and Eve, the first created man and woman; about a flood that destroyed the entire world except for one righteous individual called Noah; and about the prophet Moses, who delivered the Jews out of slavery and brought them from Egypt to their Promised Land. The Christians also told him their stories about Jesus. In addition, Muhammad learnt about the belief of the Jews and Christians in a World to Come, which was new to him as the Arabians did not believe in a life after death.

One night, which would subsequently be called the Night of Destiny or Night of Power, when age 40, Muhammad had a mind-shattering revelatory experience that would profoundly influence the direction of his life. On this night the first verses of the Qur'an were revealed to him through the heavens by the angel Gabriel. The Qur'an relates:

> *We sent it [Muhammad's revelation] down on the Night of Destiny. What will make you comprehend what that Night of Destiny is? The Night of Destiny is better than 1,000 months; on that night the angels and the Spirit descend therein with the permission of Allah with His decrees on all matters; it is all peace till the break of dawn.* (Surah 97).

Muhammad was terror-stricken by this experience. However, in the comfort of his home, his wife and relatives were able to reassure him that he had had a genuine revelatory experience.

His next revelation was 18 months later. One of Muhammad's colleagues related what Muhammad told him:

"While I was walking, all of a sudden, I heard a voice from the sky. I looked up and saw the same angel who had visited me at the cave of Hira, sitting on a chair between the sky and the earth. I got scared of him and came home and said: 'Wrap me in [blankets].' And then Allah revealed the following holy verses [of the Qur'an]: 'O thou wrapped up [in a mantle]! Arise and deliver thy warning! And thy Lord do thou magnify! And thy garments keep free from stain! And all [other goods] shun!' [1]

Allah reassured Muhammad that he was not delusional, and He instructed him to lead a pure life and begin proclaiming His message to the people and leaders of Mecca. From this point on over the next 22 years Muhammad experienced revelations from the angel Gabriel. These revelations, called an *ayah* (sign of God), were considered to be the verbatim words of God and were later transcribed by his colleagues to form the basis of the Qur'an (Muhammad could neither read nor write).

Muhammad believed he was the last of the prophets to be elected by God and that a primordial faith was being communicated to him that had previously been revealed to Moses and Jesus, but which had been received incorrectly or misinterpreted. His prophecies were the final and authentic words of God and superseded any prophecies previously communicated to others.

The Qur'an was initially transmitted orally, but the *surahs,* or chapters, were finally collected by the first caliph Abu Bakr as a book written in Arabic. A standard version of the Qur'an was made by the third caliph Uthman ibn Affan in about 650 CE. Some of this material is difficult to understand and requires the explanations of an oral tradition to fully understand it.

People in Mecca gradually became aware of Muhammad's experiences and began following him. Three years after his first revelation, he and his followers began publicly preaching his message. However, this was met with considerable resistance from the Quraishi leaders, to the extent that many of his followers had to leave Mecca. Muhammad's message involved a different understanding of Allah than they were familiar with, risked alienating their gods and was at odds with their lifestyle. Informed about a threat to his life, Muhammad and his followers fled to Yathrib some 275 miles north of Mecca, where he had

---

1   Quoted in "The Revelatory Time and the Messenger" in *Opening the Qur'an. Introducing Islam's Holy Book* by Walter H. Wagner, 122. University of Notre Dame, 2008.

previously proselytized and had a number of influential followers. This journey is known as the *hijra* and marks a major turning point in Islam.

Yathrib, or Medina as it was renamed by Muhammad, was not a town but a number of villages and forts around an oasis where two pagan and three smaller Jewish tribes lived. Muhammad was invited to govern this area which was then immersed in conflict due to blood feuds. These he halted, and he began to initiate the program described in the Qur'an: the elimination of idols, obligatory prayer and a social program with prohibitions against alcohol, gambling, usurious interest rates, spousal abuse, and mistreatment of orphans. He also introduced the *zakat* (charitable) requirement for giving alms to the poor.[2]

Muhammad realized that the Meccans would not permit him to continue living in Medina. He therefore decided to strike first and attacked Meccan caravans as recompense for the properties his followers had left behind when fleeing Mecca.[3] An engagement at Badr Springs began as a caravan raid but escalated into a full-scale battle when the Meccans brought in reinforcements. Despite being outnumbered, Muhammad won a resounding victory that he ascribed to God's intervention. This is described in the Qur'an:

> *[Prophet] say to the disbelievers: "You shall be vanquished and driven into hell, a foul resting place! There has already been a sign for you in the two groups that met face to face [at Badr], one fighting for the cause of God and the other made up of disbelievers. They [the unbelievers] saw with their own eyes that the others [believers] were twice their number; but Allah helps whomever He wills. There is truly a lesson in this for all who have eyes to see"* (Surah 3:12-13).

During the last nine years of Muhammad's life, the Muslims were involved in numerous military campaigns.[4] The Meccans eventually came to the realization that they were unable to defeat Muhammad, and they agreed to a treaty which allowed the Muslims to enter Mecca for the *Hajj* pilgrimage. Eventually, Muhammad was able to move against the city without resistance. He purified the Kaaba and removed its idols. All non-Muslims were expelled from Arabia in 635 CE.

---

2   "The Narrative about Muhammad: Hijra and the Beginning of the Muslim Era" in ibid., 129.
3   Ibid., 130.
4   "Qur'an and Conquest" in *Understanding Jihad* by David Cook, 6. University of California Press, 2015.

In a speech before his death, Muhammad summarized his beliefs and the important aspects of his religious program:

O people, listen to me in earnest, worship Allah, say your five daily prayers, fast during the month of Ramadan, and give your wealth in Zakat. Perform Hajj if you can afford to. You know that every Muslim is the brother of another Muslim. You are all equal. Nobody has superiority over another except by piety and good action. Remember, one day you will appear before Allah and answer for your deeds. So beware, do not go astray from the path of righteousness after I am gone. O people, no prophet or messenger will come after me and no new faith will be born. Reason well, therefore, O people and understand my words which I convey to you. I leave behind me two things, the Qur'an and my example, the Sunna, and if you follow these you will never go astray. All those who listen to me shall pass on my words to others and those to others again; and may the last ones understand my words better than those who listen to me directly. Be my witness, O Allah, that I have conveyed your message to your people.[5]

After Muhammad's death, Bedouin warriors enthused with the notion of holy war (*jihad)* burst into Syria and Iraq in a series of military campaigns and overthrew the established order. This was followed by the conquest of Egypt, and by 650 CE they had conquered what would become the heartlands of Islam, namely the area between Egypt on the west and the Iranian plateau on the east plus the Arabian Peninsula. Five years later, under the Umayyad dynasty centered in Syria, Muslims conquered Central Asia and Afghanistan to the northeast, Pakistan and parts of India to the southeast, Armenia and the Caucasus to the north, and North Africa and the Iberian Peninsula to the east. Their military successes were achieved because of the weaknesses of the Byzantine and Sasanian Empires, the unifying force of Islam, the warriors' anticipated rewards from *jihad*, their agile military tactics, and their focus on attacking areas that were poorly defended.[6] However, they were unable to take Constantinople from the Byzantines, and an advance into France was halted.

Conversion was not forced on the people of the countries they conquered although their victories created conditions favorable for the eventual widespread adoption of Islam.

---

5   Quoted from "The Narrative about Muhammad: Victory and Death" in *Opening the Qur'an. Introducing Islam's Holy Book* by Walter H. Wagner, 136. University of Notre Dame, 2008. The text was taken from the Alim, the Messenger's Last Sermon.

6   "The Early Conquests: Theory to Practice" in *Understanding Jihad* by David Cook, 11. University of California Press, 2015.

ATTAINING THE WORLD TO COME

Islam's fundamental beliefs are the unity of God; God's revelations through the prophets and Scriptures; and God's final judgment of humanity. This will encompass people of all faiths. As do Judaism and Christianity, Islam recognizes God as the Creator of the universe and believes that He is involved in, rather than remote from, the world He created.

The so-called Five Pillars are the fundamentals of Islamic personal behavior. One is the basic creed (*shahada*), repeated at all prayer services, in which "*I testify that there is no God but Allah and I testify that Muhammad is the messenger of God.*" The second is prayer which is recited in Arabic and contains verses from the Qur'an. At the beginning of Muhammad's missionary work, he advocated praying three times a day towards Jerusalem (as does Judaism) to attract Jews to his new religion. However, he increased its frequency to five times a day and its direction towards Mecca when it became clear to him that the Jews of Medina wanted nothing to do with his new faith. The third pillar is charity. This is a religious duty, as it is in Judaism, and even has the same name, *Sadaqah*. The other two pillars of Islam are fasting during the month of Ramadan from dawn to dusk as a means of drawing close to Allah and perfecting one's behavior, and making a pilgrimage to Mecca at least once in one's lifetime for those possessing the means to do so. This is called the *hajj*. During this pilgrimage, the Kaaba shrine is encircled seven times.

The Qur'an relates that Abraham visited the Kaaba in Mecca and made it a shrine to God; this is why Muhammad was determined to make it again a shrine for monotheism. It contains a black stone that according to Islamic tradition dates from the time of Adam and Eve. This is now in pieces held together by a ring of stone and a silver band and located in one corner of the building. Other features of Islam initially added to attract Jews and subsequently maintained are a restriction on eating pork, ritual slaughter and Friday as the main day of prayer.

Muhammad initially envisaged Islam as a religion of peace. He assumed that his countrymen would be convinced by his message regarding monotheism, that Islam would take over the Kaaba and that all of Arabia would accept Islam. But this was not how it initially turned out. When in Medina, he realized that to accomplish his goal of converting all of Arabia to Islam he would need to resort to force. This was when he developed the concept of holy war or *jihad*.

Jihad means a struggle in Arabic, although this translation does not encompass the full implications of this word. A commonly accepted meaning is warfare with spiritual significance. *Jihad* is usually authorized by a legitimate representative of the Muslim community for the sake of an issue universally recognized to be of critical importance to the entire community and against a recognized enemy of Islam.[7]

The nature of the arrangement between Allah and His fighters is evident from the following Qur'anic passage, which even invokes the Torah and gospels in its support:

> *Allah has bought from the believers their lives and their wealth in return for the Garden [Paradise]; they fight for the cause of Allah, and they kill, and they get killed. This is a true promise binding on Him in by the Torah, the gospel, and the Qur'an; and who is truer to His promise than Allah? So be happy with the bargain you have made. That is the supreme achievement"* (Surah 9:111).

The aim of *jihad* was to persuade pagans to adopt Islam. The forbidden months discussed in the following Qur'anic passage were months designated in Arabia for non-combat so that pilgrims could travel safely to the Kaaba:

> *When the [four] forbidden months have passed, wherever you encounter the idolators kill them, take them captive, besiege them, and lie in wait for them at every place of ambush; but if they repent, and establish regular prayers and pay the prescribed alms [i.e., take on the strictures of Islam], then let them go their way, for Allah is most forgiving and merciful* (Surah 9:5).

Jews and Christians were considered to be *"people of the book"* and were not required to convert, although they were obligated to pay a special poll tax and forbidden to promulgate their religion or to criticize Islam. This paradigm would govern the relationship between Muslims and those of other monotheistic faiths living in Muslim territories for many centuries:

> *Fight those of the people of the book [i.e., Jews and Christians] who do not truly believe in God or the Last Day, who do not forbid what God and His messenger have declared forbidden, who do not obey the rule of justice, until they pay the tax promptly and agree to submit* (Surah 9:29).

---

7   This definition is taken from "Introduction" in *Understanding Jihad* by David Cook, 2-3. University of California Press, 2015.

Hadiths indicate that *jihad* continued to be accepted among the faithful after Muhammad's death. Hadiths constitute a tradition later than the Qur'an and are based on the reported actions or words of Muhammad or on actions performed by his colleagues which met with his approval and which were later collected in books. The following hadith is one example among many on the subject of jihad:

There is a man who fights in the path of Allah and does not want to kill or be killed, but is struck by an arrow. The first drop of blood [dripping] from him is atonement for every sin he has committed; for every drop he sheds he gains levels in Paradise. The second type of man is one who fights desiring to kill but not to be killed and is struck by an arrow. The first drop of blood [dripping] from him is atonement for every sin; for every drop he sheds he gains a level in paradise until he bumps Abraham's knee [on the top level]. The third type of man is one who fights in the path of Allah desiring to kill and be killed, and is struck by an arrow. The first drop of blood [dripping] from him is atonement for every sin; he will come to the Day of Resurrection with a drawn sword [able to] intercede.[8]

Commenting on the importance of violent jihad in Islam, David Cook writes:

Whereas the Qur'an suffices with generalities and encouragement to fight, the hadith materials take us into a full-blown description of warfare with a heavy spiritual content. It is clear from even the cursory overview above that the subject of militant jihad was of critical concern to Muslims during the formative first three centuries of Islam, and there is no indication from any of this material that the jihad being described is anything other than military.[9]

What Cook is referring to in this last sentence is another definition of jihad, as a spiritual form of struggle or striving in the path of Islam. This non-military definition is much preferred by Islamic apologists and some non-Islamic commentators. It is described in the following Qur'anic passage:

Strive (jahidu) hard for the cause of Allah as you ought to strive (haqq jihadihi). He has chosen you and laid on you no burden, the faith of your forefather Abraham. Both in the past and in this scripture, He has called

---

8   Quoted in "Qur'an and Conquest" in ibid., 15 from reference 12, from Ibn al-Mubarak, Jihad, 104-5 (no. 125).
9   "Accounts of the jihad: the hadith literature" in ibid., 19.

you Muslims so that the Messenger can bear witness about you, and so that you may be witnesses to the people. Therefore, say your prayers regularly, give the prescribed alms and seek refuge in Allah. He is your guardian an excellent protector and an excellent helper! (Surah 22:78).

Nevertheless, it is doubtful that this definition accords with how Islam viewed jihad during Muhammad's lifetime or how it was practiced in the centuries after his death. As the Qur'an states:

Those believers who stay at home, apart from those forced by necessity, are not equal to those who fight with their goods and their persons. Allah has given those who fight with their goods and their persons a higher rank than those who stay at home. Although He has promised all believers a good reward; far greater is the recompense of those who fight for him (Surah 4:95).

The aim of all Muslims is to achieve a blissful existence in a heavenly Paradise by believing in the fundamentals of Islam and leading the type of life directed by Allah. The importance of the World to Come is evident from these Qur'anic quotations:

O you who believe! Shall I guide you to a profitable course that will save you from painful torment? Believe in Allah and His messenger and strive for Allah's cause with your possessions and your persons. That will be better for you if you only knew. And He will forgive your sins and admit you into Gardens [Paradise] graced with flowing streams, into pleasant dwellings in the gardens of eternity. That is indeed the supreme achievement (Surah 61:10-12).

As for those who are mindful of Allah, there is supreme fulfilment: gardens and vineyards, and voluptuous maidens of matching age and overflowing cups [in Paradise]. They shall not hear any idle talk or lying talk there. This will be a reward, a fitting gift, from the Lord of the heavens and the earth and everything in between, the Lord of mercy. And no one will have authority to raise their voices to Him. On the day when the spirit and the angels stand in rows, no one will speak, except for those to whom the Lord of Mercy gives permission, and who will say only what is right. That is the day of truth, so whoever wishes to, should take the path that leads towards the Lord (Surah 78:31-39).

The "*gift*" in Paradise described here will be proximity to Allah and will be extremely pleasurable. Closest to Allah in this ranking will be Muhammad, his early companions and helpers, martyrs, and extraordinary believers. For those in Paradise close to Allah, beautiful maidens will be in attendance:

> *And those foremost (in faith) will be foremost (in the hereafter). These will be those nearest to Allah in Gardens of Bliss; many from the past and a few from later generations. They will recline facing each other on thrones woven with gold and precious stones. They will be waited on by ageless youth carrying goblets and ewers and cups filled with a purest drink, neither causing headaches, nor intoxication, along with fruits of their choice and the meat of any bird they like; and beautiful-eyed maidens with large, lustrous eyes like hidden pearls shall be their recompense for their deeds. They will not hear therein vain or sinful talk, only clean and wholesome speech* (Surah 56:10-26).

In Islamic thought, all of one's thoughts, words and deeds in this world are recorded by angels. Ultimately, an archangel will blow the first trumpet blast announcing the onset of the World to Come. Everyone will die, and everything will be obliterated. On the Day of Judgment (*Yawm Din*), all the dead will be resurrected. Everyone will be judged, and every person's intentions and deeds will be weighed in the balance. Similar to Christianity, sinners will fall into an abyss of flames and eternal punishment:

> *On the day when the earth shall be changed into another earth, as shall be the heavens, and people all appear before Allah, the One, the Most Supreme. On that day you [the Prophet] shall see the guilty bound in fetters, in garments of pitch and faces enveloped by fire. Allah will requite each soul according to its deeds. Swift is Allah's reckoning* (Surah 14:48-51).

About one-third of the Qur'an relates to eschatology, namely the Day of Judgment, the punishment of the wicked and details of the World to Come. However, the Qur'an did not describe how all this will come about. This gap was filled by hadiths composed by Muslim scholars in the seventh to ninth centuries. Because of the generally cordial relations between Muslims and Jews in the early days of the Islamic empire, little was written in this eschatology about Jews, as the Byzantines were viewed as the enemy. This material was complemented by medieval Muslim writers who added apocalyptic scenarios from Jewish and Christian sources, reinterpreted as referring to Muslims.

In this literature, there will first be the appearance of Gog and Magog, who will be intent on destroying the world and who do nothing but kill, but will finally be defeated by God.[10] An Antichrist (*Dajjal*), who is Jewish, will appear at the head of an army and attempt to seduce Muslims. He finally will arrive in Jerusalem where a remnant of Muslims remain who have not been seduced. At this point, Jesus will return to earth and usher in the messianic age. In this eschatological literature, Jesus will be Muslim, rather than Christian, and he will convert all Christians to Islam.[11] In some traditions, the saving messianic figure will be the Mahdi (the rightly guided one). Either of these figures will defeat the Antichrist. Preceding this End of Days scenario will be Greater Signs of the Hour, such as major warfare, and Lesser Signs of the Hour, such as natural disasters. Peace and prosperity will reign in this messianic age. Also described are the conquest and the subjugation of non-Muslims. Sometime after this will be the resurrection and End of Days.

Muhammad's approach to Jews

There were a significant number of Jewish communities in the Arabian Peninsula at the time of Muhammad. The Jews from Yemen dated from as early as King Solomon's time. In the fifth century CE, Jews from Persia also migrated across the Gulf to the Peninsula. By the dawn of Islam, Jews dominated the economic life of Arabia. In Medina they constituted at least half its population and owned its best agricultural land.

There are many statements about Jews in the Qur'an. In the early days of his mission, Muhammad anticipated that the Jews of Mecca would join his new Abrahamic religion, and there are a number of very positive statements about Jews such as:

Children of Israel, remember how I blessed you and favored you over other people" (Surah 2:122)

and

Children Of Israel! Call to mind My favor which I bestowed on you and be faithful to [your] covenant with Me, and I will fulfill [My] covenant with you; and of Me, Me alone, should you be afraid (Surah 2.40)

However, when Muhammad arrived in Medina and took over leadership of the oasis, the Jews were highly suspicious of him. In some instances,

---

10   This sequence is described in the Qur'an 18:94 and 21:96. "Introduction to Classical Muslim Apocalyptic Literature" in *Contemporary Muslim Apocalyptic Literature* by David Cook, 10. Syracuse University Press, New York, 2005.

11   Ibid., 9.

they were decidedly hostile and even conspired against him. They, like the other Jews of Arabia, could not accept that Moses had received an inaccurate transmission from God or had wrongly interpreted the words of a primordial Torah. They were therefore not prepared to believe that Muhammad was a prophet of God or that the Qur'an contained the words of God.

None of this endeared the Jews of Medina and Jews in general to Muhammad. The males of one conspiring Jewish tribe in Medina were massacred, their women and children put into slavery and their land given to his supporters who had fled from Mecca.

No dates are given in the Qur'an for much of what was written, but the many negative statements about Jews in the Qur'an could well be from this period. The following are four examples:

> *And They say: "Our hearts are wrapped [i.e., do not hear or understand Allah's word]." But Allah has rejected them on account of their unbelief; they have little faith"* (Surah 2:88).

> *O you who believe! Do not take the Jews and the Christians for friends; they are friends of each other; and whoever amongst you takes them for a friend, then surely he is one of them; surely Allah does not guide the unjust people* (Surah 5:51).

> *Say: Shall I tell you who deserves a worse punishment from Allah? Those whom Allah has cursed and brought His wrath upon, and condemned as apes and swine, and those who worshipped evil; they are worse in rank and have strayed further from the right path* (Surah 5:60).

> *He brought down those People of the Book who supported them from their fortresses and cast terror in their hearts; some you slew, some you made captive. He bequeathed upon you their land, their houses, and their possessions, and a land you never trod. God has power over everything* (Surah 33:26).

By the time of Muhammad's death, all Jews had been expelled from the Arabian Peninsula. However, after his death, when the Bedouins emerged from the desert to engage in conquest, they were confronted with the fact that much of the population of their new empire was Christian or Jewish. The administrative talent of these people was also needed. The solution devised was the Pact of Umar, which provided protection, or *dhimmi* status, to Christians or Jews upon payment of a tax, provided they recognized the superiority of

Muslims and their religion.[12] This pact included restrictions on their building houses of worship and stipulated that these be lower in height than nearby mosques. They also had to show deference to Muslims by not striking them nor riding an animal in the Muslim way. These and the other aspects of the pact were enforced with varying degrees of strictness, depending on the historic period and the country in question. Despite these restrictions, Jews generally preferred living in Muslim rather than in Christian countries, since only the former provided them any degree of official protection. Thus, the relationship between Muslims and Jews in the Islamic Empire was generally cordial, as long as the Jews were prepared to recognize their inferior status in society.

MIDRASHIC STORIES IN THE QUR'AN AND ISLAMIC ETHICS

Muhammad was fascinated by Biblical stories told to him by the Jews of Mecca, and a number are found in the Qur'an.[13] Some were told to him embellished with midrashic explanations since bits of midrash can be found in the Qur'an. Midrash is a commentary on the Torah that seeks to fill in gaps in the Torah – with respect to Abraham, for example, to explain why he was chosen by God. Some Jews consider midrashim to be the product of Divine inspiration, although this is far from being universally accepted, and it has never been suggested that they are the words of God.

The Qur'an contains the following story about Abraham being rescued from a fiery furnace. It is not found in the Torah, but is very similar to a midrash about God rescuing Abraham from a fiery furnace after he smashed his father's idols:[14]

He [Abraham] broke them all [the idols] into pieces, except for the biggest one, so that they might return to it [for enquiry]. They said: "Who has done this to our gods? He must be a wrongdoer." Some said: "We heard a young man called Abraham talking about them." They said: "Then bring him here in the sight of all the people so that they may testify." They said: "Abraham, was it you who did this to our gods?" He answered: "No, it was

---

12   This pact is traditionally attributed to Caliph Umar ibn Khattab, although this is doubted by some scholars and alternatively attributed to ninth-century Islamic scholars or the Umayyad Caliph Umar II.

13   A pioneering book on this topic was Abraham Geiger's *Judaism and Islam. A Prize Essay*, initially published in German in 1833. It demonstrated how the Qur'an and other Islamic literature drew from Jewish sources.

14   Rashi to Genesis 11:28, based on *Bereishit Rabba* 38:13

done by the biggest of them – this one. Ask them if they can speak."' Then they turned to one another and said: "It is you yourselves who are in the wrong." Then they hung their heads and said: "O Abraham! You know very well they cannot speak." Abraham said: "So, how can you worship what can neither benefit nor harm you, instead of Allah? Shame on you and on whatever you worship instead of Allah. Have you no sense?" They said: "Burn him and vindicate your gods." But We said: "'Fire! Be cool and safe for Abraham." They planned to harm him, but We frustrated them" (Surah 21:58-70).

There are differences between the Qur'an's versions of the Biblical stories and those found in the Torah. The Qur'an's story about Noah, for example, reflects the priorities of Muhammad, particularly in relation to his struggle in Saudi Arabia against paganism. The Qur'an's version includes the following:

- Noah told the people that if they persisted in worshiping their ancestral gods they would be destroyed.

- For various reasons the people refused to believe him.

- Rumors reached Noah that the leaders were conspiring to stone him.

- With the increase in threats, Noah prayed to God that He wipe the people off the face of the earth so that potential believers would not be misled.

- Enduring the mockery of the people, he built an ark and collected animals to put in it.

- God commanded Noah to enter the ark with the few people who believed in him.

- His wife and one of his sons drowned after they decided not to join him.

- Noah was told that his true family will not be his blood relations but those who submitted to God's will.

In the Torah's version of the story, however, the sin of the generation of the Flood was not idolatry but *hamas* in Hebrew. A translation of this word is *unrighteousness*, as in *"And the earth had become corrupt before God; and the earth had become filled with unrighteousness (hamas)"* (Genesis 6:11). This noun is also found in a Torah verse about false testimony: *"You shall not bear a meritless [or false] report, do not put your hand with an evil person to be a witness of unrighteousness (hamas) [i.e., a fraudulent witness]"* (Exodus 23:1).

Hence, in the Torah, God was prepared to destroy the world because of a breakdown in civil society, whereas for the Qur'an the reason was idolatry.

There is no mention in the Bible about threats of violence against Noah, although his message to the people about a pending flood would no doubt have elicited skepticism. However, the rumors reaching the Qur'an's Noah about leaders wishing to stone him were more or less what the leaders of Mecca wished to do to Muhammad. Unlike the Qur'an's Noah, the Biblical Noah did not pray that any disbelievers be wiped off the face of the earth. Noah's wife and one of his sons did not die in the Biblical story, but this did happen to Lot's wife and Lot's two sons-in-law during the destruction of Sodom and Gomorra. The Bible also relied on a family to promote its messages and not on a group of male supporters who could well come to disagreement.

A major difference between Judaism and Islam is their approach to ethics. The Torah instructs Jews to walk in God's ways; thus, God becomes the model for all ethical behavior. The concept of imitatio Dei, or imitation of God, is also recognized by Christianity. However, because Muhammad rejected the Torah, regarding it as a distorted transmission of God's word, and considered only his prophecy as authentic, there is no concept of imitatio Dei in the Qur'an. Because of this, the Qur'an and Muhammad's own words and behavior and that of his family and friends that he approved of as reported by his colleagues and transmitted through the hadiths became the source of ethics for all Muslims. Because man, rather than God, is the model for much of Islamic ethics, this has permitted distortions of ethical behavior to be perpetrated in Allah's name, such as the murder of non-Muslims and attempted genocide of Jews. It is also noticeable that Islamic fundamentalists often seem to be functioning within a different ethical system from that of the Western world, for example in deliberately using civilians as shields during warfare.

In conclusion, Muhammad regarded himself as a prophet and not as a messiah. Nevertheless, he did have messianic-like ideas in that he wished to eradicate paganism and create ideal communities in the Arabian Peninsula. However, he was realistic enough to know that complete perfection could never be achieved and, like Christianity, he reserved his ultimate utopia for Paradise in the World to Come.

Because of Muhammad's role, the Qur'an made no mention of any messianic figure. However, over the centuries a need was recognized for a messianic person who would accomplish what a regular human being would be unable to do, and in particular hasten the End of Days. Hence, in modern Islamic apocalyptic literature a messianic figure called the Mahdi will rule a vast caliphate in which there will be mass conversion of non-Muslims to Islam. This figure will establish peace and prosperity prior to an Armageddon-type conflict that will eliminate the enemies of Islam and presage the Day of Judgment and World to Come.

Muhammad anticipated that Jews in the Arabian Peninsula would join his new religion, and the negative comments made about Jews in the Qur'an reflect his frustration that they did not wish to do so and even conspired against him. Nevertheless, he had no fundamental philosophical disagreements with Judaism or Christianity, and he believed that their adherents would also inherit the World to Come.

Hatred of Jews to the point of planning their genocide is a recent phenomenon and has been stirred up by recent Islamic apocalyptic literature, all of which is strongly antisemitic. However, the seeds of this hatred were already planted at the time of Muhammad when he struggled against the Jews of Medina and eventually expelled all Jews from the Arabian Peninsula. This is reflected in his disparaging comments about Jews in the Qur'an. Nevertheless, were it not for the creation of the State of Israel and the Israeli-Palestinian conflict, it is doubtful there would have been any conflict between the adherents of Judaism and Islam.

More about this Islamic apocalyptic literature in a later chapter.

Chapter 12

THE MESSIANIC ERA AND WORLD TO COME ACCORDING TO MAIMONIDES AND NACHMANIDES

The Talmud and midrashim discuss ideas about messianic times expressed by various sages, but no overall scheme is presented. This is in contrast to the literature of Christianity and Islam, where End of Time events were described in sequential terms. Maimonides (1138-1204) and Nachmanides (1194-1270) were *halachic* authorities, philosophers, giants of the Jewish tradition, and leaders of the Jewish world who felt it necessary to elaborate on the details of the messianic era for their generations.

Both lived at a time when the 400-year Golden Age for the Jews of Spain was unravelling. Jewish life in Spain began when the Moors, who were Muslims from North Africa, crossed the Straits of Gibraltar in 711 CE and successfully invaded the Iberian Peninsula, which was then Christian. The Jews who came with them found a welcoming home. However, this warmth ended when fundamental Islam overtook Spain and later when much of the Iberian Peninsula was reconquered by the Christians. The lives of Maimonides and his family were affected by fundamentalist Islam, while Nachmanides had to deal with the antagonism of the Christian Church.

Maimonides' monumental work, the *Mishna Torah*, is a book about halacha. However, because the messianic era is so much a focus of Jewish aspirations Maimonides felt it appropriate to include this subject in this book, and even planned for it to end with this topic. He described a future non-miraculous messianic redemption. He also placed the World to Come in the heavenly realm. A heavenly World to Come was part of the tradition of ancient Greece but had not previously been discussed in Jewish sources. Nevertheless, it accorded with his own philosophical approach and possibly with the way many Jews at that time were thinking because of the Islamic and Christian cultures around them.

A generation later, Nachmanides felt that much of what Maimonides had written about the messianic era and World to Come was not supported by talmudic and other Jewish sources, and he presented his own interpretation of traditional Jewish views on these two topics in a work called *Shaar Ha'gmul* (Gate of Reward).

A comparison of their two approaches illuminates much about the topic of messianism.

The life of Maimonides and his depiction
of a natural messianic era

Maimonides was born in Cordova, Spain, where his father was the leading rabbi. When he was a young man a fundamentalist Muslim movement, the Almohad, established an empire in North Africa and Spain and abrogated the Pact of Omar and the *dhimmi* status of Jews. As *dhimmis*, the Jews had been protected from persecution but were now faced with the choice of death, exile or conversion to Islam. Maimonides' family fled Cordova and eventually settled in Fez in Morocco. This country was also under Almohad rule, but the ruler had become more tolerant and the family was able to profess its Judaism openly.

In 1165 Maimonides left Fez for the Land of Israel, which was then under the control of the Crusaders. He stayed briefly in Acre, and may even have visited Jerusalem and the Temple Mount before making his way with his family to Fostat in Egypt. He taught himself medicine there and became a physician. Because of his reputation, he was appointed physician to a courtier of the emperor Saladin and then to Saladin himself. (This was the same Saladin who defeated the Crusaders and drove them out of Jerusalem and their Kingdom of Jerusalem). Maimonides was recognized in Egypt and the Jewish world as an authority on Jewish law and his *halachic* decisions were widely sought.

Maimonides' most significant work is his book on Jewish law, the *Mishna Torah*. The Talmud, on which much of Jewish practice is based, is arranged very broadly according to subject matter, but its discussions are free ranging, and its deliberations, even on the same topic, can be scattered throughout its 63 tractates.[1] To locate and understand a particular law can be

---

1   The Babylonian Talmud is a monumental work written over about 300 years in the centers of Jewish learning in Mesopotamia. Completed in about 475 CE, it contains discussions based on the Mishna. The Mishna was redacted by Rabbi Yehuda HaNasi at the beginning of the third century CE and is a summary of the Jewish oral tradition, which itself is based

a challenge for those without talmudic expertise. Sometimes, final decisions were left hanging. Maimonides' *Mishna Torah* is a compilation of *halachic* decisions on almost all of the Jewish written and oral tradition, arranged by subject matter in a highly original way. Whenever he felt it necessary, he included brief philosophical discussions on the subject matter he was reviewing. His other major works include a highly-regarded commentary to the Mishna, a precise compilation of Biblical laws called *Sefer Hamitzvot* and a philosophical work called in English the *Guide for the Perplexed*. This was a controversial book when released because of its attempt to blend Jewish tradition with philosophy.

Maimonides covered the topic of messianism in his *Mishna Torah*, in an introduction to his commentary on the Mishnaic tractate Sanhedrin known as *Perek Helek*, and in a pamphlet called *A Treatise on the Resurrection of the Dead*.

The belief that this current exile will eventually end and the Jewish people will be redeemed is fundamental to Judaism. The Book of Deuteronomy describes redemption within the context of the blessings and curses resulting from adhering to or not adhering to the covenant given on Mount Sinai:

> *It will be when all these things come upon you – the blessing and the curse that I have presented before you – then you will take it to your heart among all the nations where the Lord (Y-H-V-H) your God, has dispersed you. And you will return unto the Lord your God and you will listen to His voice according to everything that I command you today, you and your children, with all your heart and all your soul. Then the Lord your God will bring back your captivity and have mercy upon you, and he will gather you in from all the peoples to which the Lord your God has scattered you. If your dispersed will be at the ends of heaven, from there the Lord your God will bring you to the land that your forefathers possessed and you shall possess it; He will do good to you and make you more numerous than your forefathers. The Lord your God will circumcise your heart and the heart of your offspring, to love the Lord your God with all your heart and all your soul, that you may live* (Deuteronomy 30:1-6).

In accord with post-exilic Jewish sources, Maimonides held that redemption from this current exile will be a messianic one. Hence, not believing in the Messiah could be considered akin to not believing in redemption. The importance of these beliefs is discussed in his *Mishna Torah*:

---

on the written Torah.

Anyone who does not believe in him or does not await his coming, denies not only [the statements] of the other prophets, but [those of] the Torah and Moses, our teacher. The Torah testified to his [coming] as [Deuteronomy 30:3-5] states: "God will bring back your captivity and have mercy upon you. He will gather you [from among the nations]. . . . Even if your diaspora is at the end of the heavens, [God will gather you up from there]. . . . and [God] will bring you [to the land]." [2]

Maimonides also believed that the coming of the Messiah should be longed for by every Jew. This is based on a statement in the Talmud by the sage Rava that one of six questions that will be asked of all Jews at the time of the final judgment is whether they waited in hope for salvation.[3] He also included belief in the Messiah in his Thirteen Principles of Faith and quoted the prophet Habakkuk: "*We do not think that he will be late in coming, and even if he tarries, we await him*" (Habakkuk 2:3).

A fundamental issue is whether the messianic era will be accompanied by a change in the nature of the world, and this topic is discussed in the Talmud.[4] The view of the sage Shmuel was that "*there is nothing between this world and the messianic era except an end to the subjugation suffered in the various exiles.*" The sage Rabbi Chiya bar Abba, on the other hand, held that prophecies of Isaiah such as "*They shall beat their swords into plowshares and their spears into pruning shears; nations shall not lift up a sword against nation, neither shall they learn war anymore*" (Isaiah 2:4) and similar descriptions by other prophets refer to an unnatural and miraculous messianic era.

---

2   Maimonides, *Mishna Torah*, The Laws of Kings and their Wars 11:1. An issue raised by Moses' speech in Deuteronomy is whether repentance is necessary for redemption. See the next chapter on the Vilna Gaon. Also, Appendix A: "Repentance as a Precondition to Redemption" in *Illuminating Jewish Thought. Explorations of Free Will, the Afterlife, and the Messianic Era* by Rabbi Natanel Wiederblank, 499. Koren Publishers Jerusalem,2018.

3   TB Shabbat 31a. The Talmud's discussion revolves around the words of Isaiah 33:6 – "*the fear of God is [in] His storehouse.*" In the Talmud's list of six items, fear of God trumps all the others, which include conducting faithful business dealings and learning Torah.

4   This issue is debated by Shmuel and Rabbi Chiya bar Abba in the Talmud in TB Pesachim 68a, Berakhot 34b, and TB Shabbat 63a. Shmuel holds that weapons will be necessary in the messianic era, whereas Rabbi Chiya holds there will be world peace (TB Shabbat 63a). Rabbi Chiya holds that all the utopian prophecies found in the prophets relate to the glory and splendor of the messianic era and not the World to Come, since the latter is unknowable, whereas Shmuel holds that there will be no difference between this world and the messianic era, and even poverty will continue to exist (TB Berakhot 34b). Rabbi Chiya's view that the World to Come is unknowable is based on the verse "*No eye has seen, O God, except You, that which He will do for one who waits for Him*" (Isaiah 64:3), indicating that even the eyes of a prophet are unable to perceive the World to Come (Rashi).

They cannot refer to the World to Come since it is unknowable. In any case, the World to Come will be even more glorious than these prophecies.

The influential and earlier Jewish philosopher Saadia Gaon (882-942 CE) accepted Rabbi Chiya bar Abba's position that the messianic era will be miraculous.[5] Maimonides, on the other hand, favored Shmuel's opinion that the world would continue in its normal, non-miraculous way during messianic times. Therefore, the only difference between messianic and non-messianic times will be that the Jewish people will be independent and not subjugated and oppressed by other nations.[6] This approach also means that the Messiah will not be a miracle worker. Maimonides was unable to push these prophecies to the World to Come, not only because this is unknowable and not only because he was the ultimate rationalist, but because in his scheme of things the World to Come is a world of souls. This led him to the conclusion that the utopian visions of Isaiah and other prophets had to be interpreted allegorically. As he wrote:

> Do not presume that in the messianic age the nature of the world will change or there will be innovations in the work of creation. Rather, the world will continue according to its pattern. Though Isaiah [11.6] states: "And a wolf will dwell with the lamb, the leopard will lie down with the young goat," these words are a metaphor and a parable. The interpretation of the prophecy is as follows: Israel will dwell securely together with the wicked gentiles who are likened to a wolf and a leopard in the prophecy [Jeremiah 5:6]: "A wolf from the wilderness shall spoil them and a leopard shall stalk their cities." They will all return to the true faith and no longer steal or destroy. Rather, they will eat permitted food, at peace with Israel, as [Isaiah 11:7] states: "The lion will eat straw like an ox." Similarly, other messianic prophecies of this nature are metaphors. In the messianic era everyone will realize which matters were implied by these metaphors and which allusions they contained.[7]

By stating that the nature of the world in the messianic era will be unchanged, Maimonides was following the footsteps of Rabbi Akiva. This sage had no expectation that Bar Kochba, the military leader of the Bar Kochba Revolt whom he believed to be a messianic figure, would be a miracle worker.[8]

---

5   Saadia Gaon, *Emunot Ve-Deot*, Chapter 8.

6   *Kesef Mishna* to the *Mishna Torah*, Laws of Repentance 8:7 and The Laws of Kings and their Wars 11:1.

7   Maimonides, *Mishna Torah*, The Laws of Kings and their Wars 12:1.

8   Maimonides, *Mishna Torah*, The Laws of Kings and their Wars 11:3.

There is also no indication from textual sources that he anticipated the Bar Kochba Revolt would involve overt miracles by God.

Maimonides explained how the Messiah will be recognized:

If a king will arise from the House of David who is learned in Torah and observant of the commands, as prescribed by the written law and the oral law, as David his ancestor was, and will compel all of Israel to walk in [the way of Torah] and reinforce the breaches [in observance] and fight the wars of God, we may, with assurance, consider him the Messiah. If he succeeds in the above, builds the Temple in its place and gathers the dispersed of Israel, he is definitely the Messiah. . . . He will then improve the entire world [motivating] all the nations to serve God together as [Zephaniah 3:9] states: "I will make the peoples pure of speech that they will all call upon the Name of God and serve Him with one purpose." If he did not succeed to this degree or he was killed, he surely is not [the redeemer] promised by the Torah.[7]

In *Perek Chelek* he laid out expectations for the messianic era:

The messianic age refers to the time when the monarchy will be reestablished and the Jewish people will return to the Land of Israel. The Messiah will be great and his rule will begin in Zion. His fame will be known throughout the world, and he will be more celebrated than King Solomon. All nations will seek to treat with him, and the world will venerate his righteousness and the miracles he will bring about. Whosoever opposes him will be disabled by God and forced to surrender. . . . The world as we know it will not alter, but the Jewish nation will regain independence, as the sages said: "The only difference between this world and the messianic age is that our domination by other governments will come to an end."[9] . . . The most distinctive feature of the messianic age will be our freedom from foreign domination, which prevents us from fulfilling all the commands. Wisdom will increase, as it says: "For the land shall be filled with the knowledge of God" (Isaiah 11:9). Wars will end, as it is stated: "Nations shall not take up sword against nation" (Micah 4:3). Perfection, which grants us the merit of the World to Come will be commonplace.[10]

He also explained the overall purpose of the messianic age:

---

9   TB Pesachim 68a and TB Sanhedrin 91a and 99b.

10 "Discourse on the World to Come" in *Perek Cheleck*, translated and annotated by Avraham Yaakov Finkel. Yeshivath Beth Moshe, Scranton, PA.

We do not anticipate the messianic age because of the rich harvests or the affluence it will bring. . . . Instead, the prophets and pious have yearned for the days of the Messiah because that is when the righteous will join forces and personal conduct will be guided by morality and wisdom. The Messiah will demonstrate righteousness, integrity, extraordinary wisdom, and a closeness to God, as it says: "God said: 'You are my son; I have given birth to you this day'" (Psalms 2:7).[10]

Nevertheless, as recently pointed out by Rabbi Assaf Bednarsh, Maimonides' views were not quite those of either the sage Shmuel or Rabbi Chiya bar Abba.[11] Shmuel believed in a non-miraculous messianic era, and therefore assumed that war and poverty would continue, which is not the conclusion of Maimonides. Rabbi Chiya bar Abba, on the other hand, did envisage the elimination of war and poverty but in a miraculous messianic era.

What we see here is the originality and brilliance of Maimonides, in that he built upon the views of Shmuel and Rabbi Chiya bar Abba to create his own original synthesis. The implication of this synthesis is that Maimonides believed that the elimination of war and poverty were essential aspects of the messianic era and would be effected by non-miraculous means.

MAIMONIDES' IDEAS ABOUT THE WORLD TO COME

For both Maimonides and Nachmanides there was a link between the messianic era and the World to Come, and both scholars quoted the following talmudic statement in support of their visions of this time:

[The following was a] familiar [lesson] in the mouth of [the sage] Rav. The World to Come is not like this world. In the World to Come there is no eating, no drinking, no propagation, no business, no jealousy, no hatred, and no rivalry. Rather, the righteous sit with their crowns on their heads and delight in the radiance of the Divine Presence, as it stated: "They gazed at God, and they ate and drank" (Exodus 24:11).[12]

In the writing of Maimonides one finds for the first time in a major Jewish work the notion that the World to Come will be a world that is entirely spiritual, and one in which the intellectual faculties of the soul will be directed towards understanding God. For Maimonides, the aim of this world

---

11 "Shiur #16. The Messianic Era" by Rav Assaf Bednarsh, adapted by Leora Bednarsh in The Israel Koschitzky Virtual Beit Midrash. (https://www.etzion.org.il/en/shiur-16-messianic-era).

12 TB Berachot 17a.

was to achieve an intellectual closeness to God, and this will reach its pinnacle when the soul separates from the body and ascends to the heavenly World to Come. The soul will survive the death of the body because *"it knows and comprehends knowledge which is above matter, knows the Creator of all things, and exists forever."*[13]

But how could Maimonides write this, since the notion of an eternal soul existing in the spiritual realm was a Greek idea and not at all part of Jewish tradition? Maimonides would no doubt have replied that if the final goal of man is the comprehension of God, this can be achieved with the intellectual faculties of a soul as an angelic entity, and there is no need for the hindrance of a body.

In his *Mishna Torah*, Maimonides described the nature of a soul-bound World to Come:

> *In the World to Come, there is no body or physical form, only the souls of the righteous alone, without a body, like the ministering angels. Since there is no physical form, there is neither eating, drinking, nor any other bodily functions of this world like sitting, standing, sleeping, death, sadness, laughter, and the like. Thus, the sages of previous ages declared: "In the World to Come there is neither eating, drinking nor sexual relations. Rather, the righteous will sit with their crowns on their heads and delight in the radiance of the Divine Presence."[13] . . . From that statement, it is clear that there is no body, for there is no eating or drinking. [Consequently], the statement "the righteous sit" must be interpreted metaphorically i.e., the righteous exist there without work or labor.[14]*

Maimonides also explained the accepted idea that the punishment of being *"cut off"* described in the Torah as *"karet"* is a spiritual excision that precludes someone from inheriting the World to Come. Such individuals will go into non-existence:

> *The good that is hidden for the righteous is the life of the World to Come. This will be life which is not accompanied by death, and good which is not accompanied by evil. . . . The reward of the righteous is that they will merit this pleasure and take part in this good. The retribution of the wicked is that they will not merit this life. Rather, they will be cut off and die.*

---

13   Maimonides, *Mishna Torah,* Laws of the Foundations of the Torah 4:9
14   Maimonides, *Mishna Torah*, Hilchot Teshuva 8:1-2. Maimonides also explains that the *"crowns on their heads"* represent the knowledge the righteous acquired in this world that will enable them to experience appropriately the World to Come.

Whoever does not merit this life is [truly] dead and will not live forever. Rather, he will be cut off in his wickedness and perish as a beast. This is the intent of the meaning of the term 'karet' in the Torah as [Numbers 15:31] states: "That soul shall be cut off."[14]

But where is revival of the dead in this scheme? Surely this is a foundational aspect of Jewish thought! Could it be, his critics asked, that Maimonides did not believe in resurrection? So great was the criticism that Maimonides felt compelled to write a pamphlet entitled *A Treatise on the Resurrection of the Dead (Iggeret T'Chiat HaMeitim)* confirming his belief in resurrection. He did this even though he had previously listed resurrection as one of his Thirteen Principles of Faith and had also previously mentioned the view of the sages that anyone not believing in this doctrine would forfeit his portion in the World to Come.[15]

Nevertheless, it has to be admitted that the system Maimonides described has no real need of a resurrection. Why would a soul comfortable after death in a place of souls in the Garden of Eden have to return again to this world and then go back again to the world of souls after another death? A possible reason given by his chief critic Nachmanides (!) was that by this means the resurrected righteous will have another opportunity of achieving an even higher level of spiritual perfection and understanding of God.[16]

To summarize: According to Maimonides people will live long lives during the messianic era and also during the period of resurrection. They will then die again and return to the world of souls. This will be the beginning of the World to Come. In *A Treatise on the Resurrection of the Dead* he wrote:

It seems from these statements that these people whose souls will be returned to their bodies [at the time of the resurrection] will eat, drink, procreate, bear children, and die after a very long life like the lifespans that will exist during the messianic era. But concerning eternal life, this will take

---

15   *Introduction to Perek Chelek.* Maimonides also explained in his *Treatise on Resurrection of the Dead (Iggeret Techiyat HaMeitim)* why he omitted mention of resurrection in his *Mishna Torah*: "I saw only people discussing the resurrection. . . . while forgetting entirely about the World to Come. . . . Furthermore, though as explained there, the resurrection is one of the corner stones of Moses' Torah, it is not the ultimate purpose. Rather, the ultimate purpose is the World to Come." (Quoted in Maimonides, *Mishna Torah*, The Laws of Repentance by Rabbi Eliyahu Touger, 179. Moznaim Publishing Corporation).

16   This answer is provided by Nachmanides in his *Gate of Repentance* and is quoted in "Did Rambam Deny Techiyat Ha-Meitim?" in *Illuminating Jewish Thought. Explorations of Free Will, the Afterlife, and the Messianic Era* by Rabbi Netanel Wiederblank, 406. Maggid Books.

place during the World to Come where there is no body. For we believe, and it is the truth for anyone intelligent, that in the World to Come we will exist as souls without bodies, like angels.[17]

Below is a summary of Maimonides' ideas of the progression of the end of the world from the messianic era to the World to Come. The end of the world will comprise a non-miraculous messianic era and this will lead to the revival of the dead. Both of these will extend over an exceedingly long period:

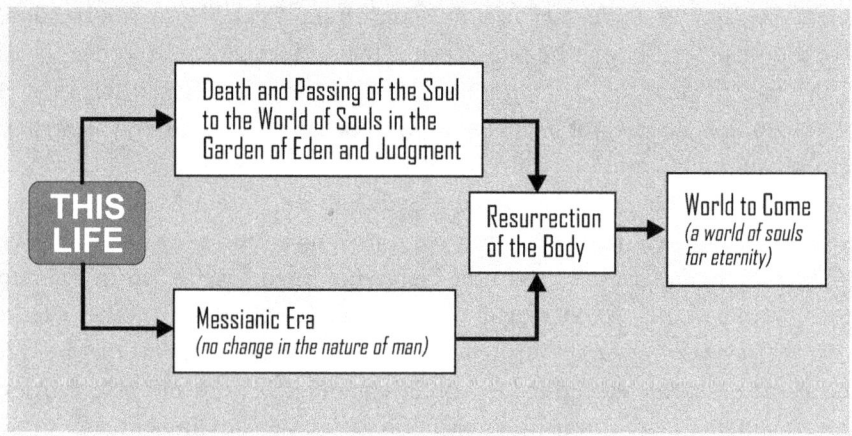

The messianic era and World to Come according to Nachmanides

Nachmanides was born a generation after Maimonides in Girona in Christian Spain. The Christians had never resigned themselves to the Iberian Peninsula being in Muslim hands and had been persistently pushing into southern Spain. By the time of Nachmanides, only a small section of the Iberian Peninsula remained Muslim. Meanwhile, as a result of Muslim persecution, many Jews moved north to Christian Spain where initially they were welcomed, although this welcome would not last.

Nachmanides studied philosophy, science and medicine. His Torah education was at three great centers of Jewish learning in Spain, Provence and northern France. These centers had different approaches to their Torah learning, and Nachmanides was able to combine them in a unique synthesis that

---

17 Translation from "Did Rambam Deny Techiyat Ha-Meitim?" in *Illuminating Jewish Thought. Explorations of Free Will, the Afterlife, and the Messianic Era* by Rabbi Netanel Wiederblank, 404. Maggid Books, 2018.

included the kabbala of Provence. He worked as a physician and also headed his own yeshiva.

His best-known work is his *Commentary to the Torah*. He adopted a more literal interpretation of the text than the commentator Rashi, who often based his explanations on midrashic sources. Aspects of messianism are discussed in a number of places in this commentary. He also wrote a book called *Torath HaAdam* (the Law of Man) that covered every facet of human thought and activity related to death, and aspects of messianism are discussed in its final chapter *The Gate of Reward* (*Sha'ar Ha'Gmul*).

Nachmanides agreed with Maimonides that in the messianic era there will be a righteous messianic figure from the seed of David, an ingathering of the exiles and the rebuilding of the Temple. The Jewish people will also help bring the world to the universal recognition of God. However, in contrast to Maimonides:

- He held that the words of the prophets describing a utopian messianic future related to a new miraculous reality and were not allegorical.

- He disagreed that the World to Come will be a world of souls. Jewish tradition has always held that the World to Come will be on earth with resurrected bodies.

- He felt that resurrection is not incidental to the World to Come, but an integral part of its initiation.

Nachmanides also believed that in the messianic era the nature of man will differ from its current state. As an analogy for this he turned to the situation before Adam and Eve were expelled from the Garden of Eden. According to Nachmanides, this was when man acted more instinctively and had no desire to sin (Genesis 2:19).[18]

Commenting on the phrase regarding redemption that "*the Lord your God, will circumcise your heart*" (Deuteronomy 30:6), he described in his *Commentary to the Torah* the new nature of man in the messianic era:

---

18   Nachmanides' interpretation of the Garden of Eden story is described in his commentary to Genesis 2:9. Nachmanides held that prior to their sin in the Garden of Eden, Adam and Eve functioned instinctively, and it was only after their sin that they obtained free will. However, many commentators have problems with this explanation and raise the issue as to how man and woman could be considered to have sinned if they lacked the capacity for free choice. They therefore provide other interpretations of the nature of Adam and Eve before and after they ate of the fruit of the Tree of Knowledge of Good and Evil. See The Garden of Eden Story in http://bible-pedia.org/the_garden_of_eden_story.

> *But in the days of the Messiah, it will be [mankind's] nature to choose the good, the heart will have no desire for the improper and no craving for it at all. This is the "circumcision" mentioned here (Deuteronomy 30:6 previously quoted), for lust and desire are the "foreskin" of the heart [blocking man's disposition to do God's will] and circumcision of the heart means that [the heart] will no longer covet or desire [evil]. Man will return at that time [to the spiritual state] he was in before the sin of the first man Adam when he did by nature that which is proper to do, and there were no conflicting desires in his will. . . . Now it is known that "the design of man's heart is evil from his youth" (Genesis 8:21) and one must educate the youth [to fear God and to follow in His ways] and [yet Scripture states that] that at that time it will not be necessary to instruct them [to avoid evil] (Jeremiah 31:32-33), [it must therefore be that] at that time [mankind's evil] inclination will be entirely abolished.*[19]

This initial period of the messianic era will be followed by resurrection in preparation for the World to Come. In the following passage Nachmanides describes resurrection as an intermediary step that will follow both the onset of the messianic era in this world and the World of Souls in the Garden of Eden after death (depending on whether the person is alive or dead) and which will continue on earth as the World to Come when body and soul unite in contemplation of God:

> *The place of reward for the souls in the World of Souls (olam ha-neshomot) [i.e., after death] is the Garden of Eden; sometimes it is called the heavenly yeshiva (yeshiva shel ma'ala). At a certain point, we hope soon, the messianic era will commence. This era fundamentally is part of this world (olam hazeh). At the end of this era, there will be a Day of Judgment and resurrection which will usher in the period of the World to Come, a time when the soul together with the body will connect to God in a more elevated way than the soul related to God when in the Garden of Eden. This existence will continue forever and ever."*[20]

Following resurrection, the faculties of the physical body will still function, although this will not be the case in the World to Come. As did

---

19 Nachmanides' *Commentary to the Torah* on Deuteronomy 30:6.

20 Nachmanides. *The Gate of Reward.* This translation is from *Illuminating Jewish Thought. Explorations of Free Will, the Afterlife, and the Messianic Era* by Rabbi Netanel Wiederblank, 372. Maggid Books. This scheme does leave the dead with no chance of participating in the beginning of the messianic era. Accordingly, there is an opinion that there will actually be two resurrections.

Maimonides, Nachmanides turned to the talmudic passage describing people not eating, drinking, nor performing other worldly functions in the World to Come and explained that resurrected individuals will survive during this time without sustenance, just as Moses survived for 40 days on Mount Sinai without eating or drinking (Exodus 34:28):

> With reference to this World to Come, the Rabbis stated in the Talmud: [The sage] Rav often said "in the World to Come there will be neither eating nor drinking, neither envy nor hatred nor competition. All [there will be] is that the righteous will sit with their crowns upon their heads and they will delight in the glory of the Divine presence." . . . This purports to state that the existence of the people who will merit the World to Come will be made possible by the light of the [Divine] glory. This is analogous to the soul's existence in the body in this world being attained by eating and drinking. This concept is akin to the verse, "In the light of the King's countenance is life" (Proverbs 16:15), which was interpreted by the Rabbis in [the midrash] Veielik Shemot Rabba as follows: "And they beheld God, and did eat and drink." It was eating and beholding.[21]

Another concept suggested by Nachmanides is that the Garden of Eden of souls after death has both a physical and spiritual location. The notion of a fiery hell with eternal torment following an adverse judgment was a Greek idea subsequently adopted by Christianity and Islam and is not found in Judaism. Nevertheless, it is generally agreed that there is a period of judgment after death limited to 12 months that takes place in a depository of souls called the Garden of Eden. During this time of judgment, sinful souls are whitewashed from sin in a place called *Gehinnom* or *Ge ben Hinom*. In this way, and in contrast to Christianity and Islam, Judaism has softened the existential anxieties related to death, and a Jew can focus on living an optimal life rather than on the punishment that could be forthcoming in the afterlife. There will also be a final judgment sometime after the resurrection. Apart from a few limited cases, every Jew, as well as all righteous gentiles, will merit

---

21 Nachmanides. *The Gate of Reward*. Translated and Annotated by Rabbi Dr. Charles B. Chavel, 109. Shilo Publishing House Inc., New York, 1983. The author points out that the last quotation is actually from *Vayikra Rabba* 20:7. In *Illuminating Jewish Thought. Explorations of Free Will, the Afterlife, and the Messianic Era* by Rabbi Netanel Wiederblank, 381. Maggid Books. Rabbi Wiederblank quotes Rabbi Bachya (Deuteronomy 30:15): "*If you argue that the physical organs will be for naught in the World to Come, [we respond] that they will not be for naught, since they will be receiving the reward and pleasure through the united body and soul just as they worked together to do the commands [in our present world].*"

the World to Come. Those not destined for the World to Come will go into non-existence.

The following is a summary of the steps comprising the messianic era and World to Come according to Nachmanides:

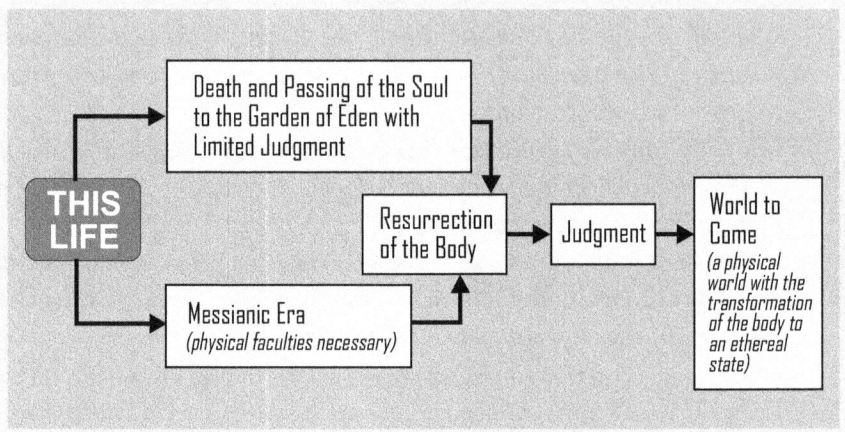

NACHMANIDES' LOVE OF THE LAND OF ISRAEL

Nachmanides and Maimonides had different approaches to living in the Land of Israel. Maimonides did not include living in Israel in his list and explanations of the 613 Biblical commandments in his book *Sefer Hamitzvot*. Nachmanides strongly disagreed with this and thought that living in the Land of Israel should be regarded as a Biblical command. His supporting Torah text is the following: "*And you shall take possession of the land and dwell therein, because I have given you this land to inherit and you shall inherit it*" (Numbers 33:53).[22]

His proof that this is an explicit Torah command also emerged from Moses' exhortation to the spies: "*Go up, take possession, as the Lord, God of the fathers has spoken to you, fear not, nor be dismayed.*" When they refused to go up, the Torah states: "*You rebelled against the commandment of the Lord and disobeyed him*" (Deuteronomy 9:23).

He wrote further:

Our sages extolled the virtues of the Land of Israel in extravagant terms. They said: "He who leaves it and lives outside the land should be regarded

---

22 "*The fourth command (mitzvah) that we were commanded [is] to conquer the land that God gave to Abraham, Isaac and Jacob, and not to abandon it to the hands of other nations or to emptiness.*" Nachmanides, *Commentary on Maimonides' Codification of Biblical Precepts (Sefer Hamitzvot)*.

as an idolater." I maintain that such hyperbolic statements were prompted by their concern to honor this explicit positive commandment of the Torah to take possession of the land and live therein. Accordingly, it is a positive commandment applying to every generation, binding on each one of us, even during the period of exile, as is clear from many passages in the Talmud.

Obviously, Maimonides did not explain why he excluded laws from his book *Sefer Hamitzvot* and much ink has been expended attempting to explain why he took the approach he did in contradistinction to Nachmanides.[23] One possibility is that Maimonides did not consider living in Israel important in the period in which he lived, as he anticipated an ingathering of the exiles in messianic times. As mentioned, Maimonides did visit Israel in 1165, although this was only a brief stop on his way to Egypt. Nachmanides, on the other hand, immigrated to Israel after his debate with Pablo Christiani.

In 1263, as the most distinguished rabbi in Christian Spain, Nachmanides was forced to participate in a four-day debate in Barcelona against Pablo Christiani in the presence of King James I of Aragon. Pablo Christiani was a Jew who had converted to Christianity and joined the Order of the Dominicans. Christiani's aim in arranging this debate was to demonstrate the truth of Christianity by referencing Jewish sources, such as the Bible and Talmud. The Church anticipated a knock-out win that would lead to a surge in Jewish conversions to Christianity. In contradistinction to similar debates in the past, Nachmanides was given a free hand to present his arguments and he demolished his opponent. After the debate, the king of Aragon presented him with prize money for his yeshiva and declared: "I have never seen a man defend a wrong cause so ably." However, the Church did not take this humiliation as calmly, and Nachmanides was hounded and forced to leave Spain. At this time, he made the bold decision to immigrate to Jerusalem. Given the uncertainties and dangers involved, neither his wife nor any other member of his family was prepared to accompany him.

The desolation that Nachmanides found when he arrived in Jerusalem in 1267 would have been overwhelming. Not only Jerusalem but the whole country was in ruins. As Nachmanides wrote to his family: *"What can I tell*

---

23 There has been much discussion as to why Maimonides did not include living in the Land of Israel as a Biblical command. Another answer suggested, besides the one in this chapter, is that Maimonides did not include broad fundamental aspects of the Torah in his listing. In contrast to Nachmanides, he may also have believed that living in Israel was a rabbinic, and not a Torah, command. For a thorough summary of this topic see https://www.mhcny. org/parasha/1043.pdf.

you about the Land of Israel? The ruin and desolation are very great. As a rule, the holier the site, the greater the desolation. Jerusalem is the most destroyed of all, and Judea more than the Galilee." Nevertheless, he continued: *"Despite all the destruction, it is still a goodly land."*[24] With this brief proviso, he demonstrated his incredible love of the Land of Israel.

Much of this destruction was due to the recent Mongol invasion.[25] However, the Mongols had been defeated by the Muslim Mamelukes, and the Mameluke sultan encouraged Nachmanides to settle in Jerusalem and rebuild its Jewish Quarter.[26]

But what could a 72-year-old man alone in a city of ruins achieve? The answer is that he succeeded in renewing Jerusalem's Jewish Quarter. When Nachmanides arrived in Jerusalem he could find only two Jews, dyers who had permission to work in the city. He first established a synagogue in a partially ruined and abandoned church on Mount Zion, and because of his reputation he was soon able to gather a prayer quorum. From this beginning, Jerusalem's Jewish population would continue to grow. The Expulsion of Jews from Spain in 1492, in particular, led to a wave of immigration to the Holy Land.

Ironically perhaps, given the Crusaders' prior bloody relationship with Jews and their massacre of the Jews of Jerusalem, a large group of prominent European rabbis was studying in the port city of Acre in the Crusader kingdom on the Mediterranean coast. Nachmanides visited them for the *Rosh Hashana* (New Year) holiday and gave a long discourse in the synagogue. At its end, he elaborated on why he had come to Israel:

> *What is all this business about God's country? Is not the whole world God's country? He created and formed all things and all is His! But the Land of Israel is the nub of the world, the Almighty's very personal and private estate that He manages directly. He appointed over it no heavenly custodian, no officer nor governor when He bequeathed it to the people who proclaim the unity of His name, His darling seed. This is the force of the texts: "You shall be to me the pick of all the peoples, for all the land is Mine. You shall be My people and I shall be your God; You shall not be subject to any other gods at all."*[24]

---

24   *Kitvei Haramban* by Rabbi B. Chavel. Mosad Harav Kook, Jerusalem.

25   Starting from northern China, the Mongols created the world's largest contiguous empire. They invaded Syria in 1260 and 1300 CE and destroyed the Abbasid Empire. They then extended their invasion into Palestine, reaching as far as Gaza. These raids were not undertaken by the main part of the Mongol army and were intended for destruction and looting, rather than empire building.

26   The Mamelukes were slave soldiers from Central Asia who comprised an elite fighting force for the sultans. They overthrew their masters and ruled Egypt and Syria from 1250 to 1517.

He brought the following sentences from the Torah as support for his assertion that the Jewish people had been allotted the Land of Israel: "*When He separated the children of men, He set the borders of the peoples according to the number of the children of Israel. For the portion of the Lord is His people, Jacob the lot of His inheritance*" (Deuteronomy 32:8-9).

He also explained the relationship of the Torah commands to the Land of Israel:

> *Judaism was designed for those living in the Land of the Lord. . . . Living in the land of Israel is equal in importance to all the commandments – this is what brought me out of my country and thrust me from my place. I abandoned my home and forsook my heritage. I made myself as the raven to my son, heartless to my daughters, because it was my desire to end my days in the bosom of my mother.*"[24]

Nachmanides also felt that Torah laws only had true value in the Land of Israel. Outside of Israel they were practice, so to speak, for when the Jewish people would return to their land.[27]

PERSPECTIVES ON THE VIEWS OF MAIMONIDES AND NACHMANIDES

Maimonides and Nachmanides have been extremely influential in explaining and promoting Jewish tradition and practice, including the concepts of messianism and Zionism. Although their approaches are different, there is some commonality. Shared beliefs include the following:

- The next redemption will be messianic.
- The messianic era will be orchestrated by a figure called the Messiah, or anointed one.
- The messianic era will presage the World to Come. According to Maimonides, these eras will be separated by a long period of time, but there will nevertheless be a connection.
- Neither described an apocalypse as being part of the messianic era or World to Come.

However, it has to be admitted that neither of their ideas fit well into the current reality in the State of Israel. Almost 50% of world Jewry now live

---

27   Nachmanides was not the only one to say this. See also Rashi to Deuteronomy 11:18 and the Sifrei 43.

in Israel, and the Jewish people continue to gather themselves from the four corners of the globe. It is difficult to deny that the Jewish people are being redeemed. It is also clear that this redemption shows none of the messianic features described by the ancient prophets of Israel or by these two giants of the Jewish tradition.

For those who participated in the second redemption from Babylon, a major issue was whether they were participating in a true redemption and whether God would support them in the rebuilding of the Temple. The issue of whether this is a true redemption is not a question for today's Jewry. Especially after the Holocaust, there can be no difficulty in believing that the creation of the State of Israel has been directed by God. Israel could never have been created without a host of unlikely steps occurring. The present ingathering of the exiles is also the result of multiple geopolitical and economic forces that have led to the Jewish people uprooting themselves from their countries of origin and heading to the Promised Land. The major question for those viewing this third redemption in religious terms is not whether God is supporting this redemption, but whether it is, or is about to become, messianic.

Three answers have been suggested:

One approach is that the words of the sages in Jewish texts have no relevance to the present State of Israel. Despite all appearances to the contrary, this return is not a true redemption. This is the view of many of Israel's ultra-orthodox Jews who cannot conceive how redemption could have been engineered by secular Jews and how a state created during a true redemption could be non-*halachic*.

A problem with this approach is that it can lead to what can be called messianic passivism. Since the messianic era will arrive in its time, there is no reason to strive to improve society, and there is certainly no reason to attempt to create a utopian state. All that is needed is personal devotion with prayer and acts of piety to speed up the arrival of the Messiah. The origins of this idea will be covered in the next chapter. This perspective regards the State of Israel as having no more religious significance than any other secular state in the world. It also permits a detachment from the functioning and visions of the state. When a significant number of people hold this view (as is the case today), this detachment and sometimes active antagonism to state bodies can become a problem for the welfare of the state itself.

A second answer, and probably the most widely held in orthodox circles, is that what was written by the prophets of ancient Israel and the sages of Israel about messianic times will indeed occur – but we are still at its very beginnings; we are in *"the heels or footsteps of messianic times"* (*Ikvot haMashiach*). Look carefully and one can see the footprints. This resembles to a certain extent the views of Rav Kook and his present-day followers, although Rav Kook believed that the messianic era had already arrived. This will be discussed in a later chapter about Rav Kook.

A third answer, and probably the least popular in the orthodox world, is to admit that neither the ideas of Maimonides nor Nachmanides quite fit the present situation, although one could say that Maimonides' non-miraculous messianic era is the closest. At the present time, a Messiah has not appeared, and war and poverty seem far from being eradicated.[28] This does not, of course, preclude the eventual eradication of war and poverty, nor viewing the Messiah as a process rather than a person.

It could also mean, however, that the ideas of Maimonides and Nachmanides need fine tuning, and redemption and messianic times will not necessarily be linked. In fact, the situation today is similar to that at the time of the return of the exiles from Babylon when there was also no connection between the two. It could also mean that God intended that the Jewish people

---

28   The roots of the notion of a messianic figure initiating and coordinating the messianic era can be traced to the Biblical period. King David was assured by the prophet Nathan that his house would be established forever (in Hebrew *ad olam*) (2 Samuel 7:13, 25, 29 and 22:51). Despite the division of the Israelite kingdom after the death of Solomon, there was still hope among the prophets that a united Davidic kingdom would again be established (Amos 9:11, Isaiah 11:10 and Hosea 3:5). The prophets Haggai and Zechariah also prophesied that a descendent of David would rule a future independent Israelite kingdom. Berman points out that the Hebrew word *olam* does not necessarily mean eternally in the Bible, but can also mean indefinitely (although Berman's discussion is not related to the issue raised in this chapter) (See "Three Misunderstood Terms: Hok Olam, Mishpat and Lo Tosif" in *Ani Maamin. Biblical Criticism, Historical Truth, and the Thirteen Principles of Faith* by Joshua Berman, 154. Maggid Books, Jerusalem. 2020). Berman suggests that when the Bible means eternally it expresses matters in a more definitive way, such as *olam va'ed* or *me'olam va'ad olam,* which have more the meaning of eternity. See also Maimonides *Guide for the Perplexed* II:28. The nature of such a promise may also depend on who is making it. One would not expect God to renege on this type of promise. Samuel, on the other hand, promised Eli the High Priest that he would serve God *"forever (le'olam),"* but later removed Eli from his position (1 Samuel 2:30-31). See also "The Messiah" in the Jewish Virtual Library including Second Temple Period, Messiah in Rabbinic Thought, and The Doctrine of the Messiah in the Middle Ages (https://www.jewishvirtuallibrary.org/messiah). Note, however, that there were sages who believed there would not be a Messiah in the future: *"Rabbi Hillel said: 'There is no Messiah for Israel for he was consumed in the time of Hezekiah.' Rav Yosef said: 'May Rabbi Hillel's Master forgive him. Hezekiah lived during the First Temple while Zechariah prophesied during the Second Temple' "* (TB Sanhedrin 99a). Rabbi Hillel's views were clearly not accepted by the sages who were not prepared to dismiss the prophecies of Zechariah. Rashi explains that Hillel believed that there would be a redemption but no Messiah.

and the nations of the world should strive (with God's help) to create their own ideal societies without the aid of a messianic figure.

As we ponder these matters, it is worth considering Maimonides' own words on the eschatological issues stated in his *Mishna Torah*:

> *All these and similar matters cannot be [definitely] known by man until they occur, for these matters are undefined in the prophets' [words], and even the wise men have no established tradition regarding these matters, but only [their own] interpretation of the verses. Therefore, there is a controversy among them regarding these matters. Regardless [of the debate concerning these questions] neither the order of the occurrence of these events nor their precise detail are among the fundamental principles of the faith. A person should not occupy himself with the aggadot and homiletics concerning these and similar matters, nor should he consider them as essentials, for [study] of them will neither bring fear nor love [of God].*[29]

---

29 Maimonides, *Mishna Torah*, The Laws of Kings and their Wars 12:2. In an essay "Messianic Wonders and Skeptical Rationalists," Hakira 6, 2008, Rabbi Natan Slifkin discusses whether aggadic interpretations of the sages of the Talmud can be regarded as definitive and whether there is therefore an obligation on Jews to believe them (https://hakirah.org/Vol%206%20Slifkin.pdf). There are certainly rabbis who have believed this, such as the Ran (Rabbi Nissim ben Reuven of Germany) who is quoted by Slifkin as saying: "*And just as we are commanded to follow their consensus in the laws of the Torah, we are also commanded to follow everything that they say to us by way of tradition with opinions and elucidation of verses, whether or not the saying is with regard to a command.*" However, this would only be with respect to a received tradition. The majority of post-talmudic sages do not regard aggadic statements as binding. See Rabbi Chaim Eisen's "Maharal's Be'er ha-Golah and His Revolution in Aggadic Scholarship – in Their Context and on His Terms", Hakira vol 4. Nevertheless, Maimonides would not have held that belief in the arrival of the Messiah and messianic period are non-binding and he includes this as one of his 13 principles of faith (found in Introduction to Perek Helek).

Chapter 13

Kabbala, Messianism and the Vilna Gaon

A new stage in the history of Jewish messianism began in the 1500s, when many Jews turned to Lurianic kabbala as a means of hastening the messianic redemption. The study of kabbala was subsequently suppressed in the mid-1600s in the wake of the Shabtai Zvi debacle, and by the 1700s it was practiced by only a few elites. However, this would change with the rise of Hasidism, a revivalist messianic movement that swept through Eastern Europe in the 1700s that popularized kabbala.

The Vilna Gaon is a pivotal figure in understanding the controversies that surrounded this new movement and its popularization of kabbala. However, one cannot but note the ironies in his involvement in this dispute. He was a scholar who wanted nothing more than to be secluded with his Torah texts, but who now found himself a leading communal figure enmeshed in the dispute between Hasidism and its opponents. He was the foremost expert in the Jewish world on Lurianic kabbala, and yet he berated the Hasidim for promoting and popularizing it. He criticized the Hasidim for their demotion of Torah study in favor of ecstatic prayer; yet it was the lack of spirituality felt by the masses and the exclusivity of the rabbinic leadership and its Torah scholarship that were significant reasons for the popularization of Hasidism.

The development and influence of kabbala

The attraction of messianic kabbala has to be viewed from the perspective of the longing for redemption that had built up in the Jewish world because of the frailty of Jewish life and lack of any other avenue to which this longing could be channeled.

Two events stand out in particular. One was the expulsion of the Jews from Spain. The reconquest of Muslim Spain by the Christians was completed by 1248, and in its wake the Church was able to extend its influence over much of the country. Violence against Jews led to the death of thousands, and many others were persecuted. Some Jews looked to emigration, while a significant number converted to Christianity. However, for many conversos their conversion was a pathway to hell, in that Jews suspected of retaining their Judaism were tortured by the Inquisition. Moreover, the Church eventually realized that only a country free of Jews would prevent the backsliding of the conversos. Under intense pressure from the Church, the order for the expulsion of all Jews from the country was signed by the monarchy in 1492 and up to 100,000 Jews were forced to emigrate. Even more converted. Most left destitute, without buyers for their properties, and many thousands died attempting to reach new places of safety.

Another trauma was the massacres of Jews by the Cossack leader Bogdan Chmielnicki between 1648 and 1656. Almost 100,000 Jews in the Polish-Lithuanian Commonwealth were murdered and 300 communities destroyed by Cossack cruelty and the attendant famine and disease. Almost no Jews took up their offer of conversion to Christianity and instead chose death. Ironically, kabbalistic calculations had indicated 1648 as being a time of messianic expectations, and many were anticipating disturbances in the world order. But their expectations bore no relationship to the horrific reality:

> *Some [Jews] were skinned alive and their flesh was thrown to the dogs; some had their limbs and hands chopped off and their bodies thrown on the road to be crushed by wagons and horses; some had wounds cut deep into them and were then thrown on the street to die a slow death.*[1]

These tragedies forced Jews to look inwards and particularly to Lurianic kabbala as a means of hastening the messianic redemption.

The scholarship of kabbala has a long history. It began in southern France in the 12th century and from there spread to Spain. Nachmanides was studying Torah in southern France at that time, and he incorporated many kabbalistic ideas in his popular Torah commentary when he returned to Spain.

Kabbala is a means of describing the attributes and actions of God. It was accepted practice not to describe the attributes of God, since any description would limit Him. The most one could do was to describe what God was not or describe His actions.[2] Nevertheless, many people felt the need for

---

1   Translated quotation from "The Rise of Chmielnicki" in *Triumph of Survival. The Story of the Jews in the Modern Era 1650-1990* by Berel Wein, 9. Shaar Press, NY. 1990.

2   King David was effusive in his praise of God. Jewish tradition holds that he wrote his Psalms with Divine inspiration which is why so much of Jewish prayer consists of psalms containing praises of God. See "With the songs of Your servant David" in *The Koren Mesorat*

something less abstract, and this need was met by the foundational book of Jewish mysticism, the Zohar. This book was discovered by Moses de Leon in the 13th century. It was allegedly written by Rabbi Shimon bar Yochai, a second-century Tannaitic sage. Tradition holds that Rabbi bar Yochai spent 13 years in a cave hiding from the Romans and was inspired by the prophet Elijah to write this kabbalistic book. Nevertheless, there was always a suspicion that Moses de Leon wrote the book himself, although this suspicion was never great enough to reject Rabbi bar Yochai's authorship or prevent the Zohar's wide acceptance.[3]

The Zohar describes the Divine attributes of the 10 *sephirot (*vessels*)*, whereby God came out of concealment and emanated His existence within the cosmos at the time of creation by successive contractions (*tzimtzumim)* of Divine abundance.

Kabbala received a major boost in the mid-1500s from a group of messianic kabbalists living in Safed in Israel. One of these kabbalists was Rabbi Moshe Cordovero (1522-1570), who systemized the kabbala of the Zohar in an encyclopedic book called *Pardes Rimonim*.

Another extremely influential kabbalistic thinker was Rabbi Yitzchak Luria (1534-1572), who lived in Safed for two years prior to his death at the young age of 40 and produced a new system of kabbala, called Lurianic Kabbala, as a development of the Zohar system. His form of kabbala would take Safed by storm and from there it would spread to the rest of the Jewish world. Rabbi Luria is usually known as *HaAri, Ha'Ari HaKadosh*, or *Arizal*. *Ari* is Hebrew for a lion and *hakadosh* means the holy one, indicating the considerable esteem in which this special individual was held.

Lurianic kabbala deals in particular with two theological issues. First, how was it possible for God to leave room for the creation of a universe when His presence is everywhere? Second, and related to this, how could God create a world out of nothing when His very presence means there is no nothing?[4]

Harav Siddur, with commentary based on the teachings of Rabbi Joseph b. Soloveitchik, 71. OU Press, Koren Publishers, Jerusalem.

3   In "The Zohar I. The Book and its Author" in *Major Trends in Jewish Mysticism*, 156. Schocken Books, New York, 1961, Gershom Scholem makes the argument, based on linguistic analysis, that the author of the Zohar could not have been Rabbi Shimon bar Yochai and must have been Moses de Leon. He points out that the Aramaic in which the Zohar was written was taken from the Babylonian Talmud and Aramaic translation of the Torah, and would not have been the Aramaic used in the time of this Second Temple Tannaitic sage, but rather it was an Aramaic translation of Arabic.

4   "Isaac Luria and His School" in ibid., 260-261.

The Ari's answers to these questions are too complicated to be addressed in this chapter, but the following is an extremely abbreviated and incomplete answer. The Ari described a process of t*zimtzum* (withdrawal), in which God, who is called the *Ein Sof* (That Which Is Without Limit), withdraws from Himself into Himself, resulting in an empty primordial space. A dynamic process involving an intermediate and the light of the *Ein Sof* then results in the formation of 10 *sefirot* (vessels) containing God's creative activity.[5] However, the Divine light is unable to be contained in the vessels of the lower *sefirot*, and this results in a cosmic catastrophe known as *shevirat hakelim* (the breaking of the vessels). This permits the presence of the demonic side of existence necessary for man to be able to choose or reject good and evil. Because of the breaking of vessels, the light of the *Ein Sof* necessary to sustain the *sefirotic* realm becomes fragmented. The task allotted to the Jewish people is for a *tikkun* (putting right) and restoration of the holy sparks to their Source. Once the *tikkun* is complete, redemption will occur not only for the Jewish people but for all mankind and with it the repair of the entire cosmic process. Reincarnation was another aspect of this system.

Rabbi Isaac Luria did not write down his system but taught it to disciples, and his teachings were transcribed by his foremost disciple Rabbi Hayyim Vital (1542-1620), who also lived in Safed, in his book *Etz Hayyim*. Commenting on the restrictions on the study of kabbala made in previous generations and the situation in his own time, Rabbi Vital asserted:

> *Every penalty revealed by this wisdom that he wrote pertains to those generations [only, when the general study of kabbala was not encouraged]. In our generations, however, it is a religious imperative and a great delight to God to reveal this wisdom and by virtue of its [revelation] the Messiah will come.*[6]

A reason for the popularity of Lurianic kabbala was its notion that each individual could influence the messianic process by reconstituting the *sefirot* with sparks of holiness and could thereby help complete cosmic perfection. This could be accomplished by keeping the commands of the Torah, not perfunctorily, but by directing one's intent towards a command, by doing good deeds and by studying kabbala. In addition, kabbalists would direct their

---

5   This is a simplified summary of Rabbi Louis Jacob's summary in *The Unity of God in a Jewish Theology* by Louis Jacobs, 21. Behrman House Inc, NJ, USA.

6   *Mishnat Hasidim*, First Introduction. Quoted in "The Messianic Window of Opportunity: 1740-1781" in *The Gaon of Vilna and his Messianic Vision* by Arie Morgenstern, 16. Gefen Publishing House, Jerusalem.

prayers towards the *Ein Sof* using hints contained within the prayers. Some felt that their living in Israel would also hasten the coming of the Messiah.

Because of the kabbalists living there, Safed became the preeminent Jewish community in Israel at that time, and the ideas and activities emanating from there would have a profound influence on the Jewish world in arousing messianic expectations. Many of the kabbalists of Safed anticipated the imminent arrival of the Messiah and their expectations were focused particularly on nearby Meron, which is the burial place of Rabbi Shimon ben Yochai who revealed the Zohar.

Rabbi Yaakov bei Rav, the leader of the Jewish community in Safed, attempted to establish the *semichah* or rabbinic ordination program that would have permitted the appointing of a Sanhedrin in preparation for the messianic redemption. However, he experienced resistance from the rabbis of other communities, particularly from Jerusalem, and this project was aborted.

His student Rabbi Yosef Caro (1488-1575), whom he ordained, wrote a scholarly work the *Bais Yosef* as a compendium of Jewish law that could be used by all of Jewry, Ashkenazi and Sephardi. This became the definitive *halachic* work of its time and had a considerable influence, second only to Maimonides' *Mishna Torah*. He was a kabbalist and included opinions from the Zohar in his book. This had the effect of ensuring the acceptance of the Zohar and kabbalah in general in Jewish life. He followed this by his *Shulchan Aruch*, which was an abridged form of the *Bais Yosef*, and which became, and still is, extremely popular. These *halachic* works created a substitute for the unsuccessful *semichah* program and would have allowed a common approach to *halacha* among world Jewry at the time of the messianic redemption.

In 1558, a heroine of the Jewish world Dona Gracia Beatrice Mendes, together with her influential son-in-law Don Yosef Nassi, supported a Jewish agricultural settlement in Tiberias. Dona Gracia was one of the richest people in the world and she used her immense wealth to rescue conversos from the Inquisition and further Jewish education, yeshivot and synagogues throughout the Ottoman Empire. This support included sages in Safed. She received permission from the sultan of the Ottoman Empire, Suleiman the Magnificent, to establish Tiberias, then in ruins, as an independent Jewish settlement. The intention was that this would become the basis of an independent Jewish state at the time of the redemption that would soon materialize. The project was eventually abandoned.

THE SHABTAI ZVI DEBACLE AND
MESSIANIC CALCULATIONS

The yearning of the populace for a Messiah and the influence of kabbala on popular thinking led in the 1600s to the Shabtai Zvi debacle, when a major part of the Jewish world threw normal checks and balances to the wind and embraced a very dubious and, as it turned out, false messiah.

Shabtai Zvi (1626-1676) was born in the Ottoman city of Smyrna where he received a traditional Jewish education, including proficiency in Talmud. At age 20 he was ordained as a *chacham,* the Sephardic equivalent of rabbi. He was much attracted to the Zohar aspects of kabbala and particularly to its practical aspects, including asceticism, multiple immersions, prolonged periods of isolation, and self-flagellation. This behavior gained him the reputation of being a holy man. He also at this time began displaying symptoms of manic-depressive psychosis, and this illness would accompany him throughout his life, although it was overlooked by his followers and considered evidence of prophecy.[7] At age 22 he started having delusions that he was the messianic redeemer. He began pronouncing the Tetragrammaton, which was a forbidden act, and announced that he had experienced visions of God. These claims and his strange behavior eventually led to his banishment by the rabbinic authorities of Smyrna.

For the next seven years he lived in various Jewish communities in Greece, Albania and Turkey. People were attracted by his charismatic personality, although many communities banished him. Eventually he made his way to Jerusalem and gathered many adherents as a result of his ascetic behavior and public acts of holiness.

On a visit to Gaza he met Nathan of Gaza, a young man of only 20, and this self-claimed prophet helped Shabtai Zvi launch his messianic career. Nathan declared himself the arisen Elijah and proclaimed the arrival of the Messiah. Threatened with excommunication when he began acting out this role, Shabtai Zvi left Jerusalem and in 1665 returned to his home town of Smyrna, where he announced that he was the Messiah. He was greeted with

---

7 "Shabtai Tzvi: Formative Years" in *Triumph of Survival. The Story of the Jews in the Modern Era 1650-1990* by Berel Wein, 21. Shaar Press, NY. 1990. An interesting question is how much of Shabtai Tzvi's messianic pronouncements were a reflection of mania from his illness. Gershom Scholem quotes one of his followers as saying *"he was like a mortal man and regretted the strange things he had done, for he no longer understood their reasons as he had understood it when he committed them."* See "Sabbatianism and Mystical Heresy" in *Major Trends in Jewish Mysticism* by Gersom Scholem, 292. Schoken Books, New York, 1995.

blowing of the shofar and cries of "Long live our King, our Messiah" in a synagogue.[8]

His fame began spreading throughout the Jewish diaspora. All caution was swept away. People sold their possessions in preparation for moving to Israel. Prayers were said for him in synagogues.[7] Prominent rabbis supported his claims, and doubts and resistance were brushed aside despite his abolishing Jewish laws such as the fast days of the 17th of Tammuz and the Ninth of Av, eating non-kosher food and issuing a new blessing permitting that which had previously been forbidden.[9]

The Sultan of Turkey initially ignored the situation because of the money coming into the coffers of the Ottoman Empire as a result of Shabtai Zvi's fame, but when Shabtai Zvi announced that he would soon liberate Jerusalem from the Sultan's rule the Sultan was forced to act. Shabtai Zvi was given the choice of converting to Islam or death – and he chose the first option, together with a state pension. Three hundred of his supporters also converted with him to Islam.

The reverberations from Shabtai Zvi's conversion and his dashing of world Jewry's messianic hopes continued for many years. The Shabtai Zvi debacle dampened people's enthusiasm for anything related to kabbala and messianism. Non-conformism in Jewish communities was attacked and the study of kabbala went underground.

Nevertheless, the Jewish people's yearning for redemption was not diminished. Over the long term, enthusiasm for the study of kabbala even increased since its study and practice were regarded as the only possible way for achieving the goals of messianism.

An influential kabbalist was Rabbi Immanuel Hai Ricchi (1688-1743). He immigrated to Safed from Italy in 1718 to increase his knowledge of kabbala and spent two years there. On his return to Italy he wrote a summary of Lurianic kabbala that he called *Mishnat Hasidism*.[9] He also calculated a date for the coming of the Messiah.

The Talmud warns against this type of calculation since failure of the Messiah to arrive on the predicted date can destroy belief in his coming.[10]

---

8   Sabbatai Zevi in Wikipedia (https://en.wikipedia.org/wiki/Sabbatai_Zevi).

9   "The Messianic Window of Opportunity 1740-1781" in *The Gaon of Vilna and his Messianic Vision* by Arie Morgenstern, 11. Gefen Publishing House, Jerusalem.

10 TB Sanhedrin 97b states: "*What [is the meaning of the verse]: 'It shall speak of the End and it shall not lie. If it tarries wait for it, because it will surely come; it will not delay' (Habbakuk 2:3). Rabbi Samuel Bar Nachmani said in the name of Rabi Yonasan: 'May the very essence of those who calculate "End" suffer agony! For they say: "Since the [date of the] End [that we calculated] has arrived and the Messiah did not come, he will never come!" Rather [one should]*

Despite this admonishment, many kabbalists were not averse to proposing a date for the beginning of the messianic era. These calculations were based on a talmudic statement in which an analogy was drawn between the six millennia of the Jewish calendar and the six days of creation:

> *The Academy of Eliyahu taught the following Beraisa: the world [is destined to exist for] 6,000 years. [The first] 2,000 [years were of] nothingness, [the second] 2,000 [years were of] Torah, [the third] 2,000 [years should have been] the days of the Messiah.*[11]

The kabbalist Nachmanides proposed the date of 1340 CE for messianic redemption,[12] explaining that since the End of Days was approaching, the prohibition against calculating a date for this was no longer applicable. Even a rationalist such as Maimonides could not resist presenting a date for messianic times.[13] The Zohar predicted messianic times as arriving in the 600th year of the sixth millennium.[14] Rabbi Ricchi therefore calculated the onset of the messianic era as being at the earliest 1740 and proceeding in a gradual process up to 1781.[15]

---

wait for him as it says: 'If he tarries, wait for him.' The Gemara asks: What [is the meaning of the phrase] 'And it declares [veyafeʹa] of the end, and does not lie'? Rabbi Shmuel bar Namani says that Rabbi Yonatan says: May those who calculate the end of days be cursed [tippa], as they would say once the end [of days that they calculated] arrived and [the Messiah] did not come, that he will no longer come at all. Rather, [the proper behavior is to continue to] wait for his coming, as it is stated: 'Though it tarry, wait for it' " (Habakuk 2:3). TB Rosh Hashona 31a and TB Kesubos 105b have the less comforting version: "*May their soul suffer agony.*" See also *Meseches Derech Eretz Rabah,* Chapter 11 that "*one who calculates the End of Days has no portion in the World to Come.*"

11   TB Sanhedrin 97a.

12   Nachmanides, *Commentary to the Torah* on Genesis 2:2. Based on a talmudic statement in TB Sanhedrin 97a and *Bereishis Rabba* 19:8, Nachmanides in his *Commentary to the Torah* on Genesis 2:2 stated that the millennium of the world (based on the Jewish calendar) accords with the numbers of days of Creation, and he estimated that the Messiah would come at the period of the "sunrise" of the "sixth" day, which parallels the creation of man on the sixth day. His prediction, therefore, for the messianic age was 1358 CE. For his rationalization on revealing messianic times see his *Sefer Hageula,* Shaar 4.

13   Maimonides in his *Iggeret Teiman* cites the injunction against revealing a date for messianic times, but then a few pages later he does just that by presenting a date passed on to him by his ancestors *(Iggeret Taiman* Chapter 3). In his defense, it could be said that he was not predicting a date, but passing on a tradition he had received.

14   The *Zohar* states: "*In the 600th year of the sixth millennium, the gates of wisdom on high and the wellsprings of lower wisdom will be opened. This will prepare the world to enter the seventh millennium, just as a person prepares himself toward sunset on Friday for the Sabbath. It is the same here. And the mnemonic for this is (Genesis 7:11), 'In the 600th year . . . all the foundations of the great deep were split.*"

15   "The Messianic Window of Opportunity: 1740-1781" in *The Gaon of Vilna and his*

The calculations of Rabbi Ricchi were widely accepted, and thousands of people began moving to the Old City of Jerusalem, which at that time was the only residential area in Jerusalem. So great was this immigration that the compound of the four Sephardi Synagogues in the Old City had to be expanded to meet the demand. Leading kabbalists also made their way to Israel, including Rabbi Hayyim ben Attar (1669-1743), who came from Morocco via Italy in 1742 and started the Yeshivat Knesset Yisrael in Jerusalem in the building now known as the Or HaHayyim Synagogue.[16] Rabbi Attar was so convinced that this was the prelude to messianic times that he called for mass *aliya (*immigration*)*. He passed away a year later during an epidemic. The Beit El Yeshiva and Synagogue were also inaugurated in the Old City in the mid-1700s, and this yeshiva was one of two well-known yeshivot studying kabbala in the Old City (which it still does).

The Vilna Gaon agreed with the dates of Rabbi Ricchi, although his views on how messianic times would come about parted ways somewhat with the kabbalists who preceded him.

THE INFLUENCE OF THE VILNA GAON

A pivotal figure in the religious issues of the 1700s was the Vilna Gaon. He was a recluse who wished to do nothing more than study and continue his scholarly work, but events in the Jewish world projected him into a leadership position.

He was born in the Polish-Lithuanian Commonwealth to a family of religious scholars.

From a young age it was apparent that he was a genius with a prodigal memory. At the age of six and a half he gave a learned discourse in the main Vilna synagogue in the presence of community scholars. He studied with a teacher until age seven but from then on taught himself. The topics he studied included astronomy, music theory, trigonometry and anatomy, all of which he felt were necessary for understanding Torah related texts. He began studying kabbala at a young age. By age 20, rabbis were submitting their difficult *halachic* questions to him.

Messianic Vision by Arie Morgenstern, 25-26, 95-96. Gefen Publishing House, Jerusalem, 2015.

16 This synagogue is named after *Ohr HaChaim*, Rabbi Hayyim ben Attar's well-known kabbalistic commentary on the Torah, as is also the street on which his yeshiva was located. The courtyard of this synagogue is also where Rabbi Yitzchak Luria was born in 1534.

His life was focused entirely on Torah, and he received financial support from the Jewish community to do this. He adopted an ascetic lifestyle. According to his children, he rarely slept more than two hours during a 24-hour period. To stop himself from falling asleep during the night, he would immerse his feet in cold water and study in a standing position. During the day, he would study with the shutters closed to avoid distraction.

His mind encompassed the entire breadth of Jewish texts. His scholarly work was voluminous. He wrote glosses to the most commonly studied texts such as the Babylonian Talmud, midrashim, the *Shulchan Aruch* (*Bi'urei haGra*), commentary on the Mishna (*Shenoth Eliyahu*), the Torah (*Adereth Eliyahu*), and commentaries to kabbalistic works such as the *Zohar* and *Sefer Yetzirah*. He was regarded as the foremost exponent of kabbala of his time.

He did not publish during his lifetime, although some of his work was published in his name. His main works were written by his disciples to whom he dictated. Of extreme value to those involved in Jewish learning have been his emendations of copyist errors that had crept into the Talmud, Mishna and other texts. Only someone of his stature and piety could have made corrections that would be accepted by everyone.

His erudition did come at a cost in that he did not relate to anyone except in learning or teaching Torah. He married at age 18 but gave over the care of his family entirely to his wife. He did not take much interest in his children's lives. His thoughts were a closed book. Arie Morgenstern quotes the words of his foremost student, Rabbi Hayyim of Volozhin: "*He was too introspective and taciturn to disclose [anything]. The little that he revealed in conversation pertained to some amazing matter and was extracted at infrequent opportunities by [my] leading the conversation.*"[17]

The Vilna Gaon had a major impact on issues of the time that were related directly or indirectly to messianism.

THE DISPUTE BETWEEN THE HASIDIM AND MISNAGDIM

The Vilna Gaon was a leader in the dispute between Hasidism and the opponents of Hasidism, or *Misnagdim* as they were called. The rabbis of Poland, where Hasidism was most active, banned Hasidism with the intent of destroying it.

---

17 Quoted in "Omission and Evasion in the Shaping of the Gaon of Vilna's Persona" in *The Gaon of Vilna and his Messianic Vision* by Arie Morgenstern, 293-294. Gefen Publishing House, Jerusalem, 2015.

Hasidism was a revivalist, kabbalistic, messianic movement begun by the Baal Shem Tov (1698-1760), which spread rapidly throughout Eastern Europe. The Baal Shem Tov succeeded in attracting talented and charismatic disciples, particularly Rabbi Dov Ber, the Maggid of Mezeritch, and he in turn attracted many disciples to spread its message.[18] An important aspect of Hasidism was its popularization of Lurianic kabbala, which after the Shabtai Zvi fiasco had been suppressed but was now seen as providing a means of speeding up messianic redemption through the cosmic effects of individual behavior. Hasidism believed in panentheism, which is the concept that God is highly immanent. In the kabbalistic ideas of Shneur Zalman of Liadi, the author of the kabbalistic work the *Tanya*, the *tzimtzum* (contraction) of the Divine essence was not as complete as in classic Lurianic thought but remained fully present, although still concealed by the natural creative processes.

The Hasidim placed mystical prayer at the center of their spiritual striving and means of *tikkun* (putting right). It was said of the Bal Shem Tov that *"the upper world was revealed to him, not because he had studied much Talmud and commentaries, but because of the prayers he had always uttered with the greatest intensity."* This approach to prayer was continued by his disciples.[19] Whereas prayer had traditionally been petitionary, under the influence of kabbala it became a means of mystical union with the Divine. This meant that Torah learning became somewhat demoted from its primary position in religious life. Hasidism approached religion with joy and encouraged its adherents to perform the commandments with enthusiasm and awareness of God's presence. It also held that evil always contained good within it.[20] This package was extremely attractive to non-scholarly Jews who lived in hamlets, had limited talmudic skills and felt a paucity of spirituality in their lives.

Of concern to the opponents of Hasidism, the *Misnagdim*, was the emphasis that Hasidism placed on prayer as a means of spiritual elevation and attachment (*devekus*) to God and on the time they spent in prayer at the expense of Torah study. The *Misnagdim* felt that this diminished the role of the Torah scholar, even though some of the Hassidic leaders were Torah scholars in their own right. As one opponent of Hasidism explained: *"They*

---

18   "Maggid of Mezeritch" in *Triumph of Survival. The Story of the Jews in the Modern Era 1650-1990* by Rabbi Berel Wein, 90. A Shaar Press publication, Monsey, New York, 1990.

19   "Mithnagdic Prayer" in *The Faith of the Mithnagdim. Rabbinic Reponses to Hasidic Rapture* by Allan Nadler, 53. The John Hopkins University Press, 1997, quoting R. Israel ben Eliezer Baal Shem Tov, Kether Shem Tov (Brooklyn, 1987, 22b).

20   "Baal Shem Tov" in *Triumph of Survival. The Story of the Jews in the Modern Era 1650-1990* by Rabbi Berel Wein, 88. A Shaar Press publication, Monsey, New York, 1990.

prolong their prayers until the sun is already in the middle of the heavens [i.e., until noon], and they thus destroy the [very] time balance of Torah study and prayer that has been established by our holy ancestors, for they try to reach the heavens."[21]

The *Misnagdim* did not object to the use of kabbala *per se*, since among them were kabbalists such as the Vilna Gaon who believed that the text of prayer did have cosmic significance and that the power of its words and formulas could contribute to the goal of universal *tikkun*.[22] Nevertheless, they felt strongly that the popularization of kabbala among the masses was inappropriate. Kabbala was for the elite and should not be part of a popular movement.

Morgenstern examines the messianic component to this dispute. Basing themselves on the writings of Rabbi Hayyim Vital, the student of the Ari, Hasidim felt that prayer would hasten the redemption and that all of Rabbi Isaac Luria's teachings had been communicated to him by Elijah the Prophet. The Vilna Gaon disputed the belief that all of Luria's teachings had been transmitted correctly by Rabbi Hayyim Vital, and he held that only part of Luria's teachings had been communicated to him by the prophet. Also, the Vilna Gaon did not believe that prayer would hasten redemption; this could only be accomplished through Torah study, discovery of the secrets of Torah and observance of halacha.[23]

Despite the opposition of the *Misnagdim*, Hasidism continued to spread and eventually it dominated Eastern Europe, other than in Lithuania and White Russia. Nevertheless, Rabbi Berel Wein suggests that the opposition from the *Misnagdim* succeeded in saving the movement from itself, by discrediting its extremists and emphasizing the primacy of intellectual Torah study and halacha in Jewish life.[24]

---

21 "Mithnagdic Prayer" in *The Faith of the Mithnagdim. Rabbinic Reponses to Hasidic Rapture by Allan Nadler*, 55. The John Hopkins University Press, 1997, quoting Wilensky, *Hasidim u-Mithnagdim*, 2:90:cf 1:138.

22 Ibid., 52.

23 "The Dispute between the Gaon of Vilna and the Hasidim over How to Hasten the Redemption" in *The Gaon of Vilna and his Messianic Vision* by Arie Morgenstern, 354-361. Gefen Publishing House, Jerusalem, 2015.

24 "Studying Kabbala" in *Triumph of Survival. The Story of the Jews in the Modern Era 1650-1990* by Berel Wein, 109. Shaar Press, NY. 1990.

The Vilna Gaon's novel ideas on
MESSIANIC REDEMPTION

The Gaon's notions on the messianic era were based on the Lurianic system of *tikkun*, but he also introduced new ideas into messianic thinking. Specifically, he believed that although redemption would be messianic, it would come about by natural means and over a period of time rather than suddenly and miraculously. He also held that Jews needed to be involved in the redemptive process by settling the Land of Israel and working on the land. He agreed with Rabbi Hai Ricchi's calculated date for the beginning of redemption, namely 5,541 years and eight months after Creation, which would be 1781 CE.[25]

The question as to whether redemption will occur at a fixed time or re-quires prior repentance had been discussed in talmudic times. Given that the Vilna Gaon accepted Rabbi Hai Ricchi's predicted dates, he clearly believed there was a fixed time for the messianic era. Nevertheless, this does seem to contradict the Torah since in Deuteronomy Moses declared redemption from exile as dependent on national repentance. In Leviticus, as well, repentance is described as a prerequisite for redemption, although equal emphasis is placed on God remembering His covenant (Leviticus 26:40-44).[26]

However, shortly before his death, Moses recited a poem about the redemption and subsequent faithlessness of the Jewish people and foretold their punishment, but mentioned nothing about the necessity for repentance (Deuteronomy 32:1-43). As Nachmanides (who also believed in a fixed time for redemption) pointed out in his *Commentary to the Torah*:

---

25 'The Gaon of Vilna Attempts to Discover the "Secrets of the Torah" ' *in The Gaon of Vilna and his Messianic Vision* by Arie Morgenstern, 353. Gefen Publishing House Ltd, Jerusalem 2015.
26 The passage in Leviticus 26:40-44 reads: *"Then [in exile] they will confess their sin and the sin of their forefathers, for the treachery with which they betrayed Me, and also for having behaved towards Me with casualness I too will behave toward them with casualness and I will bring them into the land of their enemies – perhaps then their unfeeling heart will be humbled and then they will gain appeasement for their sin. I will remember My covenant with Isaac, and also My covenant with Abraham will I remember and I will remember the land. The land will be bereft of them, and it will be appeased for its sabbaticals having become desolate of them; and they must gain appeasement for their iniquity; because they were revolted by My ordinances and because their spirit rejected My decrees. But despite all this, while they will be in the land of their enemies, I will not have been revolted by them nor will I have rejected them to obliterate them, to annul My covenant with them – for I am the Lord their God. I will remember for them the covenant of the ancients, those whom I have taken out of the land of Egypt before the eyes of the nations, to be God unto them – I am God."*

Now, in this Song there is no condition of repentance or service [of God as a prerequisite for the coming redemption]. Rather, it is a testimonial document stating that we will "commit evil deeds to the upmost" (Jeremiah 3:5) and that He, may He be blessed, will deal with us with wrathful punishments, but He will not cause our memory to cease. Rather, He will ultimately turn back from chastising us and relent and will punish the enemies "with His harsh, great and mighty sword" (Isaiah 27:1) and "forgive our sins for His Name's sake" (Psalms 79:9). This being so [that the Song foretells all of the above without predicating it on Israel's repentance], this song is a clear promise of the future redemption [of the Jewish people] – the [views of] the heretics notwithstanding.[27]

The issue of whether repentance is required for Redemption is discussed in a few places in the Talmud. One talmudic passage leans towards a requisite for repentance:

Rav said: "All the Ends [set times] have passed, and the matter [of the Messiah's arrival] depends only on repentance and good deeds." But Shmuel says: "It is enough for the mourner to endure his [period of] mourning." [The Gemara now notes that this issue has been debated previously by Tannaim]. Rabbi Eliezer says: "If the Jewish people will repent, they will be redeemed, and if not they will not be redeemed." Rabbi Yehoshua said to [Rabbi Eliezer]: "If they do not repent, they will not be redeemed? Rather the Holy One, Blessed is He, will appoint a king over them whose decrees will be as harsh [as those of] Haman [a wicked individual in the Purim story] and the Jewish people will repent and [in this way God] will bring them back to the right [path]."[28]

However, another talmudic passage which discusses a verse that refers to redemption, ("*God will hasten it in its time*" (Isaiah 60:22), sides heavily with a fixed time for the messianic era:

---

27 Nachmanides, *Commentary to the Torah* on Deuteronomy 32:40. This explanation is based on a talmudic statement in TB Sanhedrin 97a and *Bereishis Rabba* 19:8.

28 TB Sanhedrin 97b. An explanation for the words of Shmuel is that the Jewish people are the mourners who have had to suffer the exile, and just as a period of mourning comes to an end, so will the exile (Rashi). Although the Talmud suggests a parallel between the opinions of Rav and Rabbi Eliezer and those of Shmuel and Rabbi Yehoshua, they do seem to be saying different things. The Maharal resolves this by pointing out that even Shmuel would agree that some measure of repentance is required, but God will force repentance that is not self-motivated through external circumstances, whereas Rav and Rabbi Eliezer agree that repentance has to be self-motivated.

Rabbi Alexandri says: Rabbi Yehoshua ben Levi raises a contradiction [in a verse addressing God's commitment to redeem the Jewish people. In the verse: "I the Lord in its time I will hasten it" (Isaiah 60:22)], it is written: "In its time," [indicating that there is a designated time for the redemption, and it is written: "I will hasten it," [indicating that there is no set time for the redemption]. Rabbi Alexandri explains: If they merit [redemption through repentance and good deeds] I will hasten [the coming of the Messiah]. If they do not merit [redemption, the coming of the Messiah will be] in its designated time.[29]

The Talmud leaves the issue without a clear resolution. Maimonides wrote in his *Mishna Torah* that repentance was a prerequisite for redemption:[30] The Vilna Gaon, on the other hand, felt that the Jewish people were incapable of further repentance and that redemption would depend on God's mercy. He wrote:

But the final end depends not on repentance but on kindness, as it is written (Isaiah 48:11) "For My sake, for My sake, will I act" and also on the merit of the patriarchs. And that is the meaning of "He recalls the pious acts of the patriarchs and brings redemption to their children's children for the sake of His Name."[31]

According to the Vilna Gaon's son, his father planned to write a definitive work in the Land of Israel that would resolve all *halachic* disputes that had accumulated over the centuries. This would prepare the Jewish world for

---

29 TB Sanhedrin 98a. The Talmud is discussing the issue that the verse from Isaiah seems contradictory since, if the time of the Messiah is set, how then can it be hastened?

30 Maimonides, *Mishna Torah*, Laws of Repentance 7:5.

31 *Sifra de-zeni'uta* 54b on Sanhedrin 98a. Quoted and translation of Arie Morgenstern from "'Redemptive Mystical Action' to 'Redemption by Natural Means'" in *The Gaon of Vilna and his Messianic Vision* by Arie Morgenstern, 396. Gefen Publishing House, Jerusalem, 2015. (Also *Biur ha-Gra le-tiqunei haZohar* 74). The Schottenstein Edition of the Artscroll *Talmud*, Tractate Sanhedrin, 98a, Mesorah Heritage Foundation, 1995 also brings other published ideas as to how a generation that is entirely guilty can be redeemed. For example: redemption will occur even if the people are guilty (Abarbanel); the redemptive process will elevate the people to the necessary spiritual level (Radak); God will compel the Jewish people to repent by placing over them a harsh king (ibid., *Baraisa* 97b) (Maharsha); God will be forced to bring about redemption, otherwise the Jewish tradition will be lost (Chafetz Chaim in *Tzipisa LiYeshuah*). One might also say that the steadfastness of the Jewish people in keeping to the covenant during their thousands of years of exile is reason enough for God's compassion in bringing about redemption. However, this redemption will only take place when the historical circumstances are propitious for God's plans for the Jewish people and humanity.

the messianic redemption. Therefore, in 1778 the Gaon left his hometown to make his way to Palestine. However, he aborted his attempt before leaving Europe. Why he did this is unclear. All he would say was: "*I did not receive permission from heaven.*" There has been much speculation as to why he changed his mind. Morgenstern assumes that he was unable to locate mystic texts in Amsterdam that would have enabled him to finish this *halachic* work.[32]

Nevertheless, his aborted trip marked a turning point in his life. From this time on he began teaching, and for the next 18 years he would ensure that all the knowledge he had accumulated over the years was transmitted to a select cadre of disciples who were able to keep up with his demanding instruction. This teaching focused on texts that would be needed for messianic times, such as the agricultural laws and the service in the Temple. The order of *Zera'im* dealing with the agricultural laws is discussed in only one tractate in the Babylonian Talmud, but is covered in 11 tractates in the Jerusalem Talmud. However, because of corruptions in the text, these tractates are difficult to understand and were rarely studied. The Gaon now taught this material one on one to his students.

After the death of the Vilna Gaon, between 1808 and 1809, more than 500 of his followers, or *Perushim* as they were called, took the arduous 15-month journey to Ottoman Palestine to put his ideas into practice. Their organization was called *Chazon Tzion* (Vision of Zion) and it had three main objectives: to rebuild Jerusalem as the Torah center of the world, to aid the ingathering of the Jewish exile and to expand already settled areas in Palestine.

Discussing their *aliya*, Morgenstern writes:

> *Their messianic perception contrasts with that of Lurianic Kabbala. Therefore, their aliya in the early 19th century marks a dramatic change in approach from the failed attempts to hasten the redemption in mystical spiritual ways. This new-old outlook on the path to redemption called for the integration of messianic activism and the historical process or, in other words, redemption by natural means. Based mainly on the Jerusalem Talmud, which views redemption as an incremental demarche, this perspective seeks to accelerate the redemption through the rebuilding of Jerusalem and the reclamation of the Land of Israel from its desolation, rather than by means of an external, supernatural, one-off event.*"[33]

---

32 'From "Redemptive Mystical Action" to "Redemption by Natural Means" ' in *The Gaon of Vilna and his Messianic Vision* by Arie Morgenstern, 385. Gefen Publishing House, Jerusalem, 2015.

33 Quotation from "Epilogue" in ibid., 405-406.

The first major hurdle with which the immigrants had to contend was that the Ottoman authorities refused to allow them to settle in Jerusalem because of the unpaid debts of a previous Ashkenazi community. They therefore had to move to Safed and other cities, where they formed the basis of new Ashkenazi communities. However, eventually they did receive permission to settle in Jerusalem, and in 1837 they dedicated their first synagogue in the Old City, called Menachem Zion.

What was the overall influence of the *Perushim*? The *Perushim* and their progeny did have some influence on the Jews in Palestine in promoting the ideas of the Vilna Gaon and his customs of prayer, reestablishing an Ashkenazi presence in the Old City of Jerusalem, developing centers of Torah study, and creating new neighborhoods in Jerusalem, such as Mea She'arim. One of their descendants, Yehoshua Yellen, and his brother-in-law established the first agricultural settlement in Palestine in Motza, just outside Jerusalem, in the 1860s, which predated the agricultural enterprises of the First Aliya. In the late 1800s another descendent of the *Perushim*, Joseph Rivlin, was an initiator and contractor for new neighborhoods built in Jerusalem outside the Old City. All these projects conformed to the activist pathway laid out by the Vilna Gaon. Nevertheless, the *Perushim* were never able to establish a movement with mass appeal, and a substantial number of their descendants left the country during the 1930s because of Arab riots.

THE FATE OF KABBALA AND KABBALISTIC ZIONISM

The Jewish world eventually lost interest in kabbalistic messianism. Calculated dates for the arrival of the Messiah based on kabbalistic ideas came and passed without his appearance, and religious leaders were unwilling to promote further immediate expectations of the messianic era despite the sixth millennium drawing to a close. Meanwhile, other than the Lubavitch and Breslow Hasidic movements, which retained their messianic and kabbalistic emphasis, Hasidism became more interested in personal rather than national redemption. Competition in the form of the *Haskala*, or Jewish Enlightenment, provided a new outlet for the Jews of Central and Eastern Europe interested in cultural renewal, liberalism, rationalism, and integration into the societies around them. As a result of these changes sweeping Europe, Orthodoxy became more engaged in saving itself and its followers than involving itself in religious disputes and saving the Jewish world via changing cosmic reality.

The Vilna Gaon and his followers were successful in maintaining the primacy of Torah study and the Torah scholar in Jewish life, despite their failure to halt the spread of Hasidism.[34] The Gaon's foremost disciple, Rabbi Hayyim of Volozhin, established the famous Volozhin Yeshiva in Volozhin which became the prototype of all later yeshivot. These yeshivot succeeded in making Torah study the focus of Jewish religious life.[35] One could even say that the Vilna Gaon and his disciples were more successful in this than they could ever have imagined. The number of men engaged in full-time Torah study today in the State of Israel has reached the tens of thousands, to the extent that this way of life has become an issue of contention in the state because of its financial and social implications.[36]

---

34 "The Gaon of Vilna" in *Triumph of Survival. The Story of the Jews in the Modern Era 1650-1990* by Berel Wein, 100-102. Shaar Press, NY, 1990.

35 For example, the talmudic passage: *"And even if a person studies and masters all of these,* "*the fear of the Lord is his treasure," (Isaiah 33:6) [it is preeminent]. So said Rava: 'When they bring a man to judgment, they say to him: "Did you negotiate in good faith, designate times for Torah study, have children, await the redemption, and reason wisely, inferring one thing from another?'"* Rava said: *[After departing from this world], when a person is brought to judgment [for the life he lived in this world], they say to him [in the order of that verse: Did] you conduct business faithfully? Did you designate times for Torah [study]? Did you engage in procreation? Did you await salvation? Did you engage [in the dialectics of] wisdom or understand one matter from another? And, nevertheless, beyond all these, if the fear of the Lord is his treasure, yes, [he is worthy, and] if not, no, [none of these accomplishments have any value]* (Shabbat 31a). See also the *Mishna Torah* of Maimonides, Laws of Talmud Torah, Chap. 1, law 8: *"Every Jew is required to learn Torah whether he is poor or rich, whether healthy or suffering pain, whether a young man or one who has grown weak; even if he is a poor man who makes his living collecting charity by going from door to door, even if he is a husband and has young children, he must set for himself times for learning Torah during the day and night as it says: 'And you shall think about it day and night (Joshua 1:8)'."*

36 On balance, the Jewish tradition is not in favor of full-time Torah study at the expense of leaving one's family in poverty and living off charity. A Mishna in *Pirkei Avot* says: *"Rabban Gamliel the son of Rabbi Yehuda the Prince said: 'Good is Torah study together with a worldly occupation, for the exertion in both makes one forget sin. All Torah study without work will result in waste and will cause sinfulness.'"* (Avot 2:2). The Talmud states: *"One should flay carcasses in the market and earn a living. He should not say 'I am a priest, I am a great man and such work is beneath me'"* (TB Pesachim 113a). Maimonides writes: *"Whoever thinks he will study Torah and not work and will be supported by charity, profanes God's name, shames the Torah, darkens the light of knowledge, causes harm to himself and takes his life from this world. For it is forbidden to derive benefit from the Torah in this world"* (Maimonides, *Mishna Torah*, Talmud Torah 3:10). However, in the view of later *halachic* authorities the issue becomes more nuanced if the individual is able to support his own learning or if he receives a stipend. The Rama in *Yoreh Deah* 246:21, commenting on the ruling of Maimonides, writes: *"However, one who can support himself well from his own work and still occupy himself with Torah, this is a pious trait and a gift from God. But this is not the way for every man, for it is impossible for most people to occupy themselves with Torah*

The Vilna Gaon's ideas on the integration of Zionism and messianism in bringing about a messianic redemption were influential at the time, but over the longer term their impact was limited. The *Hovevei Zion* movement founded in Eastern Europe in 1881 to promote Jewish immigration to Palestine was not a messianic movement, but some of its members saw their involvement in redemptive and messianic terms and the movement was supported by many rabbis. Members of *Hovevei Zion* were part of the wave of immigration that came to Palestine between 1881 to 1903 termed the First Aliya. Among these immigrants was a remarkable young rabbi from the Russian Empire, a mystic and kabbalist called Rav Abraham Isaac Kook, who began promoting the idea that not only were the Jewish people being redeemed but this redemption was a messianic one. More about him in chapter 15.

---

and grow in its wisdom and still support themselves." For the source of these quotations and additional references, see *Mishna Berura.* Shiur #91. Simanim 155-156 by Rav Asher Meir. Yeshivat Har Etzion. Israel Koschitzky Virtual Beit Midrash (VBM). (https://www.etzion. org.il/en/simanim-155-156-appropriate-relationship-between-torah-learning-and-work).

Chapter 14

THEODOR HERZL – SECULAR UTOPIANISM AND THE FIRST STEPS IN REDEMPTION

D uring the First Zionist Congress that he arranged in Basel, Switzerland, in 1897, Theodor Herzl wrote in his diary:

Were I to sum up the Basel Congress in a word – which I shall be very careful not to do publicly – it would be this: At Basel I founded the Jewish state. If I said this out loud today, I would be answered by universal laughter. Perhaps in five years, and certainly in fifty, everyone will admit it.[1]

He was pretty close. Just a few months more than 50 years after his making this diary entry, the State of Israel was declared. That it happened at all is due in no small measure to his tireless efforts.

Herzl was the person who planted the idea into the consciousness of the Jewish people and the diplomats, politicians and leaders of the Great Powers that the Jews were a nation and deserved a state, preferably in Palestine. He was recognized as a political leader of the Jewish people, the first in thousands of years, and his First Zionist Congress would be the first step in their redemption.

Admittedly, from a reading of classic Jewish sources, Herzl was not the type of person one would have imagined leading a Jewish redemption. He was not religious. Prior to his initiation of the Zionist project, he had had no involvement with Jewish causes. He was West European rather than East European, and East Europe was where most Zionist activities were then being pursued. His book about a utopian Jewish homeland, *Altneuland*, was framed

---

1   Quoted from "The Constituent Assembly: The Basel Congress" in *Herzl's Vision. Theodor Herzl and the Foundation of the Jewish State* by Shlomi Avineri, 141. BlueBridge, New York, 2013. Shlomo Avineri is a political scientist who has written extensively on 19th-century political philosophy. This book is a classic on the life of Theodor Herzl and there are several quotations from it in this chapter.

in the humanistic values with which he was familiar and not in traditional messianic terms. His utopian state provided plenty of room for religion but was basically secular.

So why, you may be asking, would I include a chapter on Herzl in a book about messianism? There are a number of reasons. Messianism is strongly linked in Jewish sources to redemption, and Herzl was the person who placed the possibility of redemption into the minds of Jews and the great powers in the 19th century. Moreover, Herzl thought in utopian terms, although in relation to the liberal humanism of Western Europe. This was the reason for his writing his book *Altneuland* about a utopian Jewish state. It is also the case that the present State of Israel bears a far greater resemblance to *Altneuland* than that described in the Book of Isaiah. In this respect, therefore, Herzl's vision can be considered a competitor to the messianic vision.

This brings to the fore the question – is Israel to be no more than a typical state, albeit one that replicates the best that Western Europe has to offer, or does it have another mission? And finally, since it was such a big issue for Herzl, his ideas on antisemitism lead us to revisit this topic.

Herzl – from thinker and writer to Zionist activist

Herzl (1860-1904) was born in the Jewish quarter of Pest (now the eastern part of Budapest) to a secular Jewish family. His father was a successful businessman. When he was 18 the family moved to Vienna, at that time part of the Austro-Hungarian Empire. He attended a Jewish grade school and then a local gymnasium. Higher education had become fully open to Jews, and he studied law at the University of Vienna and then worked briefly in law. Herzl was enamored of German culture. He was interested in writing and wrote a number of plays that were performed in Vienna. He worked as the Paris correspondent for a Viennese paper, the *Neue Freie Presse*, which was run by Jews and converted Jews and had a large Jewish readership.

To appreciate the pathway of Herzl's life, some background is needed on the condition of Jews in Europe in the late 1800s.

Between the late 18th and early 20th centuries, Jews in Western and Central Europe obtained equality and citizenship rights as a result of the French Revolution, the Napoleonic Wars and the unification of Germany. With their emancipation, Jews began moving from villages and small towns into the larger cities, and as a result of new laws in France, Germany and the

Austro-Hungarian Empire they were able to fully participate in the academic, financial, scientific, and intellectual life of these countries.

Until this time, the people of Western and Central Europe had expressed their identity through the Christian denominations to which they belonged, but identity was now increasingly being expressed in terms of nationality. The Austro-Hungarian Empire was a large empire comprising many nationalities. However, the more the empire did on a political level to accommodate the nationalistic feelings of its people, the more they wished to express their nationalism. Herzl doubted that this empire would survive. In the meantime, the Jews were attempting to integrate into this multi-cultural cauldron, but in so doing were encountering considerable nationalistic Jew-hatred, as distinct from the religious hatred of centuries past. The more successful they were at integration, the more they were resented for it. When Herzl was still a young man, an open antisemite, Dr. Karl Lüeger, was elected mayor of Herzl's home town Vienna.

While still in university, Herzl was exposed to antisemitism. He resigned from a nationalist German student fraternity because of an antisemitic speech. He wrote to the fraternity explaining his action and was disappointed when they accepted his resignation. He was much affected by a book by Eugen Dühring that postulated that the inferiority of the Jew was inborn and not a consequence of his social and historic background. Dühring advocated that Jewish property be confiscated since all of it was stolen and that Jews be expelled from their professions and businesses. Herzl made the following comments in his diary:

> *Blood libels about murdered Christian children have been replaced, thanks to the invention of the printing press, by stories about the people's wealth and Christian property being robbed by Jewish capital. . . . Modern oil has been poured on the medieval stake. . . . Free-thinking liberals like Dühring are the true successors of the Dominicans who played that role in the malodorous Middle Ages. And after burning at the stake, robbery will follow (or the other way around) and gentlemen like Dühring will look around for booty.[2]*

The extent to which the situation of the Jewish people preyed on Herzl's mind is often not appreciated since many assume (probably incorrectly) that Herzl's conversion to Zionism came at the time of the Dreyfus trial.

---

2   Translation from "Budapest – Vienna – Paris" in ibid., 55.

Alfred Dreyfus was a Jewish officer on the General Staff of the French Army who was falsely accused of spying for Germany. In December 1894, in a public ceremony, he was stripped of his rank and sent to solitary confinement in Devil's Island. According to one version of the story, Herzl had previously been disconnected from anything Jewish and certainly from anything to do with Judaism. However, while covering the Dreyfus trial as correspondent for the *Neue Freie Presse* he was shocked to the core by the antisemitism surrounding the trial and the cries of "Death to the Jews." He realized then that the only solution for the Jewish people was a state of their own. Herzl would himself promote this version of the story in an article in the literary journal North American Review entitled "On Zionism" written four years after Dreyfus' demotion ceremony.

However, as noted by several authors, it seems clear that despite what he would write later, Herzl's conversion to Zionism had little if anything to do with the Dreyfus case and resulted from many years of contemplation about the place of Jews in Europe.[3] Herzl was a deep thinker and talented writer, and it is possible to trace the evolution of this thinking through his diaries, the many articles he wrote for the *Neue Freie Presse* and his own newspaper *Die Welt*, the plays he wrote, his first Zionist publication, *Der Judenstaat* (*The Jewish State*), and his Zionist novel *Altneuland*. His newspaper, the *Neue Freie Presse*, was aware of his Zionist work, but he was not permitted to use their paper for promotion of his Zionist views and activities.

Herzl fully bought into the official line that Dreyfus was a German spy and deserved the humiliation he was about to receive. It would eventually become apparent that Dreyfus had been framed, but his innocence was not known for many years. Herzl made no mention in his newspaper reports of any antisemitism surrounding the trial. He even mentioned in his reports that the crowds were shouting "Death to the traitor" (and not "Death to the Jews" as he later stated). There would have been no reason for him to downplay any antisemitism related to the trial in his newspaper reports. To the contrary, the large Jewish readership of his newspaper would have been interested in knowing about any anti-Jewish sentiments. His diaries also made no mention of any sudden conversion to Zionism. Rather, he would write:

> As the years went on, the [Jewish] question bored into me and gnawed at me, tormented me and made me very miserable. In fact, I kept coming

---

3   "Budapest – Vienna – Paris" in ibid., 52. Also, "Theodor Herzl's Conversion to Zionism" by Henry J Cohen in *Jewish Social Studies*, volume 32, no 2 (April 1970), 101-110. Indiana University Press and Liam Hoare "Did Dreyfus Affair Really Inspire Herzl?" *The Forward*, 26 February 2014.

back to it whenever my own personal experience – joys and sorrows – permitted me to rise to broader consideration. . . . The Jewish question naturally lurked for me around every turn and corner.[4]

Herzl assumed that antisemitism was the result of economic factors, and he elaborated on this in *Der Judenstaat*:

Modern antisemitism is not to be confounded with the religious persecution of the Jews of former times. It does occasionally take a somewhat religious bias, but the main current of the aggressive movement has now changed. In the principal countries where antisemitism prevails, it does so as the result of the emancipation of the Jews. When civilized nations awoke to the inhumanity of exclusive legislation and enfranchised us, our enfranchisement came too late. It was no longer possible legally to remove our disabilities in our old homes. For we had, curiously enough, developed while in the ghetto into a bourgeois people, and we stepped out of it only to enter into fierce competition with the middle classes.[5]

Herzl felt that as a result of their emancipation Jews had unwittingly created their own antisemitism, and neither they nor their host country had any means of extricating themselves from it.

In his novel *Altneuland* that he wrote later, Herzl described the predicament of Jews in Western and Central Europe at the end of the 19th and beginning of the 20th century:

The persecutions were social and economic. Jewish merchants were boycotted. Jewish workingmen starved out, Jewish professional men proscribed – not to mention the subtle moral suffering to which a sensitive Jew was exposed at the turn of the century. . . . As workingmen, the Jews were hated by their Christian fellows for undercutting the wage standards. As business men, they were dubbed profiteers. Whether Jews were rich or poor or middle-class, they were hated just the same. They were criticized for enriching themselves, and they were criticized for spending money. They were neither to produce nor to consume. They were forced out of government

---

4   Translation from "Between Political Fiction and Political Action" in *Herzl's Vision. Theodor Herzl and the Foundation of the Jewish State* by Shlomi Avineri, 85. BlueBridge, New York, 2013.

5   Translation from "Between Political Fiction and Political Action" in *Herzl's Vision. Theodor Herzl and the Foundation of the Jewish State* by Shlomi Avineri, 85. BlueBridge, New York, 2013.

posts. *The law courts were prejudiced against them. They were humiliated everywhere in civil life.*[6]

Revealing in this respect is a play called *The New Ghetto* that Herzl wrote before he attended the Dreyfus trial and before he returned to Vienna to become an editor for the *Neue Freie Presse*. It is a disturbing play that portrays Jewish Viennese stereotypes in an almost antisemitic way. The main character is Jacob Samuel, who attempts to live by the aristocratic ideas he has picked up through his non-Jewish education. A member of the nouveau riche, he supports himself by stock market speculation. He is sympathetic to a miners' strike, precipitated by flooding in a mine due to the owners' lack of investment in the necessary safety measures. Samuel supports the strike despite the fact that it harms the capitalists, a class of which he himself is a member. Samuel's business partners cannot understand why he is so upset about the consequences of the disaster for the miners. A rabbi at the gathering advocates communal responsibility for the poor, but also a low profile for Jews. The mirror image of Samuel is Emmanuel Wasserstein, to whom only money is of value; honor is irrelevant and he is willing to be treated like a rag. The main message of the play is that emancipated Jews have been forced into a new type of ghetto by the social forces around them that are as powerful as the restrictive forces that existed in the old ghetto. Herzl could not immediately find a theater willing to stage the play, although it was produced a few years later.

Professor Shlomo Avineri, a biographer of Herzl who downplayed the importance of the Dreyfus affair in Herzl's conversion to Zionism, made the following observation:

> *In 1894, when he wrote the play, Herzl had not yet found the answer to his dilemma, but the challenge was clearly stated. It was not the trial of Alfred Dreyfus, but Herzl's long analysis of the failure of emancipation and the rise of German and Austrian antisemitism, that led him to his radical conclusions.*[7]

From his thinking and discussions with others, Herzl concluded that the only solution to the Jewish problem was for the Jews to form their own state. In 1896 he applied his literary skills to the task of writing and published *Der Judenstaat* (The Jewish State).[8] It was widely read and disseminated among

---

6   Quoted from "Book Two, Haifa 1923" in *Altneuland. The Old-New-Land* by Theodor Herzl, 54. WLC. Published from public domain texts.

7   "Budapest – Vienna – Paris" in *Herzl's Vision. Theodor Herzl and the Foundation of the Jewish State* by Shlomo Avineri, 82. BlueBridge, New York, 2013.

8   This is a somewhat dry rather than inspirational pamphlet, containing much technical detail as to how Jews could leave their home countries and settle in a new homeland.

Jews and even became a best seller. Its ideas were supported by many, including the *Hovevei Zion* (Lovers of Zion) movement from Eastern Europe. This group was one of a variety of organizations formed in the early 1880s to promote immigration to Palestine and establish mainly agricultural settlements there. Their efforts were driven by antisemitism in Romania and Russia. On the other hand, many orthodox and assimilated Jews were critical of what Herzl had written, although for very different reasons. Nevertheless, the support engendered from his pamphlet encouraged Herzl to take the next step, which was to develop a political program to actualize his ideas. This program would consume the rest of his life.

Herzl's first step was to announce the First Zionist Congress. This took place in Basel in 1897, and its formation led to further annual congresses attended by elected dues-paying delegates. These congresses oversaw the formation of an executive committee and the establishment of a financial structure to sell shares and bonds. A newspaper he produced, *Die Welt*, became the official Zionist newspaper.

Herzl put considerable effort into trying to obtain a charter from the sultan of the Ottoman Empire that would give the Jews a degree of independence in Palestine, in return for financial incentives he thought he could arrange. However, the sultan was not interested. Herzl appealed to the leaders of the Great Powers to influence him, but they too were unsuccessful.

By the Sixth Zionist Congress in 1903, it was apparent to all that no progress had been made in obtaining permission for a Jewish homeland in Palestine, and Herzl therefore proposed an alternate location which had been tentatively suggested by the British government, Uganda in East Africa. A resolution to investigate this idea further was accepted although it almost split the Zionist body. The Russian delegates were in the main *Hovevei Zion* members who actively promoted settlement in Palestine and Jewish culture in Russia, and they were adamantly opposed to the recommendation. The Uganda option would eventually fizzle out, and a special meeting of the Zionist Executive patched up the differences with the Russian delegates. At the Seventh Zionist Congress in 1905 the Uganda option was removed from the agenda. By then, Herzl had passed away from a cardiac condition at the young age of 44.

In accordance with his will that he be buried eventually in the Land of Israel, 61 years after his death he was reinterred on Mount Herzl in Jerusalem in the section for Zionist leaders. Members of his family were later also reburied there.

Altneuland – a novel about
a Jewish utopian state

Altneuland was published in 1902 and belongs to a genre of books about utopia. But it is much more than this; it also contains the broad outlines of what Herzl regarded as a feasible plan for realizing the goals of the Zionist movement and actualizing a Jewish homeland in Palestine. As such, it adds a crucial dimension to his political program. It was written in the form of a novel, with the obvious intent of engaging people's interest, and even had a love story. The book never quite became a best seller, but it has remained the foundational text of the Zionist movement and has been translated into many languages.

The novel is set in 1902, the year the book was published. A young Jewish Viennese attorney, Dr. Friedrich Loewenberg, is jilted and sees no future for himself in his career and in life generally. Seeing a newspaper advertisement from N.O. Body for "*Wanted, an educated, desperate young man willing to make a last experiment with life*," he discovers its source to be a rich gentleman named Mr. Kingscourt. Kingscourt was formerly a Prussian nobleman called Koenigshoff who had made his fortune in America, but now has despaired of humanity and is looking for a companion to join him on his island home in the Pacific Ocean. Friedrich commits to joining him and is provided with a large sum of money which he promptly gives away to a Jewish beggar he chances upon, whose family is in considerable distress.

On their way to his island, Kingscourt offers to dock his yacht in Palestine, as it is not unduly out of their way. Neither Friedrich nor Kingscourt is impressed by what they see. The port of Jaffa is "*unpleasant*" and in "*a state of extreme decay.*" The views approaching Jerusalem by night are impressive, although "*Jerusalem by day is less alluring shouting, odors, a flurry of dirty colors. . . . The once royal city of Jerusalem could have sunk no lower.*" Herzl was probably describing here what he had seen on his only visit to Palestine four years previously.

Twenty years later, Friedrich and Kingscourt return to Vienna in his yacht for a visit, and with no particular purpose in mind stop off in Palestine. They are astounded by the changes that have taken place. David Littwak, the son of the Jewish beggar whose family Friedrich saved in Vienna, recognizes Friedrich when they dock in Haifa. He is now a senior official in this new country. Deeply grateful to Friedrich for saving his family, he spares no effort in entertaining the two visitors and showing them the country. This somewhat implausible, but nevertheless very readable, plot provides Herzl the opportunity to elaborate on the utopia that has been created in this new land through conversations with the people his characters meet.

In many ways, it is difficult for modern readers to appreciate the full dimensions of what Herzl described, since his Palestine of 1922 looked remarkably like the present-day State of Israel! However, this clearly was not the case for someone buying the book in 1902. The country was then under Ottoman rule. Palestine had always been a backwater of the Ottoman Empire, and little change would have been anticipated for the years ahead.

Herzl made a number of important points in this narrative. First, when a venture is started from scratch there are many opportunities for progress, and the chances of achieving one's objectives are much greater than when making changes to something preexisting.[9] If the beginning is right, then one is well on one's way to success.

Second, a good economic model for a country can create economic prosperity, distribute wealth, eliminate poverty, and prevent social discord. Capitalism, the book points out, leads to the accumulation of wealth in the hands of the rich and exploitation of the poor. Socialism discourages enterprise and creates the potential for violence and chaos. Therefore, Herzl's New Society is a synthesis of capitalism and socialism called "a mutualistic order" that avoids these two extremes. Private ownership is not prohibited, but the New Society promotes cooperatives – agricultural cooperatives, industrial cooperatives, newspaper cooperatives belonging to its subscribers, consumer cooperatives, and even entertainment cooperatives (theaters, for example). Thus, the entire economy is based on organizations which flourish because of everyone's efforts and from which the workers obtain appropriate reward for their efforts.

The New Society is a liberal, egalitarian, democratic, multi-cultural organization open to everyone who wishes to join, regardless of race or religion. All members receive equal rights. The one Arab mentioned in the book, a landowner who belongs to the New Society, points out that the Jews have brought benefit to everyone in the land, including to Arab villagers.

In the following passage, the host David explains to his guests the essentials of their economic system:

> *"Halt! Halt!" cried Kingscourt. "Not so fast, please! Under what kind of economic order do you live?" "A mutualistic order" [replied David Littwak]. "But please don't imagine a system of cast iron rules, rigid principles, or*

---

9   Neither Herzl nor the Torah stress this, but Jewish history comprises exiles and redemptions. Redemption provides the opportunity for starting afresh as a new beginning.

anything stiff or hard or doctrinaire. It is only a simple, flexible modus operandi. It already existed in your day like everything else you see here. All kinds of industrial and commercial co-operative societies were then in existence; and you will find all kinds operating effectively here. The whole merit of our New Society is merely that it fostered the creation and development of the co-operatives by providing credits, and – what was even more important – by educating the masses to make use of them. . . . The individual is not deprived of the stimulus and pleasures of private property, while, at the same time, he is able, through union with his fellows, to resist capitalist domination. . . . You must remember that our workingmen, as members of the New Society, are automatically insured against accidents, illness, old age and death."[10]

Members of the New Society receive a wide range of benefits, including free universal education from kindergarten through university, free medical care, retirement pensions, and old-age homes. Everyone in this society is also obliged to provide two years of national service when they are 18 years old by serving as teachers, hospital workers or caregivers for the elderly.

The country's New Society coordinates all the social programs and charitable organizations. The sick and infirm are thus taken care of and no one is left wanting:

"In philanthropy, too, we have created nothing new. We have merely systematized the old facilities, centralized them properly. Hospitals, infirmaries, orphan asylums, vacation camps, public kitchens – in short, all the types of benevolent institutions with which you are familiar have been merged here and placed under a unified administration. We are thus able to care for every sick and needy applicant. . . . Here, too, people are brought low by their own vices or lack of responsibility or misfortune – deserved or undeserved. We give medical aid to the sick and find work for the well. . . . Healthy persons caught begging are sentenced to hard labor. The needy sick have only to apply to the public charities."[11]

Herzl was describing what we would now call a welfare state and which was decades ahead of its time; it will not be until after the First World War that social welfare programs will be implemented in many countries.

The New Society proscribes situations that encourage speculation but fail to lead to the creation of true wealth. These are also situations to which

---

10   Quoted from *Altneuland. The Old-New-Land* by Theodor Herzl, 69, 73. WLC.
11   Ibid., 62-63.

Jews have typically been attracted in the past since they are easy ways of making large amounts of money quickly. There is therefore no stock market. All land bought by the New Society remains under its ownership, preventing land speculation.

It was important to Herzl that the multi-cultural aspects of his New Society be fully understood by his readers, and they were privy to listen in to an election campaign for the Congress of the New Society taking place in a Jewish village. One of the candidates is a rabbi who proposes that the New Society be only Jewish; non-Jews would not be evicted from the country but they would not be part of the New Society. This candidate is portrayed as a racist and a villain. Herzl was not about to take Jews from a racist Europe to a Jewish nationalistic state. An architect called Steineck makes a passionate speech in the campaign opposing this rabbi's approach:

> "Therefore, an anti-alien slogan is proclaimed. A non-Jew must not be accepted by the New Society. The fewer get a place near the platter, the larger the portion of each. Perhaps you believe that is to your immediate advantage. But it is not. If you adopt that stupid, narrow-minded policy, the land will go to rack and ruin. . . . I say, therefore, that you must hold fast to the things that have made us great: to liberty, tolerance, love of mankind. Only then is Zion truly Zion. You will elect your delegate to the Congress. Choose one who thinks not of the immediate advantage, but of the lasting good."[12]

Other stories are told in the book that emphasize the tolerance and pluralism of the New Society. Readers are invited to accompany Friedrich and Kingscourt to a Passover seder with David's parents; together with the Arab we have previously met, the abbot of a Franciscan monastery in Tiberius, a Russian Orthodox priest from a church in Sephorris, and an Anglican priest and his wife. The order of the evening is traditionally Jewish except that at the end of the *seder* everyone listens to a phonograph narrating how the New Society was established.

In an early conversation between David Littwack and Kingscourt, David expounds on the humanistic values of their society:

> "Let me tell you, then, that my associates and I make no distinctions between one man and another. We do not ask to what race or religion a man belongs. If he is a man, that is enough for us. . . . I shall not bore you now with our political controversies. They are the same here as everywhere else in the world. But I can tell you that the fundamental principles of

---

12   Ibid., 110.

humanitarianism are generally accepted among us. As far as religion goes, you will find Christian, Mohammedan, Buddhist and Brahmin houses of worship near our own synagogues."[13]

Technology can provide superior solutions for the country. Herzl did not invent new technology for the book, but sent the leaders of the New Society to search throughout Europe and America for the best technology for their agriculture, industry and services and applied them nationally. A Dead Sea Canal project provides electricity to the entire country. Railroads offer connections throughout the Middle East:

"All the Devils!" shouted Kingscourt, "What's that?" He pointed to large iron car running along the tops of the palms, whose passengers were looking down into the street. The wheels of the car were not underneath, but on its roof; it moved along a powerful iron rail. "An electric overhead train," explained Littwak. . . . "Overhead trains are nothing new. There was one running between Barmen and Elberfeld in the 1890's. We installed them as soon as we rebuilt our cities, because they make street traffic safer and easier. Besides, they cost less to build than elevated or surface lines."[14]

The New Society has created well laid-out cities and a beautifully cultivated countryside that looks remarkably like the countryside of Israel today:

The car had left the plain and was gliding eastward into rolling country. It took the upgrades as easily as the down. The hillsides everywhere were cultivated up to the very summits; every bit of soil was exploited. The steep slopes were terraced with vines, pomegranates and fig trees as in the ancient days of Solomon. Numerous tree nurseries bore witness to the intelligent efforts at forestation of the once barren tracts. Pine and cypresses on the ridges of the hills towered against the blue skies.[15]

This is a society that not only cares about its own members, but about all humanity. A Peace Palace on the Mount of Olives in Jerusalem works towards the peaceful resolution of international conflicts. Under the guidance of a leading scientist, readers are led through an institution seeking a cure for infectious diseases, including malaria. This was decades before the swamps of Israel's Hula Valley were drained and malaria eliminated from the country:

---

13 Ibid., 55.
14 Ibid., 51.
15 Ibid., 100.

"What do you cook there, Professor?" "Pest, cholera, diphtheria, childhood fever, tuberculosis, hydrophobia, malaria" smirked the Professor. . . . "I work here," he added. . . . "at the opening up of Africa. . . . That is to say I hope to find the cure for malaria. We have overcome it here in Palestine thanks to the drainage of the swamps, canalization and the eucalyptus forests. But conditions are different in Africa. The same measures cannot be taken there because the prerequisite – mass immigration – is not present. The white colonist goes under in Africa. That country can be opened up to civilization only after malaria has been subdued. Only then will enormous areas become available for the surplus populations of Europe." "Not only the whites!" replied Steineck gravely. "The blacks as well. There is still one problem of racial misfortune unsolved. The depths of that problem, in all their horror, only a Jew can fathom. . . . That is why I am working to open up Africa. All human beings ought to have a home. Then they will be kinder to one another."[16]

The New Society does not involve itself in matters of religion. All are free to practice their own faith in whatever way they wish. However, in Jerusalem especially, one feels the influence of Judaism *"as the spell of the Sabbath was over the Holy City."* There is also a Temple in the city which has the appearance of the ancient Temple, although it functions more as a glorified synagogue:

They reached the Temple. The times had fulfilled themselves, and it was rebuilt. Once more it had been erected with great quadrangular blocks of stone hewn from nearby quarries and hardened by the action of the atmosphere. Once more the pillars of bronze stood before the Holy Place of Israel. "The left pillar was called Boaz, but the name of the right was Jachin." In the forecourt was a mighty bronze altar with an enormous basin called the brazen sea as in the olden days, when Solomon was king in Israel. Sarah and Miriam went up the to the women's gallery. Freidrich sat beside David in the last row downstairs. . . . The great hall resounded with singing and the playing of lutes. . . . The choristers chanted a hymn that had stirred yearnings for their own land in the hearts of a homeless people for hundreds of years. The words of the noble poet Solomon Ha-Levy: "Lecha Dodi, likrath kallah (Come, Beloved, to meet the Bride)."

Because only here had the Jews built up a free commonwealth in which they could strive for the loftiest human aims. They had their own communities

---

16   Ibid., 129, 133.

in the ghettoes, to be sure, but there they lived under oppression. In the Juddengasse, they had been without honor and without rights; and when they left it, they ceased to be Jews. Freedom and a sense of solidarity were both needed. Only then could the Jews erect a House to the Almighty God Whom children envision thus and wise men so, but who is everywhere present as the Will-to-Good.[17]

Herzl wrote in his book that with the establishment of a Jewish state antisemitism would disappear. Once the Jews would leave Europe, economic competition between them and other Europeans would disappear and so would the problem. As he explained:

Jewish university graduates, men trained in the technological institutes and commercial colleges, used to flounder hopelessly; but now there was ample room for them in the public and private undertakings so numerous in Palestine. The result was that Christian professional men no longer looked askance at their Jewish colleagues [remaining in Europe], for they were no longer annoying competitors. In such circumstances, commercial envy and hatred had gradually disappeared. Furthermore, the less Jewish abilities were offered in the marketplace, the more their value was appreciated. The value of service always increased with their scarcity. Everyone knew that. Why should not this rule have applied to Jews in commercial life?

And so the effects of the improved situation had themselves felt on all sides. In countries where there was a tendency to restrict Jewish immigration [primarily to Palestine], public opinion took a turn for the better. Jews were granted full citizenship rights, not only on paper, but in everyday life. . . .

Jews who wished to assimilate with other peoples now felt free to do so openly, without cowardice or deception. There were also some who wished to adopt the majority religion, and these could now do so without being suspected of snobbery or careerism, for it was no longer to one's advantage to abandon Judaism. . . . Toleration can and must always rest on reciprocity. Only when the Jews, forming the majority in Palestine, showed themselves tolerant, were they shown more toleration in all other countries.[18]

---

17   Ibid., 193-194, 196.
18   Ibid., 139.

Religious responses to Herzl's Zionist program

Most religious leaders of Eastern and Western Europe wanted nothing to do with Herzl's secular alternative to the Jewish messianic tradition. Many also believed in a non-activist approach to redemption, based on a talmudic and midrashic injunction not to force redemption. According to this tradition, God had imposed three oaths: two on the Jewish people not to go en masse to the Land of Israel and not to rebel against the nations of the world, and one on the non-Jewish nations not to oppress Israel overmuch.[19] The talmudic commentator, the Maharal, suggests that the purpose of these oaths was to maintain the Jewish people in an unnatural state of exile among the nations of the world until the time of the final redemption. From this perspective, political Zionism could even be considered a rebellion against the wishes of God.

Nevertheless, there were leading rabbis who supported the *Hovevei Zion* movement. This was not a messianic movement, and many of its leaders were secular Jews who thought in western terms such as nationalism, economic development and social progress. However, its aims could also be aligned with a messianic vision. Their first agricultural settlement was Rishon-le-Zion, and further settlements were founded or adopted by Baron Edmond de Rothschild who lived in France. Most of the branches of the *Hovevei Zion* affiliated themselves with the World Zionist Organization when Herzl published *Der Judenstaat* and were absorbed by that organization.

Two prominent rabbis, Rabbi Judah Alkalai (1798-1878) and Rabbi Zvi Hirsch Kalisher (1795-1874), had taught that redemption would be divided into two parts: a natural phase which would be in human hands, followed by a miraculous phase. The initial phase of *athalta di-geullah* (the beginning of redemption) and of returning to Zion remained obligatory on the Jewish people since the land itself needed to be redeemed before a complete redemption could occur.[20]

There were also rabbis and religious leaders who joined Herzl's movement. Prominent among them was Rabbi Yizchak Yaacov Reines (1839-1915) from Lithuania, who was one of the first rabbis to respond to Herzl's call to

---

19   TB Ketubot 111a and *Shir Hashirim Rabba* 2:7. The three oaths are based on three verses from the Song of Songs describing the intense love between God and the Jewish people that existed in earlier times and will exist again in messianic times. See also Maimonides in his *Iggeres Taiman* with reference to violation of the oaths via false messiahs.

20   "Rabbi Avraham Yizhak HaCohen Kook: Between Exile and Messianic Redemption" by Judith Winther. (https://www.researchgate.net/publication/325420954_Rabbi_Avraham_Yizhak_HaCohen_Kook_between_exile_and_messianic_redemption).

be part of political Zionism. He was already a member of *Hovevei Zion*. He proposed that whereas medieval Jews had recognized God's hand in nature, contemporary Jews can see God's hand in history and in their surviving the exile and returning to Zion.[21] He went on to found and then head the religious Zionist movement Mizrachi, an acronym for *Merkaz Ruhani* (religious center), in 1902. This movement believed that Torah should be at the center of Zionism, but downplayed messianic expectations.

Four questions that could be asked about Herzl

Question 1. How influential were Herzl and his ideas in the overall scheme of things?
Herzl's idea of a Jewish state was not a new one. It had been discussed by Moses Hess in his book *Rome and Jerusalem* in 1862, and by Leo Pinsker in 1882 in his book *Auto-Emancipation*, a book that inspired the *Hovevei Zion* movement. It is likely that Herzl had not read any of these books before beginning work on *Der Judenstaat*. However, in contrast to these authors, Herzl succeeded in popularizing the idea that antisemitism was an international problem and that the Great Powers should be involved in its resolution. The Jews had no army and could rely only on the goodwill, guilty conscience and self-interest of the world's nations, and Herzl played on these to the fullest. He was the first acknowledged political leader of the Jewish people in thousands of years, although he did not represent all world Jewry. Nevertheless, by the time of his early death at age 44 he had been unable to establish any form of homeland for the Jewish people.

But this not the end of the story. Towards the end of the First World War, in 1917, Zionist leader Chaim Weitzman and Herbert Samuel, a Jewish cabinet member, persuaded the British foreign secretary, Arthur James Balfour, and the government of Lloyd George to issue the Balfour Declaration, in which the British promised to establish a national home for the Jewish people in Palestine. Would these Zionists have been able to wrap up this agreement with the British without the inspiration provided by Theodor Herzl? It is impossible to know. However, it was Herzl who brought to the fore the vision of a political arrangement for the Jewish people in Palestine to be engineered by the Great Powers.

One could similarly ask how influential his book *Altneuland* was with respect to the policies of the future State of Israel.

---

21 See Wikipedia Yitzchak Yaacov Reines (https://en.wikipedia.org/wiki/Yitzchak_Yaacov_Reines).

It is uncanny how much of *Altneuland* resembles what one now sees in the State of Israel, even though it never became the official Zionist blueprint for the Jewish state. Avineri notes that many of the policies of the new State of Israel were made on an ad hoc basis with no overall framework.[22] For example, once the state brought oppressed Jews to Israel, it would have been difficult not to provide them with social welfare. And when the Jewish National Fund bought land, it was a foregone conclusion that the land would continue to belong to the state and not be sold off to speculators. Moreover, Herzl's emphasis on social justice, equal rights for all citizens and being a blessing to humanity were values so ingrained in the Jewish consciousness that it would have been difficult for the Jewish state to ignore them.

Avineri also points out another aspect of Herzl's influence: "*In founding the World Zionist Organization and its agencies and subsidiaries, he [Herzl] laid the cornerstone for the representative democratic institutions, not only of the Zionist movement but of the State of Israel as well.*"[23]

Question 2. Why did antisemitism not disappear with the realization of Zionism?

Herzl believed that antisemitism was a consequence of economic factors and that when most Jews would leave Europe and move to Palestine antisemitism would disappear. The argument could even be made that this theory was the basis of Herzl's enthusiasm for Zionism. However, while economic antisemitism may well have been present in Herzl's Europe, this theory is difficult to take seriously as an overall basis for antisemitism, and there is no evidence that the creation of the State of Israel diminished antisemitism in Europe as a consequence of economic factors.

Question 3. Why Herzl?

This is a question I have never heard anyone ask. But I am going to ask it nevertheless! Given that God controls human history, why did He choose Herzl?

Despite what Herzl wrote during the First Zionist Congress, "*At Basel I founded the Jewish State,*" this was clearly an overstatement. He had put into place the first steps, but many more would be needed: a bullet in Sarajevo, the First World War, the Battle of Beersheba, the defeat of the Ottoman Empire, the Balfour Declaration, the British accepting a mandate for Palestine, ratification of the British Mandate by the League of Nations, Arab riots, the Battle

---

22 Jewish Review of Books. "Rereading Herzl's Old-New Land" by Shlomo Avineri, Summer 2012. (https://jewishreviewofbooks.com/articles/213/rereading-herzls-old-new-land/)

23 Quoted from "Toward the End" in *Herzl's Vision. Theodor Herzl and the Foundation of the Jewish State* by Shlomi Avineri, 259. BlueBridge, New York, 2013.

of Alamein, British frustration with their mandate and their leaving Palestine, the siege of Jerusalem, and finally Israel's War of Independence. If just one of these steps (plus a multitude more) had gone a different way, it is doubtful the State of Israel would have come into existence. There was a Divine plan for the creation of a Jewish state and this included Herzl.

Herzl was the right person for the right time. A religious mystic in the mold of Isaiah or someone from the seed of David discovered from genealogy lists would likely not have garnered the necessary support from the assimilated Jews of Europe and the diplomats of the Great Powers. Herzl's vision was secular because a secular vision was what was needed at that time. A mass immigration of religious Jews from Europe would not have been able to form and defend a Jewish homeland as did the Jews from the First and Second Aliyah. Also, coming mainly from Eastern Europe, messianic Jews would not have had the vision of how the best of western humanistic values could be harnessed to create an equitable and just society. Herzl broke through the religious-secular divide by ignoring it. Nevertheless, he presented the vision of a society based on social justice. He was also a journalist, a political thinker, a writer, and an expert on communication. This was what was needed at that time.

Question 4. Is Herzl's *Altneuland* an adequate model for a utopian Jewish state?

Herzl was a humanist and understood that a society without appropriate provisions for health, education, and retirement, and having problems of income inequality would lack social justice and could never become a utopian society. This is also why the State of Israel adopted, with no particular intent, many of the social provisions of Herzl's *Altneuland*.

Herzl portrays Rabbi Dr. Geyer, who is campaigning in *Altneuland* for a Jewish-only New Society, as a villain. Geyer in German means a vulture. Herzl may well have modelled him on Dr. Lüeger, the anti-Semite who had been elected mayor of Herzl's home town of Vienna. Lüeger was a European racist, and Herzl had no place for a Jewish racist in his utopian New Society. However, by arguing this point so forcefully he was also declaring that his Altneuland would be a secular, rather than religious, state.

Nevertheless, Herzl's humanitarian values were based on very solid Jewish foundations. A significant amount of Torah law is designed to provide for the disadvantaged. Ken Spiro points out that social welfare programs are a recent innovation in human history and "*a direct outgrowth of Biblical ethics and their embrace with democracy.*"[24]

---

24 "Fanning the Flames of Freedom" in *WorldPerfect. The Jewish Impact on Civilization* by

Similarly, the notions of freedom and human rights, which form the foundations of a liberal humanitarian society, are also Jewish ideas. As discussed in chapter 3, Joshua Berman notes that the Torah invented political and economic egalitarianism. Throughout human history, until fairly recently, the concept of a society of equals was unknown. Class distinctions and economic differences were universally accepted as part of the established order. The notion of slaves rising up and demanding their freedom would never have occurred in ancient Mesopotamia or in Egypt before the time of the Exodus. God giving the law on Mount Sinai to an entire nation and not just to its king or priests was unique. The idea that a people could choose its form of government and its judges was also unheard of. In the words of Berman *"Torah represents the dawn of egalitarian thought."*[25]

Nevertheless, the Bible has a dim view of the ability of mankind to create utopian societies based entirely on human-derived values. Liberal humanism is based on communal self-interest and can never be an adequate basis for an enduring utopian state. As Rabbi Jonathan Sacks so aptly puts it *"To stay free, a nation must worship something greater than itself, nothing less than God, together with the belief that all human beings are created in His image. Self-worship on a national scale leads to totalitarianism and the extinction of liberty."*[26]

However, there is no such thing as stasis in Jewish or world history. Shortly after Herzl's death, a mystic, a kabbalist, a scholar, and later the chief rabbi of Palestine will call for an integration of Zionism, liberalism, love of humanity, and Torah as a pathway to messianic redemption, a messianic redemption which he considered already underway. In effect, this was an attempt to insert God and Judaism into Herzl's humanistic utopian vision. He will also fight (verbally) the religious leaders of the Old Yishuv who strongly disagreed with his assertion that the Jews were living in a period of messianic redemption. His name was Rabbi Avraham Yitzchak Kook (1865-1935).

Herzl and Rav Kook presaged the dialectic that exists in Israel to this very day, particularly in the political realm. Israel's start-ups, its global trade relationships, its scientific know-how used the world over, and its social justice are a continuation of the secular vision of Herzl. This vision wishes Israel to be a full

Ken Spiro, 262. Simcha Press, Florida, 2002.

25 "But is it Divine?" in *Ani Maamin. Biblical Criticism, Historical Truthy and the Thirteen Principles of Faith* by Joshua Berman, 168-173. Maggid Books, Jerusalem, Israel, 2020.

26 "The Politics of Responsibility" in Covenant and Conversation. Jonathan Sacks. The Rabbi Sacks Legacy Trust, 5782/2022 (https://www.rabbisacks.org/covenant-conversation/bechukotai/the-politics-of-responsibility/).

and non-controversial member of the nations of the world, and for there to be a clear separation and non-coercive relationship between Judaism and the state.

In opposition to this is the messianic vision of the prophets of Israel promoted by Rav Kook and others who realize that just as antisemitism will never disappear, so too a complete separation of religion and state will never be realized in Israel. Their vision is of a holy people set aside from the nations of the world that acknowledges God as the source of all its beneficence and that will bring about global peace and prosperity through recognition of the God-appointed role of the Jewish people and its God-given ethics.

More about this remarkable visionary in the next chapter.

Chapter 15

THE MESSIANISM OF RAV ABRAHAM ISAAC KOOK (RAV KOOK)

R av Abraham Isaac Kook (1865-1935) was a mystic, kabbalist and visionary who brought Jewish messianic ideas into the modern age and thereby provided an alternative to Herzl's liberal humanism and the socialism of the Second Aliya as a direction for the Jewish state.

Rav Kook held that the present return to Zion marked the beginning of messianic times and that this would gradually evolve by natural means towards the creation of an ideal world. He equated Zionism allegorically with the Messiah ben Joseph.[1] He regarded messianism as an issue separate from the End of Days. He believed that humanity would be redeemed through the spiritual heights the Jewish people would achieve, and through the harmony they would create in the human and cosmic planes.

---

1   "The New Will be Holy" in *Rav Kook. Mystic in a Time of Revolution* by Yehuda Mirsky, 49. Yale University Press, 2014. This thorough and very readable biography has been used extensively in this essay, including quotations from Rav Kook's writings. In a speech commemorating Herzl's death, Rav Kook implied that the Zionist vision could be the footsteps of the Messiah ben Joseph, and he made the allegorical point that the flourishing of the body is a prerequisite for the flourishing of the soul. The notion that there will be two Messiahs, a Messiah of the lineage of David and a Messiah from the tribes of Joseph appears in a midrash (*Targum Yonatan*, Exodus 40:11), and subsequently in other midrashim and in the Talmud (TB Sukkah 52a). Different details are described but commonly a scion of the tribe of Joseph will gather and reign over the ten tribes and will battle Israel's foes at a time of great distress. It is possible that he will die during this period. Elijah will then appear and herald the appearance of the Mashiach (Messiah) ben David who will complete redemption. The topic is discussed by Rav Kook in *Ma'amarei ha'Ra'ayah*, 94. He proposed that until Israel warranted it, they would not experience the full redemption of the Mashiach ben David. The time of Mashiach ben Joseph will be one of material achievement and constitute the period of the birth-pangs of the Messiah (*chevlei Mashiach*). An excellent summary of this topic is found in "Appendix VII: Mashiach B. Yosef" in *The Ethics of Deuteronomy* by Rabbi Dr. Abba Engelberg, 355-370. Kodesh Press, New York, N.Y.

Rav Kook's influence on Jewish life in Palestine was considerable by virtue of his ideas and the religious functions he held. He is regarded by many as one of the most influential Jewish philosophers of the modern age. And his influence continues to this day.

Rav Kook in Europe

Rav Abraham Kook was born in Grivia in Latvia, then part of the Russian Empire. His father had studied in the prestigious Volozhin Yeshiva and was from a family of generations of Torah scholars. His mother was the daughter of a *Chabad* Hasid who had also studied at Volozhin Yeshiva and she maintained her allegiance to *Chabad*.

Abraham was a child prodigy. He left home at age nine to be taught by a series of rabbinic teachers in different towns, as was the custom in those days. In one of these locations, he spent time in the library of a cousin who was a follower of the Jewish Enlightenment. After getting engaged, he spent a year and a half studying at the Volozhin Yeshiva where he became the disciple of the dean Rabbi Naftali Zvi Yehuda Berlin, popularly known as the Netziv. The Volozhin Yeshiva in Volozhin, Lithuania, was the mother of all yeshivot of the 19th century. It was founded by Rabbi Chaim Volozhin, the famed disciple of the Vilna Gaon. It emphasized analytical skills in talmudic learning and the non-pilpulistic methodology of the Vilna Gaon and Rabbi Volozhin. At the time that Kook arrived, the yeshiva was at its apex and had some 250 students who represented the cream of East European talent. Learning from early in the morning until late at night, Kook received his rabbinic ordination there.

After his marriage he needed to decide how he would support himself and his wife, and he realized he had no alternative but to become a community rabbi, a profession that had little prestige at that time. While working as a community rabbi he sharpened his writing skills by contributing to many religious journals, developed his knowledge of kabbala and engaged in academic work on aggada. He was well aware of the religious and political turmoil going on in the Jewish world, and he furthered his interest in worldly matters and Jewish nationalism.

By the time he was recruited for a position in Palestine he had already developed many original ideas, and in particular the belief that the relationship between Orthodoxy and the rebellions of modernity should be dialectic rather than antagonistic.[2] He spoke Hebrew because of his interest in some of

---

2 "No Ordinary Rabbi" in *Rav Kook. Mystic in a Time of Revolution* by Yehuda Mirsky, 39. Yale University Press, 2014.

the ideas of the *Haskalah*. The *Haskalah*, or Jewish Enlightenment, entered Eastern Europe in the late 18th century and was an attempt by Jews to modernize themselves. It was unsympathetic towards Orthodox Judaism and in Eastern Europe took the form of a revival of Jewish secular culture, with its foundation stones being Hebrew and Yiddish.

A rabbi, a Zionist and *Hibat Zion* member, visited Rav Kook's community in Boisk shortly before Rav Kook left for Palestine and described his time with him:

> *"I spent three days in the city of Boisk and spent several hours each in the rabbi's home. We discussed various matters in halacha, the aggada, and life questions. I saw before me no ordinary rabbi following well-worn paths, but a man of the spirit, paving his own way. He had not found it yet, but was searching for it, in all the length and breadth of Judaism. He was diving into the seas of the Talmud, midrashim, philosophy, kabbala, Hassidism, and the new Hebrew literature, and bringing up precious stones with which to pave his way."*[3]

RAV KOOK IN PALESTINE

Rav Kook was born in the Russian Empire, served as a community rabbi for the Jews of the Russian Empire, and continued to look after their spiritual welfare when he immigrated to Palestine. It is helpful, therefore, to look at the many changes in Russia during the 19th century that influenced Jewish life there.

The Jews of Russia constituted the largest concentration of Jews in the world, and because more of them immigrated to Palestine at that time than from anywhere else, they had a major influence on Jewish Palestine. They also brought with them the sociological, religious and intellectual undercurrents then present in the Russian Empire.

Whereas the Jews of Western and Central Europe were able to integrate into the business and cultural life of their host countries, this was not the case in Eastern Europe. Russia itself contained few Jews, but with the expansion of the Russian Empire following the partition of Poland the Jewish population of the empire increased to more than 1.3 million.[4] The czars of Russia were not enthused to have so many Jews in their country and considered them their "Jewish problem." Their intention was that the Jews either convert (which few

---

3   Ibid., 41.
4   "Russian Oppression under the Czars" in *Triumph of Survival. The Story of the Jews in the Modern Era 1650-1990* by Berel Wein, 162. A Shaar Press Publication.

did) or leave. Jewish settlement was confined to the Pale of Settlement, which included eastern Poland, Lithuania, White Russia, the Ukraine, the Crimea, and Bessarabia. In the early 1800s Jews were restricted in their employment opportunities, and efforts were made by bureaucratic means to curtail the full expression of Jewish life.

Life improved little for Jews throughout most of the 19th century until Russia experienced rapid industrialization in the later part of the century. The subsequent changes in society encouraged assimilation and secularism. Many Jews were attracted to the Enlightenment, secular humanism, Marxism, agnosticism, atheism, and Jewish nationalism. Jewish nationalism was far more of an East European phenomenon than a West European one.[5] A minority of radical left-leaning Jews were drawn to trade unionism, socialism, communism, anarchism and revolution. However, despite the many sociological changes occurring in their country, most Jews in Russia prior to the First World War maintained their religious commitment.

Beginning in 1881 there began substantial Jewish immigration to America, and by the beginning of the First World War there were more than 2 million Jews living in the United States. There was also a significant, although much smaller, stream of immigration to Palestine. The first Zionist wave of immigration between 1881 and 1903 consisted of about 60,000 Jews and is known as the First Aliyah. Many of these immigrants were traditional in observance and worked as artisans, in small trades or in agriculture. Many, almost half, would return to their home country because of the difficult conditions in Palestine. The agricultural workers belonged to a loose organization called *Hibat Zion*, which was founded in 1881 for the purpose of establishing Jewish settlement, primarily agricultural, in Palestine. Members called themselves *Hovevei Zion* and their activities were supported by many leading European rabbis.[6]

A subsequent wave of immigration, the Second Aliyah, took place just before the First World War, between 1904 and 1919, and consisted of about 35,000 Jews. These people were in the main idealistic, secular and socialist, and their intent was to be a new type of Jew who would create a new type of country based on prophetic ideals of social justice.[7] They believed in the sanctity of labor and the rights of the proletariat and were opposed to capitalism and the influence of religion.[8] They formed the core of Labor Zionism

---

5 "New Yearnings," ibid., 201.
6 "0Return to Zion", ibid., 223-228.
7 "The Second Aliya", ibid., 258.
8 Ibid., 259.

and were responsible for developing the kibbutzim. They eschewed Arab labor. Their utopia was a Marxist future and the triumph of the international worker. Rabbi Berel Wein describes them thus:

> The new Jew, whom they idealized, would speak Hebrew, not Yiddish, Ladino or Arabic, be a farmer, laborer, warrior, and intellectual. He would be idealistic, selfless and honest, indifferent to material wealth, concerned with the society and not the individual. He would also be irreligious (if not anti-religious) and view Jewish tradition as an anachronism and an unnecessary burden. The communes of these new Jews knew nothing of Sabbath or Yom Kippur, and had no synagogue or kosher kitchen. A new Passover seder service based upon Marx and Engels was composed, Shavuot became a purely agricultural holiday, the Bible became literature, and religious ritual was deemed repulsive and hence prohibited.[9]

These new immigrants were not the only Jews then in Palestine. From the time that Nachmanides arrived in Jerusalem in 1267 during the Mameluke period its Jewish population had been slowly increasing, mainly with Sephardi Jews. During the late 18th and early 19th centuries there was increased European immigration to Palestine by followers of the Vilna Gaon and the Hasidic masters, who settled in Jerusalem, Safed, Tiberias, and Hebron. These immigrants constituted what was known as the Old Yishuv. Most were not self-supporting, as there was little economy in Palestine until the later waves of Jewish immigration. They were supported by charity from their home city or country, distributed by the *kollel* (community gathering) they were in. These people considered themselves to be preserving a Jewish presence in Jerusalem and Palestine until the advent of the Messiah, and they engaged in Torah study and deeds of piety. As previously discussed, the philosophy of the Vilna Gaon stressed not only the importance of Torah study but also working the land, and some descendants of his disciples, including the family of Yoel Moshe Salomon, were active in building up Jerusalem and in establishing an agricultural settlement.

The leader of the Jews of Jerusalem throughout much of the 19th century was Rabbi Shmuel Salant. In the late 1800s the Old Yishuv was joined by Lithuanian and Hungarian rabbis who also held leadership positions. By 1885 there were 25,000 Jews in Palestine, of whom 17,000 lived in Jerusalem. Rav Kook came from the same background in Torah learning as the Jews from the Old Yishuv. However, for many reasons the Old Yishuv was at first suspicious

---

9   Ibid., 260.

of him, and as they became more aware of his activities and philosophy this suspicion turned to outright hostility.

Rav Kook was recruited for a position in Jaffa as a different kind of rabbi from those of the European mold. He arrived there in 1904 at the beginning of the Second Aliya, two months before Theodor Herzl's death. He was then 38 years old and slightly older than many of his wider community.

Jaffa was a mixed Jewish-Arab city and had a Jewish population that numbered about 5,000 people. It was also the main urban hub in Palestine for a growing number of Jewish agricultural settlements. Rav Kook considered himself responsible for all these people, although his interest in them was not necessarily reciprocated. Many of them wanted nothing to do with what he stood for, although they may have grudgingly admired him as a person.

Yehuda Mirsky quotes a wonderful passage from Joshua Radler-Feldman's *From the Weave* describing the effervescent place that Jaffa was and the arrival of its new Rabbi:

> *Jaffa, a small community. . . . but very strange. All shuddering, boiling and bubbling. Taut and ready. All kinds of parties and streams, directions and inclinations. Wars among them, of words, of course. . . . Everything is floating, changing, shifting forms. And there's a rabbi, a genius, rhetorician, and bit of a poet, so different from the rabbis you've known or even appreciated in your life. Yet when it comes down to it, you can't really grasp him either.[10]*

Rav Kook immersed himself in this environment with communal duties such as helping the sick and poor, adjudicating in his rabbinical court, mediation, answering *halachic* enquiries, officiating at civic ceremonies, charitable work, and building synagogues and ritual baths. He soon developed a reputation as a *tzadik* (righteous person). Biographers mention that he regularly gave away his household possessions and signed as guarantor for paupers' loans, until his family convinced the local loan society not to honor his signature.

Four years after his arrival he wrote to a colleague in Europe:

> *"Thank God who made me this kind of self, a spirit and soul living and feeling all the different movements and agitations with all their birth pangs and travails, but also with all the strength of their life force and faith in redemption, the things all palpably meet in me, and I must deal with them in deed and action, and endure all the breakers of the different waves and the height of their pounding. And hear the hidden, secret voice within them."[11]*

---

10   "The New Will be Holy: Jaffa" in *Rav Kook. Mystic in a Time of Revolution* by Yehuda Mirsky, 43. Yale University Press.

11   Ibid., 49.

Nine years after his arrival in Palestine Rav Kook began an initiative which he thought could bring reconciliation between the New Yishuv and the Old: a series of visits to new agricultural settlements in Samaria and the Galilee for purposes of teaching and encouraging religious revival. Included in his party were local rabbis and Rabbi Yosef Chaim Zonnenfeld, one of his chief critics from the Old Yishuv in Jerusalem. In the course of a month they visited 26 communities. Their visits went well and led to religious initiatives in settlements established during the First Aliyah. Settlements from the Second Aliyah, on the other hand, were not interested in returning to what they had just left. On balance Rav Kook was encouraged by this experience, while Rabbi Sonnenfeld was strengthened in his opinion that there could be no compromise with such people.[12]

Rav Kook was stuck in Europe during the First World War. Upon returning to Palestine after the war, he was appointed Ashkenazi chief rabbi of Jerusalem. He was now living in the hornet's nest of his critics, and the Jerusalem rabbis continued to be extremely hostile to him. Two years later he was appointed Ashkenazi chief rabbi of Palestine.

Rav Kook died in 1935. Nearly one-third of Jerusalem residents followed his coffin, and thousands more watched from sidewalks and apartments. Memorial services were held all over Palestine and far beyond. The zealots, however, continued to hound him even after his death. A poster hung on city walls read: *"Our doctrine regarding that man is clear, that is, we find him to be the greatest destroyer of our land and polluter of Orthodox Judaism, and [our] war against him has no limit."*[13]

THE UNDERPINNINGS OF RAV KOOK'S PHILOSOPHY

Rav Kook believed that the Jewish people were at the beginning of a messianic redemption and not just in its "footsteps." This led him to construct a messianic vision of ever-increasing holiness. This would proceed through the hidden providence of unity that guides humanity and all creation and through the Divine light permeating all reality.

All this was based on kabbalistic underpinnings beginning with the unity of God.

The unity of God is not a uniquely kabbalistic idea, but a fundamental

---

12 "The Second Aliyah" in *Triumph of Survival. The Story of the Jews in the Modern Era 1650-1990* by Berel Wein, 262. A Shaar Press Publication

13 "Conclusion: Afterlight" in *Rav Kook. Mystic in a Time of Revolution* by Yehuda Mirsky, 219. Yale University Press.

principle of Judaism. One of the most important declarations of Judaism is *"Hear O Israel, the Lord our God, the Lord is One."* At its most basic level, this means there is only one God and there is an absolute prohibition against idolatry. However, the concept of the unity of God can be taken much further than this for if God is Oneness and God created the universe, then the entirety of His creation also manifests oneness.[14] This was discussed by the medieval philosopher Maimonides in his philosophical work, the *Guide to the Perplexed*:

> *Know that this Universe, in its entirety, is nothing else but one individual being: that is to say, the outermost heavenly sphere, together with all included therein, is as regards individuality beyond all question a single being.*[15]

Nevertheless, our perception of the world around us suggests that it is not at all unified but rather in a state of disunity and fragmentation. In kabbalistic terms, this fragmented world is called an *alma di-peruda*. Rav Kook's aspiration was a world of harmony and sanctity that embraced everything, an *alma de-yihuda*. In Lurianic kabbala, this state of cosmic unity will only be attained in the eschatological future. However, in the mystical awareness of Rav Kook an interconnected, organic wholeness already exists in our physical and spiritual worlds. That it appears otherwise is only due to our flawed perception of reality.[16] He wrote:

> *Greater than this is the mystical quest, which by its nature penetrates to the depths of all thought, all feelings, all tendencies, all aspirations, and all worlds, from beginning to end. It recognizes the inner unity of all existence, the physical and spiritual, the great and the small, and for this reason there is, from its perspective, no bigness or smallness. Everything is important and everything is invested with marked value. . . . Because of this advantage, mystical vision, in being able to embrace within itself all thoughts and all sparks of the spiritual, is alone fit to chart for us the way to go. . . . The far-reaching unity of the mystical dimension embraces all creatures, all conditions of thought and feeling, all forms of poetry and exposition, all*

---

14   "Principle of Unity" in *The Mystical Dimension. Volume One. The Mystical Tradition* by Jacob Immanuel Schochet, 46. Kehot Publication Society, New York.

15   *Guide to the Perplexed*, Translation by M. Friedlander, 1:72. Dover Publications Inc, New York.

16   "Harmonism, Novelty, and the Sacred in the Teachings of Rav Kook" by Norman Lamm in *Rabbi Abraham Isaac Kook and Jewish Spirituality*, eds Lawrence J. Kaplan and David Shatz, 159. New York University Press, 1995.

expressions of life, all aspirations and hopes, all objectives and ideals, from the lowest depths to the loftiest heights.[17]

However, if one only focuses on one's own aspect of reality, one fails to see the totality of existence. The result is human conflict:

All the defects of the world, the material and the spiritual, all derive from the fact that every individual sees only the one aspect of existence that pleases him and all other aspects that are uncomprehended by him seem to deserve purging from the world. And the thought leaves its imprint in individuals and groups, on generations and epochs, that whatever is outside one's own is destructive and disturbing. The result is the multiplication of conflict.[18]

How far was Rav Kook prepared to take this notion of cosmic wholeness? Can the holy and profane be unified, for example? This seems to be at odds with the direction of Judaism. The *halacha* recognizes that holy and profane are distinct entities, as evident by the separation between Sabbath and weekdays and kosher and non-kosher.

Rav Kook was not a Hasid, but he was attracted to some of the kabbalistic ideas of Hasidism. It was Hasidic thought that began blurring the distinction between the holy and profane, with its ideas of the extreme immanence of God and the panentheistic notion that the presence of God fills the universe.[19] In Hasidic thought the holy gains greater power, reaches out and envelopes the secular and thereby transforms the secular into the holy. The opponents of Hasidism, on the other hand, the *Misnagdim*, under the leadership of the Vilna Gaon, were opposed to what they regarded as the exaggerated immanentism of Hasidism. As an example, they faulted the Hasidic idea that one could contemplate words of Torah in a latrine. Rav Kook was well aware of this debate and therefore tread with extreme care in explaining the transitory nature of the separation between sacred and profane and its ultimate dissolution:

The distinctions between the sacred and profane are [to be found] in the entire cosmos. . . . The profound cognition and awareness of these distinctions are a source that bears much spiritual fruitfulness. However, after this [cognition and awareness] one comprehends with a clear understanding that all these [distinctions] are transient matters, and that the elevation

---

17   *Orot Hakodesh* I, 9-10. Quoted from *Rabbi Abraham Isaac Kook and Jewish Spirituality*, eds Lawrence J. Kaplan and David Shatz, 27. New York University Press, 1995
18   *Orot Hakodesh* I:120. Quoted from ibid., 26.
19   "Harmonism, Novelty, and the Sacred" by Norman Lamm in ibid., 169.

of all [being] toward sanctity and harmony and non-differentiation and refinement is the eternal idea that always dwells in noble spirits, while the careful effort to make distinctions is an ephemeral matter that arises from temporal life.[20]

With this understanding, one can appreciate what Rabbi Norman Lamm calls Rav Kook's "theory of harmonism," although this was not a phrase that Rav Kook used.[21] Rav Kook's harmonism is totally embracing and affects ideas, human relations and the inner life of the individual. This theory fitted well with his personality in that he was a peace-loving individual who wished to harmonize differences and not leave them to fester.

Another important aspect of Rav Kook's philosophical approach was his ready acceptance of the new. Judaism does not readily espouse novelty. This stance can be regarded as a positive, since Judaism provides stability in a world that by its nature is always changing. However, Rav Kook appreciated that much of the Judaism practiced in his time had developed over thousands of years of exile and that new emphases were needed as the Jewish people came into contact with innovative ideas in science and ethics.

The rabbis of the Old Yishuv strongly disagreed with this. It was Rabbi Moses Sofer (1762-1839), one of the leading rabbis of Hungary and the author of the work *Chatam Sofer*, who felt that in this age in which everything around was changing, the Jew needed to hunker down, and he pronounced the *halachic* ruling (out of context as it was) that *"hadash asur min haTorah"* ("what is new is forbidden by the Torah").

In contrast, Rav Kook wrote:

This is the force that proclaims that it is our duty to revitalize the spirit of God in our people and to gain respect for the Torah and the commandments through the acquisition of all cultural resources active in the world. . . . We must take whatever is good from any source where we find it to adorn our spirit and our institutions.[22]

As chief rabbi of Palestine, Rav Kook needed to issue *halachic* rulings

---

20 Quotation from "The Land of Israel and Historical Dialectics in the Thought of Rav Kook: Zionism and Messianism" by Ella Belfer, in ibid., 263. See also "Harmonism, Novelty and the Sacred in the Teachings of Rav Kook," in ibid., 170.
21 "Harmonism, Novelty, and the Sacred in the Teachings of Rav Kook" by Norman Lamm in ibid., 161.
22 *Orot Hakodesh*, vol II, 484. Quoted from "Introduction" in *Abraham Isaac Kook - The Lights of Penitence, Lights of Holiness, the Moral Principles, Essays, Letters, and Poems* by Ben Zion Bokser, 15. Paulist Press, New York, 1978.

that affected all Jews in the country. Nevertheless, one can sense his anguish in his recognition of the discordance between his vision of ultimate holiness and the constraints of ancient *halachic* texts that he felt were incapable of expressing the full power of spirituality (and one can also appreciate the suspicion and antagonism towards him from the Old Yishuv):

> *Great anguish is experienced by one who leaves the wide horizons of pure contemplation, suffered with feeling, with poetry of the most exquisite beauty, and enters the study of the confined world of halachic enactments. . . . A person who is stirred by a soul ennobled with the splendor of holiness suffers frightful anguish at the chains of confinement when he leaves the one branch of study for the other.[23]*

RAV KOOK'S IDEAS ON MESSIANISM AND UNIVERSAL REDEMPTION

With this background, we can examine Rav Kook's ideas on redemption and messianism from six perspectives:

- The Land of Israel
- National religious Zionism
- A vital and receptive Judaism
- A sympathetic ear to humanistic ideas promoting social justice
- The innate drive of God's creation towards increasing holiness
- Universal redemption

(i). Rav Kook's approach to the Land of Israel

Rav Kook had a far more expansive approach to the Land of Israel than anyone before him, other than perhaps the poet and philosopher Rabbi Yehuda Halevi (1075-1141). Nachmanides had written that individual Torah observance was deficient outside the land of Israel and that Torah practice in the diaspora was only practice, so to speak, for the time of redemption.[24] Rabbi Yehuda Halevi in his book, *Sefer HaKuzari*, postulated that the perfection of any Jew, including the ability to prophecy, could only be achieved in the Land of Israel.[25] Like Nachmanides, he immigrated to Israel in his later years.

---

23   Ibid., 5.
24   Nachmanides to Genesis 26:5. Also Rashi to Deuteronomy 11:18 and *Sifrei* 43.
25   *Sefer HaKuzari* II:9-24.

Rav Kook regarded the longing for a return to the Land of Israel as an integral aspect of Judaism and its severance as a risk to Judaism itself. He considered every facet of Jewish life to be inferior in the diaspora. He felt that only in Israel could the mystical bond between the land and its people blossom and Jewish creativity flourish. Moreover, only in Israel was one able to appreciate that one is surrounded by spirituality and holiness. All this is apparent from the following two quotations from his writings:

> *A valid strengthening of Judaism in the diaspora can come only from a deepened attachment to the Land of Israel. The hope for the return to the Holy Land is the continuing source of the distinctive nature of Judaism. The hope for the redemption is the force that sustains Judaism in the diaspora; the Judaism of the Land of Israel is the very redemption.*[26]

> *A Jew cannot be as devoted and true to his own ideas, sentiments, and imagination in the diaspora as he can in the Land of Israel. Revelations of the holy, of whatever degree, are relatively pure in the Land of Israel; outside it, they are mixed with dross and much impurity. . . . In the Holy Land, man's imagination is lucid and clear, clean and pure, capable of receiving the revelations of Divine truth and of expressing in life the sublime meaning of the ideal of the sovereignty of holiness; there the mind is prepared to understand the light of prophecy and to be illuminated by the radiance of the Holy Spirit. In gentile lands the imagination is dim, clouded with darkness and shadowed with unholiness, and it cannot serve as the vessel for the outpouring of the Divine light.*[27]

(ii). Rav Kook's approach to Zionism and Jewish peoplehood

Rav Kook's approach to Zionism and Jewish peoplehood was original and would have important consequences for Orthodox Judaism.

As discussed in the previous chapter, there were (and still are) four different approaches within Orthodoxy to the secular-Zionist revolution and secular Jewish nationalism.[28] One approach is total rejection; this was the path of the Old Yishuv and much of European Orthodoxy. To them, Herzl's secular Zionism could never be an alternative to the traditional belief in the Messiah.

---

26 Quoted from "Rabbi Kook: The Dialectics of Redemption" in *The Making of Modern Zionism. The Intellectual Origins of the Jewish State* by Shlomo Avineri, 199. Reprinted by permission of Basic Books, an imprint of Hachette Book Group Inc.

27 Quoted from ibid., 198.

28 "The Land of Israel and Historical Dialectics in the Thought of Rav Kook: Zionism and Messianism" by Ella Belfer in *Rabbi Abraham Isaac Kook and Jewish Spirituality*, eds Lawrence J. Kaplan and David Shatz, 257. New York University Press, 1995.

It was also unimaginable to them that a secular Zionist leadership could be part of any messianic vision.

A second approach, articulated by Rabbi Yitzhak Breuer, was to accept that national revival could be viewed in messianic terms and to call for a counterrevolution against secular Jewish nationalism.

A third response which was adopted by a number of orthodox rabbis active in the Zionist movement, including Rabbi Yitzhak Reines, was to ignore any messianic implications of Zionism and to recognize political Zionism as a necessary solution to the plight of diaspora Jewry. These rabbis held that messianic belief and political Zionism were not in conflict because they dealt with different realities. This is why Rabbi Reines was even willing to vote for the Uganda option at the Sixth Zionist Congress. These rabbis were also prepared to accept the socialism brought into the country with the Second Aliya.

The fourth and harmonizing approach was that of Rav Kook, who regarded the secular Zionist pioneers who devoted themselves to reclaiming the land in consonance with their nationalist or socialist ideology as being part of God's cosmic plan for redemption. These pioneers did not recognize themselves as participating in the process of redemption, but in actuality they were. Furthermore, the nationalist values espoused by these pioneers contained within them sparks of holiness:

> *How should men of faith [that is, religious Judaism] respond to an age of ideological ferment which affirms all these values in the name of nationalism and denies their source, the rootedness of the national spirit in God? To oppose Jewish nationalism, even in speech, and to denigrate its values is not permissible, for the spirit of God and the spirit of Israel [that is Jewish nationalism] are identical. What they must do is to work all the harder at the task of uncovering the light and holiness and implicit in our national spirit, the Divine elements which are at its core. The secularists will thus be constrained to realize that they are immersed and rooted in the life of God and bathed in the radiant sanctity that comes from above.*[29]

According to Rav Kook, the atheist and anti-religious thinking of these pioneers is mistaken. Eventually, they will recognize their error. Moreover, secular Zionism has no staying power and its eventual fate will be to imbibe more holiness:

29　Quoted from "Rabbi Kook: The Dialectics of Redemption" in *The Making of Modern Zionism. The Intellectual Origins of the Jewish State* by Shlomo Avineri, 202. Copyright © 1981. Reprinted by permission of Basic Books, an imprint of Hachette Book Group Inc., which in turn was quoted from Kook, "Lights for Rebirth" by Arthur Hertzberg, in *The Zionist Idea*, 430. New York, 1969.

Nationalist movements are temporary phenomena, which are due to be transcended as man responds to the more universal claims of his nature, A secularly oriented Zionism has sufficient potency to be a theme of propaganda, and to some extent, win adherents for a limited span of time, but secularity cannot offer us a permanent directive for life.[30]

(iii). The responsiveness of Torah to the new age

To achieve its messianic goal, Rav Kook felt that Judaism needed to become more responsive to all aspects of the present age and its intellectual ethos:

The life of the Jewish people, which is constantly being renewed in the Land of Israel, causes us to renew and exalt our thought processes and our logic. The specific form of this novelty must be felt in all disciplines – in halacha and in aggada, in all areas of science and ethics and in our weltanschauung. The general content of this newness must be the establishment of all spirituality of the collective life of the nation and the establishment of all of national life on its highest spiritual basis, and the complete coordination of secular life and physical life with spiritual life in general.[31]

Moreover:

The reason for combining Torah with wisdom [i.e., secular knowledge] is not to make up for some deficiency [in either of them], but in order to create new combinations and phenomena.[32]

He also wrote

As long as Orthodoxy maintains stubbornly: No, we shall concern ourselves only with the study of Talmud and legal codes, but not aggada, not ethics, not kabbala, not scientific research, not the knowledge of the world, and not Hasidism, it impoverishes itself, and against all this I shall continue to wage battle.[33]

---

30   Quoted in *Introduction to Abraham Isaac Kook. The Lights of Penitence, Lights of Holiness, the Moral Principles, Essays, Letters, and Poems* by Ben Zion Bokser, 11. Paulist Press, New York. 1978.

31   "Ne'eder baKodesh in Ma'amarei haRe'ayah (Jerusalem 1984), 413. Quoted from "Harmonism, Novelty, and the Sacred" by Norman Lamm in *Rabbi Abraham Isaac Kook and Jewish Spirituality,* eds Lawrence J. Kaplan and David Shatz, 165. New York University Press, 1995.

32   *Orot haKodesh* I 63 (paragraph 46). Quoted in ibid., 167.

33   *Igrot,* vol letter 602, quoted from *Introduction to Abraham Isaac Kook. The Lights of Penitence, Lights of Holiness, the Moral Principles, Essays, Letters, and Poems* by Ben Zion Bokser, 14. Paulist Press. New York. 1978.

(iv). Accepting social justice as a humanistic value

Rav Kook was prepared to listen sympathetically to the ideas of social justice that the Zionist pioneers had brought with them, and he recognized their underlying value:

> *Dreadful sorrows and travail have made [this generation] determined and fierce. . . . It can't be stooped and bent even if it wanted to. . . . A generation like this, which is willing to die bravely for what, to its mind, are noble ideals, among them the sense of righteousness, justice and knowledge that it feels within it, can't be lowly. Even if its goals may be utterly wrong, its spirit is exalted, great and awesome.[34]*

(v). The drive of creation towards holiness

Rav Kook believed that an innate spiritual force together with increasing goodness and perfection would drive the messianic process forward:

> *Nothing remains the same; everything blooms, everything ascends, everything steadily increases in light and truth. The enlightened spirit does not become discouraged even when he discerns that the line of ascendance is circuitous, including both advance and decline, a forward movement but also fierce retreats, for even the retreats abound in the potential of future progress.[35]*

Judith Winther suggests that Rav Kook was influenced in these ideas by the evolutionary theories of Charles Darwin, and especially those of the French Jesuit theologian, philosopher and paleontologist Pierre Teilhard de Chardin, who developed the theory that a vitalist evolutionary process was moving the world towards universal Divine goodness.[36]

(vi). The belief in universal redemption

Rav Kook held that the entire world would be redeemed as a result of the spirituality of the Jewish people. In this way, the physical and spiritual aspects of all existence would be brought into a state of unity:

> *All the civilizations of the world will be renewed by the renaissance of*

---

34 Kook, *Ikvei haTzon*, III. Quoted in "The New Will be Holy" in *Rav Kook. Mystic in a Time of Revolution* by Yehuda Mirsky, 59. Yale University Press, 2014.

35 *Orot Hakodesh*, vol II, p484. Quoted in *Introduction in Abraham Isaac Kook- The Lights of Penitence, Lights of Holiness, the Moral Principles, Essays, Letters, and Poems* by Ben Zion Bokser, 21. Paulist Press, New York. 1978.

36 "Rabbi Avraham Yizhak HaCohen Kook: Between Exile and Messianic Redemption" by Judith Winther. (https://www.researchgate.net/publication/325420954_Rabbi_Avraham_Yizhak_HaCohen_Kook_between_exile_and_messianic_redemption)

our spirit. All quarrels will be resolved, and our revival will cause all life to be luminous with the joy of fresh birth. All religions will don new and precious raiment, casting away whatever is soiled, abominable and unclean. They will unite in imbibing of the dew of the holy lights that were made ready for all mankind at the beginning of time in the well of Israel. The active power of Abraham's blessing to all the peoples of the world will become manifest, and it will serve as the basis of our renewed creativity in the Land of Israel.[37]

THE LONG-TERM INFLUENCE OF RAV KOOK

Rav Kook is regarded by many as one of the most influential Jewish philosophers of the modern age. It is helpful, therefore, to review what he was able to accomplish – and, just as important, what he was unable to achieve.

His ideas of "harmonism" enabled a more enthusiastic engagement of Modern Orthodoxy with the Zionist enterprise than might otherwise have been the case. This is not to say that Orthodoxy would not otherwise have engaged with Zionism. Even before he came to Palestine there were orthodox rabbis involved in political Zionism. However, following Rav Kook, this engagement became more vigorous and passionate. An obvious example of this is the enthusiastic involvement of the *hesder yeshivot* and many adherents of Modern Orthodoxy with the Israeli army.

For comparison, one need look no further than the relative non-engagement of many haredi Jews, or the ultra-orthodox, with the Jewish state. Haredi Jews are the inheritors of the approach of the Old Yishuv. For many, their allegiance to the State of Israel is half-hearted at best because of the secular nature of the country. Even when in the government, they often view their role as protecting the interests of other haredi Jews and not necessarily the interests of all the Jewish people.

Rav Kook also began the process of creating a more modern form of Orthodoxy in the Holy Land, and in this he succeeded. His yeshiva, Mercaz HaRav, was the first in Palestine to use Hebrew as the language of instruction, to study other aspects of Torah besides Talmud, including Bible, philosophy and kabbala, and to produce a new type of rabbinic leadership that was attuned to the times and able to engage with the people. His small yeshiva, initially in the synagogue in his home, became the nucleus of a burgeoning modern

---

37   Quoted from "Rabbi Kook: The Dialectics of Redemption" in *The Making of Modern Zionism. The Intellectual Origins of the Jewish State* by Shlomo Avineri, 203. Copyright © 1981. Reprinted by permission of Basic Books, an imprint of Hachette Book Group Inc.

orthodox yeshiva movement. He also laid the foundations of the Talmudic Encyclopedia. (A similar modernizing influence on Orthodox Judaism occurred in America, with its nucleus Yeshiva University in New York and its philosophical mentor, Rabbi Joseph B. Soloveitchik).

On the other hand, his followers were unable to mobilize a spirit of holiness, religiosity and awareness of God in the country that would have been channeled into Rav Kook's messianic age. Rav Kook accepted non-religious nationalism and socialism as appropriate for the time but as the appeal of these movements waned, his followers were unable to create a religious substitute that would engage the secular world. Thus it was that start-ups, buy-outs and liberal humanism became the ethos of much of the Jewish state and not Divine morality, love, fear and reverence of God, and knowledge and practice of the Torah commandments, all of which would have raised the spiritual level of the country and brought it closer to the ultimate messianic perfection.

There were many reasons for this. One was that Rav Kook did not produce a systematic philosophy. His most widely read books, *Orot HaTeshuva* and *Orot HaKodesh,* were published by others from notes he wrote over many years. The ideas in these books are often abstract and hard to grasp. Mystical ideas also tend to defy systemization and can be difficult to convey. His ideas were studied by his followers and those interested in Jewish philosophy, but they rarely entered the secular world.

Many people also had doubts about aspects of his vision. One of these was whether the Jewish people were truly on a natural path to increasing holiness, or whether his optimism about this was misplaced. Another concern was whether a philosophy that assiduously avoided confrontation and conflict was the optimal way of dealing with evil in the world.

Rav Kook did not write much about evil, but the cat came out of the bag when one of his followers, Rabbi Ya'akov Charlap, discussed the subject. Rabbi Charlap would later become head of the Merkaz HaRav Yeshiva after the death of Rav Kook. No doubt echoing the teachings of his rabbi, although more in relation to the sinners of Israel than evil as a concept, Rabbi Charlap proposed that good and evil were not external categories, but rather products of the visions of goodness and evil that people carried in their minds and enacted with their wills. If everyone would purify their minds and wills, evil would cease to exist: "*Revealing the interior to heal the exterior. . . . to learn how to look with a piercing eye into the interiority of everything and whip it upwards.*"[38]

---

38   Charlap, Tovim Meorot (Jerusalem, Lunz, 1920, 9, 13). Quoted in "Dear, Wounded

In a similar vein, Rav Kook suggested that over time the profane would become absorbed by holiness. In the interim, he validated multiple pathways to holiness. As topics for study these ideas can be exhilarating, but whether they offer realistic ways of dealing with the realities of the world can be questioned.

Shlomo Avineri also points out that Rav Kook did not regard an independent Jewish state as the ideal vehicle for his messianic vision, in that statehood would force the Jewish people into issues of power and the corruption attendant on power.[39] Rav Kook could not envisage a Jewish state becoming the vessel for redemption of the world through its righteousness and justice if the state itself was in an unredeemed condition. He wrote:

> *It is not fitting for Jacob [speaking of the Jewish people] to engage in political life at a time when statehood requires bloody ruthlessness and demands a talent for evil.*[40]

Rav Kook proposed his ideas while the Jews in Palestine were under Turkish rule and, following this, under the British Mandate. However, political independence was always the aim of the Zionist movement.

Absent an overall framework, there has been a tendency for the alumni of his yeshivot to split Rav Kook's messianic vision into parts. One of these has been an emphasis on Jewish settlement in Judea and Samaria.

Rabbi Zvi Yehuda Kook, Rav Kook's son, took over the leadership of the Merkaz HaRav Yeshiva after the death of Rabbi Yaakov Charlap. Just before the Six-Day War, when the military crisis was already unfolding, he addressed his students and mentioned almost prophetically why he had been unable to join in the communal rejoicing in 1947 following the announcement of the United Nations partition vote on Palestine:

> *"Where is our Hebron – are we forgetting it? And where is our Shechem – are we forgetting it? And our Jericho . . . our East Bank? Where is each and every clod of earth? Every last bit, every four cubits of the Land of Israel? Can we forgo even one millimeter of them? God forbid! Shaken in all my body, all wounded and in pieces, I could not then rejoice."*[41]

Brothers" in *Rav Kook. Mystic in a Time of Revolution* by Yehuda Mirsky, 167. Yale University Press, 2014.

39   Quoted from "Rabbi Kook: The Dialectics of Redemption" in *The Making of Modern Zionism. The Intellectual Origins of the Jewish State* by Shlomo Avineri, 202. Copyright © 1981. Reprinted by permission of Basic Books, an imprint of Hachette Book Group Inc.

40   Ibid., 205.

41   Quoted from "Conclusion" in *Rav Kook. Mystic in a Time of Revolution* by Yehuda Mirsky,

Following the victory of the Six-Day War, new settlements were established in the captured Jordan Valley by the Labor movement as part of the Yigal Alon Plan. After the trauma of the Yom Kippur War, Religious Zionists were revitalized and established a movement called *Gush Emunim* for the purpose of establishing religious settlements in newly liberated areas of Judea and Samaria. Its platform was decidedly messianic and declared that it sought *"fulfillment of the Zionist vision. . . . complete redemption of the people of Israel and the entire world."*[42] However, the settlers of *Gush Emunim* tend to live in remote parts of the country, and their active messianism is not as obvious to the Israeli population than if they had been living in the center of the country, other than on a political level.

Hence, much of the active messianism within Israel today is focused on the Temple Mount. More about this in the next-to-last chapter concerning the messianic struggle over the Temple Mount.

---

226. Yale University Press, 2014.

42 Quoted from "Rabbi Kook: The Dialectics of Redemption" in *The Making of Modern Zionism. The Intellectual Origins of the Jewish State* by Shlomo Avineri, 226. Copyright © 1981. Reprinted by permission of Basic Books, an imprint of Hachette Book Group Inc.

Chapter 16

THE GENOCIDAL PROGRAM OF HAJ AMIN AL-HUSSEINI

The notion that murdering Jews and planning their genocide guarantees a privileged place in Paradise is a recent development in Muslim thought. The place of Jews in Islamic countries during the Muslim, Mameluke and Ottoman periods had its ups and downs since they were regarded as second-class citizens. Nevertheless, they were protected by their dhimmi status and only rarely was this removed. Thus, Jews generally preferred living in Muslim countries than in Christian Europe where there was no such protection. This is why many Jews fled to the Ottoman Empire following their expulsions from Spain and Portugal in 1492 and 1496.

It is often not appreciated that one Palestinian, Amin al-Husseini (1895-1974), was largely responsible for stoking up the conflict between Palestinians and Jews in British-controlled Palestine and initiating what would become a religious messianic struggle between Muslims and Jews. The Israeli-Palestinian struggle is often dismissed as a territorial issue or a matter of freeing Palestinians from Israeli oppression (although most Palestinians in Judea and Samaria are under self-rule). However, recognizing this struggle as primarily a religious one permits a more objective analysis of this conflict.

Ironically, al-Husseini was not foremost a Palestinian nationalist. His goal, as was that of the Muslim Brotherhood of which he was a founding member, was the creation of a greater pan-Islamic state of which Palestine would become a part. In fact, his dream could well have been realized if Hitler had not been defeated during World War II.

Al-Husseini invented anti-Jewish terrorism, and his technique of spreading fear within the Jewish population would be continued by the Palestinians long after his death. It would also be adopted by other radical Islamic movements in their struggle against the West. Nevertheless, in Palestine, at least, this tactic failed to achieve any of his long-term goals.

Al-Husseini was very familiar with the Holocaust, and while in Germany, he encouraged the Nazis to proceed with their Final Solution. Together with the Germans, he also planned the extermination of Palestine's Jews. This was to take place after the anticipated victory of Field Marshall Erwin Rommel's Africa Korps over the British, and Germany taking control of the Middle East.

Hence, from its very beginnings many in the Palestinian movement promoted hate and genocide, and through the efforts of Amin al-Husseini this message would spread throughout the Muslim world. This hatred continues to be fueled by recent Islamic eschatological literature that describes a messianic apocalyptic struggle prior to the End of Days, the destruction of the Jewish state and the genocide of Jews living in Israel.

THE BRITISH MANDATE IN PALESTINE

First, we need to look at some history of this period.

In October 1914 the Ottoman Empire entered World War I on the side of the Central Powers Germany, Austria-Hungry and Bulgaria against the Allies (Great Britain, France, Russia, Italy and Japan). Anticipating the defeat of the Central Powers, Great Britain and France negotiated the secret Sykes-Picot agreement, in which they reached an understanding with the Russian Empire and Italy about a division of their respective spheres of influence once the 400-year Ottoman Empire would come to an end.

The beginning of this end came about when the British-led Egyptian Expeditionary Force under the command of General Edmund Allenby captured Beersheba in October 1917. The British had failed to take over Gaza from their base in Egypt, and they decided instead to attack Beersheba. This was not anticipated by the Turks, as the British had planted information they would be attacking Gaza again. It was a desperate bid. Much of the British army was cavalry, and if they failed to capture the desert fortress at Beersheba their horses would die of thirst.

Initially, the British were unable to make progress against the 2,000 Turkish defendants. Allenby then decided on another tactic. Facing artillery and machine gun fire, mounted Australian cavalry charged the defendants with open bayonets. The Turks were unable to direct their fire accurately at such close quarters, and the cavalry successfully overran the city with surprisingly few casualties. The route to Jerusalem was now open. The Turks retreated, and Jerusalem was captured six weeks later without a shot being fired. Within a year, Turkey capitulated following its defeat at the Battle of Megiddo.

The Battle of Beersheba would have major consequences for the course of Jewish history. In the weeks between the capture of Beersheba and Jerusalem, the British foreign secretary, Arthur James Balfour, issued to the British Jewish leader Lord Rothschild a letter containing the Balfour Declaration, in which the British government promised support for the establishment of a Jewish state in Palestine. The declaration read as follows:

> *His Majesty's Government view with favor the establishment in Palestine of a national home for the Jewish people, and will use their best endeavours to facilitate the achievement of this object, it being clearly understood that nothing shall be done which may prejudice the civil and religious rights of existing non-Jewish communities in Palestine or the rights and political status enjoyed by Jews in any other country.*

This declaration was the result of heavy lobbying by the Zionist leader Chaim Weitzman and the English politician Sir Herbert Samuels, a member of the Anglo-Jewish elite, a Zionist and a cabinet member in Lloyd George's government.

Why did the British issue this declaration? The British probably hoped it would rally global Jewish support for the Allies and that Jewish settlement in Palestine would help protect the approaches to the Suez Canal. Many British Christians also believed that the establishment of a Jewish state in Palestine would presage the arrival of the Christian messianic era and the Second Coming of Jesus.

The Balfour Declaration was endorsed by the Allied powers, was included in the British mandate over Palestine, and was formally approved by the newly-created League of Nations in July 1922.

Initially, the British attempted to fulfill the provisions of their mandate, and partition plans under discussion would have provided self-determination for both Jews and Palestinians in Palestine. Nevertheless, the British would eventually renege on their commitment to the Jews. Even shortly after the Balfour Declaration was issued there were those in the British military who sought to undermine it. By the 1930s, Jewish immigration to Palestine had become critical with the rise of the German Nazi party and Nazi persecution. However, the Middle East had also become an important arena for the Allies, and it was crucial that the Arabs not join the Axis powers. A White Paper issued by the British government in 1939 effectively reversed the Balfour Declaration by severely restricting Jewish immigration to Palestine.[1] Thus, when increased immigration was most needed, the door was locked. Only

---

1   This policy of restricted immigration was maintained by the British even after the Second World War. Foreign Secretary Ernest Bevin had no love for the Jews and brought Jewish immigration almost to a halt.

when the British left Palestine and the State of Israel was declared in May 1948 did Jewish immigration again become unrestricted.

AL-HUSSEINI'S CAMPAIGN AGAINST THE JEWS AND BRITISH IN PALESTINE

Amin al-Husseini (1897- 1997) was born to an influential Palestinian family that traced its roots to the grandson of Muhammad. His brother was mufti of Jerusalem, his father had served as mufti and his cousin was then mayor of Jerusalem.

Al-Husseini attended schools in Jerusalem and Cairo and briefly studied at Al-Azhar University, the most prestigious university for Sunni Islamic learning, although he never completed his degree nor qualified as an Islamic cleric or scholar. During the First World War he enlisted in the Turkish Army as an artillery officer. After the defeat of the Turks, he returned to Jerusalem and worked first as a clerk in the office of the Arab advisor to the British military governor and then as a teacher. The Balfour Declaration had been issued shortly before al-Husseini's return to Jerusalem and this radicalized many Palestinians, including al-Husseini, who rejected the authority of the British to issue such a declaration. Using his naturally-endowed political skills, he began mobilizing Arabs who supported his views.

Much of the controversy surrounding al-Husseini is due to the fact that he did not publish, and most of his scheming was done in secret. Even the British, for whom he began working, could never be quite sure how involved he was in civil disturbances. His ideologies therefore have to be gleaned in large measure from his activities. This often becomes colored by who is writing the history and their stand on the Israel-Arab conflict (and I have to include myself in this).

Al-Husseini's first anti-Jewish activities were in April 1920 during the annual Muslim festival of Nebi Musa, celebrating the birth of Moses. He organized rioting in Jerusalem during which five Jews and four Arabs were killed and many Jews injured. The British held him directly responsible for this pogrom and sought his arrest. He managed to escape to Transjordan and was sentenced in absentia to 10-years imprisonment.

The Jews in Palestine were at first ecstatic when Sir Herbert Samuel was appointed Palestine's first high commissioner, and his arrival in Jerusalem in June 1920 was viewed in almost messianic terms. On his first Sabbath in Palestine, he prayed in the Hurva Synagogue in the Old City of Jerusalem and was invited to read the weekly portion from the prophets. This section from the prophet Isaiah (Isaiah 40:1-26) describes the redemption of the Jewish people, and Sir Samuel's recitation brought the congregation to tears. However, their love affair with him soon cooled when he appointed Amin al-Husseini mufti of Jerusalem, when this position became available on the death of his older brother. Sir Herbert Samuel had pardoned those involved in the previous anti-Jewish riots, including al-Husseini.

Al-Husseini had not been a strong candidate for this position in the elections, but Sir Herbert Samuel was subjected to strong pressure from Arabists in the British Foreign Office to appoint him as they believed that it would be useful to coopt an extreme Palestinian to work with them. There was also the desire to balance influential positions between his family and the Nashashibi family, both of whom dominated Palestinian politics.

As mufti of Jerusalem, al-Husseini gained control of the religious life of the city. In May 1922, Sir Herbert Samuel also supported his appointment as president of the Supreme Muslim Council, a body newly created by the British to administer the Islamic religious courts, mosques, schools, Muslim social services, and the Muslim Religious Trust, the Waqf. In his attempt to be impartial, Sir Herbert Samuel had appointed a radical, who hated Jews and the British alike, as the religious and political leader of the Palestinians.

Al-Husseini's organizational skills for perpetrating terror against Jews would soon become apparent. In May 1921, shortly after al-Husseini had been appointed as mufti, anti-Jewish rioting broke out, allegedly because of the increasing Jewish population in Palestine. This rioting resulted in the death of 47 Jews and the wounding of 146. Sir Herbert Samuel temporarily suspended Jewish immigration, leading al-Husseini to the conclusion that violence paid off and the Jews to the conclusion that the British were committed to a policy of appeasement.[2] Anti-Jewish violence broke out again in August 1929 with rioting in Jerusalem, Hebron, Safed, Jaffa, and Haifa, and led to the deaths of 135 Jews and 136 Arabs. An official enquiry did not hold al-Husseini responsible for initiating these riots, although it did hold him partially responsible for the disturbances. Others, however, were convinced that he had been aware of these raids from early on.

An anti-Jewish and anti-British riot in which he was clearly involved was the Arab Revolt of 1936. The Arab Higher Committee, of which the mufti was a leader, called for a strike because of continuing Jewish immigration, and

---

2   "Appeasement" in *Icon of Evil: Hitler's Mufti and the Rise of Radical Islam* by David G. Dalin and John F. Rothman, 26. Transaction Publishers, 2009.

this was followed by attacks on Jewish properties and settlements through-out the country. Syrian and Iraqi volunteers began arriving in Palestine.[3] The Arab Higher Committee was eventually outlawed and al-Husseini was sought by the British police. However, he was tipped off and escaped to Lebanon, where the committee was reconstituted and continued to organize violence until May 1939.

Now living outside Palestine, al-Husseini was involved in a short-lived pro-German coup in Iraq in 1941, which the British crushed by sending in troops and planes. Following this, the mufti incited a pogrom in Baghdad that was responsible for the deaths of 110 Jews.[4] He sought refuge in neighboring Persia but remained there only four months, as the pro-Nazi Shah was forced to abdicate in favor of his young son when Great Britain and Russia sent in troops. Despite being pursued by the British, he managed to escape to Turkey and then to Italy, an ally of Germany. From Italy he made his way to Germany.

AL-HUSSEINI IN GERMANY

Al-Husseini's activities in Germany are a subject of controversy. The debate centers on how much he knew about the Final Solution, whether he visited Nazi concentrations camps and whether he was instrumental in furthering the Final Solution. These questions are of more than just academic interest. One of the claims of the Palestinians is that they have been made to suffer unfairly from the consequences of European antisemitism, the Holocaust, and the re-sulting immigration of European Jews to Palestine. However, this claim loses much of its validity if the leader of the Palestinian people, Amin al-Husseini, was actually involved in the Final Solution in Europe.

Almost all historians agree that al-Husseini was familiar with the Final Solution, that he approved of it, and that his diplomatic activities were re-sponsible for the deaths of thousands of Jews in the concentration camps. However, there is no consensus as to his influence on the Holocaust and whether he even visited concentration camps. Many historians point out that the Germans needed no encouragement or assistance in carrying out their Final Solution, and therefore al-Husseini's influence, if any, was mini-mal. Nevertheless, there are historians who disagree with this. After the war Great Britain, France and Yugoslavia considered pushing for al-Husseini's

---

3   "The Mufti, the Arab Revolt of 1936-1938, and the Jews of Palestine" in ibid., 33.
4   "On the Road to Berlin, April-November 1941", ibid., 46, quoting Daniel Carpi, *The Axis of Anti-Semitism*, 9, Quebec, Canada. La Compagnie de Publication. Dawn Publishing Company Ltd, 1985.

indictment in the Nuremberg trials, but the Allies were reluctant to prosecute him for fear of upsetting the Arab nations.

Al-Husseini had been making overtures to Germany from as early as the late 1930s, reflecting a general Arab sympathy for Nazi aims. The forces of German Field Marshall Erwin Rommel's were advancing within Egypt, and with Britain alone confronting Germany it seemed but a matter of time before Germany would control the entire Middle East.

Al-Husseini was treated royally when he arrived in Italy and was greeted warmly by Mussolini in his office in the Palazzo Venetia. Mussolini was supportive in his opposition to a Jewish state and spoke openly about the extermination of Jews. He is quoted as saying: *"We have here in Italy 45,000 Jews, but none will be left. They are our enemies, and there will be no place for them in Europe."*[5]

From Italy, al-Husseini made his way to Berlin where he was welcomed equally warmly. Soon after his arrival, in November 1941, he met with Adolf Hitler and his hopes were fully fulfilled by this meeting. Hitler was obviously willing to overlook his prior writings in *Mein Kamp* about the racial inferiority of Arabs. He was not prepared to provide al-Husseini with a public statement supporting the elimination of a Jewish homeland, but he did reassure him that Germany had no territorial claims on Arab lands and that he fully supported the elimination of the Jews of Palestine. Hitler is quoted as saying: *"Germany has resolved, step by step, to ask one European nation after the other to solve its Jewish problem, and at the proper time, direct a similar appeal to non-European nations as well."*[6] Moreover, when Germany had defeated Russia and broken through the Caucasus into the Middle East, it would have no further imperial goals of its own and would support Arab liberation. After this *"Germany's objective would then be solely the destruction of the Jewish element residing in the Arab sphere under the protection of British power."*[6]

Al-Husseini was appointed as a propagandist for the Axis Powers and made regular radio broadcasts directed at Arab public opinion. He was paid extremely well for this and was provided with a chauffeured Mercedes limousine and accommodation in fancy homes and luxurious hotel suites.

---

5   "On the Road to Berlin, April-November 1941", ibid., 46, quoting Daniel Carpi, *The Axis of Anti-Semitism*, 9, Quebec, Canada. La Compagnie de Publication. Dawn Publishing Company Ltd, 1985.

6   Wikipedia, Amin al-Husseini, quoting Christopher Browning, "Bibi's self-serving, Palestinian-blaming version of Nazi history is just plain wrong," Foreign Policy, 22 October 2015.

His extreme antisemitic views are evident from his broadcasts. For example, in a typical broadcast on Radio Berlin in November 1943 he said: *"The overwhelming egoism which lies in the character of the Jew, their unworthy belief that they are God's chosen nation and their assertion that all was created for them and that other people are animals makes them incapable of being trusted. . . . They cannot mix with any other nation but live as parasites among the nations, suck out their blood, embezzle their property, corrupt their morals. . . . The divine anger and curse that the holy Qur'an mentions with reference to the Jews is because of this unique character of the Jews."*[7]

In March 1944, on a broadcast on Radio Berlin, he urged: *"Arabs, rise as one man and fight for your sacred rights. Kill the Jews wherever you find them. This pleases God, history and religion. This saves your honor. God is with you."*[8]

During his four years in Germany he had close working relationships with Nazi leaders, including Joachim von Ribbentrop, Hitler's foreign minister; Heinrich Himmler, the architect and administrator of the Final Solution; and Adolf Eichmann, also an organizer of the Final Solution. The decision to carry out the extermination of European Jewry was made two months after al-Husseini arrived in Germany, although this could be coincidental.[9] Von Ribbentrop established a division within the Foreign Ministry, the "Anti-Jewish Action Abroad," designed to help in the *"physical elimination of Jewry . . . thereby to deprive the race of its biological reserves,"* and al-Husseini became one of its advisors.[10]

In their book *Icon of Evil: Hitler's Mufti and the Rise of Radical Islam*, Dalin and Rothman note that one of Adolf Eichmann's senior deputies, Dieter Wasliceny (who was subsequently executed as a war criminal), testified at the Nuremberg trials that al-Husseini *"was one of Eichmann's best friends and had constantly incited him to accelerate the extermination measures. I heard him say that, accompanied by Eichmann, he had visited incognito the gas chamber of Auschwitz."*[11]

---

7   "Hitler's Voice to the Arabs: The Mufti and Nazi Radio Broadcasts to the Middle East" in *Icon of Evil. Hitler's Mufti and the Rise of Radical Islam* by David G. Dalin and John F. Rothman, 54. Transaction Publishers, 2009. (Quoted from Elias Cooper in "Forgotten Palestinian. The Nazi Mufti," 26, American Zionist LXVIII, no 4, March-April 1978, 5-37.)

8   Wikipedia, Amin al-Husseini. Their reference is *Aliyah: The People of Israel* by Howard Morley Sachar, 231. World Publishing Company. 1961.

9   "Escaping Indictment at Nuremberg" in *Icon of Evil. Hitler's Mufti and the Rise of Radical Islam* by David G. Dalin and John F. Rothman, 62. Transaction Publishers, 2009.

10 "The Mufti's Relationships with German Leaders", ibid., 49. Referenced to Michael Bloch, *Ribbentrop: A Biography*, 401-402. New York, Crown, 1992.

11 "The Mufti's Relationships with German Leaders", ibid., 51. Referenced to Peter Z. Malkin and Harry Stein, *Eichmann in My Hands*, 38. New York, Warner Books, 1990.

Eichmann denied this at his trial in Israel in 1961. Nevertheless, the Jerusalem court believed the authenticity of this conversation and accepted the assertion that al-Husseini had aimed to implement the Final Solution.[12] Others, however, regard the evidence as uncorroborated.[13]

Dalin and Rothman also describe that in June 1944 Dieter Wasliceny told a Hungarian Jewish leader: *"The importance of the mufti's role must not be disregarded. . . . The mufti had repeatedly suggested to the various authorities with whom he was maintaining contact, above all to Hitler, Ribbentrop and Himmler, the extermination of European Jewry."*[14]

These authors also report that Bartley Crum, a member of the Anglo-American Committee on Palestine, was able to view relevant archives while at the Nuremberg trials: *"An Army intelligence officer, at three o'clock one afternoon, made it possible for me to enter a room and sit down at a table upon which was a thick file of documents. I opened the file and began to read. The record of the ex-Mufti's intrigues was fantastic. The file showed clearly that he climaxed a record of fascism, anti-British intrigues and anti-Semitism by helping spearhead the extermination of European Jewry."*[15]

Al-Husseini was also responsible for the deaths of thousands of Jews as a result of his blocking proposed exchanges, due to his fear that those released would settle in Palestine. The following is an example of a letter he sent to the Hungarian foreign minister on learning about a transfer of 900 Jewish children and 100 adults. In effect, this letter was requesting that the Jews be sent to Polish concentration camps: *"I ask your Excellency to permit me to draw your attention to the necessity of preventing the Jews from leaving your country for Palestine, and if there are reasons which make their removal necessary, it would be indispensable and infinitely preferable to send them to other countries where they find themselves under active control, for example, in Poland, thus avoiding danger and preventing damage."*[16]

---

12 Wikipedia, Amin al-Husseini, quoting Moshe Pearlman, *The Capture and Trial of Adolf Eichmann.* Wedenfield and Nicolson, 1963.

13 Rafael Medoff "The Mufti's Nazi Years Re-examined" in The Journal of Israeli History, 17, 317–333, 1996. *Semites and Anti-Semites: An Inquiry into Conflict and Prejudice* by Bernard Lewis, 1999. *Eichmann before Jerusalem* by Bettina Strangneth, 43-44. London, The Bodley Head, 2004.

14 "Escaping Indictment at Nuremberg" in *Icon of Evil. Hitler's Mufti and the Rise of Radical Islam* by David G. Dalin and John F. Rothman, 61. Transaction Publishers, 2009, quoting Joseph B. Schechtman *The Mufti and the Fuhrer: The Rise and Fall of Haj Amin al-Husseini,* 159. Thomas Yoseloff, New York, 1965.

15 "Escaping Indictment at Nuremberg" in ibid., 62, quoting Bartley C. Crum, *Behind the Silken Curtain,* 109-110. Simon & Schuster, New York, 1947.

16 Wikipedia Amin al-Husseini. (Quoting from Joseph B. Schechtman, *The Mufti and the Fuehrer: The Rise and Fall of Haj Amin al-Husseini,* 154-155. New York, Thomas Yoseloff, 1965.

By 1942 the Germans and al-Husseini were together planning the liquidation of Palestine's Jews.[17] On a number of occasions, al-Husseini urged Himmler and other Nazi leaders to bomb Jerusalem, Tel Aviv and other Jewish military targets, but these requests were rejected by Hermann Goring, head of the German air force, for logistical reasons. Nevertheless, anticipating the victory of Erwin Rommel, a special Einsatzgruppe Egypt SS squad was formed for action in Palestine and stood by in Athens. This unit was attached to Rommel's Afrika Korps and led by SS Obersturmbannfuhreer Walther Rauff, one of Eichmann's trusted deputies.

The seminal event confounding al-Husseini's plans for Palestine's Jews was the defeat of Field Marshall Erwin Rommel's Afrika Korps at the Battle of El Alamein during the Second World War. The fate of the Middle East hung in the balance between October and November 1942. A German victory would have meant the end of hopes for a Jewish state and the destruction of much of the remnant of the Jewish people.[18] The Germans would have advanced into Palestine. The mufti and his Nazi friends would have followed soon after and would have called upon the SS waiting patiently in Greece. The Jews in Palestine had plans to fight the Germans in this eventuality, but it is hard to see how their resistance would have been effective. The Jews of Palestine would have been annihilated, and no one would have been able to lift a finger to save them.

AL-HUSSEINI AND THE MUSLIM BROTHERHOOD

Al-Husseini was a founding member of the Muslim Brotherhood, and was instrumental together with them in formulating the anti-Jewish stance of radical Islam. The Muslim Brotherhood was formed by Hassan al-Banna (1906-1949) in 1928 when he was only 22, and branches of this movement spread rapidly throughout Egypt and beyond.

---

17 "Exterminating the Jews of Palestine" in *Icon of Evil. Hitler's Mufti and the Rise of Radical Islam* by David G. Dalin and John F. Rothman, 60. Transaction Publishers, 2009, quoting Thomas Krumensackeer, "Nazis planned Holocaust for Palestine Historians," Washington Post, Reuters, April 7, 2006.

18 "The Mufti's Reflection: What if Germany Had Conquered Palestine and Britain?" in *Icon of Evil: Hitler's Mufti and the Rise of Radical Islam* by David G. Dalin and John F. Rothman, 69. Transaction Publishers, 2009. This is an interesting and imaginative chapter on what might have been if Germany had postponed its invasion of Russia and if Germany had provided Rommel with sufficient men, ammunition and fuel to win the Battle of El Alamein.

Al-Banna believed in a new Islamic order in which Islam would not just be a personal religion, but the Qur'an and *Sunnah* (the sayings and practices of Muhammad) would become the basis of the constitution of the state. He rejected Arab nationalism in favor of a Pan-Islamic state in which the artificial boundaries between the states created by the Great Powers would be eliminated. His organization involved itself in propagating its message, teaching the illiterate and organizing social welfare programs in public health.

Within a decade the Muslim Brotherhood had mushroomed to about 50,000 active members. It did not advocate revolution in Egypt but aimed for a gradual moral reform, although it did have a secret military wing. Its enemies were Zionism and the British colonial governments throughout the Muslim world. It supported the replacement of current political Arab leaders, whom it felt had been corrupted by Western values. Al-Banna was assassinated by the Egyptian secret police.

Another Muslim Brotherhood figure who was extremely influential in developing the major doctrines of radical Islam was Sayyid Qutb (1906-1966). He was also intensely antisemitic. Christian antisemitism had infiltrated into the Arab world in 1840 with the Damascus Blood Libel and was maintained by the wide circulation of the pamphlet, *The Protocols of the Elders of Zion*. This was, and still is, a popular book in the Muslim world, and Sayyib Qutb was heavily influenced by it. This forgery was first published in Czarist Russia in 1903 and describes a conspiracy by a group of powerful, malign and satanic Jewish elders, or leaders, to take over the world.

In an infamous 1950s essay "Our Struggle with the Jews" Qutb wrote:

> *Jewish wickedness, deception and plotting keep the Muslim world in a state of estrangement from the teachings of the Qur'an, thereby depriving it of the real sources of knowledge and power. . . . Their history reveals the sort of mercilessness, [moral] shirking and ungratefulness for Divine guidance as does this one. . . . The Jews perpetrated the worst sins of disobedience [against Allah], behaving in the most disgustingly aggressive manner and sinning in the ugliest way. Everywhere the Jews have been they have committed unprecedented abominations. From such creatures who kill, massacre and defame prophets, one can only expect the spilling of human blood and any dirty means which would further their machinations and evilness.*[19]

---

19   Sayyib Qutb, "Our Struggle with the Jews," Saudi Arabia, 1970, quoted by Gabriel Schoenfeld in *The Return of Anti-Semitism*, 41. San Francisco, Encounter Books, 2004.

As well as being one of the founding fathers of the Moslem Brotherhood, al-Husseini was its leader in Palestine, and he strongly supported the pan-Islamic ideology of this movement. Until 1920 his efforts were focused on creating a Greater Syria in which Palestine would have been a southern province. This project collapsed after the French defeated Arab forces in the Battle of Maysalum in July 1920, entered Damascus and overthrew Faisal I in accord with the Sykes-Picot agreement. In August 1928, an assembly convened by the French in Syria was hastily adjourned when calls were made for a reunification with Palestine. Al-Husseini was among those calling for a unified monarchial state under the son of Ibn Saud.[20]

MUSLIM APOCALYPTIC LITERATURE

About one-third of the Qur'an relates to eschatology, specifically the Day of Judgment, the punishment of the wicked and the World to Come. However, it does not describe how this will come about, and this gap was filled by hadiths composed by Muslim scholars in the seventh to ninth centuries CE.

Other than describing the anti-christ as being Jewish, this early material was not particularly antisemitic with the exception of a single hadith, which must rank as one of the most odious statements in the history of religion:

> *The Day of Judgment will not come about until Moslems fight the Jews, when the Jew will hide behind stones and trees. The stones and trees will say "O Moslems, O Abdulla, there is a Jew behind me, come and kill him."*[21]

Especially since the Six-Day War, there has been a profusion of apocalyptic literature, penned, not by Muslim scholars, but by Muslim writers who have attempted to update this earlier material. These works proclaim that the End of Days is approaching and they borrow from Biblical and Christian apocalyptic ideas to explain how this will come about. The precise details depend on the author, but the main characters of the early narrative are brought into the modern era. Many of these books have been extremely popular in the Islamic world; some have become best sellers. This material is highly antisemitic and draws on ideas from *The Protocols of the Elders of Zion*, with the Jews portrayed as devils and deserving the fate in store for them. As an example, one book warns:

---

20   Wikipedia. Amin al-Husseini (https://en.wikipedia.org/wiki/Amin_al-Husseini).
21   Sahih al-Bukhaim 4:52:177.

At a glance at The Protocols of the Elders of Zion. . . . you are amazed at how these [Zionists] began to plan corrupting the entire world, all of its nations and peoples, and how they used knowledge, progress, nudity, vilification of morals and values, and how they made all of these into implements for their goals that they attained, using all monstrous lies and deception, breaking of treaties, and biting the hand that is extended to help them, and destruction of countries, killing of the sons of nations that work for their benefit. In short, they have surrounded themselves with all of the implements that make them into a terrifying and frightening race to all who deal with them.[22]

Other than being Jewish, little was said about the antichrist in the early eschatological literature, but in this later material he is described as being a world leader, the epitome of evil and a seducer of Christians and Jews. In these books he attacks the Muslim messianic figure, the Mahdi, and this struggle ends with the complete annihilation of the Jews either by the Mahdi or by Jesus, depending on the author. Note the appearance in the following passage of the early hadith just quoted describing how the Jews must be annihilated so that Islamic eschatology can proceed:

This battle will finish with the final and complete purification of the earth from the Jews when the stones and the trees will speak, and everything behind which a Jew is hiding will speak and say: "O Abdalla [servant of God], there is a Jew behind me, come and kill him."[21] The killing of the antichrist and his Jewish and non-Jewish followers in their totality and their uprooting from the earth will be counted as the uprooting of the great corruption [of the Jews] and the judgment upon the corruptive arrogance of Banu Isra'il [Israelites] in the third and final stage, and there will be no further Jews upon the face of the earth until the Hour.[23]

In this apocalyptic literature, the Mahdi will establish a caliphate that will take over the Muslim world either peacefully or violently. The Mahdi will not appoint himself but will be recognized by his abilities and qualities:

---

22 "Classical Muslim Apocalyptic Literature" in *Contemporary Muslim Apocalyptic Literature* by David Cook, 25. Syracuse University Press, 2005, quoting Muhammad 'Amaluhu. (Mawdu'iyyat al-Islam fir muwajahat al-Sihyawniyya, 160-161. Tripoli. Manshurat Kulliyat al-Da'wa al-Islamiyya, 1992).

23 "The Figure of the Antichrist" in ibid., 193, quoting Abdallah Zilzal al-ard al'-'azim, 129, Cairo, 1994.

He [the Mahdi] will announce that the Islamic caliphate has been estab-lished to fulfill the truth and to destroy wrong, and that anyone who is not satisfied with it is fighting God and His messenger, or [anyone who] wants peace with those who desire to fight us. The entire Muslim world, whether its leaders submit their authority in the oath of allegiance to the caliph of the Muslims, or whether the Islamic armies are compelled to take posses-sion of every inch [of their territory], its people will submit to the laws of God without spilling blood – if the surrender is to the will of God; if not there is nothing wrong in the legal fighting for the realization of the truth and the raising of God's word [to the highest]. There can be no restraint in war with infidels, even if they wear the clothes of belief or of Islam.[24]

Israel will be invaded and become a Muslim country:

Jerusalem is truly the city of peace, God is peace and Islam is peace. . . . Jerusalem is Arab Muslim, and Palestine - all of it, from the river to the sea – is Arab Muslim, and there is no place in it for any who depart from peace or from Islam, other than those who submit to those standing under the rule of Islam. They will have to pay the jizya if they wish peace or life under the shadow of Islam keeping their own religions, or submit to God, loving what was before it [i.e., the previous faiths] or fighting will decide between us and God will judge in our dispute – God is the best of judges and we are marching on Palestine.[25]

The Mahdi will rebuild Jerusalem and it will become his capital. The technology of the West will be transferred to the Mahdi's empire. He will rule the entire world either by conquest or conversion and will establish justice and righteousness.[26] The enemies of Islam will be annihilated in an Armageddon-type battle, and this will be the prelude to the Day of Judgment and the World to Come.

Islam's messianic struggle with Jews and the world

An Islamic obsession with Jews was already present in the Qur'an, but the relationship between Muslims and Jews in the modern era need not have

---

24 "The Mahdi and World Conquest" in ibid., 132, quoting M. Da'ub Al-Mahdi al-muntazar 'ala al-abwab, 113, Cairo, Dar Randa Amun, 1977.

25 Ibid., 138-139, quoting M. Da'ud, Al-Mahdi al-muntazar 'ala al-abwah, 179-80, Cairo, Dar Randa Amun 1997. Compare H. 'Abd al-Hamid Isharat al-Islam wa-l-kutub al-samawiyya ila al-harb al-'alamiyya al-qadima fir al-sharq al-awsat, 56-58. Cairo, 1998.

26 "Classical Muslim Apocalyptic Literature" in ibid., 10.

evolved in the way it did. The Qur'an even contains a few complimentary comments about Jews. However, Amin al-Husseini and leaders of the Muslim Brotherhood viewed Zionism and a potential Jewish state as a threat to Pan-Islamism and a future pan-Islamic empire, and hence to Islam itself. This was reason enough to hate Jews, murder them and destroy them as a people. Al-Husseini was a spokesman for these ideas and the one who successfully mobilized the Palestinians and much of the Arab world in their support.

It is very likely that the territorial disagreements between the Zionists and Palestinians could have been resolved at an early stage if the Palestinians had been willing to do so. Palestine at the end of the 19th century was a barren and fairly empty land. It had never been the intention of the early Zionist pioneers to forcibly take over Arab lands. Their settlements were built on land bought from Arab landowners. Some of this was marginal land on the coast and in the Jezreel Valley that was unsuitable for agriculture. There were Palestinian leaders, such as members of the prominent Nashashibi family, prepared to come to an accommodation with the Zionists in some form of partition plan as devised by the British and United Nations, but they were politically neutralized.

The eschatological dimensions of Israel's current conflicts with its enemies are often not appreciated. Hamas is a Palestinian movement that rules the Gaza Strip and is an avowed enemy of Israel. Until it was considered judicious to remove it, the early hadith about the killing of Jews was part of its 1988 charter. Hence, article 15 of the Hamas Covenant of August 1988 explains that "*The day that enemies usurp part of Moslem land, jihad becomes the individual duty of every Muslim. In face of the Jews' usurpation of Palestine, it is compulsory that the banner of* jihad *be raised.*"

As has been pointed out:

Hamas is a radical Islamic movement whose worldview is marked by an Islamic eschatology in which the Jews occupy a central place. Its apocalyptic vision of a final confrontation with Israel. . . . Far from being merely an epiphenomenon. . . . constitutes the very core of its political-religious doctrine.[27]

Since 2017 when it took over Gaza, Hamas has had four major military conflicts with Israel and there are expectations on both sides that violent conflict will continue.

---

27 "Hamas and Islamic Millenarianism: What the West Doesn't Recognize" by Paul Landau, World Political Review, Jan 2008. (https://www.worldpoliticsreview.com/articles/1481/hamas-and-islamic-millenarianism-what-the-west-doesnt-recognize).

The self-governing Palestinian Authority in Judea and Samaria is considered a secular nationalistic movement, but this does not mean it has disavowed its Islamic eschatology. To the contrary. Despite the promise of the Palestine Liberation Organization chairman Yasser Arafat to Israeli Prime Minister Yitzhak Rabin before he would agree to sign onto the Oslo Accords, the Palestinian National Charter has never been changed. Its article 15 states that: "*The liberation of Palestine, from an Arab view point, is a national (qawmi) duty and it attempts to repel the Zionist and imperialist aggression against the Arab homeland, and aims at the elimination of Zionism in Palestine.*" Their "pay for slay" Martyrs' Fund, which provides monthly remunerations to those injured or imprisoned for attacking Israelis and to their families, also indicates that the Palestinian Authority is still in the radical Islamic camp. In this program, the longer the prison sentence (and thus the more heinous the crime), the greater the payment. A monthly stipend is also provided to families of Palestinians killed during attempted attacks on Israelis. This program now accounts for 8% of the budget of the Palestinian Authority. The lack of censure by the Palestinian Authority of Jewish murders and its subtle encouragement in its school educational material to Palestinian children to kill Jews are similarly part of this murderous ideology. No nationalistic aims are achieved by these murders. Their motive is religious.

The following are sections of a speech given by Mahmoud Abbas, the PLO Chairman and president of the Palestinian Authority following Arafat, to Palestinian university students:

> "*In the name of Allah, the Merciful and Compassionate. . . . Allah, the Supreme, spoke the truth. We will continue to stand firm and carry out Ribat [religious war for Muslim control] in Jerusalem and its surroundings until Judgment Day. Then the believers will rejoice in the victory of Allah.*"[28]

This eschatology would explain why many Israelis are not prepared to accept a new Muslim state on their doorstep that categorically refuses to disavow a messianic agenda. Moreover, its messianic beliefs make the Palestinian Authority unable to make the necessary compromises that would satisfy Israel and lead to a resolution of the Israeli-Palestinian conflict. Chief among them is an agreement to end the conflict. This would explain why no Palestinian leader has ever availed himself of the many opportunities offered in the past to establish a Palestinian state. Also, why many regard a two-state solution as

---

28 Quoted from "Is the PA capable of ceding once Islamic-held land for peace?" by Eric R. Mandel in The Jerusalem Post, Friday Sept 24, 2021. Mandel is the Director of MEPIN (Middle East Political Information Network).

a two-state illusion, for the simple reason that no Palestinian leader is capable of signing onto it. Moreover, recent polls within the Palestinian Authority territory consistently show its population to be more supportive of the aims of Hamas and its armed struggle with Israel than the ambiguous aims of the Palestinian Authority.[29]

It is well recognized that since its 1979 Islamic Revolution, the leadership of Iran has also been following an apocalyptic agenda. Iran's majority Shi'ite sect is called the Twelvers, and it believes that the 12th imam, Muhammad al-Mahdi, who was born in the mid-ninth century, is still alive and has been hidden until the End of Days. Eventually, when Allah directs, his presence will be revealed. This sect also believes that the Mahdi will destroy the Jewish state and annihilate its Jews, and preparation for this is part of the political agenda of the Iranian leadership. This accounts for Iran's interference in the affairs of Lebanon, Syria, Iraq, Gaza, and Yemen; its intention being to create a ring of hostile states around Israel that will deter Israel from attacking Iran and will join or even initiate its genocidal program. This is also why a nuclear weapons program is so important to the Iranian leadership and why its prevention is such a high priority for every Israeli government.

Many Europeans and Americans are being sucked into the messianic struggle between Islam and the Jews. Antisemitism is on the rise in Europe and the United States. It is related in the main to the Israeli-Palestinian conflict and is promoted by liberals and the Left and sometimes by ultra-nationalists. It looks favorably on Palestinian claims, and attempts to equate Israelis with Nazis in their treatment of the Palestinians. It regards Israel as a racist colonial white power oppressing a powerless minority and portrays Jews as immoral and controlling world affairs in a modern form of *The Protocols of the Elders of Zion*. Its overall aims are to blacken the reputation of the Jewish state, prevent it from achieving dominance in the Middle East and on the world stage, limit its territorial expansion by diplomatic means, and enable the formation of a Palestinian state without the compromises necessary for a negotiated settlement. Much of this antisemitism has its roots in Islamic and Christian messianism. Many of its supporters are carried along by its factually inaccurate rhetoric about human rights and are ignorant of the underlying issues; including the violent Islamic messianism beneath the slogans. This form of antisemitism is difficult to eradicate since it has little to do with intolerance of differences but has religious and political motives. It is a disaster for multicultural countries such as Europe and the United States since it leads to

---

29   Index PSR Polls in Policy and Survey Research (http://pcpsr.org/en/node/154).

a splitting apart of the fabric of society by promoting hate rather than civility as the basis of societal interactions. It may even be an indication that the glue that should be holding society together is already becoming unstuck.

However, it is not only Israel and Jews that are in the sights of radical Islam. Sunni movements such al-Qaeda and ISIS think in eschatological terms. Their aim is to establish an Islamic caliphate that practices pure Islam and that will rule the Near East and eventually the entire world as a prelude to the onset of the World to Come. This will be accomplished by jihad. Muslim Europeans and Americans are not immune from being attracted to these ideas.

The Taliban is a fundamentalist Islamic movement that has succeeded in establishing a legitimate government in Afghanistan. It is a rural, tribal movement that has been traditionally antagonistic to the urban elite in the country and opposes many aspects of modernity.[30] In the past, it has outsourced its global jihad mission to al-Qaeda. Its long-standing struggle for control of Afghanistan has debilitated the country. Its reintroduction of its repressive rule of the 1990's restricting freedoms and the rights of women almost guarantees that Afghanistan will continue to be a basket case dependent on Western aid. Whether it can continue to obtain handouts from Western countries, while at the same time advocating and even working towards their destruction through an association with al-Qaeda, remains an open question.[31]

In conclusion, Al-Husseini's legacy of hate and religious war between Islam and the Jewish state is a sad one and has been a disaster for many Palestinians, particularly those who were displaced during the 1948 war. This includes their families who have inherited the status of Palestinian refugees. Iran's messianic struggle with Israel has also brought nothing but misery to the people of Iran, Syria, Lebanon, Yemen, and Gaza, who have been dragged onto the front lines of this messianic conflict.

However, all is not gloom for the Jews. Ironically, it was the success of Amin al-Husseini in promoting himself as the leader of the Arab world and

---

30   "Afghanistan and the Taliban in Classical Muslim Apocalyptic Literature" in *Contemporary Muslim Apocalyptic Literature* by David Cook, 172-183. Syracuse University Press, 2005. Also, *Messianism in the Shiite Crescent* by David Cook. Hudson Institute, April 8, 2011 (https://www.hudson.org/research/7906-messianism-in-the-shiite-crescent) and "The Taliban, Radical Islam and Afghanistan" by Amalendu Misa. Third World Quarterly, vol 23. No 3, 577-589, 2002 (https://library.fes.de/libalt/journals/swetsfulltext/13640302.pdf).

31   "Al-Qaeda successfully played 'long game' in Afghanistan, FBI and UN official say" by Jerry Dunleavy (https://www.yahoo.com/news/al-qaeda-successfully-played-long-193800578.html).

mobilizing the Palestinians and neighboring Arab nations to support his geno-cidal agenda that has been most responsible for the territorial expansion and strengthening of the State of Israel. Because of the opposition to its existence, Israel was forced to develop its military capabilities, and using technology, in-genuity and resolve, it has been able repeatedly to defeat the military forces ar-rayed against it. The Six-Day War resulted in an even greater Israel territorially. All this, of course, was the very opposite of everything al-Husseini intended.

There are also now Muslim countries, predominantly Sunni, prepared to ignore this recent Islamic eschatology and who are cooperating with Israel under the Abraham Accords to their mutual advantage. The hope must be that the resulting increase in trade, personal interactions and religious understand-ing will have an enduring effect on the relationship between Jews and Muslims.

Chapter 17

THE MESSIANIC STRUGGLE FOR THE TEMPLE MOUNT

"The Temple Mount is in our hands!"

These now-famous words spoken by "Motta" (Mordechai) Gur, Chief of Staff of the Israel Defense Forces (IDF), in June 1967 during the Six-Day War would herald the beginning of a new reality for the Jewish people.

Israel had had no plans for taking over the Old City of Jerusalem, East Jerusalem or the West Bank of the Hashemite Kingdom of Jordan during the Six-Day War. The Israeli government begged Jordan to stay out of the conflict. But when the Jordanians continued shelling Jerusalem under the prearranged command of the Egyptians, Israel had no option but to open a third front.

In six days, the IDF defeated the armies of Syria, Egypt and Jordan. Jerusalem became a united city (geographically, that is) and the West Bank of Jordan, which once constituted the Biblical heartland of the Jewish people, was once again in Jewish hands. In the history of warfare, no territorial conflict like this against three enemies had ever been settled definitively in six days.[1] The conquest of Judea and Samaria, the Old City of Jerusalem and the Temple Mount had occurred almost by accident.

It seemed as if history was proclaiming the beginning of the messianic era. It was time to dust off the prophecies of Isaiah:

> *And many peoples shall go, and they shall say, "Come, let us go up to the Lord's house, to the house of the God of Jacob, and let Him teach us of His ways, and we will go in His paths," for out of Zion shall the Torah come forth, and the word of the Lord from Jerusalem (Isaiah 2:3).*

---

1   Hagi Ben-Artzi in *The Six-Day War Scroll*, Sifriat Beit-El, Jerusalem, 2016 points out the numerous "coincidences" that occurred during the Six Day War war. This is one I like a lot. Prior to waves of Israeli planes bombing all of Egypt's airbases, the Jordanians attempted to alert Egyptian Intelligence from their new radar station, but Egypt was unable to receive their message as the code had been changed that morning. In the end, Israel's 200 mostly old French planes were able to destroy 450 of Egypt's 600 modern Soviet planes with a loss of 46 Israeli planes.

and

And I will cause them to rejoice in My house of prayer, their burnt offerings and their sacrifices shall be acceptable upon My altar, for My house shall be called a house of prayer for all peoples (Isaiah 56:7).

An influential figure who definitely appreciated the messianic implications of Israel's victories was Rav Shlomo Goren, then chief rabbi of the Military Rabbinate of the IDF with the rank of general. Shortly after the capture of Jerusalem, he blew shofar blasts on the Temple Mount. A photograph of him blowing the shofar at the first ceremony at the Western Wall has been widely disseminated.

This shofar blowing on the Temple Mount and Western Wall accorded with a number of messianic Biblical verses, such as:

On that day a great shofar will be sounded, and those who are lost will come from the land of Assyria, and those who were banished, from the land of Egypt, and they will worship God at the holy mountain in Jerusalem (Isaiah 27:13).[2]

With the capture of Judea and Samaria and its Palestinian population, this victory created a new phase in the Israeli-Palestinian conflict. Eventually, it would also have the effect of awakening Jewish messianism in relation to the settlement of Judea and Samaria, and to initial steps in reclaiming the Temple Mount. Much of Israeli society will become involved in the spin-off from this messianism. This is because there is not one messianic narrative connected to the Temple Mount, but two – a Jewish and a Muslim one.

I need to say at the outset that this chapter is not intended to be an opinion piece about any particular theological position or course of action that the Israeli government should take. I cannot deny that I have opinions on these matters, but this book was not intended to be a forum for expressing them. This is a book about the history of ideas related to messianism, how they are related to the historic events of that era, and the effects of messianism on that period.

First, the evolution of the current situation.

---

2   Other sources are Isaiah 18:3, Joel 2:1 and Amos 2:2.

The rabbinic ban on Jews ascending the Temple Mount

Throughout the centuries prior to the 1948 War of Independence, an exposed part of the Western Wall of the Temple Mount, the closest part of the Western Wall to the former Holy of Holies, functioned as a Jewish prayer area, although no more than an alleyway. Within three days from the end of the Six-Day War, volunteer contractors were instructed to demolish the 135 Arab houses in the densely packed Mughrabi Quarter to make room for a large plaza in front of the Western Wall. The Mughrabi Quarter was an old residential area that was part of the Muslim Quarter and extended to adjacent to the Western Wall. This demolition was completed within a few days. Defense Minister Moshe Dayan, together with his staff officers then sat together with the Waqf and informed them that Israel would now be responsible for security on the Temple Mount, but it would otherwise continue to be run by the Jordanian-controlled Islamic Waqf. Jews would be able to ascend the Temple Mount, but they would be forbidden to pray there. Nor would they be permitted to bring onto the Temple Mount religious items such as prayer books or phylacteries. The Temple Mount would be exclusively an Islamic prayer area, and Jews would pray at the Western Wall as they had done (when permitted) for the last two millennia. Thus was born the new "status quo" for the Temple Mount.

Moshe Dayan had good reasons for planning separate prayer areas for Jews and Muslims. The Israeli government wanted to avoid religious conflict with the entire Muslim world; a backlash could have made it more difficult to establish control over the whole of Jerusalem. There was also the hope that Arab nations involved in this war would agree to a comprehensive peace settlement in return for the captured territory.

This turned out to be wishful thinking. At their 1967 Khartoum Conference, the Arab world issued three resounding noes: no to recognition [of Israel], no to negotiations and no to peace with the Jewish state. Nevertheless, at least one of Dayan's aims was met in that he succeeded in dampening Jewish messianic expectations.

Nevertheless, it could well be asked how Dayan was able to get away with this, in that at a single meeting with the Waqf he had relinquished 2,000 years of Jewish aspirations. Since its destruction, rebuilding the Temple had always been foremost in Jewish thought and central to much of Jewish daily prayer. The first project of the returnees to Zion from Babylon was the construction of a Temple. At the time of the Roman Emperor Julian (reigned

361-363 CE) Jews began rebuilding the Temple although circumstances halted this. Why were there not demonstrations throughout the country? At the very least there should have been a debate in the Knesset. Could it be that the Jewish people no longer cared about rebuilding their Temple?

Ironically perhaps, Jewish concern for the Temple Mount was expressed by agreeing with Dayan that Jews should stay away from the Temple Mount. In fact, a notice issued by Israel's Chief Rabbinate soon appeared outside the Mughrabi Gate, the main entrance to the Temple Mount for non-Muslims, forbidding any Jew from ascending it. This was not a law of the land and had no enforcement provisions, but rather a *halachic* ruling by the most authoritative religious body of the state.

The Chief Rabbinate issued it for a number of reasons:

- They thought it likely that many Jews would ascend the Temple Mount without due reverence for the site and without the required ritual purity (to be discussed).

- They thought that Jews might walk on prohibited areas for which sufficient ritual purity cannot be achieved nowadays.

- The exact place where the Temple once stood was not known, and people might inadvertently step on holy areas.

- Since the destruction of the Temple, all the great sages of the generations had prohibited entrance to the Temple Mount.

- There is no religious obligation (*mitzvah)* to ascend the Temple Mount.

- The Western Wall has been the place for Jewish prayer for thousands of years because of its proximity to the Temple, and its importance should not be diminished.

It may also be that the rabbis comprising the Chief Rabbinate believed that the Temple would only be rebuilt in messianic times and any Jewish initiative on the Temple Mount should be delayed until those times.[3] As Maimonides explained:

---

3   Two possibilities are considered in the Talmud as to how redemption will take place. One is a miraculous redemption; in which case the Temple will probably also be rebuilt miraculously. There are a number of references in the Talmud to the Temple being rebuilt in this way (TB Rosh Hashana 30a and TB Succah 41a). There is also a ruling in the Talmud (which is not normative practice) that priests should not drink alcohol lest the Temple be built miraculously. If they had recently imbibed alcohol, they would not be permitted to officiate at the Temple service (TB Sanhedrin 22b). An addition to the important Eighteen Benedictions prayer on the Fast of Tisha B'av says: "*For you O Lord consumed it with fire, and with fire You will rebuild it in the future.*" On the other hand, if redemption does not

In the future, the messianic king will arise and renew the Davidic dynasty, returning it to its initial sovereignty. He will build the Temple and gather the dispersed of Israel. [Then] in his days, [the observance of] all the statutes will return to their previous state. We will offer sacrifices, observe the Sabbatical and Jubilee years according to all the particulars mentioned by the Torah.[4]

It does not always happen this way on philosophical matters, but on this issue ultra-Orthodox and National Religious (*dati leumi*) Israelis saw eye to eye. Many of the latter were followers of the late Rav Abraham HaCohen Kook, and they practiced a more modern form of Orthodoxy. Both groups agreed that the Temple Mount should not be ascended, although for different reasons. Rav Kook held that the Zionist return to then-Palestine was part of redemption and the beginning of the messianic era. He also believed that spirituality would increase among the Jewish people, and this would lead eventually to the coming of the Messiah and the rebuilding of the Temple. In the meantime, the spiritual status of the Jewish people was insufficiently elevated. Or put another way, the Jewish people were not yet ready. Therefore, the Temple Mount should not be ascended.

---

occur miraculously, it will take place in its designated time and will be a gradual process. Rabbi Tokzinski in his book *The Holy City and the Temple* (in Hebrew) suggests that if the redemption is non-miraculous, then the building of the Temple will also be non-miraculous (Part 5, Chapter 1). There are a number of sources for a non-miraculous redemption and building of the Temple. TY Berochot 81 suggests that the redemption will start slowly and progress. TY Ma'aser Sheni 85 suggests that the Temple will be built by human hands (by the House of David with permission of the nations of the world). It is generally agreed that whether redemption comes miraculously or slowly depends on whether the Jewish people repent. Hence, TB Sanhedrin 98a discusses a verse from Isaiah which talks about redemption but seems to be internally inconsistent: *"Rabbi Alexandri says: Rabbi Yehoshua ben Levi raises a contradiction [in a verse addressing God's commitment to redeem the Jewish people. In the verse: "I the Lord in its time I will hasten it" (Isaiah 60:22)], it is written: "In its time," [indicating that there is a designated time for the redemption], and it is written: "I will hasten it," [indicating that there is no set time for the redemption. Rabbi Alexandri explains]: If they merit [redemption through repentance and good deeds] I will hasten the coming of the Messiah. If they do not merit [redemption, the coming of the Messiah will be] in its designated time. Rabbi Alexandri says: Rabbi Yehoshua ben Levi raises a contradiction [between two depictions of the coming of the Messiah]. It is written: "There came with the clouds of heaven, one like unto a son of man. . . . and there was given him dominion and glory and a kingdom. . . . his dominion is an everlasting dominion" (Daniel 7:13–14). And it is written: "Behold, your king will come to you; he is just and victorious; lowly and riding upon a donkey and upon a colt, the foal of a donkey" (Zechariah 9:9). Rabbi Alexandri explains: If the Jewish people merit [redemption, the Messiah will come in a miraculous manner] with the clouds of heaven. If they do not merit redemption, the Messiah will come lowly and riding upon a donkey."*

4   Maimonides, *Mishna Torah*, The Laws of Kings and their Wars 11:1

He wrote:

> *And when through God's infinite mercy, a fragment of the light of the emergence of salvation has begun to shine, the Rock of Israel will, with God's help, add the light of His mercy and truth, and will reveal to us the light of His full redemption, and bring us speedily our true redeemer, the redeemer of justice, our just Messiah, and will speedily fulfill all the words of his servants the Prophets, and will build the Temple, speedily in our days. . . . And, until then, all Israel shall as friends associate in a single union to steer their hearts toward their Father in Heaven, without bursting out and without departure, without any demolition of the fence and without any hint of transgressing against the prohibition of profanity and impurity of the Temple and its holiness.[5]*

At the time of the liberation of Jerusalem, Rav Avraham Kook was no longer alive, but his son and chief disciple Rabbi Zvi Yehuda Hacohen Kook was then head of the Merkaz Harav Yeshiva, the central yeshiva of the National Religious movement. For the same reason as his father, he held that it was prohibited to ascend the Temple Mount. He also advanced the argument that the holiness of the Temple would be elevated by refraining from ascending the Temple Mount. Accordingly, he held that it was forbidden to even touch the Temple Mount, including placing a note in the Western Wall. Thus it was that the majority of orthodox Israeli rabbis approved of the rabbinic ban on ascending the Temple Mount, a position which had been held by most (although not all) Jewish sages throughout the generations.

Nevertheless, there were those who disagreed. After the war, Rav Goren maintained a small synagogue on the Temple Mount, and he and some supporters held a prayer service two months after the war on the important fast day of Tisha Be'Av which commemorates the destruction of the Temples. He also announced he would be holding religious services on Yom Kippur. However, following Muslim violence on the Temple Mount as a result of the Tisha Be'Av service, this was thwarted by a ministerial committee.

Rav Goren was later appointed to the position of Ashkenazi Chief Rabbi of Israel, and he made a presentation to rabbis of the Chief Rabbinate, arguing that the prohibition against ascending the Temple Mount should be rescinded. However, his proposal was rejected and the prohibition remained.

---

5   Avraham Yitzhak Kook, Mishpat Cohen, 203. Jerusalem, 1984 (Hebrew). Quoted by Motti Inbari in his essay "Religious Zionism and the Temple Mount Dilemma – Key Trends," Israel Studies, Summer 2007, 29-47. (https://libres.uncg.edu/ir/uncp/f/Religious%20 Zionism%20and%20the%20Temple%20Mount%20Dilemma.pdf)

He also failed to persuade Menachem Begin to ease restrictions on Jewish prayer on the Temple Mount.[6]

There is a little-known story told by Gershom Gorenberg that at Rav Goren's initial visit to the Temple Mount during the Six-Day War, he requested General Narkis, the commander who had liberated the Old City, to blow up the Dome of the Rock since he realized this would be the only opportunity the Jewish people would have of being able to do this.[7] General Narkis refused and threatened to have him arrested if he made this request again. Rav Goren subsequently denied ever saying this.

The 1993 Oslo Accords between Israel and the Palestinians were a wake-up call for some of the politically-minded rabbis of the *Gush Emunim* movement. Issues of sovereignty over the Temple Mount had become a point of discussion in the negotiations with the Palestinians. These rabbis realized that contrary to the intentions of Rabbi Zvi Yehuda Kook, once something is out of sight it easily becomes out of mind. The non-religious then assume that the Temple Mount has no importance to religious Jews. As a result of these fears, there was a split within the *Gush Emunim* movement and Merkaz Harav Yeshiva, and a number of rabbis organized themselves to form a new political organization, the Yesha Council. This group issued a ruling that not only was it permissible to ascend the Temple Mount, but it should be encouraged. As a spokesman for the Yesha Council stated:

> *We send out to the Arabs a message of weakness by forfeiting our physical presence on and around the Temple Mount even in places where there is a rabbinic consensus that Jews are allowed to walk. The Arabs believe the Jews have no right to the Temple Mount and the Chief Rabbinate is helping them believe that.*[8]

One might well ask, however, what were the aims of the Yesha Council, given that Muslims have no intention of vacating the Temple Mount? Their ruling was clearly an attempt to make it difficult for the Israeli government to relinquish the Temple Mount within the context of a peace agreement.[9] A

---

6   "Religious Zionism and the Temple Mount Dilemma – Key Trends," Israel Studies, 37, Summer 2007, 29-47.

7   "For God and Country" in *The End of Days. Fundamentalism and the Struggle for the Temple Mount* by Gershom Gorenberg, 100. Oxford University Press, 2000. Also, Temple Mount, Shlomo Goren, Wikipedia. (https://en.wikipedia.org/wiki/Shlomo_Goren).

8   Quotation of Rabbi Daniel Shilo, spokesman of Yesha Council, reported in the Jerusalem Post, Feb 14, 2007.

9   The Council of Yesha Rabbis in "Religious Zionism and the Temple Mount Dilemma – Key Trends", Israel Studies, 37, Summer 2007, 38-42.

greater number of visitors would increase pressure on the Israeli government to agree to more favorable policies for Jews on the Temple Mount, such as granting them equal prayer rights. It could be considered an incremental step in the rebuilding of the Temple. It is also possible that members of the council believed that God could be prodded into speeding up the rebuilding of the Temple if passion about the Temple Mount was more widespread.

Rabbi Yehudah Glick, a longtime Temple Mount activist, rabbi and former member of the Knesset, is quoted as saying:

> *God chose the Jewish people, and He chose the Temple Mount as His one resting place in the world, and as a result we have a common destiny which is to declare God's kingdom from the Temple, which will be a house of prayer for all people, and where all nations will announce that God is One and His name is One. . . . We can only do that from the Temple Mount, which is where God chose to place His palace. We cannot choose anywhere else.*[10]

The rescinding of the ban on ascending the Temple Mount by these rabbis has had a marked effect on the number of Jews visiting the Temple Mount. While there are still many religious Jews in the ultra-Orthodox and National Religious camps who will not ascend the Temple Mount, a permissive attitude to ascending has become acceptable and even advisable, especially among National Religious Israelis. In 2009 only 5,658 Jews visited the Temple Mount. The figure was 33,523 in 2021, an almost 500% increase in 12 years.

Temple Mount activists admit that they are participating in a long-term project and they have no intention of taking drastic steps. Nevertheless, within these few years their campaign has had a number of significant effects:

- A division of the Temple Mount between Jews and Muslims is completely unacceptable to Muslims. Hence, the very fact that more Jews are walking on the Temple Mount means that tensions are ratcheted up a notch.

- These tensions have brought the issue of the Temple Mount to the forefront of Israeli politics.

- This campaign has struck a chord with many Israelis, including those with no messianic leanings, primarily because of issues of freedom of

---

10   Quoted in "Ascending the Mount" by Jeremy Sharon in Frontlines Section, the Jerusalem Post, Friday July 30, 2021.

religion and Israeli sovereignty. Many feel it is unacceptable that freedom of religion in Jerusalem applies to everyone but Jews, with Jews being restricted on when they can go to the Temple Mount and from praying there. And Israelis are the ones who captured this site! In the history of warfare there has probably never been an instance when a victorious army handed over control of its primary religious site to its adversary as a gesture of good will.

- A recent Israel Democracy Institute poll of 601 Hebrew speakers (hence mainly Jews) found that 50% of those polled supported Jewish prayer on the Temple Mount while 40% opposed it. Three-quarters of those who supported Jewish prayer held this view "because it is proof of Israel's sovereignty." It has been noticeable that Israeli police on the Temple Mount seem to be less strict with Jewish visitors than they were previously, and silent Jewish prayer is now permitted, albeit unofficially.

From the perspective of this campaign, all this can be considered a tremendous success.

To fully understand where all this may be heading, we need to go deeper into the significance of the Sanctuary in the wilderness and the subsequent Temple.

What was the purpose of the Sanctuary?

Shortly after leaving Egypt and while still in the wilderness, the Israelites were instructed to build a Sanctuary. What was its purpose?

A place of holiness for containing God's presence

The Torah introduces the topic of the Sanctuary with the following words: *"They shall make Me a Sanctuary (mikdash) – and I will dwell among them"* (Exodus 25:8).[11] This Sanctuary was not only a place for revering God, but for the Jewish people to experience the fact that God's presence was *"among*

---

11 The Hebrew word for Sanctuary is *mikdash*, derived from the word *kodesh* or holy. I follow here the interpretation that the laws of the Tabernacle were given on Mount Sinai. However, based on a midrash (*Tanchuma* 8), commentators such as Rashi and Sforno suggest that God originally did not intend that a Tabernacle be built at all and He only felt it necessary after the sin of the golden calf. The fact that the sin of the golden calf is not in the appropriate place in the Torah does not negate this explanation since the words of the Torah are not always in chronological order. However, Nachmanides believes that the Tabernacle was always intended to be the central focus of religious life for the Israelites, and this is why the topic of the Tabernacle constitutes a major part of the Book of Exodus.

them." Hence, the Book of Numbers described the Sanctuary as being at the very center of the Israelite camp, with the tents of the 12 tribes placed around it in groups of three and the tents of Moses, Aaron and the sons of Levi adjacent to it (Numbers 1:47-2.34). In this way God's presence had truly come to dwell "*among*" His people.

Jewish commentators have elaborated on why the concept of appreciating God's presence was so important. Abarbanel suggests that the purpose of the Sanctuary was to instill in the Jewish people the knowledge that God resides not only in heaven but also on earth, that He dwells among them and constantly watches over them. Yehuda Nachshoni summarizes Abarbanel's explanation as follows:

> *Through it [the erection of the Sanctuary] Israel would be taught that God (Y-H-V-H) dwells in their midst. His Providence accompanies them at all times and He carefully observes their deeds. Such was the symbolism of the Sanctuary, causing these principles to take deep root in the Jewish people.*[12]

The need for awareness of God's presence would explain several physical representations present within the Sanctuary:

- **The cherubim**. The Ark of the Covenant was a wooden box placed in the Holy of Holies that was covered in gold and contained the two tablets of the Ten Commandments.[13] It also had a golden lid, and from this lid projected two golden cherubim at each end (Exodus 25:18-20). According to a talmudic tradition, these had the faces of a male and female child facing each other and wings like that of a bird stretched upwards.[14] The purpose of this lid was to permit God and Moses to communicate with each other between the two cherubim as they had done

---

12 "Building the Mikdash – a Mitzvah for All Time" *in Studies in the Weekly Parashah, Shemos* by Yehuda Nachshoni, 525. Mesorah Publications Ltd, Artscroll, Jerusalem, 1998.

13 A fascinating question is what happened to the Ark of the Covenant. During the time of the monarchy, the kingdom of Judah oscillated between monotheism and paganism. The Bible relates that Josiah, the 16th king of Judea, "*placed the Holy Ark back in the Temple*" (2 Chronicles 35:3), possibly indicating that his father Manasseh had placed graven images there in its stead. A rabbinic tradition interprets a Mishnaic verse "*after [the Ark] was taken away*" as indicating that Josiah hid the Ark of the Covenant in a specially concealed subterranean chamber prepared by King Solomon to prevent the Babylonian king Nebuchadnezzar from taking it to Babylon (Tosefta, Sotah 13:1 and TB Kareithot 5b). In any event, the Ark of the Covenant is not mentioned in the Bible as one of the items taken from the Temple to Babylon (2 Chronicles 36:7) (TB Yoma 53b). A tradition from the Book of Maccabees is that Jeremiah hid the Ark of the Covenant on Mount Nebo, in present-day Jordan, prior to the Temple's destruction by the Babylonians (2 Maccabees 2:7).

14 TB Succah 5b. The Hebrew word for a cherub is *k'ruv* and the Aramaic for like a child is *k'ravya*.

at Mount Sinai (25:22). A number of places in the Bible suggest that the cherubim represented the footstool of the throne of God.[15]

- **God's presence filling the Sanctuary**. After the dedication of the Sanctuary, the end of the Book of Exodus described God's presence filling the Sanctuary as a cloud, to the extent that Moses was unable to even enter the Tabernacle:

The cloud covered the tent of meeting and the glory of God (Y-H-V-H) filled the Tabernacle (mishkan). And Moses was not able to come to the Tent of Meeting, for the cloud rested upon it, and the glory of God filled the Sanctuary (Exodus 40:34-35).[16]

From its focus in the Tabernacle, holiness would emanate to the rest of the Israelite camp and God "will *walk among you, I will be a God to you and you will be a people to me*" (Leviticus 26:12). In this way, the cloud established that the arena for God's interaction with the Jewish people was not in the heavenly realm but within the Jewish camp.

- **The candelabrum and showbread**. The Sanctuary contained a *menorah* (candelabrum) and a table with showbread. One way of looking at these objects is that symbolically they represented furniture for a God who resided within His Sanctuary.[17]

A place to offer sacrifices

At its most basic level the Sanctuary was a structure for offering sacrifices, and this remained its main function throughout Temple times:

A replica of Mount Sinai

An idea raised by Nachmanides was that the Sanctuary was intended to replicate the experience of the Jewish people at Mount Sinai. Hence, at Mount

---

15 Three references to this concept are as follows: "*God has reigned. Let peoples tremble before Him Who is enthroned on cherubim, let the earth quake*" (Psalm 99:1); "*The name of the Lord of hosts who dwells upon the cherubim [being] upon it*" (2 Samuel 6:2); and "*King David rose to his feet and said: . . . 'It is with my heart to build a house of rest for the Ark of the Covenant and for the footstool of our God'*" (1 Chronicles 28:2).

16 Rashi points out that Moses did enter the Tabernacle (Numbers 7:89). How then can this contradiction be resolved? He suggests, based on a midrash (*Toras Kohanaim,* Yud Gimmel Middos 8), that his actions depended on the cloud over the Tabernacle. Only when the cloud was upon the Tabernacle was he unable to enter. Nachmanides in his commentary to Exodus 40:34-35 suggests that God would call Moses to step within the cloud as at Mount Sinai.

17 The Sforno on Exodus 25:23 points out that a table and lamp are essential furnishings for a guest room (2 Kings 4:10).

Sinai, God's glory was located within a cloud. Similarly, the Tabernacle was witnessed by the Israelites as being enveloped in a cloud or fire. Moses was required to await a Divine summons to enter both these clouds. The Sanctuary contained the tablets of the Ten Commandments given at Mount Sinai that had been placed in the Ark of the Covenant. God also communicated with Moses above the covering of the ark and between the cherubim and He continued to provide explanations about the covenant as He had done at Mount Sinai. Thus, one way of viewing the Sanctuary was as a portable version of Mount Sinai.[18] As such, it would have been a powerful reminder not only of God's presence but also His covenant.

FROM SANCTUARY TO TEMPLE

Maimonides derives the directive to build a Temple in the Land of Israel from the Torah command to build a Sanctuary in the wilderness. He summarizes this in his *Sefer Hamitzvot* (*Book of Commandments*) as follows:

> *By this injunction we are commanded to build a Sanctuary [in the Land of Israel] for His service. There sacrifices are to be offered and the perpetual fire is to burn, thither the [prescribed] pilgrimages are to be made, and there the festivals and assemblages are to be held every year, as will be explained. This injunction is contained in His words exalted be He: "And let them make Me a Sanctuary" (Exodus 25:8).*[19]

The Torah also directs that this Temple be at a single location and there

---

18 Nachmanides, *Commentary to the Torah*, Introduction to the Book of Exodus. In his commentary to Exodus 40:34-35 Nachmanides suggests that in kabbalistic terms the Tabernacle was supposed to be a representation of Mount Sinai. He writes: "*The esoteric significance of the Mishkan [the Tabernacle] is that the glory that rested upon Mount Sinai [at the time of the giving of the Torah] should rest upon the Tabernacle, [but unlike at Sinai] in a concealed manner. And just as it is written there [regarding Mount Sinai] (24:16) 'The glory of Hashem rested upon Mount Sinai,' regarding the Tabernacle it says twice 'And the "glory" of God filled the Tabernacle'* " (Exodus 40:34-35). See also, "Of Parts and Pieces: The Instructions and Assembly of the Mishkan" by Rav Chanoch Waxman in *Torah Mietzion. New Readings in Tanach. Shemot*, eds Rav Ezra Bick and Rav Yaakov Beasley, 521. Maggid Books, Jerusalem, 2012.

19 Maimonides, *Sefer Hamitzvot*, Positive Commands #20. See also his *Mishna Torah,* The Laws of the Temple 1:1. The Talmud also learns other laws about the Temple from the next verse, Exodus 25:9 (TB Sanhedrin 16b and Shavuos 14b). The Smag disagrees with Maimonides and feels that this commandment was only for the wilderness. His source for the construction of a Sanctuary or Temple in the Land of Israel is Deuteronomy 12:11: "*Then there shall be a place which the Lord your God shall choose to cause His name to dwell there.*"

should not be multiple sanctuaries throughout the country:

> *Only at the place that the Lord your God will choose from all your tribes to place His Name there, you shall seek out His resting place and come there. And you shall bring your olah-offerings. (Deuteronomy 12:5-6).*[20]

Fulfilling this command was a continual struggle throughout the monarchial period, and only a minority of Judean kings were able to establish centralized worship as distinct from a profusion of shrines throughout the country.

At a speech he gave at the dedication of his temple, King Solomon elaborated on an idea not previously discussed in the Bible; that his Temple should not only be the exclusive place for sacrifice, but also the focal point for Jewish prayer. This raised the obvious question: How can pray be directed towards one location when God's presence is everywhere? Solomon's answer to his own question was a request to God that He make it so:

> *But will God (Elohim) really dwell on earth? Behold, even the uttermost reaches of heaven cannot contain You; how much less this temple I have erected. Yet turn O Lord my God to the prayer and supplication of Your servant, and hear the song and prayer which Your servant prays before You this day. May Your eyes be open toward this house night and day, toward the place which You said: "My Name will be there" to heed the prayers that Your servant will pray toward this place* (1 Kings 8:27-29).

Solomon also requested from God that his Temple be the place towards which the Jewish people pray whenever they are in distress and these prayers should be accepted by Him:

> *So, too, if there is a famine in the land, if there be pestilence, blight, mildew, locusts, or caterpillars; if their enemy besiege its gates in the land, whatsoever plague, whatsoever sickness. Any prayer, any supplication offered by any person among all Your people Israel, each of whom know his own affliction, and spreads forth his hands toward this house. Then hear in Your*

20　The Tabernacle in the desert was a temporary tent-like structure. After the conquest of Canaan, the Tabernacle was moved to the town of Shilo and given more permanence by enclosing it with stone walls, although its roof was still covered by curtains. The Sanctuary remained in Shilo for 369 years during the pre-monarchic period. Shilo was eventually destroyed by the Philistines, and the Ark was captured. When the Ark was returned to the Israelites, the Sanctuary was reestablished at Nov and then at Gibeon until Solomon built his Temple in Jerusalem. King David intended to build a permanent structure for God, but was told by the prophet Nathan that this task would devolve onto his son Solomon (2 Samuel 7).

heavenly dwelling place, and pardon, and take action, and render to every man according to his way as You know his heart to be, for You, alone, know the hearts of all the children of men (8:37-39).

King David was told by the prophet Nathan that contrary to his wish, he would not build the Temple but rather his son Solomon. In the Book of Chronicles, David described his interpretation of how God's "*Name*" would be placed on the Temple built by his son:

And David said: "Solomon my son is young and tender and the House that is to be built for God must be magnified on high for fame and for glory to all lands. . . ." (I Chronicles 22:5)

This idea was elaborated on further by Solomon who proposed that his Temple should not only be a house of prayer for Jews, but for all people who hear of God's great "*Name*" and come to pray at His house:

And also concerning the stranger, who is not of Your people Israel, who will come from a distant country for the sake of Your Name. For they shall hear of Your great Name, and of Your mighty hand, and of Your outstretched arm, when he will come and pray toward this house, o' hear in Your heavenly abode, and grant all that the stranger asks of You. Thus, all peoples of the earth will know Your name, to revere You, as do Your people Israel, and they will recognize that Your name is called upon this house that I have built (ibid., 8:41-43).

Finally, Solomon discussed that the location of the Temple should be the direction to which Jews pray whenever they are in straits:

When Your people are struck down before the enemy, because they sin against You, and shall turn again to You, and acknowledge Your name, and pray and make supplication to You in this house. Then hear in Heaven, and forgive the sin of Your people Israel, and bring them back to the land which You gave to their fathers (ibid., 8:33-34).

But what if there is no longer a Temple? Should Jews pray towards a ruin, or even to the shrine of another religion? Solomon did not raise this issue but later religious authorities will need to. It is related to the question – what holiness does the location of the Temple possess in the absence of a building? Is God's presence still there?

JEWISH REVERENCE FOR A NON-EXISTENT TEMPLE

For many centuries, the Temple Mount has contained just Islamic structures. To all intents and purposes, this is an exclusively Islamic prayer area.
Nevertheless, Jews never gave up hope that one day their Temple would be rebuilt. This hope is expressed in the veneration still accorded to the area where
the Temple once stood.

The Book of Leviticus instructed that the Sanctuary be approached with
reverence (Leviticus 19:30). This is summarized by Maimonides as follows:

> There is a positive commandment to hold the Temple in awe, as [Leviticus
> 19:30] states: "And you shall revere my Sanctuary" (ibid., 19:30).
> Nevertheless, it is not the [physical building of] the Temple which must
> be held in awe, but rather, He who commanded that it be revered. . . .
> Everyone who enters the Temple Courtyard should walk in a dignified
> manner in the region where he is permitted to enter. He should conceive of
> himself as standing before God, as [1 Kings 9:3] states: "My eyes and my
> heart will be there forever." One should walk with awe, fear and trembling,
> as [Psalms 55:15] states: "We would walk in the House of the Lord with
> fervor."[21]

And he continues:

> Even though the Temple is now in ruin because of our sins, a person
> must hold its [site] in awe, as one would regard it when it was standing.
> [Therefore] one should only enter a region which he is permitted to enter."[21]

Maimonides supported this last statement with a midrash that noted
that because the Temple and the Sabbath are mentioned in the same verse, the
Temple has the same eternal sanctity as the Sabbath:

> "You shall observe my Sabbaths and you shall revere My sanctuary"
> (Leviticus 19:30) [explaining the analogy between the two commands, the
> Sages comment]. Just as the observance of the Sabbath [applies] for eter-
> nity, so too, the reverence for the Temple must be eternal.[22]

In his *Mishna Torah* Maimonides raised a related issue. It is accepted
that the Land of Israel became holy when Joshua conquered the Land of Israel,
but this sanctification was nullified during the exile following the destruction

---

21 Maimonides, *Mishna Torah*, Hilchot Beit Habechirah 7:1 and 5. Leviticus 19:30, *Sifra*.
22 Maimonides, *Sefer Hamitzvot*, positive commands #21. Also, Leviticus 19:30, *Sifra*.

of the First Temple.[23] Therefore, Ezra needed to re-sanctify the land when the Jews returned from the Babylonian exile. This renewed sanctity, which related mainly to Jewish agriculture laws, was at a rabbinic and not Torah level. How then could Maimonides say that the sanctity of the Temple persists forever, when the land itself never had eternal sanctity?

Maimonides' answer is that the sanctity of the Second Temple stemmed not from the land on which it stood, but from the holiness of God's presence within the Temple. This never disappeared:

> *Why do I say that the original consecration [at the time of David and Solomon] sanctified the Temple and Jerusalem for eternity, while in regard to the consecration of the remainder of the Land of Israel (Eretz Yisrael) in the context of the Sabbatical year, tithes, and other similar [agricultural] laws, [the original consecration at the time of Joshua] did not sanctify it for eternity? Because the sanctity of the Temple and Jerusalem stems from God's presence (the Shechina) and the Shechina (God's presence) can never be nullified. Therefore, [Leviticus 26:3] states "I will lay waste to your sanctuaries." The sages declared: "Even though they have been devastated, their sanctity remains."*[24]

The view that the area where the Temple once stood retains extreme sanctity was not held by all rabbinic authorities in the past, although it is accepted nowadays as normative *halacha*.[25] Hence, all orthodox rabbis today

---

23   There was therefore no need to keep any of the agricultural laws pertaining to the Land of Israel during the Babylonian exile.

24   Maimonides, *Mishna Torah,* Hilchot Beit Habechirah 6:16. Also TB Megilla 28a.

25   There is debate in Jewish sources regarding the sanctity of the Temple area in post-Temple times. On the Talmud's statement in TB Shavuot 16b *"because its sanctity is an everlasting sanctity,"* Rashi, in his commentary to the Talmud, writes that what constituted its sanctity was that from the time the Temple was built it was no longer permitted to offer sacrifices on private altars. Tosafos notes that the permanence of the Temple's sanctity was that even if it were destroyed, a new Temple would be erected only on this site. This could imply that both authorities would not regard the Temple Mount site as currently having extreme holiness. The Ra'avad, who wrote notes to Maimonides' *Mishna Torah* and who not infrequently disagreed with him, says: *"This is [the Rambam's] opinion. I am not aware of his source. . . . According to the opinion in the Talmud which states that it was not originally consecrated for eternity, no differentiation was made between the Temple, Jerusalem and the remainder of the Land of Israel."* Which means that the Temple will only be reconsecrated in messianic times. However, the Ra'avad's opinion is not generally accepted. Rav Avraham Kook attempted to clarify this debate in an original way. He explained that no one disagrees that the Temple Mount still has a degree of sanctity; the question is how much. Objects that have been used for a holy purpose are not summarily discarded after their use is terminated. The covering for phylacteries, for example, has the same degree of holiness

consider the area of the Temple compound (which is only a section of the Temple Mount) to have enduring sanctity because of God's presence. Accordingly, it is forbidden by Jewish law to walk on this area in a state of ritual impurity, and the Torah's penalty of *karet* (spiritual excision) applies if this area is stepped upon. All Jews nowadays are considered to be ritually impure by virtue of their possible defilement by contact with the dead, and there is no way of removing this other than by the ashes of a red heifer, ashes that do not exist (although for all other areas on the Temple Mount ritual immersion is sufficient).

THE TEMPLE MOUNT IN ISLAM

Jerusalem's Muslim period began in 638 CE when the caliph Omar ibn al-Khattab (584-644 CE) captured the city from the Byzantines. He was a senior companion of Muhammad and the second caliph after Abu Bakr. He became one of the most powerful caliphs in history and considerably expanded the territory ruled by the caliphate. He cleaned up the Temple Mount, which had been left as a garbage site during the Christian period, and built a mosque on the Temple Mount to the south of the Foundation Stone. Other than this, he had little interest in the Temple Mount or in Jerusalem.

The Islamic Empire was subsequently ruled by three dynasties. The Umayyad dynasty came to power in 661 CE and their caliphs held Jerusalem in considerable esteem. In 682 CE, 50 years after Muhammad's death, there was a succession crisis for leadership of the Islamic Empire following the assassination of Ali, the fourth caliph and husband of Muhammad's daughter Fatima, and Muslims in Syria and Palestine were unable to go on pilgrimage to Mecca. At this time the Umayyad dynasty promoted the idea that the al-Aqsa Mosque was the *"remotest sanctuary"* referred to in the Qur'an, and it became a new site of pilgrimage.

The Qur'an relates that Muhammad was told to take his horse El Burak to the *"remotest mosque"* or *"al-Aqsa,"* and it is from here that he went up to heaven to meet the prophets Moses, Elijah and Jesus. As the Qur'an relates: *"Praise be to Him who made his servant journey in the night from the sacred sanctuary to the remotest sanctuary"* (Sura 17:1). It was probably also

---

as the phylacteries themselves, and is not thrown away but placed in *geniza* (storage). On the other hand, a set of the Four Species that is no longer needed after the holiday of Succot (Tabernacles) is wrapped up in a respectful way before being discarded. Is the destroyed Temple similar to this or does it have enduring holiness like the covering of the phylacteries? On this matter, Maimonides and the Ra'avad disagree.

during the Umayyad dynasty that the Final Judgment foretold by the Qur'an was given a geographic location the Temple Mount. As a result of these traditions, the Temple Mount became the third holiest site to Sunni Muslims after Mecca and Medina.

The Dome of the Rock was completed by the fifth Umayyad caliph, Abd al-Malik. This shrine (it is not a mosque) was given this name because it was built on top of exposed rock at the highest part of the Temple Mount. This rock is called in Arabic the *al-Sarah al-Mušarrafah* or Noble Rock. The Dome of the Rock was (and still is) the highest and most prominent building in the Old City of Jerusalem.

This same rock is called the Foundation Stone or *"even ha-shetiya"* in Hebrew. It is mentioned in Mishna Midot as being the location of the Holy of Holies. The Roman historian Josephus also stated that the Temple was located on the highest part of the Temple Mount. Hence, there can be no doubt that the Dome of the Rock was built over the Foundation Stone and the site of the Holy of Holies of the Jewish Temple. It is not entirely clear why al-Malik built this structure, but it is surmised from inscriptions on the building that denounce the Christian doctrines of the Trinity and divinity of Jesus that its function was to demonstrate the preeminence of Islam over Christianity and Judaism. Al-Malik's sons rebuilt the al-Aqsa Mosque at the site of Omar's original mosque.[26]

Nevertheless, it is highly questionable whether Muhammad ever journeyed to Jerusalem, even mystically. Jerusalem held no significance for him, and it is never mentioned in the Qur'an. There was a time in the early Mecca phase of his preaching when he and his followers turned towards Jerusalem in prayer to attract Jews to his new faith, but when Muhammad moved to Medina and found the Jews to be either apathetic or hostile to him and his new religion, he changed the direction of prayer to Mecca. A hundred years or so after its designation as a holy place, historians were already questioning whether the *"remotest sanctuary"* was really in Jerusalem. A book by the Muslim historian and geographer al-Waqidi (747-823 CE) described two *"masjeds"* (places of prayer) in al-Gi'irranah, a village between Mecca and Ta'if, one of which was *"the closer mosque (al-masjid al-adna)"* and the other was *"the further mosque (al-masjid al-aqsa)."* He relates that this was where Muhammad would pray whenever he went out of town. It is noteworthy that Jerusalem never became holy to the Shi'ites since they had no need for an additional holy site.

---

26 The al-Aqsa Mosque has been rebuilt several times since it was first constructed, mostly because of earthquake damage. Much of the current building dates from 1929.

Nevertheless, almost no Sunni Muslim nowadays would question the significance of the al-Aqsa Mosque. One could even say that the true location of the *"remotest mosque"* is irrelevant. Throughout the centuries, Jerusalem and the Temple Mount have been held in considerable esteem by Muslims and their places of worship on the Temple Mount are holy to them. The struggle between the Crusaders and the Muslims was primarily a struggle over Jerusalem, but for Muslims it was also about the Temple Mount.

As discussed in the previous chapter, a major driving force for anti-Jewish sentiment in much of the Muslim world today is its apocalyptic literature. This literature already existed by the first and second centuries of the Islamic period, and its rudimentary outlines were formulated at that time. It was based on the historical events of that period, and there was no particular focus on Jews. However, Islamic apocalyptic literature exploded after the Six-Day War. In these books Israel will cease to exist and a caliphate will be ruled by a messianic-like figure called the Mahdi. Jerusalem will become Islamic and will become the capital of the caliphate.

Islam presently has only partial control over the Temple Mount since the Israeli police have the final say over everything that happens on this site. Only when Muslims are able to break out of this stranglehold can they hope for the establishment of their caliphate, the victory of Islam over Judaism and Christianity and the final Day of Judgment. Hence, it is unimaginable that any Sunni Muslim authority would ever voluntarily agree to share the Temple Mount for Jewish prayer, and even more to consent to the erection of a Jewish Temple.

The Temple Mount has become the focus of the struggle between Palestinians and Israelis. Israeli police actions against rioting Muslims and the fear of changes in the status of the Temple Mount are used as a rallying call by Hamas, who is calling on all Muslims within Judea and Samaria, and even within Israel itself, to rise up in violence against Israelis. This position has wide support among Palestinians. All this is nothing new. Just under a 100 years ago, Amin al Husseini also appreciated the effectiveness of calls to Muslims to defend al-Aqsa, even when the provocation was fabricated. Except in this instance, it is not completely fabricated in that there is indeed an attempt by messianic Israelis to change what they and many others regard as an unacceptable "status quo" on the Temple Mount.

Nevertheless, the calls by Muslims for a return to the "status quo" is somewhat disingenuous. The true demands of the Palestinians are hardly for the status quo. As the Jordanian Foreign Minister Ayman Safadi was quoted as saying: "*Our demands are clear that the al-Aqsa and Haran al-Sharif in all its area is a sole place of worship for Muslims.*" Moreover, the waqf has made many changes to the status quo since it was formulated, such as paving over new pathways, building outdoor prayer platforms and constructing three new mosques (the latter so as to leave no room for Jewish worship).[27]

Maimonides, sacrifices and the Temple

Throughout the centuries it has been a given in religious Jewish writings that the Temple will one day be rebuilt and the sacrificial rites restored. The only dissenting voice of influence in the orthodox world has been that of Maimonides writing in the Middle Ages.

Maimonides' works have been extremely influential in the development and dissemination of Jewish law and have gained wide acceptance. An exception to this is his book *The Guide for the Perplexed*. It was written for Jews having difficulty harmonizing the ideas of then current philosophy with Jewish thought. However, it also contains many "modern" ideas regarding other important philosophical issues. It influenced several major Christian and Muslim philosophers and was quoted by them. Many Jews appreciated the book, but others found its ideas problematic, and even heretical. For a time, it was banned in the Jewish world. It is rarely studied in ultra-orthodox yeshivot, but is regarded by many Jews as a valuable addition to Jewish scholarship.

This is what Maimonides wrote about the Temple and its sacrifices:

> *It is namely impossible to go suddenly from one extreme to the other; it is therefore according to the nature of man impossible for him suddenly to discontinue everything to which he has been accustomed. . . . But the custom which was in those days general among all men, and the general mode of worship in which the Israelites were brought up, consisted in sacrificing animals in those temples which contained certain images, to bow down to those images, and to burn incense to them. . . . It was in accordance with the wisdom and plan of God, as displayed in the whole creation, that He did not command us to give up and to discontinue all these manners of service; for to obey such a commandment it would have been contrary to the nature of man, who generally cleaves to that to which he is used. . . . For this reason, God allowed these kinds of service to continue. . . .*

27 "Israel's ignominious Temple Mount dismount. Israel asserts no unambiguous Jewish claim to the Temple Mount" by Yisrael Medad in the Jerusalem Post, May 24, 2022.

By this Divine plan it was effected that the traces of idolatry were blotted out, and the truly great principle of our faith, the existence and unity of God was firmly established; this result was thus obtained without deterring or confusing the minds of the people by the abolition of the service to which they were accustomed and which alone was familiar to them.[28]

Maimonides is saying here that God adapted His instructions according to man's natural disposition during a particular historic period and that sacrifices in the Sanctuary and Temple were a concession. He further suggested that since "*supplications, prayers, and similar kinds of worship are nearer to the primary object and indispensable for obtaining it,*" this was the reason that this type of worship was limited to one place. Hence, "*All these restrictions served to limit this kind of worship, and keep it within those bounds within which God did not think it necessary to abolish sacrificial service altogether. But prayer and supplication can be offered everywhere and by every person.*"[28]

Maimonides did not say specifically that the Temple was also a concession, but he did link together sacrifices and the primary location of the cult, and this could be read into his words, especially as "*prayer and supplication can be offered anywhere.*"

These were radical ideas and were accepted by no one of any standing in the Jewish world.[29] They even contradicted his own words that he wrote in his *Mishna Torah*:

In the future, the Messianic King will arise and renew the Davidic dynasty, returning it to its initial sovereignty. He will build the Temple and gather the dispersed of Israel. [Then] in his day, [the observance of] all the statutes will return to their previous state. We will offer sacrifices, observe the sabbatical and jubilee years according to all the particulars mentioned by the Torah.[4]

It should be recalled that it was the Jews who developed a concept that would fundamentally change their own religion and would eventually be adopted throughout the monotheistic world: a Temple is no longer necessary for worshipping God and seeking atonement. Instead, it is possible to bring God's presence into a "small Temple" or synagogue.[30]

---

28 "Why did God give laws to oppose idolatry instead of uprooting it directly" in *The Guide for the Perplexed*, Part 3, Chapter 32 by Moses Maimonides, translated by M. Friedlander, 322-327. Dover Publications Inc, New York.

29 For example, Nachmanides, *Commentary to the Torah*, Leviticus 1:9.

30 A talmudic passage states: "*The verse states: "Yet I have been to them as a little sanctuary in the countries where they have come" (Ezekiel 11:16). Rabbi Yitzhak said: This [is referring*

Most people would agree that the evolution of the synagogue was an extremely positive development within monotheism in that it permitted worshippers to become actively involved in their relationship with God rather than being primarily observers of the activities of priests.

Should ideas like those of Maimonides be brought into present day discussions or are they so far from Jewish tradition as to be completely unacceptable? I would suggest that these should be discussed, even if they are in the end rejected.

For thousands of years Jews have not had autonomy. The State of Israel is an experiment in bringing Judaism to the place it truly belongs – as the guiding force in the spiritual and ethical life of the nation. That a person of the stature of Maimonides could write that it might be possible to dispense with sacrifices brought this view into the open. As such, his words provide support nowadays to those Jews who continue to pray for the return of God's presence to the Temple Mount but who find distasteful the idea of a return of the sacrificial rites.[31]

The rebuilding of the Temple on the Temple Mount clearly constitutes a tremendous question mark. One could well argue that the religious and political questions raised are so difficult to answer that in the absence of a prophet providing guidance the easiest path is to push them off to messianic times. However, as soon as Jews engage in any form of messianic activism on the Temple Mount, including promoting increased visiting (which many would agree they are in any case entitled to), these questions make their way to the fore.

WITHER NOW?

Much of Jewish messianism in the 21st century is focused on the Temple Mount. Where is it heading?

It will be recalled that it was the Jews who brought the concept of hope to civilization and the notion that it is possible to create an ideal God-focused society that would influence the rest of humanity. Part of this concept is that

---

to] *the synagogues and study halls in Babylonia. . . . Rava interpreted [a verse] homiletically: What is the meaning of that which is written: "Lord, You have been our dwelling place in all generations" (Psalms 90:1)? This is referring to the synagogues and study halls"* (TB Megilla 29a). See also comments of Rashi and Radak to Ezekiel 11.16.

31 According to the Talmud, with the lack of prophecy, the *Shechina*, or presence of God, and the Holy Spirit present in the First Temple were already lacking in the Second Temple (TB Yoma 21b).

the Name of God and His universal ethics should be recognized by all humanity. The prophets of ancient Israel realized that such an ideal world could never be realized without the overt intervention of God. Thus was born the notion of a messianic era. Rebuilding the Jewish Temple was an integral part of this vision.

But where does the rebuilding of the Temple fit in nowadays? At this moment in time, this relates to the question as to whether Israel should permit public Jewish prayer on the Temple Mount as a first step in reclaiming use of the Temple Mount.

On this, there are currently two opinions. One is that Jews should stay away from the Temple Mount, either because the Jewish people are not yet at a sufficiently high spiritual level (following the opinion of Rav Kook) or because messianic times have not sufficiently progressed, or even started. The second opinion is that public prayer should be permitted. In reality, for the majority of Israelis who think this way, their opinion has next to nothing to do with religion (in fact, they may not even be Jews who pray regularly) but more to do with establishing sovereignty over the Temple Mount and obtaining equality for Jews. The cheerleaders for this project are a small group of messianic activists who wish to establish Jewish prayer as an incremental step in the rebuilding of the Temple.

There could also be a third way. This is to say that the messianic activists are correct in their desire for a Temple and for promoting Jewish visiting (as long as it does not become excessive), since one day a Temple will be built on the Temple Mount for the glory of God and to promote His Name among the nations. Private prayer is also the right of any individual. However, public prayer is another matter. The sentiment is correct, but the timing may not be.

It is worth recalling that at the time of King David, the Temple was considered to be the icing on the cake so to speak and not the cake itself, since there was already an alternative place for worshiping God (II Samuel 7:1, II Chronicles 22:18). Moreover, the prophetic refusal in acceding to David's request to build a Temple in favor of his son could well have been based on an interpretation of verses in Deuteronomy:

> *When you cross the Jordan and settle in the land that the Lord your God causes you to inherit and He will give you rest from all your enemies all around, so that you dwell securely. Then it shall be that the place where the Lord your God will choose to cause His Name to dwell there – there shall you bring everything that I command you: your elevation offerings and your feast offerings. . . .* (Deuteronomy 12:1-11)

Israel is hardly at rest from its *"enemies all around."* Moreover, the Temple is to be a building of peace for all nations and this can only happen when Israel is truly at peace with all its neighbors.

Israel has too many other priorities at this time to allow the Temple Mount to become a focus of Palestinian and Islamic rage and for it to become a rallying call for Muslims who reject the presence of Israel in the Middle East. From a religious perspective the gains are almost nil. A prayer quorum on the Temple Mount is the same prayer quorum as one at the Western Wall. God will listen in either case. And the distance to the former Holy of Holies is about the same.

There is still much for Israel to accomplish in its relationship with the Islamic world without Jewish activities on the Temple Mount being a hindrance. A number of influential Islamic countries continue to pursue their messianic mission of eliminating Israel from the globe. Chief among them is Iran. This has brought and continues to bring economic disaster and misery to the people of these countries. The neutralization, and even defeat, of these countries is a priority for the Jewish state.

It is also readily apparent that cooperation with Israel brings in its wake *"blessing"* to all concerned and that the Abraham Accords have the potential to being about a new reality to this part of the world. These accords constitute an alliance of Middle Eastern countries against messianic Islamic fundamentalism and they open the possibility for Muslims to become partners with Jews in building prosperity for themselves and a kinder golden age for the Middle East.

Glossary of Hebrew terms

Aggada   Non-legalistic exegesis appearing in the classical rabbinic literature of Judaism, particularly in Talmud and midrash.

Aliya   Ascending. Often used to refer to the immigration of Jews to Israel.

Ashkenazim   Jews whose ancestors came from Central and Western Europe and who continue their traditions

Baraita   A text of a tradition in Jewish law that was not incorporated into the Mishna.

Haggadah: A compilation of blessings, prayers, midrashic comments and psalms recited on the Passover eve in celebration of the Israelite release from Egyptian slavery some 3,500 years ago.

Halacha   Jewish law and related to Jewish law.

Halachist   A Jewish sage involved in developing and formulating Jewish law.

Haredim   A sect within Orthodox Judaism that practices strict adherence to Jewish law. They are often referred to as ultra-orthodox Jews.

Hasidim   A Jewish revivalist sect founded in Poland in about 1750 CE.

Hasidism   The practices and beliefs of the Hasidim.

Hesder   An Israeli program combining advanced talmudic study with military service in the Israel Defense Forces.

Kabbala   Esoteric Jewish mysticism.

Kollel   A "gathering" or "collection" of scholars for full-time advanced study of the Talmud and rabbinic literature.

Menorah

Hebrew for a lamp. The menorah in the Sanctuary and Temple was a seven-branch lamp/lampstand made of pure gold.

Mezuzah
mezuzot (pl.)

A small parchment scroll on which is written a specific passage from the Torah. It is enclosed in a case and affixed to the doorposts of Jewish homes.

Midrash
plural
midrashim
(noun),
midrashic (adj.)

An exposition or explanation that is part of Jewish tradition and that interprets Biblical narrative, explores questions of ethics or theology, or creates homilies and parables based on the text. There are two types of midrashim. A halachic midrash is concerned with law and religious practice. A midrash aggada contains aggadic and non-halachic material.

Mishna
(noun),
mishnaic (adj.)

The first major written collection of the Jewish Oral Law or oral tradition. It was compiled around 200 CE.

Paschal lamb

The sacrifice slaughtered by the Jews before the Exodus from Egypt. It was mandated by the Torah to be ritually slaughtered on the day before Passover and eaten on the evening of Passover. In the absence of a Temple, this ritual is no longer performed.

Perushim

The word means "separated ones." They were disciples of the Vilna Gaon who left Lithuania at the beginning of the 19th century to settle in Palestine.

Sanhedrin

A legal body. The Lesser Sanhedrin had 23 judges and functioned in every city. The Great Sanhedrin was the equivalent of a Supreme Court, had 71 judges, and functioned only in Jerusalem. After the destruction of Jerusalem, a number of ordained rabbis functioned as the Sanhedrin.

Seder

The ritual ceremony held at the beginning of Passover in the evening and celebrated with a narrative and feast.

Shulchan aruch

The most widely consulted compilation of Jewish law, written in Safed by Joseph Karo in 1563 CE.

Sephardi
(noun and adj.),
Sephardim (pl.)

Strictly speaking this refers to Jews from the Iberian Peninsula, but commonly includes Jews from Western Asia and North Africa whose families continue their traditions.

Sifra	A halachic midrash to the Book of Leviticus. It is frequently quoted in the Talmud.
Sifrei	Either of two midrashic works on the Book of Numbers and Deuteronomy.
Talmud (noun), talmudic (adj.)	The central text of rabbinic Judaism and the primary source of Jewish law. It comprises the Mishna and Gemara, the latter being a commentary on the Mishna. The Jerusalem Talmud was completed in about 350 CE. The Babylonian Talmud was transcribed in about 500 CE and continued to be edited for another two centuries.
Tanna (noun), Tannaim (pl.), Tannaitic (adj.)	A Jewish sage whose views were recorded in the Mishna and who would therefore have lived from about 10 to 282 CE.
Torah	Hebrew for instruction, teaching or law. It can have a number of meanings depending on the context. Specifically, it refers to the entire Written Law, or Pentateuch, handed down by God to Moses, but it can also refer to all of Jewish tradition, including Biblical and rabbinic texts.
Tosefta	A compilation of Jewish Oral Law that is supplemental to the Mishna, written in the same period as the Mishna, in the 2nd second century CE.
Yeshiva (noun), yeshivot (pl.)	A Jewish educational institution that focuses on the study of traditional Jewish religious texts, such the Talmud, the Torah and halacha.

www.ingramcontent.com/pod-product-compliance
Lightning Source LLC
Chambersburg PA
CBHW060856120626
46553CB00001B/109